● Town/settlement
▪ ▬ Road/track
▪▪▪ Railway

MEDITERRANEAN SEA

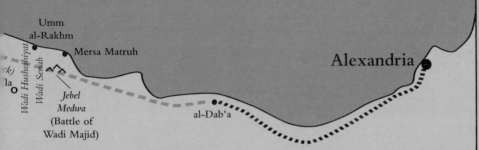

Umm
al-Rakhm
● Mersa Matruh

Alexandria ●

Wadi Hushehiyat
Wadi Serhab

k)
la ○

Jebel
Medwa
(Battle of
Wadi Majid)

al-Dab'a ●

QATTARA DEPRESSION

EGYPT

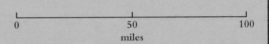

0   50   100
miles

THE
SANUSI'S LITTLE WAR

THE
SANUSI'S LITTLE WAR

The Amazing Story of a Forgotten Conflict
in the Western Desert, 1915–1917

Russell McGuirk

Arabian Publishing

The Sanusi's Little War

The Amazing Story of a Forgotten Conflict in the Western Desert, 1915–1917

© Russell McGuirk, 2007

First published in 2007 by Arabian Publishing Ltd

3 Devonshire Street, London W1W 5BA

Email: arabian.publishing@arabia.uk.com

Editor: William Facey

A catalogue card for this book is available from the British Library

ISBN-10: 0-9544792-7-0

ISBN-13: 978-0-9544792-7-5

Typesetting and digital artwork by Jamie Crocker, Artista-Design, UK

Printed and bound in the UK by Creative Print and Design (Wales), Ebbw Vale

Perfect peace here, except on the West, where there is a little war going on

T. E. Lawrence, in a letter home from Cairo,
28 December 1915

Contents

Acknowledgements

During the long process of putting this story together many people have given me generous help and encouragement. I am especially grateful to the descendants and family members of officers of the Egyptian Coastguard Administration. I owe special thanks to Archie and Mirabel Hunter for access to the Hunter family archives and photographs. Thanks are also due to Vickie Bucknall, Angela and Donald Cordess, Hugo von Dumreicher, Jennifer Hart Dyke (Vaudrey), Lieutenant-Colonel R. L. V. ffrench Blake, Arnold Hoghton, the late Lieutenant-Colonel Anthony D. Hunter, Lady Veronica Maclean, Rhoddy A. Macleod, Ann Mills, Netta Butterworth Morice, and Andrew and Pauline Tweedie.

I am grateful to: Julia Armor, David Burgess-Wise, Edmund Carr-Saunders, Mrs Mair James, R. G. Jones, Henry Keown-Boyd, John Pulford, Jim Routledge, Dr Janet Starkey, Dr Philip H. Stoddard, J. C. C. Sworder, Huw Williams, Glenn Wright, Siân Wyn-Jones, Jim Harold, Stella Overbye, Derek A. Hamilton, Maureen Marsh, and Omar Ziad Al-Askari; to Jane Hogan, Archives and Special Collections, Durham University; to Clare Brown and Debbie Usher, the Middle East Centre, St Antony's College, Oxford; to the Royal Geographical Society, London (especially Shane Winser, Pauline Hubner, Sarah Strong, and Huw Thomas); to Richard Burnell of the Holyhead Maritime Museum (and to Mrs J. Moss of Holyhead); to Firestone Library at Princeton University, especially Annalee Pauls, Margaret Sherry Rich, and Ben Primer; to Barbara Henson at the Center for Middle Eastern Studies, Harvard University; to Michael Hopper, Middle Eastern Division, Widener Library, Harvard University; to the Duke of Westminster's Office, the Grosvenor Estate, Chester, and the Cheshire Record Office; to Beverly Owen, Archives Assistant, Gwynedd; and to Anne Venables at the Llangefni Record Office; to the staffs of the National Archives in Kew, the Imperial War Museum, the National Army

Museum in Chelsea, the Library of the School of Oriental and African Studies, the Liddell Hart Centre for Military Archives at King's College London, the British Library, and the German Historical Institute in London; to Gabriele Teichmann of the Sal. Oppenheim Jr. & Cie. in Cologne; to Kornelia Rennert of the Mannesmann-Archiv, Mülheim an der Ruhr; and to Dr Kurt Erdmann of the Bundesarchiv in Freiburg; to Professor Mohammed el Sharkawi at the Egyptian Education and Cultural Office in London; to Muhammad Ali Ibrahim, Editor-in-Chief of *The Egyptian Gazette* in Cairo; to Dr Samir Gharib and Dr Mohammed Gallal Ghandour of the Egyptian National Library and Archives in Cairo; to Dr Mursi Saad el-Din; to Dr Aida Nosseir, Director of the National & Middle Eastern Services at the American University in Cairo; to 'Izz al-Din 'Atiyah Hamad in Burg al-'Arab; and to my friends Jill Hassan and Dr Sayed Madbouli.

To Dr Faraj Najam I am grateful for important Arabic and other source material, and for providing numerous interesting photographs.

I wish to thank Dr Jay Spaulding, who, many years ago in the Siwa Oasis, first fired my interest in the Sanusi; Brigadier Rupert Harding-Newman, who shared with me his knowledge of the early use of motor vehicles in the deserts of Egypt; and, although I only met him once and that was long before I began this book, I must also mention the late Brigadier Ralph Bagnold, who gave me the great honour of inviting me to his home to discuss the use of Model T Fords in the Western Desert.

I am also deeply grateful to William Facey, of Arabian Publishing Ltd, for his unstinting interest in this project, and for his sound advice and unfailing encouragement to a hesitant author; and to Jamie Crocker for his work on the page layouts, photographs and maps.

My final thanks are for my family, who have been so encouraging – especially to my wife, Sheila, who has been my principal support throughout the writing of this book; and to my brother, Murray McGuirk, for his help in enhancing the quality of the old photographs.

Russell McGuirk
2007

Illustrations

Between pages 206 and 207

26. HMS *Tara*, formerly SS *Hibernia* of the London and North Western Railway Company. By courtesy of the Trustees of the Imperial War Museum, London, and the family of Sub-Lt. Albert Marsh.

27. The *U-35* off the Adriatic port of Cattaro. By courtesy of the Imperial War Museum, London (Q24049).

28. Kapitänleutnant Waldemar Kophamel, commander of the German submarine *U-35*. By courtesy of the Imperial War Museum, London (HU53919).

29. View from the Western Frontier Force camp at Mersa Matruh. By courtesy of the Sudan Archive, Durham University Library.

30. The Egyptian Coastguard fort at Mersa Matruh. By courtesy of Angela Cordess.

31. View from the Western Frontier Force (WFF) camp at Mersa Matruh, looking south towards the desert. By courtesy of the Sudan Archive, Durham University Library.

32. The Dorset Yeomanry resting at Umm al-Rakhm after the Battle of Wadi Majid, Christmas Day 1915. By courtesy of the Sudan Archive, Durham University Library.

33. Column of cavalry moving down Umm al-Rakhm hill towards Mersa Matruh late on Christmas Day 1915, after the Battle of Wadi Majid. By courtesy of the Sudan Archive, Durham University Library.

34. Ja'far al-'Askari, wounded and taken prisoner by the British, arriving at Sidi Barani after the Battle of al-'Aqaqir. By courtesy of Omar Ziad al-Askari.

35. The burnt-out Coastguard station at Sidi Barani as it appeared when the WFF arrived on 28 February 1916. By courtesy of the Sudan Archive, Durham University Library.

36. Supplies arriving by ship at Sidi Barani, late February or early March 1916. By courtesy of the Sudan Archive, Durham University Library.

37. The WFF's two BE2c biplanes at Sidi Barani after the Battle of al-'Aqaqir (late February or early March 1916). By courtesy of the Sudan Archive, Durham University Library.

50. Sayyid Ahmad al-Sharif al-Sanusi and ex-Coastguard officer Muhammad Saleh Harb, after the two men had left Libya in a German U-boat. By courtesy of Dr Faraj Najem.

MAPS

Abbreviations

AA	anti-aircraft
ADM	Admiralty
AIR	Air Ministry
ASC	Army Service Corps
Berks	Berkshire
Bucks	Buckinghamshire
CIGS	Chief of the Imperial General Staff
CO	Commanding Officer
DSO	Distinguished Service Order
EA	Egyptian Army
EG	*The Egyptian Gazette*
FDA	Frontier Districts Administration
FO	Foreign Office
GHQ	General Headquarters
GOC	General Officer Commanding
ICC	Imperial Camel Corps
LCP	Light Car Patrol
MC	Military Cross
NCO	non-commissioned officer
Notts	Nottinghamshire
OC	Officer Commanding
QF	quick-firing
RAF	Royal Air Force
RAMC	Royal Army Medical Corps
RFC	Royal Flying Corps
RHA	Royal Horse Artillery
RNACD	Royal Navy Armoured Car Division
RNVR	Royal Naval Volunteer Reserve
SNO	Senior Naval Officer
VC	Victoria Cross
WESTFORCE	Western Frontier Force (telegraphic address)
WFF	Western Frontier Force
WO	War Office

Introduction

IN THE NORTH-WESTERN corner of Egypt the town of Sollum runs along the edge of a small bay and, on its western side, stops abruptly against a 600-foot high wall of reddish sandstone. Alexandria is 320 miles away to the east. The coast is flat and featureless, with stretches of unsightly beach communities between occasional desert towns like al-Alamein, Mersa Matruh and Sidi Barani. At Sollum, the sand and gravel of the Western Desert become rock, and the coastline turns to the north-west. To the south, the escarpment sweeps round behind the town and heads off to the south-east, the edge of a tableland that descends all the way to the Nile. This escarpment and the Libyan Plateau dominate the landscape and Sollum.

It is November 2001 and this is my second visit to Sollum. Thirty-five years ago, as a young student of Arabic, I shared a ramshackle taxi from Benghazi, in the Kingdom of Libya, to Alexandria – a trip of over 600 miles that cost me $7. I remember the car reaching the edge of the plateau at sunrise, a time when the colours of rock, sand and sea are at their best, and then zigzagging down to the Egyptian plain below with the Mediterranean on our left, a sparkling turquoise in the shallows, an opaque cobalt blue in the deep. It was my first trip to Egypt and the scene was all the more beautiful for being entirely unexpected.

This time, my wife and I have come from the opposite direction. Our driver is a young school teacher with connections at the Mersa Matruh Tourist Office, who finds it more lucrative to drive foreigners to the beaches and oases of the Western Desert. It has taken two hours to reach

Sollum at his mercifully relaxed pace, the plateau to the south gradually rising until, to the front of us, the Libyan heights come into view.

At the outskirts of Sollum we stop at a checkpoint where a guard looks at our passports and our official permission to be here. I ask if we can drive up to the plateau; he nods and waves us through. We move on with the Mediterranean on one side, a dreary collection of buildings on the other, including Sollum's only hotel and a British Second World War cemetery. The heights bristle with antennae and radio towers; we can see the shoe-lace pattern of the road leading to the top and, half a mile beyond, the yellow buildings of the Egyptian border post. An overhead sign tells us that the Libyan post is ten kilometres further west. There is no indication on it that Libya has changed – that the Kingdom of Libya is now the Socialist People's Libyan Arab Jamahiriya, run by Colonel Gaddafi.

We wind our way to the top and pull off the road so that I can walk back to the cliff edge. The view is still stunning, but the beauty of the sparkling bay is in sharp contrast to the scattering of drab housing compounds and office blocks spreading to the east for about a mile.

Situated in the lee of such a wall of rock, is Sollum protected by its geography or threatened by it? History suggests the latter and that is why I am here. Sollum is no resort: it is a border town, here exclusively for the serious business of border control. Over the past century it has been the military objective of numerous armies seeking to hold Egypt. In the 1940s the people of Sollum saw Italian, German and British armies repeatedly weave through the mountain passes here, sometimes going east, sometimes west. But perhaps the strangest army to sweep down from the plateau in the 20th century was an Arab army, in alliance with the Turks and Germans, which invaded British-occupied Egypt in 1915. It was the Bedouin army of Sayyid Ahmad al-Sharif al-Sanusi.

This is the story of that invasion and of the British campaign to contain it. It is the story of Sollum, the Sanusi, and of a British officer named Leopold Royle.

As in most stories of war this one has heroes, and they are to be found on both sides of the conflict. But for the author Royle is the principal hero. He was an exceptional officer in the Egyptian Coastguard Camel Corps before the war; and during the war he was a Royal Flying Corps officer, in action over Sinai, the Western Desert and Palestine, as well as an Intelligence officer throughout the Sanusi campaign. While his presence is woven into the story from beginning to end, the pattern it makes is sometimes bright and obvious; at other times it is but a thread, barely visible. Yet Royle is there at almost every engagement in Egypt, and the denouement of the story – the rescue of the *Tara* crew from captivity in Libya – was only possible because of his knowledge of the desert and his rapport with his Bedouin guides. Curiously, although he has been an unsung hero in his own country, in the first years of the 21st century the author encountered old Bedouin in the Western Desert who still remembered the name of Leopold Royle.

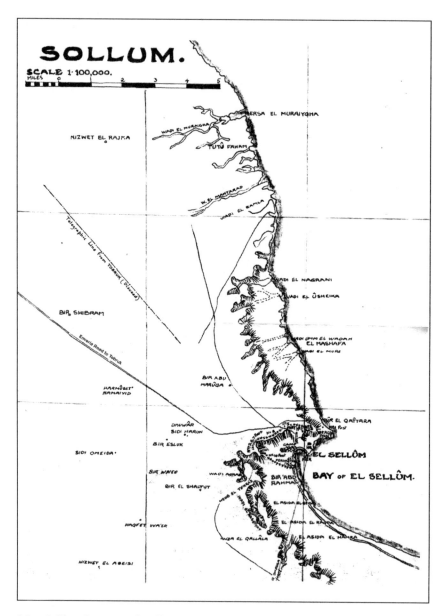

Map 2 Sketch map of Sollum and environs.

Prologue
The Tara Incident, November 1915

WEEKS AFTER THE EVENT it became clear that the war on Egypt's western frontier – a little war within the Great War – had begun with the sinking of HMS *Tara* on Friday, 5 November 1915.

That morning the *Tara* had been steaming westward along the coast of Egypt bound for Sollum. She should have arrived at this last outpost on the Egyptian side of the frontier about 11am. In fact, at 10am she was only eight miles away. The headland above Beacon Point was within sight. The fort on the plateau 600 feet above Sollum camp may have also been visible but not the few stone buildings and tents of the camp itself huddled below the escarpment at sea level. Of the several hundred Turks and several thousand Sanusi Arabs said to be threatening both fort and camp there was, at that distance, no sign, but they were there on the plateau.

The *Tara* had arrived from England two weeks earlier, and this was her second patrol between Alexandria and Sollum. Her crew, mostly Welshmen from Holyhead and fresh from the Irish Sea, had begun to think that cruising along the Egyptian coastline, searching for contraband on fishing boats and otherwise doing routine work in the Mediterranean sunshine, was rather pleasant. An account published by the *Tara*'s captain, R. S. Gwatkin-Williams, describes a scene on deck that morning not unlike that of a holiday cruise, "the weather calm and bright", the ship "nosing smoothly into a gentle swell", while "most of the officers were under the boat deck awning ... smoking or reading".[1]

At 10am on that day, with the sun just beginning to be hot, the holiday atmosphere was shattered when the lookout on the mast-head suddenly began to shout and point frantically to starboard. Tables and chairs went flying as men rushed to the rails in time to see a white furrow on the water's surface racing toward the ship.

The torpedo struck on the starboard side of the engine room, blowing away a portion of the main deck and throwing wreckage high into the air. Those in the engine room or adjacent cabins had no chance of survival. The ship's gunner, who had spotted their attacker's periscope and got off several rounds, died because he did not know how to swim. Of the ten life-boats only three got away. Eight minutes after the explosion, in a great vortex of spars, rafts, canvas and other debris, the *Tara* sank. Twelve crewmen were dead; ninety-two were still alive.

The German submarine that had fired the torpedo was the *U-35*. She approached this scene on the surface, many of her crew on deck with firearms ready. Life-boats were prepared for towing, while some of the men in the water were helped into them where there was space. The rest were taken on board the submarine. The *U-35* then turned and headed for the nearby port of Bardia on the Libyan side of the frontier.

An Egyptian Army detachment was garrisoned in the fort above Sollum camp. If anyone there had heard the explosion and looked seaward with binoculars, he would have easily seen the *Tara* sink and the survivors being towed away. But no one heard it, and no one was watching.

In command at Sollum was Lieutenant-Colonel Cecil Longueville Snow of the Egyptian Coastguard. Fifty-two years old, Snow had spent most of the past four years in this lonely outpost – ever since 1911, when the Italians had invaded Turkey's Libyan provinces and provoked a war with Turkey and the Libyan Arabs. Snow's task had been to keep the frontier secure and to gather intelligence about the activities of Sayyid Ahmad al-Sharif, the Grand Sanusi, whose Libyan-based Sanusi Brotherhood had thousands of devotees in Egypt's Western Desert and even in parts of the Nile Valley. In September 1914, Sayyid Ahmad and his army had unexpectedly arrived at the border and camped on the Libyan side, at Amsa'id, two miles from Sollum. The Turco-Italian War had ended in 1912. The Turks had lost, but the Libyan Arabs, including the Sanusi,

[1] Gwatkin-Williams (1919), *Prisoners of the Red Desert*, p. 14.

were still fighting the Italians. But now, in November 1915, Sayyid Ahmad was still at Amsa'id. Turkey was now on Germany's side in the world war, and Turkish soldiers had in recent months reassembled at the Sanusi camp. To make matters worse, Italy had now joined the war on the side of Britain and her allies. How long could the neutrality between the Sanusi and the British in Egypt survive the strain?

At Sollum camp on 5 November, Cecil Snow was preoccupied with a report he had just received from one of his Arab agents at Amsa'id. According to the agent, sixty Sanusi regulars had arrived at the Sanusi camp with four machine guns and thirty camel-loads of captured Italian rifles.[2] In recent months there had been many unsettling reports. Nuri, the brother of Enver Pasha, Turkey's Minister of War, was said to be at the Sanusi camp; and there was at least one German, the agent Otto Mannesmann, in the vicinity. Snow knew that the Turks and Germans were arguing for a Sanusi invasion of Egypt right here at Sollum. Perhaps the success of the Turkish defence at Gallipoli would influence Sayyid Ahmad. After all, the tribesmen of the Western Desert were pro-Sanusi, and Egyptian nationalists in the Nile Valley were anti-British. A Sanusi attack co-ordinated with a rise of Egyptian nationalism … or perhaps another Turkish attack from Sinai on the Suez Canal … these disturbing scenarios were continually being pondered, not just by Snow, but by the General Staff in Cairo and by Kitchener, Britain's Minister of War, in London.

With his agent's report on his mind, Snow would scarcely have noticed when HMS *Tara* did not make her scheduled appearance at midday. In any case, the *Tara* was on patrol. The more vessels there were to search, the longer she would take to reach Sollum. Besides, the ship had a wireless set. At Sollum there was only the telegraph, but Snow could receive messages from the *Tara* via Alexandria or Port Said, and so far he had received nothing.

Sollum was a lonely outpost. Although this corner of Egypt could be beautiful at times, especially when the sun was near the horizon, it could be hell in the full heat and glare of a summer's day, or when the spring sandstorms blew down a cataract of grit and dust from the plateau above. There were some comforts, however. The Coastguard had built Snow a stone house near the path up the escarpment. And, since the Coastguard

---

[2] FO 371/2356, Western Desert Intelligence, p. 316.

cruisers called at Sollum at least twice a week, he could occasionally get away to spend a few days with his family in Alexandria, although the present tensions on the frontier had made such escapes increasingly rare.

With Snow at Sollum in November 1915, in addition to the Egyptian Army unit, was a small contingent of Coastguard Camel Corps – mostly Sudanese with a few native Egyptian officers and NCOs. There was also a party of convicts serving as a labour force and living in tents on the beach. There were only two fellow-Englishmen. One was Captain Richard Bazley-White, in command of the Egyptian soldiers. The other was Captain Leopold Royle, formerly one of the Coastguard Camel Corps' most experienced officers. Royle knew the Grand Sanusi personally – in fact, he had been the first Englishman ever to meet him. Royle had since joined the Royal Flying Corps and would normally have been with his squadron near the Suez Canal, but when British–Sanusi relations became tense Kitchener had personally arranged for Royle to drop his RFC work and join Snow at Sollum. If this was frustrating for Royle, who loved flying, at least he and Snow got along well: for thirty-three year old Leo Royle was Cecil Snow's nephew.

That was the situation at Sollum on the day that HMS *Tara* was sunk eight miles away to the north-east. Snow and his men still had no knowledge of that event, but at 5.15pm that same day they too were attacked by the enemy submarine.[3] The *U-35* surfaced in the Bay of Sollum and brazenly moved to within a few hundred yards of the harbour, where two Coastguard cruisers, the *Abbas* and the *Nour al-Bahr*, were at anchor. The submarine's gunner manned the single 7.5 cm gun on deck and opened fire, aiming for the waterline of the two cruisers. The *Abbas* was sunk, and the *Nour al-Bahr* was badly damaged. He then turned his attention to targets ashore, as everyone at Sollum camp – coastguards, soldiers and prisoners – ran for cover. Explosions rang out among equipment, tents, and buildings. Miraculously, no one was killed. The German gunner's rate of fire was only a few shells per minute, and targets were difficult to spot from that distance and angle with the result that the destruction was relatively light. To the defenders' frustration there was little

---

[3] Most accounts of this event give the day of the attack as 6 November. This was because Snow was unable to report the attack until the day after it occurred, but there is no doubt that it occurred on the 5th. See ADM 137/193 No. 184, 6 November 1915; and WO 33/714, GOC Egypt to WO, No. 2140, 6 November 1915.

they could do to retaliate. Incredibly, they had no artillery with which to return fire: the camp was completely exposed.

At one point during the shelling Snow noticed that there was a man on the heights observing the attack. With his field glasses Snow saw that the man looked European, and he suspected that this was Otto Mannesmann. As will become apparent, Snow's suspicion was almost certainly correct.

The attack lasted forty-five minutes. Then, in the failing light, the *U-35* turned to the north and sailed away.

The immediate danger past, Snow rushed to the telegraph hut to inform naval headquarters at Port Said of what had happened. More frustration: the telegraph was not working. There was no apparent damage to the telegraph lines in camp, so Snow assumed the lines were down somewhere along the coast to the east. He sent an Egyptian repairman out in the dark to find the problem and fix it. Sometime later the unfortunate man was back in camp having been waylaid by Sanusi soldiers and beaten before he could carry out the repairs. Snow realized that the line had been deliberately cut. Was the Grand Sanusi aware of what was going on? Was this the start of the invasion? Snow had no way of knowing but suspected the worst. He sent a message to Sayyid Ahmad complaining about the ill-treatment of the repairman. It is not clear when the reply came – probably on the morning of the 6th – but at least its tone was conciliatory. Sayyid Ahmad wrote that he regretted the assault on the repairman and that he was sending his soldiers to guard the telegraph line. He did not acknowledge the obvious: that his soldiers had cut the line in the first place. Snow could only hope that the message meant that the Sanusi was still neutral.

On 6 November the lines were still down, so Snow sent a messenger to Sidi Barani, a small Coastguard station sixty miles along the coast, where the telegraph was working. Finally, at 3 o'clock in the afternoon on the day after the attack the news was received at Alexandria that Sollum had been attacked by submarine. Only then did it begin to dawn on the naval authorities that something was amiss with the *Tara*.

Over the next few days the mood of crisis deepened as reports of other submarine attacks began to arrive. HMS *Lunka*, ordered on the 6th to get to Sollum as fast as possible, picked up the crew of British steamer HMS *Woolwich*, which had been sunk by *U-35* two days before her attacks on the *Tara* and Sollum. On the 7th the SS *Moorina* was sunk, and two days later her crew came ashore at Baqbaq, between Sollum and Sidi Barani. His telegraph now functioning again, Snow arranged to send them food and to bring them to Sollum.

In the meantime, the Sanusi camp was abuzz with wild rumours. By the time HMS *Lunka* arrived at Sollum on the 7th Snow's agents were reporting conflicting accounts from excited Turks and Arabs who had actually been at Bardia on the 5th and had seen the *Tara* crew and the German submarine. Snow reported to the captain of the *Lunka* that he had "very reliable evidence" that the *Tara* had been attacked "by two submarines, one small, and one large", and that there were "about seventy saved, including probably [Captain] Gwatkin-Williams", and this information was sent by ship's wireless to Port Said. Snow also began trying to negotiate with the Sanusi for the release of the survivors.[4] Sayyid Ahmad disclaimed all knowledge of their whereabouts, although he said he would try to get news.

On 10 November, Captain Royle went along the coast to try to find physical evidence that the *Tara* had been torpedoed.[5] He took a small sailboat in the direction of Baqbaq and on the way he found what he was looking for. Among a mass of flotsam off the coast Royle counted some fifty deck rafts. He also found one body. The *Woolwich* had been sunk at a point half way to Crete; the *Moorina* had gone down a considerable distance to the north-west of Sollum and far out to sea. This wreckage almost certainly came from the missing *Tara*. Royle hauled the body into his boat and sailed back to Sollum.

In Cairo during the First World War, a two-storey building stood just off the little roundabout known then as Midan Suarès and today as Midan Mustapha Kamel. A rare contemporary photograph shows a sentry box to the right of the main door; the sentry, in uniform and pith helmet, is British. The windows on the ground floor are barred. Above the door are a balcony and three casement windows. Between door and balcony is a marble plaque that reads "HEADQUARTERS OFFICE, ARMY OF OCCUPATION".

On 9 November, four days after the *Tara* was lost, a twenty-seven-year-old intelligence officer with the rank of second lieutenant left his room at

---

[4] ADM 137/193, No. 196, 8 November 1915.
[5] FO 371/2356, Western Desert Intelligence, 12 November, p. 327.

the Continental Hotel in Opera Square and made his way by bicycle to the Military Intelligence Office located in the above-mentioned building. The distance was no more than 500 yards. The obvious route would be to turn right out of the hotel and go due south along the edge of the square turning right again onto Qasr el-Nil Street. The Headquarters' building was on the left just before the roundabout.

At Headquarters the situation at Sollum had commanded more attention than usual over the past three days. General Maxwell had received Snow's message late on the 6th concerning the attack on Sollum, but he was unable to reach Kitchener who was *en route* to the eastern Mediterranean to confer with his generals about the situation at Gallipoli. Maxwell sent a telegram to the War Office stating the bare facts of the occurrence, time and place of the attack and then left for the Greek island of Lemnos to participate in the conference of generals.[6] Kitchener would want to know all the details, and Maxwell would have the opportunity of discussing the attack with him in person in a few days.

However, when Maxwell left Cairo the attack on HSM *Tara* was still unconfirmed and so of secondary importance. Only after his departure did Snow's subsequent report, with its curious errors concerning the attack on the *Tara*, arrive at Army HQ in Cairo. This was forwarded to London by British naval authorities in Port Said; whereupon the Admiralty in London sent an encoded single-sentence announcement of the sinking of HMS *Tara*, with the errors, to the Military Intelligence Office in Cairo.

At Army HQ on 9 November, the young intelligence officer perused the latest military and political telegrams, saw the announcement concerning the *Tara*, and included it in the day's Intelligence Summary for the General Staff.

Secret
Military Intelligence Office
War Office, Cairo
9th November 1915

[6] "6 November 1915. An enemy submarine opened fire yesterday afternoon on our Coastguard cruisers in Sollum Bay and fired about 50 rounds. 'Abbas' was sunk and 'Nur el Bahr' hit. At dark the submarine submerged and disappeared north. No casualties are reported." See WO 33/714.

Censored Telegram from London to "Mokattam", Cairo – 8th November
1915 – Admiralty announces that British armed boarding steamer *'Tara'*
was sunk by two submarines in the Eastern Mediterranean, 34 lives being
lost.[7]

The factual errors are incidental. What commands attention is the name
of the officer who was responsible for that week's Intelligence Summaries
and whose signature is on the front of the Summary of 9 November. It is
signed "T. E. Lawrence".

In November 1915 Lawrence had been in Egypt for nearly eleven
months, one of five officers sent by the War Office at the end of 1914 "to
form the nucleus of a Military Intelligence Department" in Cairo.[8] Each
of the five men was considered to be a specialist in the Ottoman Empire,
and not one was a professional soldier: they were Captain George Lloyd,
Captain Aubrey Herbert, Lieutenant Leonard Woolley, Lieutenant James
Hay, and Second Lieutenant Thomas Edward Lawrence. The officer in
charge of these "five musketeers", as they were called,[9] was Captain

---

[7] WO 157/697.
[8] WO 95/4360, GHQ GS War Diary, entry for 20 December 1914.
[9] Liddell Hart (1934), *T. E. Lawrence: In Arabia and After*, p. 96
[10] Lt. James Hay is of particular interest despite his rather limited role in this story. He
appears to have been the outsider of the "five musketeers", and is rarely even
mentioned by historians, some of whom, indeed, have doubted his very existence. His
disappearance from one of the most raked-over periods of military history is probably
due to the fact that Hay had nothing to do with the Arab Revolt; he was simply
working on another front and so is scarcely ever mentioned in the usual "Lawrence of
Arabia" sources. Moreover, there are so many J. Hays in the *Military Lists* of the period
that it has seemed impossible to track him down. He is the only one of the musketeers
about whom no biographies have been written and no articles published. A Scotsman
from Aberdeenshire, he was born in 1880, which made him the same age to within a
year as Herbert, Woolley and Lloyd. In 1915 they were all around 35 years old, while
Lawrence was fully eight years younger. Later in the war Hay became Assistant Provost
Marshal, GHQ – in other words, a senior officer in the Military Police. This fact,
together with his known specialisation in matters involving the Turks in Libya, suggests
the possibility that like Col. W. H. Deedes and Lt.-Col. C. J. Hawker, both of whom
worked on occasion for Cairo's Military Intelligence, Lt. Hay may have previously
worked for the Ottoman Gendarmerie in Libya.
[11] M. R. Lawrence (1954) (ed.), *The Home Letters of T. E. Lawrence and his Brothers*, letter
of 23 June 1915.
[12] WO 95/4437, War Diary entries for 9 and 10 November 1915.

Stewart Newcombe; and the unit as a whole worked for the Director of Intelligence, Captain Gilbert Clayton. Eleven months later the musketeers were mostly dispersed. Apart from Lawrence the only other "musketeer" left in the office at Midan Suarès was the one whose area of specialisation was Turkish activity in Libya, James Barromew Hay.[10]

Lawrence's duties were many and various. In a letter home he had described them as consisting of "drawing & overseeing the drawing of maps: overseeing printing & packing of same: sitting in an office coding and decoding telegrams, interviewing prisoners, writing reports, & giving information from 9am till 7pm".[11] In fact, his intelligence and powers of organisation were such that he had become the office jack of all trades. The most junior officer of the five musketeers had become one of the most indispensable intelligence officers at Army HQ, with access even to General Maxwell.

Working with Lawrence on the Intelligence Summaries in November 1915 was an Irishman named Mervyn Sorley Macdonnell. Like Hay, Macdonnell was a specialist in "Tripoli", that is, he tried to keep informed about what the Turks were up to on the western frontier and in Libya. He reappears in our account of the Sanusi War later.

As for Hay, on 9 November he was preparing to leave for the Western Desert.[12] That afternoon he would take the train to Alexandria; the next morning he would take another along the Mariout Line to the railhead at al-Dab'a, where an Emergency Squadron of the Royal Naval Armoured Car Division (RNACD) was already assembling to bolster British and Egyptian positions in the Western Desert. Hay's job was to liaise between the RNACD and Army HQ in Cairo.

This is where matters stood as of 9 November. With Hay due to arrive at al-Dab'a on the 10th, it must have been assumed at Army HQ that any urgent Intelligence matters would be handled from there by him. In fact, there would be many such matters, although Hay's participation in the events of the next few months was to be minor. He recedes into historical oblivion, but within days Lawrence himself would be visiting Sollum and conferring personally with Cecil Snow.

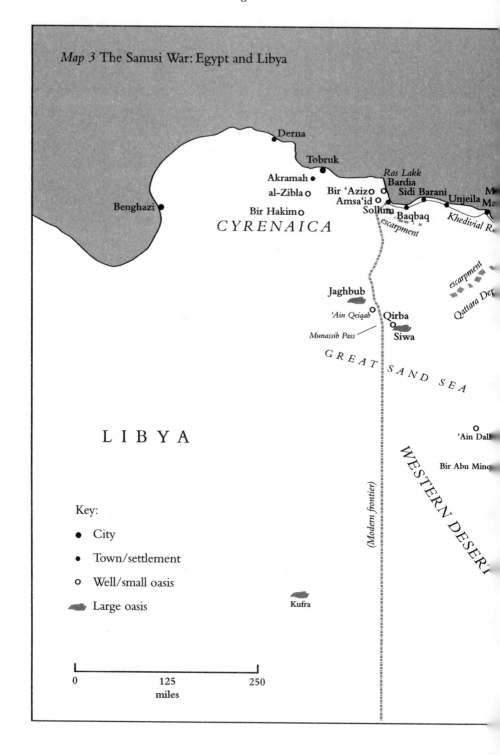

Map 3 The Sanusi War: Egypt and Libya

Derna

Tobruk

Ras Lakk

Akramah
al-Zibla   Bardia
                Bir 'Aziz   Sidi Barani
                Amsa'id   Unjeila   M
Benghazi   Sollum   Ma
                Bir Hakim   Baqbaq
CYRENAICA   escarpment   Khedivial R

                                    escarpment

                              Qattara De

Jaghbub

'Ain Qeiqab   Qirba
Munassib Pass   Siwa

GREAT   SAND   SEA

LIBYA
                                    'Ain Dall

                              Bir Abu Minq

Key:

● City

● Town/settlement

○ Well/small oasis

🝖 Large oasis   Kufra

(Modern frontier)   WESTERN DESER

0   125   250
              miles

PART I

1

The Sanusiyya

IN OCTOBER 1912 the Turco-Italian War officially ended, and to everyone's surprise, especially to that of the hard-pressed Italian invaders, it was won by Italy. The First Balkan War had suddenly broken out and, with Constantinople now directly threatened, the war in Libya was no longer viable for the Ottoman Government. They had no choice but to sue for peace, a treaty was signed on 18 October at Ouchy in Switzerland, and the Libyan provinces were lost forever to the Turks' dwindling Empire.

A few days before the Treaty of Ouchy was signed, the Egyptian coastguards guarding the frontier were surprised to receive a message from Sayyid Ahmad al-Sharif, the Grand Sanusi.[1] The letter was delivered to coastguard Leopold Royle, officer commanding at Qirba, where his detachment was guarding one of the principal passes to and from Libya. It was an invitation to one of Royle's Egyptian officers to go to the Sanusi "capital", Jaghbub, and to meet with Sayyid Ahmad. To be thus contacted by the Grand Sanusi was such an unexpected development that Royle immediately wired Lt.-Col. Cecil Snow, OC at Sollum, who forwarded his telegram to Coastguard Headquarters in Cairo, where Director-General George Hunter in turn sent it post-haste to British Agent and Consul-General Lord Kitchener at the British Agency. Royle reported that he had

[1] FO 141/732, telegram 13 October 1912.

given the Egyptian officer permission to go to Jaghbub with a desert guide
and that, although no Englishman had ever met Sayyid Ahmad, he sensed
that he too might have the opportunity to visit Jaghbub. "May I go if
invited?" he asked. "Would be quite safe [and] should only be away five
days." Snow and Hunter both recommended that Royle be given
authorization to go. Kitchener's cautious reaction is written in his own
hand on the telegram, "Royle must report if he is invited and not go until
he receives permission. K." But Kitchener's curiosity was obviously
piqued, or perhaps he perceived an unusual opportunity, for he then added
the following afterthought: "He might report on general situation and
Senoussi's intentions when he gets reliable news."[2]

In the event Royle's hopes that he would be able to follow his two men
into Libya came to nothing – at least on this occasion. Nevertheless,
communications were opened for the first time between the British and
the Sanusi, and it was Royle who for the next two years would be the
principal intermediary. In the meantime a succession of Egyptian
coastguards and native agents began to cross the frontier, in the process
accumulating information about Sayyid Ahmad al-Sharif and the Sanusi
Brotherhood.

The Sanusiyya arose in Libya in the mid–19th century, and its founder was
an Algerian named Muhammad bin 'Ali al-Sanusi.

Muhammad al-Sanusi was born in 1787, and even as a youth he was
known for his intelligence, learning and religious devotion. He received
his basic Islamic education at Fez in Morocco. He left that city when he
was in his thirties and began a prolonged period of travelling. He stayed
and taught in Cairo and at Mecca, but at both these places he managed to
upset the religious authorities, despite the fact that his teachings generally
conformed to orthodox Sunni Islam. His difficulties with the Islamic
establishment may have been due to his charismatic personality: wherever
he went he acquired disciples.

In the 1840s Muhammad al-Sanusi tried to return to Algeria. Intent on
establishing his own Sufi brotherhood among the Bedouin, his plan to
return to his native land was thwarted by the recent French occupation.
He decided to settle in Cyrenaica instead. In this easternmost province of
Libya, bordering on Egypt, he could proselytise without interference from

---

[2] FO 141/732, telegram 13 October 1912.

religious or political authority. There the Bedouin lived in poverty, despised by Turks and Arab town-dwellers alike, and could greatly benefit from acts of charity.

The new Sanusi movement was uncomplicated in structure. The Bedouin formed the main body of adherents. Disciples who could read and write, called *ikhwan* (brothers), recited the Koran and led the prayers. Muhammad al-Sanusi himself, the head of the movement, became known as the Grand Sanusi, and this title was adopted by his successors. At the heart of the Sanusi system was the *zawiya*, a place of religious teaching, but also a staging post for caravans, a hostel for travellers, and a centre of agricultural development. Muhammad al-Sanusi did not impose the creation of *zawiya*s on the desert Arabs. They were not built unless they were asked for by the local population, but since the Bedouin were being offered precisely what they needed to improve their lives, there soon developed a widespread network of these centres. Whatever the Bedouin felt about Muhammad al-Sanusi's theology and erudition, they clearly saw in his charismatic personality and charity a degree of *baraka*, blessing and good fortune, that was normally absent from their lives.

In the mid-1840s Muhammad al-Sanusi had two sons, Muhammad al-Mahdi and Muhammad al-Sharif, both born in Cyrenaica. In 1854 he moved to Jaghbub, deep in the Libyan Desert near the Egyptian border, and established his headquarters there. When Muhammad al-Sanusi died in 1859, the Sanusi Brotherhood was flourishing.

The founder's first-born son was his successor. Only fifteen when he became Grand Sanusi, Muhammad al-Mahdi had extraordinary organisational talents that over the next forty years turned the Sanusiyya into the most influential religious movement in all of North Africa. Under his leadership the establishment of *zawiya*s gained momentum. The Sanusi colonized the desert by taking maximum advantage of the caravan routes that criss-crossed the Sahara. Their main focus was on a thriving route that ran through Cyrenaica from a sub-Saharan region called Wadai to the Mediterranean port of Benghazi, but the Sanusi also developed other routes, some of them thousands of miles long. By the end of the 19th century there were about a hundred *zawiya*s in the three provinces of greater Libya, more than thirty in Egypt's Western Desert, over a dozen on the Arabian coast of the Red Sea and a similar number in the Sudan. To the west there were *zawiya*s all along the caravan routes to Timbuctu and beyond, to Nigeria and Senegal. The speed and scale of Sanusi success suggest an obvious comparison with the meteoric spread of Islam in the 7th century. However, it is important to emphasize that from the start of the Sanusi movement in the 1840s to the dawn of the 20th century its sole purpose was to bring better living conditions and religion to desert nomads. At no time in this period did Sanusi leaders show any interest in converting religious and economic influence into political power.[3]

With the coming of the new century, however, Sanusi expansion was suddenly checked by the interference of the Great Powers in Central Africa. In 1898 Kitchener met Marchand at Fashoda in southern Sudan, and French colonial ambition, confronted by British colonial ambition, was diverted away from Sudan towards the regions of Chad and Wadai to the west. In 1901 the French attacked a *zawiya* sixty miles from Lake Chad, setting off the Franco–Sanusi War, which continued intermittently until 1911. From this point on the Sanusi movement was to become increasingly political, and its destiny was to clash with three Great Powers one after another.

Muhammad al-Mahdi died in 1902. Since his first-born son, Muhammad Idris,[4] was too young to assume the leadership, it was decided that the position should go to Ahmad al-Sharif, the oldest son of Muhammad al-Mahdi's younger brother Muhammad al-Sharif. Sayyid Ahmad al-Sharif, the third Grand Sanusi, continued the war against the French, and it was he who rallied his followers in support of the Turks against the Italians in 1911.

Because the Sanusi heartland was the Saharan interior, few Europeans – other than French and Italian soldiers – ever came into contact with them. In Egypt, at least among the European communities there, the Grand Sanusi was an enigma. From time to time *The Egyptian Gazette* would refer to this mysterious leader and his Brotherhood in terms which were a

---

[3] That is, they shunned the sort of political power that might challenge, for example, the Ottoman position in Libya, or provoke reactions from European colonial powers. They stayed as far away as they could from both Turks and Europeans, preferring to operate in the political vacuum of the desert. Indeed, Muhammad al-Mahdi went so far as to move Sanusi headquarters from Jaghbub to Kufra (in the south of Libya) and then to the Gouro Oasis in Tibesti (northern Chad).

[4] King of Libya from 1951 to 1969; overthrown by Col. Gaddafi in September 1969.

farrago of fact, legend, and the less than objective views of the French, whose armies were beset with an awkward desert war.

> [1901] From a French source we learn that ... a large number of letters [have been] found in Arabic from the famous chief Senoussi ... proving that this remarkable man was making strenuous efforts to combine the [local tribes] into an anti-European league for the purpose of establishing a powerful Mussulman Empire in the heart of Africa ... he is still a force to be reckoned with, for his agents are spread over the whole of Northern and Central Africa, from Morocco to the Nile, and from the Mediterranean to Lake Chad.[5]

And

> [1902] ... the French at present act as a buffer between the Senoussists and the British, and no immediate trouble is apprehended, but in certain quarters it is thought possible that this great Mohamedan movement may in the near future become a formidable sequel to the Mahdiism of the Egyptian Sudan, and it is held that it should be watched carefully.[6]

When the second Grand Sanusi, Muhammad al-Mahdi, died in August, 1902, *The Egyptian Gazette* printed a long editorial on the possible threat that the Brotherhood represented to Europeans in Africa.

> A telegram this morning from Tripoli states that Sheikh El Senoussi has died at Kanem. This personage has been figuring in the European Press for some years past as the great African Bogey Man, and the echoes and vague rumours that have reached the outer world from the back of the beyond of the Sahara have all tended to invest the ... figure of the Sheikh with an awe-inspiring and mysterious personality, just as in the Middle Ages was the personality of Prester John of Ethiopia ...
>
> The last appearance of the Sheikh on the African stage was a few months back when it was reported that a French expedition had suffered a severe reverse in Kanem at the hands of the followers of El Senoussi, and soon news reached the Mediterranean ports that the Sheikh had

---

[5] *EG*, 31 January 1901.
[6] *EG*, 11 June 1902.

collected a large army, in whose ranks were found not only the wild
tribesmen of the Sahara but numbers of recruits from Algeria and Tunis
...

The movement of which the late Sheikh was the head was not anti-
British nor anti-French, but anti-European, and its leaders do not
recognise the political frontiers which have been traced on the map of
Africa in London, Paris, and Berlin ... The celebrated African traveller
[Gerhard] Rohlfs remarked in his work ... : "What specially characterises
them, almost above every other Mohamedan order or sect, is not merely
the fanaticism within their own religion, but their burning hatred of
Christians ..." The actual subjects [of the Grand Sanusi] number, it is
estimated, about four or five millions and owing to its perfect
organization so vast a combination is necessarily fraught with danger to
the peace of Africa.[7]

Nevertheless, Egyptian experience of the Brotherhood seemed to
suggest that this foreboding was ill-founded. Not only had Muhammad al-
Mahdi flatly rejected the Sudanese Mahdi's call to *jihad* in 1884; Sanusi
influence had already spread to Egypt without bringing problems. There
were *zawiya*s all along the northern coast, the Siwa Oasis was a notable
Sanusi centre, as was Fayoum, and their influence was increasing in the
Nile Valley. The British in Egypt came to consider their presence as benign
and, in fact, this assessment was accurate since, if not interfered with, the
movement was religious, not political.

In late 1909 there occurred an incident in the Siwa Oasis that seemed
both to test and confirm this point of view. The Sanusi agent in Siwa, who
was also the headman of the oasis, was Sheikh 'Uthman Habbun. Habbun
was perceived by the Egyptian Government to be a bad-tempered and
awkward individual who disdained their authority – regardless of whether
its representatives were British or Egyptian – and eventually he became
involved with Libyan gun smugglers. When the Government's senior
representative in Siwa, the *ma'mour*, went to Habbun's house to confront
him about this involvement, he was shot dead, apparently by one of
Habbun's two sons. It was 'Uthman Habbun, however, who was tried and
sentenced to be hanged, while for their part in the affair the sons were
sentenced to long-term imprisonment. The Khedive,[8] 'Abbas Hilmi II,

[7] *EG*, 16 August 1902.

confirmed the sentences, and the caravan bearing the official executioner, his gallows tied to the back of a camel, began the twelve-day trek from Alexandria to Siwa. Meanwhile, the Egyptian press speculated excitedly about what the Sanusi would do if Habbun were hanged. Even *The Egyptian Gazette* warned that Sanusi warriors were preparing to attack from Jaghbub and rescue their agent. On the last day of 1910 Egypt held its collective breath as the sentence was carried out. Habbun was executed in the presence of 5,000 Siwans, all followers of the Sanusi, but neither they nor their brethren across the border tried to stop the course of justice.[9] The case of 'Uthman Habbun brought no repercussions, whereas the Turco-Italian War, which broke out a year and a half later, turned the whole Libyan Desert, including the Western Desert, into a hornet's nest.

Two events took place in September 1911 which had far-reaching consequences for the Sanusiyya, for the Western Desert Arabs, and for the Turks. First, Kitchener arrived in Egypt as British Agent and Consul-General; and, second, the Italians declared war on the Ottoman Empire and invaded Libya.

These events occurred within forty-eight hours. On the 27th, Italy presented the Turks with an ultimatum demanding that they agree to allow the Italians to occupy Libya. On the 28th, Kitchener arrived in Egypt. On the 29th, Italy declared war and the invasion force sailed.

The Italian claim on Libya was transparently spurious. It was in essence based on the fact that Libya had once been a province of ancient Rome – and now Italy wanted it back. At the Congress of Berlin in 1878 Bismarck had remarked when overseeing a discussion of the division of Ottoman spoils, "the Italians have such a large appetite and such poor teeth". But newly reunited Italy, taking her seat among the Great Powers, wanted an empire. For years France and Britain had been taking choice parts of the Ottoman domain, while Germany, which in the time of Bismarck had not wanted overseas colonies, was now, in the period of Wilhelm II, actively set on catching up with them. In 1896 Italy's teeth failed her when she

[8] The Khedive was the semi-independent hereditary ruler of Egypt, who owed allegiance to the Ottoman Sultan. His relations with Cromer and Kitchener, both British Consuls-General in Egypt, were often strained.

[9] *EG.* The incident unfolds through numerous articles between 8 October 1909 and 12 January 1910.

suffered ignominious defeat in Abyssinia. She had since set her sights on
Libya in the hope that the inefficient and sometimes corrupt Turkish
administration there would lead the local population to welcome a
change. It was certainly true that the Libyans were not overly fond of the
Turks. But when the Italian battle-fleet sailed for Libya, Italy was so clearly
the aggressor that the Turks were suddenly cast in the role of heroic
defenders of the faith.

The Italians bombarded Turkish forts in the area of Tripoli and occupied
the town. They also landed at points along the Libyan coastline and
established bridgeheads. The Turks withdrew into the interior,
reorganized, and fought back with the unexpected assistance of thousands
of Libyan tribesmen who flocked to join them.

In neighbouring Egypt there was nearly universal support for the
Turkish cause. For one thing there were over 30,000 Turks living in Egypt,
many of them people of wealth and influence. The Khedive was descended
from Muhammad 'Ali Pasha, an Albanian-Turk. Egypt's aristocracy was
mostly Turkish, and many had homes on the Bosphorus as well as on the
Nile. But Arab Egyptians were also outraged by the invasion. Young
Egyptians from all classes and walks of life volunteered to enlist in the
Turkish Army. The Bedouin tribes living in Egypt, many of whom were of
Libyan origin anyway, were ready to send volunteers. Egyptians who were
unable to fight contributed money and jewellery for the cause.

This situation presented Kitchener with a dilemma. Italy had cleared
her intention to seize Libya with the Great Powers. These had signed secret
agreements in which they acknowledged the Italian claim and in return
received Italian support for their own foreign adventures. The British
Foreign Office had been involved in these secret deals, and Kitchener –
employed by the FO – knew about them. He declared, therefore, that
Egypt would remain strictly neutral in the dispute. Neither volunteers nor
arms would be allowed across the border, although humanitarian and
medical assistance would be permitted.

British attention was now drawn to the fact that Egypt's western border
had never been precisely delineated. To the Turkish Sultan the exact
boundary had been of no concern because Libya and Egypt were both
part of his Ottoman Empire.[10] On the coast the obvious natural border was
the escarpment of the Libyan Plateau. In the interior the oasis of Siwa was
generally acknowledged to be part of Egypt; west of Siwa by some sixty

miles was the oasis of Jaghbub and this by general agreement had always been part of Libya. The British now began to make unprecedented claims for land on behalf of Egypt.

Early in November 1911 Mark Sykes,[11] who had recently visited the Western Desert, stood up in Parliament and asked the Foreign Secretary whether the oasis of Jaghbub was in "Anglo-Egyptian" or Libyan territory. The following exchange was reported in *The Times*:

> (Sir Edward Grey:) His Majesty's Government consider Jaghbub to be in Egyptian territory and both the Porte [ie Turkey] and the Italian Government are aware of this view.
> (Earl of Ronaldshay:) May I ask whether the Italian and the Ottoman Governments accept the view taken by His Majesty's Government?
> (Sir Edward Grey:) I am not sure that their acceptance has been asked. We have made the statement and to it we intend to adhere. (Cheers!)[12]

With the Turks now fully occupied with the Italian invasion Kitchener took steps to make territorial gains for "Anglo-Egypt" in the important coastal region. In December he sent a detachment of Egyptian Coastguard, commanded by Coastguard Director George Hunter, and another of the Egyptian Army to seize that part of the heights that overlooked Sollum. *The Egyptian Gazette* printed an account of the take-over as reported by an Egyptian officer involved:

---

[10] In fact, this was also the position of the British Foreign Office, which until the First World War officially defined Egypt's status as "a semi-independent tributary state of the Ottoman Empire". Until December 1914 Egypt was neither a British protectorate, nor a dependency. Britain had been there temporarily since 1882 to put things right. Of course, this pretence was nearly as absurd as the Italian claim to Libya.
[11] Mark Sykes was related by marriage to George Hunter, the Director-General of the Egyptian Coastguard Administration. Both men were married to sisters of Sir Eldon Gorst, Kitchener's immediate predecessor as British Agent and Consul-General. Sykes visited the Awlad 'Ali tribe (who were Sanusi followers) in the Western Desert in 1910 and wrote: "Now if you take the train at Alexandria and travel westward you come to another land – a land neither of the Arabs nor of the fellahin of Egypt, but of the folk who call themselves 'sons of the Weled Ali' ... Frankly, I do not like these people." Mark Sykes (1915), *The Caliph's Last Heritage*, p. 504.
[12] *The Times*, 7 November 1911.

We reached here from Alexandria on Wednesday, December 20, and found Hunter Pasha encamped with his men on the hills behind the port of Sollum ... while the fort which we had come to take over from the Turks stands just in front of the harbour on the top of a hill. We pitched our camp on the west, or Tripoli, side of the harbour and the fort and at once set to work throwing up entrenchments, though we were wet to the skin from the rain which had fallen steadily all the way from Alexandria.

As soon as we had made ourselves secure negotiations were opened with the Ottoman commander for the handing over of the fort. At first he absolutely refused to evacuate and we greatly feared what might be the result of his obstinacy ... At last the Turkish commander was compelled to yield ... They are moving out today (December 21) and we shall go in tomorrow.[13]

The success of the operation caused much excitement back in Cairo. The Khedive, who was usually at odds with Kitchener, was delighted and left immediately to inspect his new territory.[14] George Hunter went back to Cairo to report to Kitchener in person. Kitchener's *aide-de-camp* Oswald Fitzgerald, present at the interview, described the scene at Sollum as related by Hunter:

Lord Kitchener since he has been here has insisted that the boundary line runs as shown on map attached, and that the Turkish troops in Sollum must move out ... I have just received reports to say the Turks evacuated the post on 21 December 1911, and we occupied it the next day with Capt. Kyrke and 50 men of the Egyptian Army. The Turks have moved to a camp that we pitched for them two miles west. This is still within our boundary but was the best that could be done; we had to lend them tents and pitch them also to make sure of their moving. The Officer who was there representing Egypt, Hunter Pasha, head of the Coastguards, says it was the funniest procession he had ever seen – a long-legged Coastguard officer pacing while the Turkish officer stopped every hundred yards to

---

[13] *EG*, 17 January 1912

[14] Nevertheless, the Khedive was generally indignant that Kitchener usurped Egyptian Government prerogatives by giving direct orders to the Coastguard Administration. He remained friends with the Hunter family, however, and after the war Hunter's eldest son became the then exiled Khedive's Private Secretary.

protest that he would die sooner than give up more territory.

This boundary you will notice is west of Jaghbub, a strong Sanusi centre of no use to us, except that in the future we will be able to give it up as a concession for something else we want. You had better inform the Mapping Section of this boundary as all the maps have it wrong.[15]

In the meantime Kitchener closed the border and sent patrols to the northern coastline to keep Turkish soldiers, Egyptian volunteers, and armaments from reaching the Turkish defenders. These patrols were primarily the job of the Coastguards, although the Alexandrian police and the Egyptian Army reinforced them in the early stage of the Turco-Italian War.

A description of these activities was given by a young Thomas Russell, later Russell Pasha of the Egyptian Police, in a letter to his father on Christmas Day, 1911:

[There are] about 200 Sudanese police and coastguard camel corps with 13 English officers stationed at different points along the coast from Alexandria to the Tripoli frontier, which is 300 miles roughly from Alex. There is a private railway of the Khedive which runs as far as [al-Dab'a] and I am in charge of the coast so far with two of our English Alexandrian police officers under one Captain Smith of the Egyptian Army, who is in charge of railhead and 50 camel corps. The whole coast and the desert behind is divided up into patrols of about 30 miles long. A tracker and a man has to cover each of these beats in as short a time as possible every day after dawn to see if there are any tracks of people landing stuff from the sea or caravans on the desert roads. They sleep at the end of their beat and do the same patrol back the next day unless they find tracks when, of course, they have to ride in fast to the main post and give word to the officers ... I fear there is little chance of them trying to run any more. Everyone wishes they would as it's precious dull patrolling the desert if there's nothing to be caught.

I came here yesterday to visit Smith and go back tomorrow half way to Alex. I don't think we shall be out here more than another week or 10 days as the Coastguards will take it all over after they have handed over

---

[15] WO 106/218, letter of 1 January 1912.

Sollum, the frontier station, to the Egyptian Army, who have sent 50 men
there. In fine weather it wouldn't be at all bad but it's pelting with rain
and blowing a gale every day from the coast … The Sudanese are capital
fellows to be with. Always cheery though often wet through.[16]

In fact, these efforts to seal the border served more to demonstrate
British neutrality to the Italians than to stop men and equipment reaching
the defenders of Libya. The Western Desert was simply too large and the
imposed neutrality was never accepted by the people of Egypt. In any case,
the Young Turks had already crossed the border.

On 15 October 1911, a major in the Ottoman army known simply as
"Enver" disembarked in disguise from a ship in Alexandria harbour. He
had shaved off his moustache, put on sunglasses and a black fez and
assumed the identity of "a doctor", hoping that he would not be
recognized by the Egyptian port authorities. For Enver, not yet thirty-years
old, was already world-famous as a leader of the Young Turk movement
and a hero of the Turkish Revolution of 1908. Abdul Hamid II had been
overthrown; his brother Mehmed V was now Sultan and Caliph, and Enver
was engaged to Mehmed's niece, an imperial princess. Enver believed he
was destined for great things and without doubt at this stage in his life his
star was rising.

Five other Turkish officers, likewise incognito, were in the crowd
waiting to pass through immigration. All made it through, Enver simply by
presenting a false identity card.

The Turkish officers stayed in Alexandria for a week while
arrangements were made for travelling to the western frontier. Enver
stayed in a dingy and ill-lit room near Muhammad Ali Square. On 21
October he changed his identity again. He also swapped his European-
style clothes for Arab robes, a white burnous over a long blue under-robe.
Characteristically – for he was invariably a vain man – he put on a white
kafiya with gold braid for a headdress, a strange choice for someone trying
to look inconspicuous. On the 24th Enver and his men travelled west by
train along the northern coast of Egypt to the railhead at al-Dab'a. They
travelled third class and, as a sandstorm was raging outside, their hair and

[16] Private Papers Collection, The Middle East Centre, St Antony's College, Oxford.
Thomas Russell, letter to his father, Christmas Day, 1911.

faces were covered with dust even though the windows were closed. At the railhead, on the 25th, they were given horses and joined a caravan that was leaving for Libya. They travelled within sight of the sea nearly all the way to Sollum and then turned inland to cross into Libyan territory, which they did on 28 October. Enver was pleased with the reception he received from the Awlad 'Ali. Referring to himself in his diary he wrote: "The morale of the Arabs is improving every day. The unexpected arrival of a relative of the Caliph has made a great impression on them."[17] That diary gives no hint that the party was detained *en route* by the Egyptian authorities. Nevertheless, another source indicates that they were detained and very fortunate not to be sent back; this minor incident was to assume major relevance in the light of certain events that would occur later.

A young Egyptian coastguard named Muhammad Saleh Harb was at this time part of the British-imposed cordon in the Western Desert. From Aswan Province, he was a graduate of the Cairo Military Academy; he was religious, without being fanatical; and he was an Egyptian nationalist, ready to help the Turks in defiance of British orders.[18] Shortly before his death in the 1960s, Saleh Harb went on record as having been instrumental in getting Enver's group across the border. According to his account Enver and his men were stopped by a Coastguard detachment commanded by Saleh Harb, who then gave them advice on how to get through the cordon.[19]

Curiously, another party of disguised Turkish officers left Alexandria a week later, and among them was Mustafa Kemal, who after the First World War, as Atatürk, would become the first president of the new Turkish republic. This group also crossed into Libya successfully with the help of a sympathetic border patrol.

The letter from Kitchener's *aide-de-camp* reporting the British occupation of Sollum goes on to confirm that the British realized that their attempts to seal the border were ineffective.

[17] Enver Pascha (1918), *Um Tripolis*.
[18] FO 371/27432 includes a biographical profile of Saleh Harb written by British Intelligence during the Second World War.
[19] Philip Hendrick Stoddard, "The Ottoman Government and the Arabs, 1911 to 1918: A Preliminary Study of the Teshkilat-ı Mahsusa" (unpublished Ph.D thesis, Princeton University, 1963).

We are having great trouble now because the Turks are running officers, men, and munitions of war, through Egypt, and so breaking our neutrality. Posts have been established along our coasts and frontiers, but these are so long, and all the inhabitants are in sympathy with the Turks, that effective guarding is nearly impossible with the means available.[20]

By this time – December 1911 – Enver was a lieutenant-colonel (having received a double promotion) and overall commander of Turkish forces in Libya. As if to presage events in 1914 he also had a number of German officers advising him at his headquarters near Derna, some of whom would be back in the region four years later during the First World War. Enver was also assisted by his younger brother Nuri Bey, who at twenty-one was now getting his first experience of war. In 1915 Nuri would be at Sollum and his enemy then would be the British in Egypt.

Despite the final outcome of the Turco-Italian War, the Turks were quite successful in Libya. Some 5,000 regular troops, assisted by large numbers of Bedouins, generally managed to keep the Italians pinned down in their bridgeheads on the coast. The Turks were now appreciated by the Libyan Arabs to a degree they could have only dreamed about before the Italian invasion.

In Cyrenaica the main source of Bedouin warriors was the Sanusi Brotherhood. Enver had arrived in Libya unsure of Sanusi support and was much relieved to find that he had it. Sanusi warriors had been fighting the French in the central Sahara for ten years and, thus battle-hardened, readily joined forces with the Turks to repel the Italians.

Another mark of Turkish success was that foreign correspondents covering the war for newspapers in Europe tended to favour the Turks (except in Italy of course). Even *The Egyptian Gazette*, representing the British point of view in Egypt, generally applauded Turkish successes and treated Enver as a romantic hero, as when one of their correspondents, openly cheering the failure of the British cordon, wrote: "At the beginning of the war ... the guarding of the frontier was not remarkably successful and this helped Enver Bey and the other Turkish leaders in organising their wonderfully successful resistance."[21]

The image portrayed by these correspondents was so positive that a small stream of European volunteers began to arrive to fight for the

[20] WO 106/218, letter from FitzGerald, 1 January 1912.

Turkish cause. *The Egyptian Gazette* reported that an Englishman named Mr Smallwood, "as fine a figure of a man as one could wish to see", had crossed the frontier at Sollum in the company of two Germans and been killed fighting the Italians.[22]

A German correspondent named von Pernull, interviewed by *The Egyptian Gazette* just after the Turco-Italian War, gave an interesting account of Enver. At one point in the interview von Pernull revealed an interesting insight into Enver's character. He described the scene at the battle of Derna in July 1912 when he had "stood beside Enver throughout the day and greatly admired his coolness".

> On the morning of that day [von Pernull] remarked to Enver. "There will
> be great slaughter today, I fear."
> "Soldiers are meant for that," replied the Turk.[23]

As patriotic and brave as Enver was, this ruthless side to his character was to become increasingly apparent in his later career.

As soon as the Italians realized that they were in danger of losing the war in Libya, they began to look for ways to hit at the Turks elsewhere. In late February 1912 their fleet bombarded Beirut; in April they struck at the forts guarding the Dardanelles; in May they occupied Rhodes and several of the Dodecanese islands. To the consternation of the Great Powers the Italians were destabilizing the whole eastern Mediterranean. Turkish resolve merely hardened. In the early autumn of 1912 Italy finally hit upon a way to force the Turks to the negotiating table. The King of Italy, Victor Emmanuel III, was married to the daughter of Nicholas I of Montenegro. Montenegro was enticed into settling her quarrels with her Balkan neighbours, at least temporarily, and joining with Bulgaria, Serbia and Greece in rising against the Ottomans. It was at this point that the First Balkan War broke out, in October 1912, and the Turkish war effort in Libya collapsed.

This unexpected development caused Enver considerable embarrassment. He had been the war's most inspiring figure; thousands had died, many of them tribesmen loyal to the Sanusi; moreover, the Turks had been winning, or at least not losing. Enver decided he had better

---

[21] *EG*, 18 July 1912. [22] *EG*, 18 July 1912. [23] *EG*, 3 December 1912.

explain Turkey's defeat in person to Sayyid Ahmad al-Sharif. On 19 November he travelled by automobile from Tobruk to Jaghbub, arriving the next day.[24] This was an epic desert journey, the first of its kind in the Libyan Desert, but the feat was dwarfed to insignificance by the enormous disappointment occasioned by Turkey's withdrawal from the country. Enver explained to Sayyid Ahmad the reasons behind the peace treaty and said that he would go immediately to see the Sultan, and either return himself or write fully. Sayyid Ahmad was nevertheless angry that Libya was to be abandoned. It was decided that some Turks, including Enver's brother Nuri, would stay in the country.[25] This was in breach of the peace terms, but it went some way to assuage the feelings of the Sanusi.

A few days later Enver returned to Egypt. He left the way he had arrived, although it would appear from a short item in *The Egyptian Gazette* that he made less effort this time to keep his presence there a secret. "Enver Bey, who commanded the Turkish forces in Tripoli, arrived at Alexandria incognito last night ..."[26] From there he returned to Constantinople.

On 18 October 1912, the very day that the peace treaty was signed ending the Turco-Italian War, Royle's Egyptian officer and the guide arrived back at Qirba from their visit to Jaghbub. Royle debriefed them and wrote a detailed report about the nature of the desert between Qirba and Jaghbub. "[T]he going on the whole is good," he wrote, "except for sandy passes ... broken country as far as ['Ain Qeiqab]; from there onwards the route lies between the sand dunes on the south and the hills leading up to the plateau on the north." He also reported on the town of Jaghbub, till then a complete mystery. "[It is] built on the form of a square with the tomb of Sidi Muhammad al-Sanusi and other members of the family on the north side ... [and the] houses are all one-storeyed"; and he added that 'Ali

---

[24] FO 141/732. Intelligence Dept., Cairo. Report of 4 January 1913.

[25] "The Turkish soldiers who remained in Cyrenaica were drawn from every part of the Ottoman Empire – Albanians, Kurds, Syrians, Iraqis, Circassians, Anatolians, Macedonians, and Thracians – and were practically mercenaries who lived by the sword. Slovenly though they were, they were fine fighters and frugal as well, being content to campaign on rice, potatoes, bread, and an occasional helping of meat; and in Enver Bey they had an inspiring leader." (Evans-Pritchard (1954), *The Sanusi of Cyrenaica*, p. 115.)

[26] *The Times*, by-line Cairo, 2 December 1912.

Muhammad (the Coastguard officer) and the guide "were very well received and most generously treated during their two days there". He went on:

> on the first day Sidi Ahmad sent for them, and received them in his house, the walls and floor of which were covered with good rugs and behind Sidi Ahmad against the wall were his arms which consisted of a magazine carbine and two swords, one of them being that recently given him by the Sultan of Turkey ... [then at midnight 'Ali Muhammad was sent for] and had a private interview with Sidi Ahmad alone ... and explained that he was very grateful to me [Royle] and the patrol for not worrying their caravans and agents, and would like to meet me, but these days it might cause embarrassment ... meaning, I think, that the Turks and Bedouins would think that he was intriguing with the Christians ... He also said he wished to avoid all friction and trouble with the Egyptian government with whom he was friendly.
>
> The Arabs relate with joy a rather significant incident. Before Sidi Ahmad's arrival the Turks had hoisted the Turkish flag and, when requested to take it down ... Nuri Bey [Enver's brother] refused saying who were they to order the Sultan's flag to be taken away. On the arrival of Sidi Ahmad he sent for Nuri Bey ... and told him to take the flag down at once, and as soon as Nuri Bey had left his house he sent twelve of his Sudanese to see that his order was carried out.[27]

Over the next few months there were further communications between Sayyid Ahmad and the Coastguard. With British interest in Sanusi affairs now aroused, they sent a number of native agents to gather information. In January 1913 one unnamed agent went directly to the Grand Sanusi and a full report, marked "Secret", was compiled by the Intelligence Department of the British Army of Occupation in Cairo.[28] This confirmed that the Sanusi was greatly upset by the Turkish withdrawal and that he was determined to continue the war without them. To that end he had exacted an oath from the sheikhs of his *zawiya*s to stand by him for as long as it took to get their country back from the Italians.

The Sanusi asked the agent if there was any news for him from the

[27] FO 141/732, Royle's report of 20 October 1912.
[28] FO 141/732, Secret report of 16 January 1913.

Khedive, to whom he had sent two female slaves, and from whom there had been no acknowledgement of receipt. The agent told Sayyid Ahmad that he had nothing to do with the Khedive; that he was simply a devotee of the Sanusi Brotherhood, although apparently he was not believed. Sayyid Ahmad instructed the agent to inform the Khedive that the Sanusi were in need of more ammunition despite the cargoes now being delivered by steamer to the Libyan coast.

Some Sanusi adherents visiting from the 'Asir near Yemen complained to Sayyid Ahmad that Royle's men had searched their baggage, and they talked openly of murdering Royle. This was expressly forbidden by Sayyid Ahmad, who said that Royle was better than "the others", and they should let him do his job.

Sayyid Ahmad was also described as being scholarly, spending considerable time cataloguing his books and manuscripts. He was depicted as being of medium height, a bit stout, with a beard and "a firm, determined face… [and is] about 40 years old".

There were other communications from Sayyid Ahmad that were addressed directly to Royle, but still no invitation to go to Jaghbub. Instead, Sayyid Ahmad sent his brother Sidi Hilal to make Royle's acquaintance. They met in Qirba, near Siwa, on 25 February 1913.[29] As far as the British knew this was the first time that a member of the Sanusi's own family had visited Egypt since the original Grand Sanusi had passed through the country on his return from Mecca in the 1840s. It was an occasion that called for appropriate ceremony and competent hosting. The honour fell to Leo Royle to keep his eminent guest entertained and he rose to the occasion using what resources he had available. He organized parades with his Sudanese troopers, who were the Coastguard rank and file. He paraded them mounted on camels; and he paraded them dismounted. Then he drew them up into two teams and had them play a football match. Royle then showed Hilal a collection of illustrated magazines and pointed out portraits of Turkish ministers and officers. Hilal was astonished to see pictures of Enver in a top hat and frock coat and sporting a "German moustache" like Kaiser Wilhelm's.

As for Hilal, he was a young man, apparently in his early twenties. He was "well-built, medium height, no hair on his face, has excellent manners … very quiet … most intelligent … has a good sense of humour, is very

[29] FO 141/732, Royle's report from Qirba, 2 March 1913.

fond of laughing, and looks one straight in the face". Among his bags he carried a wind-up gramophone given to him by a member of the Egyptian ruling family who liked to hunt in Libya, and Hilal entertained Royle with this by putting on records of native Egyptian singers.

Hilal had arrived in Qirba with a retinue of about 130 armed tribesmen. Royle was impressed by Hilal's saddlery, which he describes as "magnificent ... all inlaid and worked with silver and gold. His own bridle seems to be entirely composed of gold and silver coins and beads, the reins being a silver cord."

On the 27th Royle escorted Hilal to Siwa.

> [At first there] came a giant Sudanese on foot carrying a big *chassepot* at the slope; some twenty paces behind him came Sidi Hilal on horseback, and from his girths spreading out in a straight line from him on either side about 80 men on foot, 40 either side with rifles ... at the slope; behind Sidi Hilal in line came the horsemen who happened to be with the party ... [then] came the baggage and people on donkeys and walking in a crowd ... sometimes he rode at a trot and those on foot had to run![30]

A mile outside Siwa Oasis a thousand men met the procession with flags, war drums and muskets. "It was a very fine sight as they rushed firing and shouting to meet us, Sidi Hilal's party also firing as fast as they could load." Royle also mentioned in his report that the people of Siwa were "for the first time quite pleased to see us".

Royle had brought a Kodak camera and Hilal allowed himself to be photographed. Amusingly, Royle had hurriedly to send a telegram to Cairo: "[H]e desires a Kodak and day-light developing gear. May this be sent to me at earliest convenience at my cost or otherwise. If it catches next post shall probably be in time to explain working of it before he goes west." Royle's guest also admired his Colt 45 automatic and asked if he could have it. In fact, the British had recently sent one to Sayyid Ahmad as a gift. But this time Royle felt that his guest was asking too much. He told Hilal that it was Government property and not available in Egypt. On 12 March Hilal finally left Egypt (with his new camera). His last request was for Royle to pass "his salaams" to Lord Kitchener and to ask him to

---

[30] FO 141/732, Royle's report from Qirba, 2 March 1913.

send a Colt 45. Then he left, intending to go first to Jaghbub and then to join the "holy war" against the Italians.

Thanks to Royle good relations had been established with the Sanusi, and the Government of Egypt was grateful – at least to the extent of awarding him its "Fourth Class Osmanieh" medal when the next Khedivial honours were announced. Perhaps Kitchener was more impressed then the Khedive because from this point on he showed special interest in Royle. As for Sayyid Ahmad, he was clearly pleased with the reception given to his younger brother. On 26 March a special messenger arrived from him with a gift of a goat for Royle and a letter for Lord Kitchener containing seventy Turkish pounds and a shopping list. At the bottom of the list requesting the supply of various rifles and telescopic sights was the Sanusi's order for sixteen Colt 45s.

2

Bimbashi Royle

IN AN EXTRAORDINARY PHOTOGRAPH, taken at Qirba in 1911, Leo Royle is standing by a pool of water amidst clumps of high swamp grass. His workaday Coastguard uniform rather suggests that of an unkempt Boy Scout: shorts reaching to the knees; shirt sleeves rolled up his forearms, the shirt's two front pockets stuffed full and sagging; around his neck a kerchief knotted in front. He also wears a wide military-style belt with several pouches and a sheathed dagger aslant behind it. On his head is the customary fez of an Egyptian official, but this one, with the attached plume, identifies the wearer as an officer of the Coastguard Camel Corps.

What is extraordinary, however, is Royle's face. He is not yet thirty years old, but for twelve years he has lived in the desert, chased armed smugglers, experienced tribal warfare and feuds; and it is the distillation of that harsh and sometimes violent existence that seems etched into the face and character of the man who is staring at us. It is not just that he is so thin; or that his facial skin is like saddle leather; or that his eye-lids and lips appear to have been sand-blasted. It is the eyes themselves that give the impression that he is now "at home" in conditions of extreme deprivation. But his look reflects more than the soldierly virtues of dignity, honesty, courage – there is something hard and humourless about it as well.

And yet there was clearly another side to the man. His cousin Gladys, daughter of George Royle, was an English rose who charmed Cairene society at this time.[1] She was often mentioned in the social columns after dances at the Savoy, banquets at Abdin Palace, receptions at the British Agency ... In later life, she would remember Leo as her "favourite cousin", which suggests that we have been misled by the look in the photograph, that he did have a sense of humour and could be good company. Alas, there is a paucity of such personal information as would enable one to complete this portrait with confidence. No family letters have survived, and there are only a few anecdotes remembered by Royle's descendants. One, told by a nephew, is that when on home leave in England Leo seemed to eat incessantly.[2] Another used to be related by Leo's brother, Guy Royle, to shock the ladies: that Leo had a "native wife", but as Leo never married we can only surmise whether this was just a joke or an indiscreet reference to some lady of the night.[3]

Yet to supplement this sketchy information there is enough elsewhere to confirm that he was an exceptional figure both in the world of Egyptian public security and, as soldier and airman, in time of war.

Leopold Victor Arnold Royle was born on 9 April 1882, the eldest child of Dr Arnold Royle and Cecily Jane Longueville Snow. Dr Royle was the personal physician of Prince Leopold, the haemophiliac youngest son of Queen Victoria. In fact, Leopold Royle was Prince Leopold's godson. The Prince died in 1884 leaving a bequest of £1000 to the doctor and a smaller amount to young Leo. The Royle family was allowed to continue living at Albany Lodge, in Esher, Surrey, on the Prince's estate and did so until Dr Royle's death in 1919.

The Royle family had strong links with Egypt even before Leo was born. Arnold Royle had two brothers who had lived and worked there since the 1870s, that is, since before the British Occupation in 1882. Both were ex-Navy men and qualified barristers, and both became pillars of Anglo-Egyptian society. George Royle went to seek his fortune in Port Said shortly after the opening of the Suez Canal and had a long and

[1] Leo and Gladys were, in fact, "double cousins", that is, their fathers were brothers and their mothers were sisters. In 1905 Gladys married Charles Wilberforce Maclean; their only child, Fitzroy Maclean, was born in Cairo in 1911. In fact, Sir Fitzroy Maclean's full name was Fitzroy Hew Royle Maclean.

[2] Related by Mr Arnold Hoghton, son of Leo's sister Sybil, in correspondence with the author.

[3] Related by Mrs Ann Mills, a relation of the wife of Leo's brother Guy, in an interview with the author.

successful business career. Charles Royle practised law in Alexandria, eventually becoming a judge of the Egyptian Court of Appeal. He was also one of the founders of *The Egyptian Gazette* and the author of an authoritative history of the Occupation and the Sudanese War. By the early 1900s both brothers were living in Cairo.

It was, however, a third relative, a brother of Leo's mother Cecily, who opened the door to Leo's career in the Egyptian Coastguard. Cecil Longueville Snow, having served five years in the Canadian North-West Mounted Police, joined the Egyptian Coastguard in 1891. By 1899 he had worked his way up to head the Coastguard's Directorate for the region of Port Said and the Suez Canal, and in the summer of that year he returned to England to get married. One can easily imagine that this family event was the occasion when Leo's prospects for work in the Coastguard were seriously discussed. Leo was 17 and had left Wellington College the previous year. The Coastguard was expanding, and several new recruits had recently been accepted. When Snow returned to Egypt with his new bride, he would have discussed the possibility of employing Leo with Coastguard Director-General George Hunter. Hunter was clearly amenable, because in 1900 Leo arrived in Egypt via P&O steamer – his uncle George Royle had been P&O agent in Port Said – to begin his new career.

In 1900 the Egyptian Coastguard Administration was in a period of great expansion and administrative change. Founded in 1876 the Coastguard "Service", as it was then called, had been a small and under-funded sub-department of Customs within the Egyptian Ministry of Finance. It had proved its worth in the fight against the smuggling of tobacco and salt, both Government monopolies, and more recently against the smuggling of hashish. By the 1890s the Coastguards had both a Marine Service, with its own cruisers for patrolling the Mediterranean and Red Sea coasts, and a Land Service, with its own Camel Corps. It was in this latter division that Leo Royle was employed.

In the western part of Alexandria, on the narrow neck of land between the sea and Lake Mareotis, stands the Shefakhana Fort, almost completely hidden today amidst the tumble-down urban sprawl of Mex district. At the start of the 20th century this relic from the time of Muhammad 'Ali, still with moat and drawbridge, was the Coastguard station where the training of European recruits took place. A colourful description of that training

occurs in the memoirs of Thomas Russell Pasha, who, though a police
cadet, received the same training as the Coastguard recruits at Shefakhana
in 1902, two years after Royle, "to be drilled in the ranks and pushed
about by native drill sergeants just like any Egyptian cadet officer."

> From the Coastguard point of view I was a raw recruit who had to be
> trained from the very beginning, and it would have been quite useless to
> explain that I had commanded my Cadet Corps at school ... there were
> two things I did not know, one was the Arabic language and the other
> was the words of command which were still given in Turkish ... My
> instructor was a huge Egyptian sergeant without a single word of
> English, possessed of a voice like a bull and a deep-rooted conviction that
> the way that he had been trained was the only way to train others ... The
> first morning at seven o'clock punctually I paraded in tarbush, sweater
> and flannel trousers and was served out with my first equipment,
> consisting of leather belt, cartridge-pouch and bayonet frog: the sergeant
> then produced a tin of soap, a small dry sponge and a piece of heel-ball.
> I deduced that his intention was that I should apply the soap to the belt
> for cleaning purposes and, seeing no water handy, I made a sound like
> "*moiya*", meaning water, to which the sergeant reacted by shaking his
> head and saying "*mafish moiya*" – "there is no water". He then took the
> tin of soap and, with some deep preliminary throat-sounds, proceeded to
> spit generously into it and show me how to produce the necessary lather
> with my little bit of sponge. Thus it was on the first day and thus it was
> everyday for the belt and pouches ... Having passed with credit as a
> private of horse and foot in a squad composed only of myself, I was then
> put in as No. 2 in the front rank of a squad of fifty Sudanese infantry
> recruits whose friendly black hands caught hold of mine and pulled me
> into place when I missed the Turkish word of command ... Finally I was
> made to drill the squad myself, the sergeant quietly giving the Turkish
> words of command for me to repeat in a bellow to the squad.[4]

When Royle received his basic Coastguard training at Shefakhana, the
Libyan Desert reached right to the western fringes of Alexandria, and
there Egyptian Government authority virtually stopped. Smuggling was
rife both in the ports and in the desert. In the port areas the coastguards,

[4] Thomas Russell Pasha (1949), *Egyptian Service: 1902–1946*, pp. 15–16.

especially those of the Marine Service, worked with police and Customs; but the fight against smuggling in the desert regions was the sole responsibility of the Coastguard Administration, primarily the Land Service. Their attempts to curtail such activities were mostly launched from Shefakhana and did not go very far beyond the city limits.

The officer in command at Shefakhana during Royle's stay there was Gordon Morice Bey, while Morice's second in command was a twenty-year-old officer named Charles Armstrong. Both of these men were in a position powerfully to influence Leo's imagination. Morice was the son of Major James Morice, the first head of the Egyptian Coastguard, who died at the battle of El Teb (near Suakin in the Sudan) in 1884, as well as being the godson of Gordon of Khartoum. Charles Armstrong had no such glorious antecedents, but the work he carried out based right there at Shefakhana was adventurous enough to stir the sensibility of any raw recruit. The following account of one of his anti-smuggling operations is from an official report quoted by *The Egyptian Gazette* in 1901.

> While a Coastguard patrol of 9 men under Mulazim Awal [First Lieutenant] Armstrong was patrolling the desert to the west of Nubarieh Canal, they seized a caravan of 11 camels and 6 Bedouins with over 1,400 kilos of hashish.
>
> A few days later, on hearing that there was more hashish in the desert, they proceeded on patrol, and discovering tracks of a caravan, followed them up and seized a further 600 kilos.
>
> While making this latter seizure, they were heavily attacked by upwards of 60 Bedouins, who kept up a continual fire on the patrol for over an hour, but were eventually driven off, and the hashish was successfully brought into the nearest Coastguard station.[5]

The fact that Lt. Armstrong died of smallpox three years later is a sufficient reminder that the coastguards faced other perils than simply armed smugglers.

The head of the Coastguard Camel Corps (and the Desert Directorate) in this period was a German of Danish extraction named André von Dumreicher, who wrote memoirs which brilliantly depict what this work was like, though they are frustratingly vague about personal details and

[5] EG, 6 August 1901.

dates. On the other hand, they were written a quarter century or more after the events they describe, and von Dumreicher's vagueness may be the result of painful memories. As the Egyptian Government official most directly responsible for administering the country's deserts, he had unparalleled direct knowledge of, and sympathy for, the Bedouin, whose way of life was changing forever; and he disapproved of Government policy toward them, which inflexibly sought to apply "the letter of the law" to a people with ancient laws and customs of their own. His partiality for the Bedouin brought him into conflict with certain British officials, especially the Adviser to the Ministry of Justice, Malcolm McIlwraith, and this eventually cost von Dumreicher his job despite his excellent relations with his British colleagues and with Kitchener.[6]

Royle and Armstrong were two of only four young European officers apprenticed to von Dumreicher. The other two were a German named Gärtner and a third Englishman, named Johnston; both appear to have left the Coastguard by 1906. Leo Royle, the youngest of the four, stayed in the service for fifteen years, until the First World War.

Royle's first years in the Coastguard were spent in the Eastern Desert between the Nile Valley and the Red Sea. Von Dumreicher portrays Royle while still a teenager showing great enthusiasm and a sense of adventure.

> At Asyut I crossed the Nile in sailing-boats with Yousbashi Radwan, Royle, ten Sudanese, and two guides … To return to mundane things, we had an excellent dinner. Royle, who all day long ate snacks from his saddle-bags while riding, was always surprised that he never felt really very hungry. However, that evening he devoured a quarter of a ham, half a Dutch cheese, and other dainties. I soon lay on my camp-bed, dreaming of clear, rippling brooks in Europe and slept till dawn. Royle, who had been reading *The Last of the Mohicans*, lay in the open and waited in

[6] In 1907 von Dumreicher married the niece of George Hunter. He left the Coastguard 1 January 1910, at the height of the 'Uthman Habbun affair, and went to work for the Ministry of the Interior organising the *ghafirs* (village watchmen) in the Nile Valley. When war broke out between Britain and Germany he was personally vouched for by several high-ranking British officials, including Kitchener. However, after the latter's death in June 1916 von Dumreicher was given the choice of being interned in Malta or in England. He opted for England and remained there until 1919.
[7] André von Dumreicher (1931), *Trackers and Smugglers in the Deserts of Egypt*, pp. 140 and 148.

ambush the whole night for the salt-thieves, though these had no reason to march during that bitterly cold night.[7]

In general the coastguards were reluctant enforcers of the salt monopoly, which pre-dated the British Occupation. In the desert there are frequent salines, or salt pans, where anybody can scoop up as much salt as he wants off the ground. But to do this was illegal in Egypt because of the Government monopoly. The British recognized the injustice of this situation but were slow to correct it, mainly because the monopoly was a major source of revenue for the impecunious Egyptian treasury, and the ostensible reason for the British being in Egypt was to put Egyptian accounts into order. While Cromer declared that he had finally balanced Egypt's books by the early 1890s, he did not end the monopoly until 1 January 1906, and until then the Government expected the Coastguard to put a halt to salt "smuggling". The officers tried to turn a blind eye in cases where poor villagers collected salt for their own use; but there were still plenty of men who would collect salt to sell at a price less than the Government's price, and these people were usually armed and on the look-out for Coastguard patrols. On the day after the above-quoted occasion Royle was fired upon by an armed smuggler. He fired back from 150 yards and the man fell dead. It was the sort of tragedy that could not have happened but for the delay in abolishing the hated monopoly.

In March 1902 Sir Eldon Gorst, the Adviser to the Ministry of Finance and future successor to Cromer as British Consul-General,[8] joined von Dumreicher in a visit to the Eastern Desert, crossing on camels to the north-east from Qena (north of Luxor) to the Gulf of Suez. The then nineteen-year-old Royle, who was commanding officer at Qena with the rank of *yousbashi* (captain), was sent with his patrol several weeks earlier to ensure that this part of the desert was clear of smugglers. Von Dumreicher's party

struck [Royle's] track now for the first time at El Kattar [near the Red Sea]. He had tried to climb up the perpendicular cliff of the waterfall with the camp-ropes. Naturally he did not succeed, and I was glad that he had not broken his neck. As Royle loved his camels and was very proud of his patrol, his ambition was always to establish new records. He

[8] And, incidentally, Coastguard Director George Hunter's brother-in-law.

declared that he never drove his camels too fast, but this I did not believe, since from his tracks I could establish positively the fact that for hours on end he kept up a speed of eight miles an hour, which is too fast going for heavily laden camels on a long trek. However, since his camels were in good condition I could not reproach him seriously.[9]

While stationed at Qena Leo Royle encountered the gifted tracker named Husayn Faris. Husayn was a Bishari from that mountainous part of Upper Egypt between the Nile and Red Sea which straddles the Tropic of Cancer. Like the Bushmen of southern Africa the Bisharin have an uncanny ability to read the desert's signs and tracks and to tell in detail what has happened there, a gift which can seem almost supernatural to the uninitiated. Royle received from Husayn an "education" in desert tracking and survival.

Hussein soon became a favourite with all my young English officers, who admired him immensely; and after saving Royle's life in the mountains when the latter nearly fell over a precipice, the two became inseparable friends ... [Royle] was about the same age as Hussein, and one could not help delighting in these two boys. Much as they differed in appearance, education, and ideas, they were similar in character, equally fearless, daring, and persevering, and they were both under the spell of the desert. Hussein showed Royle how to live there independently of civilization. The patrols always took with them provisions for six weeks, but Royle, with Hussein and another Bishari, remained six months in the wilds. They left their camels in shady ravines and climbed the high mountains. They hunted gazelle and hare, and shot grouse and partridge. On coral reefs they found lobsters and mussels. In one or two bays of the Red Sea they found rock-oysters, which are better than the ordinary kind, and when necessary they contented themselves with simpler fare. Once, as *hors d'oeuvre*, they partook of an oyster-like mussel a foot long, which would have poisoned twenty ordinary men, but did not upset their ostrich-like digestion, and, to round off their meal, they devoured a whole stork, the toughest of birds, with the exception of beak and legs, and declared both dishes excellent. Royle spent the happiest years of his life with Hussein. He was the only European who could read a track

[9] Dumreicher (1931), pp. 150–1

1. Bimbashi Royle, photographed at Qirba in 1911.

2. Lieutenant-Colonel Cecil Longueville Snow of the Egyptian Coastguard, Officer Commanding at Sollum. The fact that Snow was Leopold Royle's maternal uncle seems to have been kept secret, as it is never mentioned in the sources.

3. *Left*: Leo Royle (far right) on home leave from the Egyptian Coastguard in the summer of 1903. With him at this beach near Bexhill are his brother Guy and sisters Victoria (next to Leo) and Sybil. Their uncle George Royle had a home nearby.

4. *Below*: Coastguard Douglas "Roy" Tweedie on his motorcycle. Tweedie joined the Royal Flying Corps with Royle in September 1914.

5. *Left*: George Hunter, Director-General of the Egyptian Coastguard Administration. Both he and Mark Sykes were married to sisters of Sir Eldon Gorst, British Agent and Consul-General in Egypt from 1907 to 1911.

7. *Opposite page*: Detachment of the Coastguard Camel Corps at Qirba before the First World War.

6. *Below*: The camp of the Egyptian Coastguard detachment at Qirba in 1911. The coastguards were guarding the passes on the frontier to prevent smuggling from Libya. There were three campsites at Qirba, but the layers of rocky shelf against the hills suggest that this may have been the site of the battle on 3 February 1917.

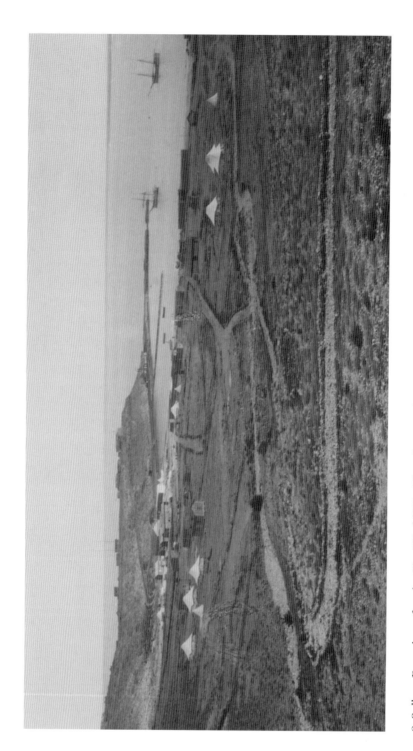

8. Sollum Bay, taken after the First World War. The photographer is standing near the bottom of the path that wound up the escarpment.

9. The Turkish fort above the escarpment at Sollum. At the instigation of Kitchener the fort was occupied by the Egyptian Army in 1911, at the start of the Turco–Italian War.

10. Lord Kitchener (in civilian dress, first row centre) and General John Maxwell (sitting at Kitchener's left), with officers and NCOs of the 21st Lancers at Cairo Barracks shortly before the First World War. Where the barracks were, the Nile Hilton now stands.

11. General John Maxwell at Mudros (near Gallipoli) to meet with Kitchener in November 1915.

12. A rare photograph of the "Headquarters Office, Army of Occupation" at Midan Suarès in Cairo. T. E. Lawrence worked here for a year, until British Army Headquarters moved to the Savoy in December 1915.

Savoy Hotel au Caire.

L'hôtel qui se trouve juste

13. The Savoy Hotel, to which British Army Headquarters, including the Intelligence Department, moved in December 1915.

14. *Left*: T. E. Lawrence at British Army Head-quarters (the Savoy Hotel) in Cairo.

15. *Below*: A Maurice Farman, flying over Sinai in February 1915. The observer, sitting in the forward seat, is Roy Tweedie.

16. Sulayman al-Baruni, Libyan hero of the Turco–Italian War and member of Enver's Special Organization. At the start of the First World War, Enver sent al-Baruni to Cyrenaica to urge the Sanusi to attack the British in Egypt. (Al-Baruni had vowed not to cut his hair so long as Libya was occupied by the Italians.)

Sayyid Ahmad, the Grand S...

17. *Above left*: Enver in Libya during the Turco-Italian War, 1911–12.

18. *Above right*: The Grand Sanusi, Sayyid Ahmad al-Sharif al-Sanusi, at Amsa'id. (This picture and the following two pictures are from General Maxwell's own photo album and were almost certainly taken by Royle.)

19. *Below left*: The Grand Sanusi's younger brother, Hilal.

Sayid Hilal el Senussi.

Sayed Idris el Senussi

20. *Above*: Sayyid Muhammad Idris al-Sanusi, Sayyid Ahmad's nephew. Sayyid Idris eventually became the head of the Sanusiyya and (in 1951) King of Libya. He was overthrown by Colonel Gaddafi in September 1969.

21. *Left*: This picture of Ottoman officers was taken at Edirne in November 1913, shortly after the ending of the Balkan War. The man in the centre (with the white moustache) is General Khorshid Pasha. To his right (in the front row) is Enver Pasha. Standing just behind Enver's right shoulder is his younger brother, Nuri. At the far right of the group is Ja'far al-'Askari. The robed Libyan to the rear is Muhammad Jibani, who sailed with Nuri and Ja'far on their mission to the Sanusi in January 1915.

22. *Left*: The wealthy and gifted orientalist, Baron Max von Oppenheim, who worked as an *attaché* at the German legation in Cairo from 1896 to 1910. Against the Occupation, he regularly upset the British in Egypt, especially Lord Cromer, because of his contacts with Egyptian nationalists. In 1914 he wrote a German master plan for defeating the British in the East.

23. Baron Max von Oppenheim, dressed as an Arab. He occasionally walked around Cairo in this attire, probably more for his own amusement than for professional reasons.

24. Otto Mannesmann, German agent in Cyrenaica, was the youngest son of industrialist Reinhard Mannesmann.

25. Ja'far al-'Askari in Sanusi robes. The photo was taken in Alexandria on 27 April 1915, while Ja'far was on his secret mission to visit Jemal Pasha in Jerusalem.

easily, and he could find the wells by following the trail of the wild animals going to drink. He naturally became the idol of the bedouins.[10]

By 1904 Royle had risen to the rank of *saghkolaghasi* (adjutant-major) and is listed in the *British Garrison Directory* of that period as officer commanding the Suez Canal at the Victoria Barracks, just south of the town of Suez. These barracks had been used before the Suez Canal as a staging area for British troops going to and from India – the stretch between Alexandria, Cairo and Suez in those days was made by train for most of the distance and on foot for the rest. Since the opening of the Canal the Barracks had been redundant, and the Coastguard took them over in 1904 as a base for patrolling the west coast of the Gulf of Suez. In this period Royle reported directly to his uncle, Cecil Snow, who was based in Port Said.

> When the smugglers of Suez and the Red Sea, like their brothers of the Libyan Desert, realized that their safety depended on the swiftness of their camels, we had to build four wooden stations between Suez and Cape Zaffarana, eighty miles farther south, and patrol this coast night and day. About twenty miles further inland Bisharin trackers busily examined any camel-tracks which might have gone to the shore to fetch hashish. Thus the smugglers, who rode only at night to avoid being seen by the guides, could not reach the coast before 11 p.m. Sometimes ten well-armed Maaza smugglers on the swiftest riding camels, with only a very light load in their saddle-bags, would start at midnight on their hundred miles' journey from the Gulf of Suez to the Nile, and, when the patrols picked up their tracks at daybreak, the smugglers would already be half-way to Cairo, so that further pursuit was useless.[11]

Around 1906 the main focus of the Coastguard's fight to control hashish and arms smuggling was in the Western Desert. Virtually all the hashish smuggled into Egypt at this time came from Greece, and most of it was delivered by boat to the Mediterranean coast of Egypt or Libya, where it was picked up and run to the Nile Valley by camel caravan. The Egyptian Coastguard had developed an effective intelligence network not only among the Western Desert Arabs, but also in Greece and Libya, so that the

[10] Dumreicher (1931), pp. 116–17. [11] Ibid., p. 164.

annual amounts of hashish seized was increasing until, in early 1906, a boundary dispute in the Sinai resulted in the withdrawal of a large Coastguard force from the Western Desert to the Sinai Peninsula. "As soon as it was known that the frontier was practically unguarded," wrote Percy Machell,[12] the Adviser to the Ministry of Interior, to Lord Cromer, "hashish poured into Egypt."[13] It was in these circumstances that the Coastguard Administration sent Leo Royle to the Western Desert.

In the six years since Royle had left Shefakhana, the Coastguard Administration had made great progress in bringing the Western Desert under the control of the Egyptian Government. Moving westward along the coast they had established Coastguard posts at regular intervals, the main one being at Mersa Matruh, with its natural harbour. There would soon (1907) be a post at Sidi Barani, which at the time was considered the westernmost position they could occupy without upsetting the Turks who were at Sollum. The narrow-gauge tracks of the Khedivial Railroad, meanwhile, were laid following the westward progress of the Coastguard. Its railhead would eventually be near al-Dab'a, mid-way between Alexandria and Mersa Matruh.

As the Western Desert was now safer to visit, the Egyptian Government began to pay more attention to the outlying Siwa Oasis. Shortly after his transfer Royle, in charge of a twelve-man patrol, accompanied von Dumreicher and an Egyptian officer named al-Mesiri on a visit to that oasis, where some of the more intrepid smugglers entered the country from Libya. Also of the party was Major Arthur Reginald Hoskins, whom von Dumreicher describes as "a friend", but who was in fact in charge of the intelligence branch of the Army of Occupation. The party was not well-received by the inhabitants of Siwa, nor by headman 'Uthman Habbun. This would not have been surprising, since it was common knowledge that several European travellers had been roughly handled there during the preceding decade. Nevertheless, al-Mesiri was able to soothe ruffled feelings among the Siwans, and the coastguards were able to explore the smugglers' route from Libya and then leave in peace.

---

[12] Machell had also been Director-General of the Egyptian Coastguard from 1896 to 1898, during which period George Hunter, who later succeeded him, was Deputy Director-General.

[13] Parliamentary Papers (Great Britain): Egypt No. 1 (1907), "The Annual Report for 1906".

A Maghrebi Arab named 'Abd al-'Ati al-Hasuna earned himself particular notoriety around this time for his daring smuggling operations from Libya. He was wealthy and, according to von Dumreicher, smuggled primarily "from a spirit of adventure". His route, incredibly, was often across central Egypt, in other words, hundreds of miles from the coast.

> [He] was well-educated, had been brought up in France and spoke several languages ... was a brave and daring man and equipped his bodyguard, which consisted of the boldest outlaws, with the most modern magazine rifles.[14]

Curiously, two German archaeologists, excavating ruins thirty miles west of Alexandria, may have personally encountered 'Abd al-'Ati in 1907, without knowing that he was one of the most hunted outlaws in Egypt. Since the notorious smuggler was about to become part of the Royle legend, it is worth including their account of the meeting.

> [We] met two handsome Arabs in spotless burnous, and armed in a way not usually found in the desert. They carried Martini rifles, and their cartridge-belts slung across the shoulder certainly fulfilled the purpose of making the necessary impression. When they saw us, they greeted us very politely, and one of them took some papers from his red-leather bag and said, "I come from the district of the great Gássabe (Marmarika), and only want a letter read for me which I have carried about for a long time, and must otherwise take to Alexandria." The letter was in German, and from a Viennese lady who, in affectionate terms, invited the man to go to Vienna, described the route via Alexandria and Trieste, and, as is usual in such cases, concluded with more expressions of affection. The lady also promised to send money for the journey, and did so, for months after the man came again and stayed until one of us went to Alexandria, where a sum of 10 or 12 pounds was awaiting him. The two strange men who appeared so suddenly ... were hashish smugglers; one of them had carried on an excellent business at Vienna in selling cigarettes, and spoke a little German – the Viennese dialect, naturally – and was glad to find some one who could read his letter. We did not consent to write the

[14] Dumreicher (1931), p. 159.
[15] J. C. Ewald Falls (1913), *Three Years in the Libyan Desert*, pp. 168–9.

reply for him – mistrust of all was our best safeguard – and so with many
expressions of thanks the smugglers departed, after they had been
permitted to rest for an hour in one of the tents.[15]

In pursuit of 'Abd al-'Ati Leo Royle performed an extraordinary feat of
desert exploration, one that his Coastguard colleagues and others involved
in desert security regarded as unprecedented for a European. In 1907–8,
Royle spent six months patrolling from Qirba (near Siwa) south to 'Ain
Dalla, and even to a well called Bir Abu Minqar, over 200 miles south of
Mersa Matruh. Presumably Husayn Faris was with him (although that is
uncertain since the Bishari tracker ended his service with the Coastguard
around this time) and Royle must have had at least a small patrol. One
wonders if even his loyal Sudanese could have remained unfazed at having
to spend half a year without a break so far into the desert.

In mid-1908 a Coastguard patrol finally battled it out with their greatest
enemy in the dunes south of Siwa. Seven smugglers were killed, including
'Abd al-'Ati's brother and two cousins. 'Abd al-'Ati himself escaped with
the remainder of his men. Royle was not involved in the battle because
after his long desert ordeal he had been temporarily sent to work at 'Ain
Shams, near Cairo, but he was soon back in the Western Desert, and that
is where he stayed until the outbreak of the First World War.

It all amounted to a remarkable apprenticeship for Leo Royle, who was
finally to meet the Grand Sanusi, Sayyid Ahmad al-Sharif, in November
1914.

3

Egypt, 1914

A T THE START OF THE First World War, Egypt in effect had two rulers and both were out of the country. The Khedive, 'Abbas Hilmi II, had sailed to Constantinople on his yacht to spend the summer on the Bosphorus. There, four weeks after Archduke Franz Ferdinand was assassinated by a Serbian student, the Khedive was attacked in similar circumstances by an Egyptian student, who approached the khedivial carriage and fired ten shots from two Browning revolvers, wounding 'Abbas Hilmi in the cheek and left forearm. The assailant was killed on the spot in circumstances that raised suspicion that responsibility for the attack lay not simply with extremist Egyptian nationalists, who hated their "reactionary" ruler almost as much as they hated the British, but also with high officials in the Turkish government. It was established that numerous policemen had been present at the scene, including two senior officials from the Ministry of Interior, and that the would-be assassin had nevertheless been able to empty both revolvers, and only then, when he could easily have been arrested, was he shot dead. The Khedive was convinced that the Young Turks were behind the plot[1] and was anxious to get home as soon as possible. By the time he had recovered from his wounds, however, the world was at war, and the British had informed him – by telegram! – that he would not be allowed to return to Egypt.

The other man who ruled Egypt, Lord Kitchener, was in England. On 3 August, with war imminent, he hurried to Dover hoping to be able to return to Egypt. Before Kitchener's Channel steamer could sail, however, Prime Minister Asquith recalled him to London. Two days later Kitchener was appointed Secretary for War. Neither he nor 'Abbas Hilmi would ever see Egypt again.

Kitchener's new appointment necessarily resulted in changes at the British Agency in Cairo. The *chargé d'affaires*, Milne Cheetham, was temporarily placed in charge for the Foreign Office, while Lieutenant-General John Maxwell was ordered to Egypt to take charge of military affairs. The war caused a shift in the relative importance of the two top positions, political and military. For the first time since the beginning of the Occupation the senior British military officer in Egypt had greater authority than the senior Foreign Office official. This was further accentuated by the fact that Maxwell was a long-time friend and colleague of the new Secretary of War in London, and so willingly fell into the habit of reporting to him regularly, often daily, about the situation in Egypt. Kitchener was thus able, despite his massive workload, to continue his involvement in Egyptian affairs.

Britain's most urgent problem in Egypt immediately after the outbreak of war was what to do with some 10,000 Germans and Austro-Hungarians who were still in the country on 4 August.[2] The Germans represented only a quarter of that figure but were nevertheless the particular focus of British concern. Some, like Royle's mentor André von Dumreicher, had been in Egyptian Government service for many years. The Germans had their own schools, hospitals, churches, and banks; there were German beer halls and German newspapers. In fact, it was the newspapers that gave the British an early excuse to take action against the German community despite Egypt's neutrality. Soon after the fighting started in Europe the locally-published *Ägyptische Nachrichten* published "sensational" news of German victories in Belgium, and the British authorities responded by closing it down.

---

[1] Sir Ronald Storrs, Oriental Secretary at the British Agency in Cairo, subscribed to the theory that the Turks were responsible. In *Orientations* he placed the blame on the Ottoman Grand Vizier, Prince Muhammad Saïd Halim, who himself would have become khedive of Egypt if 'Abbas Hilmi's grandfather, Ismaïl, had not succeeded in changing the line of succession. According to this theory Halim had conspired with a disaffected former instructor in Arabic at Oxford named 'Abd al-'Aziz Shawish, who was wanted by the Egyptian authorities for acts of political violence, including involvement in the 1910 assassination of Egypt's Coptic Prime Minister, Butros Ghali.
[2] According to the *EG*, 6 October 1914.

In early September German and Austrian diplomatic and consular staffs received notice that they were being expelled. To his credit the German *chargé d'affaires* exhorted his compatriots to remember that they were guests in the country and to behave accordingly, and this was reported in *The Times*. The diplomats were expelled on 10 September.

Another British problem was the presence of German ships at the ports of Alexandria, Port Said and Suez. Many of these had rushed to Egyptian waters in the hope that official Egyptian neutrality and the international status of the Suez Canal would afford them protection from seizure. In the event such hopes proved futile as the British seized the ships as prizes and took about one hundred and fifty German crew members prisoner.

Before long all Germans and Austro-Hungarians domiciled in Egypt were required to register or be arrested. This resulted in the detention of over 500 men of military age who were shipped to Malta for internment.

As the months passed it became clear that Turkish-Egyptians would pose a greater problem for the British than the European enemy aliens. There were more than 30,000 members of this community[3] and, on the whole, they had accepted the Occupation better than Egypt's Arab population had. But Egypt, despite nominal semi-independence, was by international law part of the Ottoman Empire, and signs were already mounting that the Young Turks would align that Empire on the side of Britain's enemies.

For the first three months of the war the Turkish government in Constantinople had agonized over which side to join. Enver's pro-German stance was common knowledge, but the country's entry on the side of the Central Powers was not a forgone conclusion, as Enver's colleagues in the ruling triumvirate, Talaat and Jemal, were less enthusiastic than he about joining with the Central Powers. In the end it was the British and the Germans who forced a decision.

In the final days before the war Winston Churchill, as First Lord of the Admiralty, had requisitioned for the Royal Navy two battleships that were being built for the Turks on the River Tyne. The order had cost Turkey an immense sum that she could scarcely afford. The British, as if determined to push Turkey into the German camp, then refused to discuss compensation.

---

[3] The Census of 1907 gives a figure for that year of 27,000.

While the British pushed, the Germans pulled. On 29 October a German admiral named Souchon, with German sailors dressed as Turks and his German ship flying the Turkish flag, bombarded the Russian fleet in the Black Sea. The Russians, deceived by this ruse, declared war on Turkey on 2 November. Three days later Britain and Turkey were also at war.

In Constantinople the Sultan formally and officially confirmed the state of hostilities with a second declaration on 11 November. More ominously for the British, who were in occupation of (mainly) Islamic Egypt, this was followed on the 14th by a declaration of Holy War. Mobilisation had already begun in Turkey. At the railway station at Haidar Pasha on the Asian side of the Bosphorus, Jemal Pasha was cheered by a vast crowd as he left to take command of the Turkish 4th Army in Syria. He was hailed as the "Saviour of Egypt" and as the train departed he declared, "I shall not return to Constantinople until I have conquered Egypt!"[4]

These events naturally made the security situation in Egypt delicate. How would the Turks there react? How would the Muslim population in general respond to the call for Holy War? And how would the Sanusi react to that call?

Since Turkish-Egyptians had been relatively uncritical of the British occupation, General Maxwell correctly assumed that the vast majority of them would not react at all. Nevertheless, there were some very distinguished Turks in Egypt who were also senior officers in the Turkish Army, and these had to be individually interviewed and, no matter how anglophile they were, sent abroad for the duration upon their word of honour that they would not participate in the conflict. One of these was the Khedive's cousin, Prince 'Aziz Pasha, who was an Ottoman general and a personal friend of General Maxwell. The Prince understood and sympathized with Maxwell's position, but when he came to say good–bye before leaving for Italy, he cheerily predicted that the British would face attack on two fronts, from the east and the west, as well as a general rising of the Muslim population in Egypt.

The British were acutely aware of the anti–British and pro–German feeling among the Arab Muslim population in general. It was particularly strong among Egyptian Army officers, which was why most of these were kept out of the way in the Sudan, but many Egyptians in government

[4] Henry Morgenthau (1918), *Ambassador Morgenthau's Story*, Ch. 15.

employment, as well as many students, also resented the British presence. The student population, especially, had been fertile ground for nationalist ideas, although the British-controlled Ministry of Interior had so far kept them in check.

As for the Sanusi, notwithstanding that he had never caused any trouble in Egypt, he was still unpredictable, and some Egyptian ministers were openly nervous about his power to cause religious ferment. In November Maxwell considered sending troops into the Western Desert to secure that side of the country. Kitchener, however, advised against the action on the grounds that the force might have to be recalled quickly, which would create a bad impression, and he suggested that Maxwell should use police and coastguards instead.

The day the Turks entered the war (2 November) General Maxwell declared Martial Law in Egypt; six weeks later (18 December) Egypt was at last declared a British Protectorate; and the next day the Khedive was deposed. In his place (in a clear provocation aimed at the Ottoman Sultan, Mehmed V) 'Abbas Hilmi's anglophile paternal uncle, Husayn Kamel, was proclaimed "Sultan" of Egypt.

In the meantime, Egypt waited for the Turks to attack from the east. Maxwell decided to withdraw British and Egyptian forces from Sinai and to place his main line of defence along the west bank of the Suez Canal. A rumour began to spread that the Turks would attack on 27 January 1915, since on that day there would occur a rare conjunction of the birthdays of the Kaiser and the Ottoman Sultan. (Wilhelm's birthday was a fixture on the Gregorian solar calendar, while that of his Turkish ally was tied to the shorter Islamic lunar year.) It was indeed a rare coincidence, and the notion that it would be too auspicious a date for the Turks to pass up was to prove surprisingly accurate.

4

"Senoussi is at Sollum ... all looks favourable." [1]

IN AUGUST 1914 THE western frontier was unusually quiet. Egyptian Army officer Bimbashi Hewitt, in temporary command at Sollum, had a discipline problem with his men. A patrol had captured 800 kilos of hashish from a caravan descending the Augerin Pass. The contraband drug was brought back to the fort in sealed bags and put under guard. Three days later, on transferring it to a Coastguard cruiser in the harbour, three slabs of hashish were found to be missing. Hewitt made enquiries and discovered that four of his native soldiers were the culprits. The crushing boredom of life on the frontier was no excuse as far as he was concerned and he severely cautioned the detachment. [2]

The level of excitement rose in September when agents in Alexandria learned that an emissary from Constantinople, a Libyan deputy in the Ottoman parliament named Sulayman al-Baruni, had slipped into Egypt on a special mission to the Sanusi. Royle, who had been invited to the Arab camp at Amsa'id on the 20th, was able to ascertain that al-Baruni was indeed expected. [3] The Mariout Railway was carefully watched and a

[1] WO 33/714, Maxwell to Kitchener, 19 November 1914.
[2] WO 157/687, Bimbashi Hewitt's Report for 16–31 August 1914.
[3] WO 157/687, Royle's telegram of 20 September 1914.

description of al-Baruni circulated. The search was futile: like Enver, Mustapha Kemal, and numerous others before him, al-Baruni was able to cross the Western Desert undetected and enter Cyrenaica.

But while the search for al-Baruni was underway there was suddenly major excitement of a different kind. The Sanusi's younger brother Hilal again visited Egypt, this time travelling to the *zawiya* at Umm al-Rakhm, half way along the coast towards Alexandria. Royle spent a day and a half with him there and received the astonishing news that the Grand Sanusi himself was coming to Amsa'id, only two miles from Sollum, to celebrate the Bairam feast among his followers. Hilal clearly enjoyed the look of surprise on his friend's face, and – knowing exactly how the British received their information from the Libyan side of the border – Hilal asked Royle if he could be enlisted as a "paid informer".[4] There is no record of how the British received this suggestion but one assumes that the offer was gently declined.

Notwithstanding Ahmad al-Sharif's imminent arrival Royle was restless to get away from the Western Desert. He wanted to contribute more to the war effort, that is, to do something more useful than chasing smugglers or elusive Ottoman deputies, or even being Britain's primary contact with the Sanusi. He applied for, and was given, permission to join the new Royal Flying Corps.

For years Royle had been trying to convince the Coastguard Administration to invest in an aeroplane. By this time there were several of these machines in Egypt and it seemed absurd to continue doing Coastguard work from the back of a camel when from an aeroplane one could scan vast tracts of desert efficiently in an hour's flight. On 30 September 1914 he was in Cairo and received his commission as a captain in the RFC, assigned to be an "observer", that is, to serve as the second man in the two-seater biplanes, the one whose task was to observe the terrain, enemy movements, changes in the weather, etc., and generally to collect visual military intelligence.

Enlisting with Leo Royle was fellow-coastguard Douglas Royle Tweedie. Known to his friends as "Roy" Tweedie, he was not – despite his middle name – a relation of Leo's. Roy Tweedie's father had been a close family friend of Leo's uncle George since the 1880s, and the name was merely a token of that friendship.

[4] WO 157/687, Royle's telegram of 12 September 1914.

The two new RFC cadets were for the time being restricted to being trained in the theoretical aspects of their work. Kitchener had had the foresight to order an RFC detachment to Egypt several days before the start of the war, but it was not due to arrive until mid-November. In the meantime, they were simply two more British volunteers, among thousands in Egypt, caught up in the turmoil of preparing for the likelihood of Egypt's eventual involvement in the hostilities.

Three weeks after Royle joined the RFC there was another surprising development on the western frontier, and it caused the temporary suspension of his RFC training. The British received a message from the Grand Sanusi, who was still making his way to Amsa'id, to the effect that he wished to meet personally with Leo Royle. The news spread quickly through Army Headquarters and the British Agency in Cairo, and from there to the offices of Kitchener and Sir Edward Grey in London. Royle's personal reaction to the news can only be guessed. There was no question but that he had to return to Sollum, but was he disappointed to go back? Was he fated, after all, to spend the war as a coastguard "diplomat" acting on behalf of his government at a desert encampment? Perhaps, after the disappointments of two years earlier, it was some consolation to know that he would be the first Englishman actually to meet the Grand Sanusi. As such, it was an event which would, briefly at least, hold the attention of Grey and Kitchener, two of the great men in his country's history.

Royle, accompanied by Cecil Snow, returned to Sollum aboard the Coastguard cruiser *Rasheed* on 27 October 1914. The Bairam feast had come and gone, yet Sayyid Ahmad had still not arrived at Amsa'id. On 2 November the following telegram from Royle reached Clayton's desk at Army Headquarters in Cairo.

> Sheikh not yet arrived, [but] said to be four hours from here; have written to him to make an appointment … All notables at Arab Camp gone to meet him with exception of al-Barouni whom I hear on good authority has never met Sheikh Senoussi. Sidi Hilal went up the pass last night … [but I] did not have chance to meet with him.[5]

The next day another message arrived from Royle saying that the Grand Sanusi was now due on the 6th and that al-Baruni had now in fact

[5] WO 157/688, 2 November 1914.

met with him. Royle sent four *fantasses*[6] of Nile water to Hilal and asked permission to send more to Sayyid Ahmad when he arrived. Apparently Bimbashi Hewitt begrudged giving away water that had to be especially delivered to Sollum by Coastguard cruiser. Royle sent another message, "Please instruct Hewitt … These little attentions much appreciated by Sanusi and therefore necessary". Hewitt was duly reminded of the importance of Royle's mission and told that the water should be made available.[7]

Clayton may have feared that two officers of the same rank might clash, for he took the further step of telegraphing Hewitt that all restrictions that had been in place regarding the camp's food and water supplies were now to be removed. Hewitt replied that the message was "thoroughly understood". There was also a hint from Hewitt that Royle was getting impatient.

> Have removed all restrictions as regards foodstuffs to West. Royle says Senoussi at Zoweit near [Bardia] and expected here daily … Royle has got Sidi Hilal to write and ask Senoussi if he may go to meet him if he is not arriving soon at Sollum … Sidi Hilal most friendly and agreeable. Royle lunched with him today.[8]

On the same day Royle asked for authorisation to spend eight pounds from Sollum petty cash "for sheep, sugar, etcetera" in case he had the opportunity to return the hospitality that he was likely to receive at the Sanusi camp.[9]

Sayyid Ahmad finally reached Amsa'id on 14 November, having been delayed by all the tribes entertaining him along the way. But when the celebrations began at Amsa'id, they went on for so long that Royle found that he had to wait several days more before he could get the Sanusi's attention.

The weather, while staying dry, turned cold, and for three days a strong westerly gale blew, casting a pall of sand over the escarpment and onto Sollum camp. Finally, on the 17th, Royle went up to Amsa'id. He had been waiting for this moment for nearly two years; he was excited and no doubt a bit nervous; and expectations were high in both Cairo and London.

---

[6] Arabic: *fintaas*, a water can.   [7] WO 157/688, 6 November 1914.
[8] Ibid., 10 November 1914.   [9] Ibid., 10 November 1914.

But what actually happened that day was completely unanticipated. Royle arrived at the Arab camp only to find that he was kept waiting with scarcely any notice being taken of him. This was a very conspicuous breach of Arab hospitality for an invited guest. Could it be merely an oversight? Or was it a deliberate insult, and if so, why? Three days had passed since Sayyid Ahmad's arrival, and the camp was still effervescent with excitement. Perhaps the offhand treatment was merely a lapse in customary etiquette due to this excitement. But when Sayyid Ahmad did finally appear he seemed preoccupied and unfriendly, and he curtly demanded a letter confirming that Royle was authorized to represent the British authorities in Cairo.

Royle, who had not asked to be there but had come because of a personal invitation from Sayyid Ahmad, was in an impossible position. He did not have such a document, the need for it never having been mentioned, and there was little he could do but leave right away to get one. He returned to Sollum. The next morning (18 November) he boarded the *Rasheed* to begin the long trip back to Alexandria and Cairo. Late in the afternoon of the following day he saw General Maxwell and told him what had happened.

Royle gave the impression of being philosophical about the inconvenience and the snub implicit in his present mission, and the General, similarly, downplayed the annoying episode – in fact, he skipped over it entirely in a telegram he sent that evening to Kitchener: "Senoussi is at Sollum … Royle will go out tomorrow to visit him. In this direction, I think, all looks favourable."[10] Cheetham, however, was annoyed. He wrote to the Foreign Secretary that "this refusal [to discuss matters during the meeting with Royle on 17 November] was all the more unreasonable as the officer in question had gone to meet the Sheikh at the latter's own request."[11]

The letter of authorisation that Royle was given comprised a single sentence over the signatures of both Maxwell and Cheetham.

20 November 1914

To El Sayed Ahmed el-Sherif,

This letter is to inform Your Excellency that Bimbashi Royle is entrusted

[10] WO 33/714, No. 306E, 19 November 1914.
[11] FO 371/1971, Letter of 7 December 1914.

by us, the representatives on behalf of Earl Kitchener of His Britannic Majesty's Government and the Government of Egypt, with power to discuss with your Excellency any questions which it may be desirable to settle between us, and that the said Bimbashi Royle has our full authority and confidence.

J. G. Maxwell, Lieutenant-General
General Officer Commanding His Majesty's Troops in Egypt

Milne Cheetham
His Britannic Majesty's Acting Agent and Consul-General in Egypt[12]

Royle hurried back to Sollum and on to Amsa'id bearing the necessary credentials. This time he was properly and graciously welcomed. He had two sessions with Sayyid Ahmad on 22 November. When he returned to the Sollum camp, he was bearing an elaborate Arab robe presented to him by his host and a letter from Sayyid Ahmad for Maxwell and Cheetham. Royle briefly described that day's encounters with the sheikh and the substance of their discussions in a telegram to his superiors. In it he was optimistic about the Sanusi's attitude toward the war.

> Two most successful interviews … First, assured me of friendly intention; said he never had otherwise and cared nothing for Turks or Germans. Said he would give me a letter to this effect … Second, bargain for arms and ammunition. Told him not possible, he then suggested loan of money. Told him thought it impossible; impressed on him importance of our allowing him food … Told me to come and fetch letter tomorrow evening; expect more bargaining … Hope to leave here tomorrow night [23 November]. Royle[13]

He left as anticipated and again hurried to Cairo, where he had meetings with both General Maxwell at Army HQ and with Cheetham at the Agency.

Royle's diplomatic mission to the Sanusi was now over, but there remains the mystery of Sayyid Ahmad's strange behaviour at their first

[12] FO 371/1971.
[13] WO 157/688, Royle at Sollum to Coastguard, Alexandria, 22 November 1914.

meeting. For a plausible explanation we need only to consider the presence of al-Baruni and the numerous Turkish soldiers at the Sanusi camp. We know that Sayyid Ahmad had seen al-Baruni before he saw Royle; and that al-Baruni had been especially sent by the Turks to try to convince Sayyid Ahmad to join them against the British. Sayyid Ahmad was not at this point swayed by al-Baruni's arguments; but if the latter, knowing that Royle had been invited, had commented that the Grand Sanusi was demeaning himself by negotiating with a mere English "bimbashi", one can well imagine that the comment would have stung. In fact, there is evidence that something like this actually happened. Eighteen months later, when Sayyid Ahmad was losing the war in Egypt, he wrote to his agent in Cairo that attacking Egypt had never been his idea, but that since the Turks, his allies in the war against Italy, were at war with the English it had been difficult for him to speak freely; that his pro-Turkish followers had begun to disapprove of his peaceful relations with the British in Egypt, and were talking behind his back. "Among the things they said," he wrote, "was that the Grand Sanusi was *'an English bimbashi'*." [author's italics][14]

Royle returned to his RFC duties, reporting to Camp Moascar at Ismailia, on the Suez Canal. During his brief mission to the Western Desert the RFC had received their aeroplanes from England. For the immediate future it was Egypt's eastern frontier that was to have his attention.

As for the letter that Royle had brought back from the Sanusi,[15] it fell short of both Maxwell's and Cheetham's expectations. Maxwell wrote to Kitchener that it was "distinctly non-committal",[16] but he adhered to his

---

[14] Sir John Maxwell Papers, Princeton University Library, letter from Sayyid Ahmad to his agent Muhammad al-Sharif al-Idrisi, 7 April 1916.

[15] Sayyid Ahmad's letter (FO 371/1971):

We have met your agent, Bimbashi Royle, and have discussed with him those matters which required our care and attention in the present circumstances. The reasons for our journey to the Egyptian frontier are merely that we may meet our master, El Sayed Mohammed Idris El Senussi.

We desire that you convey our highest compliments and deepest respect to His Excellency Earl Kitchener.

God is the one who only gives good counsel.

El Sayed El Mahdi Ahmed El-Sherif El-Senussi

[16] WO 33/714, (No. 327E) 25 November 1914.

earlier optimism and would soon adopt a policy of writing regular personal letters to Sayyid Ahmad as a means of maintaining friendly relations.

Cheetham was less sanguine. He sent Grey a long report on British-Sanusi relations, attaching a translation of Sayyid Ahmad's letter without specific comment.[17] In the report, however, he made clear his opinion that Britain had not received from the Sanusi the firm commitment that was needed if Egypt's western frontier was to be considered secure. He was uneasy on several accounts. He had recently seen intelligence about the Fayoum Oasis, near Cairo, where the Sanusi had numerous followers. Cheetham cited "symptoms of unrest among the Egyptian Bedouins" and his certainty that "Turkish and German agents ... have unquestionably been intriguing with the Egyptian Bedouins in the Western Desert". He also mentioned a newspaper article that had just been published in Constantinople claiming that Sanusi tribesmen "have begun their march on Egypt", and which went on to exhort its readers to "imagine the situation of our enemies who are going to find themselves caught between the Ottoman armies marching towards Suez ... and the warriors of Sheikh Senoussi rushing across the west of Egypt". This was precisely the scenario predicted by Prince 'Aziz Pasha to General Maxwell, and, as we shall see, it was one relished by others at this time in Berlin.

The clear-sighted conclusion to Cheetham's report is particularly noteworthy considering the outbreak of hostilities on the western frontier a year later.

> If the situation remains favourable to the British cause, it is most improbable that [the Sanusi] will adopt a hostile policy which would be obviously detrimental to their interests; but should the general situation develop unfavourably for us, we must be prepared for a quite different attitude on the part of the Sheikh and his followers. Hence, while there appears to be no cause for immediate apprehension, it is necessary to keep as closely as possible in touch with the state of feeling among the western Bedouins and to maintain a careful watch on our western frontier.[18]

[17] FO 371/1971, Cheetham to Grey, 7 December 1914.
[18] Ibid.

The credit for this insight rightly belongs to an Intelligence officer working for Clayton, a man called Wilfred Jennings Bramly. Bramly was a specialist on the Egyptian Bedouin, and he had recently written a report that was the basis for Cheetham's conclusion. Bramly was a great admirer of Royle and his long desert experience, but his assessment of the situation was dispassionate and uncannily accurate.

> If Sidi Ahmad is greatly influenced, as I believe, by personal feelings, how do we stand with him now in comparison to the Turks.
>
> The Turks gave him Enver, and Enver, by his personal bravery and [the power of his] personality, has certainly made for himself a place next only to Sidi Ahmad with the Bedouins of the West. Where his tent stood the Arabs have built a mosque. Twice he left them for Turkey.[19] His success there, the officers sent by him, and the money sent by him, have kept his fame among them as fresh as on the day he left.
>
> We have, to counteract this personal influence now directly against us, "Royle". How Royle has been able to obtain the influence he has over Sidi Ahmad is very astonishing when we consider how little he has had to work with … Sidi Ahmad … must have formed a personal liking, but the basis of this friendship can only be put down to a sense of obligation to Royle for his sympathy and treatment of the Awlad Ali, and the aid he has been allowed to render the Senoussi by the passing through of foodstuffs.
>
> But if Sidi Ahmad is influenced by … the obligations to Royle, how much more should he be influenced by his obligations to Enver; how much more should he be influenced by his obligations to Turkey who supplied the money for the foodstuffs which we only allowed to pass through our country. Is he not constantly reminded of his obligations to Turkey by Enver's officers? Add to this, there is the great influence of religion to bias him to the side of Turkey.
>
> In all probability, therefore, an appeal from Turkey to fight will outweigh the friendship to Royle[20]

Turkish soldiers in Cyrenaica were already appealing to the Sanusi to

---

[19] The author knows of only one stay by Enver in Libya and so only one departure.
[20] To his own report Cheetham attached that of Jennings Bramly's, also to be found in FO 371/1971.

make common cause with them against the British in Egypt. In two months Enver would back up this appeal by sending a second special mission to Sayyid Ahmad, one more effective than that of al-Baruni. In four months the British would put their position and status in Egypt at risk by attempting to break through the straits at Gallipoli.

Almost from the moment he arrived in Egypt (8 September) General Maxwell had to face the fact that nearly all military personnel under his command were required on the Western Front in Europe. The six thousand-man Army of Occupation, the force behind Britain's presence in Egypt for the past 32 years, departed at the end of September, while a Division of raw East Lancashire Territorials arrived in replacement. More fully-trained and battle-hardened units were promised for Egypt, generally from India, but no sooner would these arrive then they too would be sent to France.

Maxwell complained to Kitchener: "I cannot spare more Staff Officers ... The inexperience of the Territorials will add to the work and all departments are shorthanded."[21] Eventually a partial solution to this problem was found in the many retired British officers then in Egyptian government employment. Maxwell was given permission to give these men appropriate local and temporary rank. He assured Kitchener, "This involves no question of payment".[22] In other words, the Egyptian government would pay!

In this way, Coastguard director Hunter Pasha was sent to the Suez Canal as a General Staff Officer with the local and temporary rank of colonel; and Captain Gilbert Clayton, already in the important position of Director of Military Intelligence, was given the more suitable local and temporary rank of lieutenant-colonel.

In the first week of November the War Office in London began an exchange of telegrams with General Maxwell that would have great historical significance for Britain and the Middle East, and in a minor way become part of the history of the Western Desert campaign of 1915–16:

War Office: "We are receiving offers of service from various British civilians who have knowledge of Turkish language and of Asia Minor

[21] WO 33/714, (No. 609E) 26 September 1914.
[22] Ibid., (No. 243E) 4 November 1914.

generally. Please state whether a few carefully selected persons of this sort would be of service to you."[23]

Maxwell: "Yes, a few."[24]

War Office: "The following are being sent out to you for special service:- Lieut. G Lloyd … Lieut. C L Woolley … Lieut. J Hay … 2nd Lieut. T E Lawrence[25]

In the end five "specialists" arrived in Cairo to work on the General Staff of Army HQ in December 1914, the fifth (unmentioned in the above exchange) being the eccentric, amusing, and nearly blind Aubrey Herbert. Herbert and his friend George Lloyd had had parallel careers: both knew Turkish, both had worked at the British Embassy in Constantinople, and both had been Members of Parliament; Leonard Woolley and T. E. Lawrence both knew Arabic and had worked together as archaeologists at Carchemish on the upper Euphrates in northern Syria; the outsider of the group was James Barromew Hay, a Scot whose pre-war career remains a mystery, although it is likely that he had worked for the Ottoman Gendarmerie in Libya.[26] By November 1915 only Hay and Lawrence were still working at Army Headquarters in Cairo.[27]

Among the Indian units assigned to General Maxwell in Egypt were some which had been chosen because of their expertise in desert warfare. In late October the Bikanir Camel Corps arrived for duty on the Canal, and within three weeks it was involved in Egypt's first skirmish of the war. The Coastguard Camel Corps – Egypt's own *élite* desert force – was also involved, albeit in a way that was hugely disappointing for George Hunter and the other British officers who had worked in the Egyptian Coastguard.

[23] WO 33/714, (No. 3501 MO 16) 6 November 1914.
[24] Ibid., (No. 254E) 8 November 1914.
[25] Ibid., (2092) 16 November 1914.
[26] See footnote on p. 12.
[27] Stewart Newcombe, to whom the five had reported, had also moved on by this time. It is interesting to note that General Maxwell had originally requested that Newcombe be assigned to Egypt "for observation work" with the Royal Flying Corps because of his expertise in the geography of Sinai [WO 33/714, (No. 323E) 24 November 1914]. Newcombe never became an RFC observer over Sinai, whereas the two coastguards from the Western Desert, Leo Royle and Roy Tweedie, did.

On 19 November a Bikanir patrol of forty men, commanded by one Captain Chope, arrived at a well called Bir al-Nuss, in the north of Sinai just east of the Canal. A detachment of twenty coastguards was already there, and Captain Chope ordered their Egyptian officer to make camp at a point 300 yards away from the Bikanir's camp and to report at 6am. It is not known whether Chope issued this order for defensive reasons, nor whether the coastguards were insulted by a tone of voice or an arrogant look. In any event, the next morning the coastguards were nowhere to be seen. Captain Chope went to the now empty coastguard campsite with twenty Bikanirs and found tracks of many camels and of men on foot, all of which apparently indicated a force far larger than that of the twenty coastguards of the previous day.

Captain Chope, who still had only half his force with him, moved east in search of the missing detachment. After an hour he stopped to allow his men to adjust their saddles when they suddenly saw twenty men on white Coastguard camels – Bedouin camels were brown – waving white flags. Chope was immediately suspicious. He told a fellow officer acting as interpreter to shout in Arabic that only one man would be allowed to advance. All twenty of them came forward slowly. At thirty yards, they suddenly opened fire on the Bikanirs. Chope's men scrambled to find cover and returned fire, but then another party appeared, this one clearly of Bedouin. His own men now dangerously outnumbered, Chope tried to get them away, but as they mounted their camels "several hundred" more Bedouin horsemen appeared and joined the attack. The Arabs rode "rings around [the Bikanirs], firing from horseback".[28] Thirteen of Chope's twenty men were killed in the action. The survivors somehow made it back to the twenty Bikanirs who had stayed at Bir al-Nuss. Nothing further was ever seen of the native Coastguard patrol.[29]

Hunter was at Qantara, on the Canal's eastern bank, when Captain Chope's unit returned, and it fell to him to head the enquiry. His report does not mention the word "desertion". Its conclusion was that his

[28] WO 157/688, Intelligence Report No. 12, 21 November 1914.
[29] Ibid.
[30] WO 33/714, (No. 325E) 24 November 1914. British Intelligence had learned of four German officers who were based in Gaza, dressed as Arabs, and worked with the Bedouin in Sinai.
[31] Ibid., (No. 314E) 21 November 1914.

Egyptian coastguards "were surrounded and surrendered to Bedouins, *who were under the command of a German officer* [!]".[30] But General Maxwell reported to Kitchener in more damning terms: "I regret that the Egyptian coastguards are untrustworthy. It is believed that … twenty have deserted to the enemy."[31] The final indignity for the Coastguard Camel Corps was a subsequent order from Maxwell that all the camels belonging to the coastguards stationed along the Canal were to be handed over to the Bikanirs.

As a result of this incident Maxwell concluded that patrols of camel-mounted natives were not the best way to gather information about enemy movements in Sinai. The merits of using aircraft instead of camels had suddenly become obvious, and, fortunately for the British, the Royal Flying Corps formation at Ismailia was now ready to take over the surveillance of the peninsula.

5

Baron Max von Oppenheim

PRINCE 'AZIZ PASHA'S prediction in November 1914 that a Turkish attack on the Canal would signal a Sanusi invasion from the west and a nationalist uprising in the Nile Valley bore a striking similarity to certain German war objectives in the Near East outlined in a memorandum written for the German Foreign Office in Berlin early in the war. Its title was "Promoting revolution in the Islamic regions of our enemies", and its author, who was well-known to British officials in Cairo, was Baron Max von Oppenheim.

Oppenheim was one of Germany's most distinguished orientalists. He had worked at his country's consulate in Cairo from 1896 to 1910, and his intellectual brilliance was but one facet of a complicated and colourful personality: he was also enormously wealthy, a renowned socialite, and – with connections to many disparate elements of Egyptian society (including the Khedive, the nationalists, the Turks and the Sanusi) – had a penchant for upsetting the British. This last trait had often embarrassed his colleagues at the German consulate, but it had delighted the Kaiser, with whom he was personally acquainted, and the Kaiser's very delight in his friend's habit of annoying the British had made it impossible for the German Foreign Office to call him to account. His long sojourn in Cairo was followed by three years in the upper Euphrates region, where he had a concession from the Ottomans to excavate the ancient site of Tell Halaf. At the end of 1913 he returned to Berlin to write up the results of his expedition and to organize the many crates of antiquities that the Turks had allowed him take to Germany.[1] The outbreak of war the following summer found Oppenheim still in the German capital. At fifty-four years of age he was too old to be a soldier, but as a leading expert on the Islamic world he could still be of use to his country. He set aside archaeological research and offered his services to his former employers at the German Foreign Office. The result was the above-mentioned memorandum whose grandiose aim was to bring down the British Empire.

Max von Oppenheim was born in 1860 into a wealthy Jewish family from Cologne. As his background would occasionally subject him to anti-Semitism, particularly at the German Foreign Office, it is interesting to note that his mother was Catholic and his father a Catholic-convert.

As a young man Oppenheim rejected any notion of a career in his family's well-established banking business. Instead he decided to devote his life to travel and to studies of the Arabic language and Islam. On his path to becoming an orientalist two milestones are of interest. The first is his relationship with Gerhard Rohlfs, who in the 1870s and '80s was the first European to cross (and re-cross) the Libyan Desert. It was the period when the Sanusi Brotherhood was expanding and flourishing under the leadership of the founder's son, Muhammad al-Mahdi. Rohlfs' accounts of his expeditions by camel caravan made him a hero to several generations of Libyan Desert explorers, and he became Europe's main source of information about the Sanusiyya. In old age Rohlfs became Oppenheim's friend and mentor.

The second milestone in Oppenheim's career was his encounter with European colonialism. Early travels through French-occupied Tunisia and Algeria and British-occupied Egypt resulted in Oppenheim becoming ardently anti-colonialist. Many of his fellow-Germans opposed French and British colonialism simply because Germany had lagged behind in the European scramble for colonies, but Oppenheim's motive appears to have stemmed from a romantic view of the Arab world, and he wanted that world to remain unspoilt by European imperial adventures of any kind.

---

[1] Tell Halaf is a hundred miles east of Carchemish, another Hittite site, where T. E. Lawrence and Leonard Woolley were engaged in similar work at roughly the same time. Lawrence had the highest respect for Oppenheim as an archaeologist and map-maker but came to regard him as Germany's arch-villain in the Near East.

Later he would modify his view to the extent of accepting German meddling in the region if the result would upset the imperial plans of France and Britain.

In 1887 Oppenheim applied for a position in the German Foreign Service, but despite his intelligence, wealth, social rank, and uncommon expertise in the Arabic language and culture, his application was rejected. A blunt note by Secretary of State Herbert von Bismarck, son of the German Chancellor, states that the application was rejected because of the applicant's Jewish ancestry.[2] A second application in 1892 was also unsuccessful. Finally, in 1895 the father of Oppenheim's close friend Hermann Graf von Hatzfeldt made a direct appeal to Otto von Bismarck on his behalf. A compromise was reached whereby Oppenheim would be allowed to work for the Foreign Service as an *attaché* at the German legation in Cairo, but he was not, and never would be, formally accepted into the German diplomatic corps.

It so happened that the restricted position of *attaché* in Cairo was the perfect job for a man of Oppenheim's talents, and he soon became a prolific writer of reports on all aspects of Egyptian life and politics – and on the British Occupation. He was, in fact, the German Consulate's equivalent to what the British called the "Oriental Secretary" at their own Consulate, a position held by his contemporaries Harry Boyle and Ronald Storrs.

When not working at the legation, Oppenheim enjoyed the glittering social scene of *Belle Epoque* Cairo with its multitude of balls, "small dances", and elegant dinner parties. In 1898 the Savoy opened on Midan Suleiman Pasha and immediately gained a reputation as the most exclusive hotel in the Near East. Oppenheim became a *habitué* of the Savoy dining-room and inevitably would have developed at least a nodding acquaintance with fellow regular customers George Royle and his family, and later with Charles Royle.[3]

Oppenheim's private life centred on the large and beautiful house that he rented in Cairo's Bab al-Luq district, near the Abdin Palace. His unpublished memoirs reveal an interesting arrangement he had with certain "agents" who annually provided him with a "temporary wife".

[2] Teichmann *et al.* (2001), *Faszination Orient*, pp. 27–8.
[3] Oppenheim's social activities in the period 1900–10 are abundantly chronicled in the social columns of *The Egyptian Gazette*.

Except for one single occasion I was always able to make such a choice
that I kept that "temporary woman" with me at home until the final day
of my stay in the year in question. Then I discharged her. In three
instances I asked her to come back to me when I returned to my house
on the Bab el Louk ... All the "temporary women" I had at my house
on the Bab el Louk were charming, young, mostly cheerful creatures.
Needless to say, I only chose really pretty ones ... Throughout my
thirteen years' service in Cairo I managed to keep my life with my
"temporary women" absolutely secret. My servants kept silent, as did my
secretaries, who no doubt suspected these things but could never enter
the interior of my house. To all strangers, and even to my most intimate
friends and the members of my own service, the staircase with the harem
on the first floor and the basement remained permanently closed.[4]

Another eccentricity of Oppenheim's private life was his habit of
dressing up as an Arab and slipping out of his house through a side door
to mingle with the native population in streets where Europeans seldom
ventured.

In 1898 Oppenheim wrote a long report which brought him to the
attention of Kaiser Wilhelm II.[5] Its subject was the rising "pan-Islamic"
movement, which aimed to bring about an Islamic renaissance and to end
the subjugation of Muslims by the European powers. Oppenheim argued
that Pan-Islam could be a useful tool in the shaping of a German policy
for the region. The Kaiser was preparing to visit Constantinople and the
Holy Land later in the year and Oppenheim's report made an impression
on him.

The German emperor's tour of the east was a great success and well-
reported by the European press. When it was over Oppenheim began to
receive occasional invitations to dine with the Kaiser at Potsdam.
Referring to these occasions Oppenheim used to like to relate an
anecdote, that as his favourite dish was lobster Wilhelm would ensure that
it was always on the menu, but that his host was a fast eater and the dishes
would be cleared away before Oppenheim could finish.[6] In any case, the

---

[4] M. Stürmer, G. Teichmann, and W. Treue (1994), *Striking the Balance: Sal. Oppenheim
Jr. & Cie. A Family and a Bank*, p. 250.
[5] Fritz Fischer (1967), *Germany's Aims in the First World War*, p. 121 ff.

Kaiser was delighted to hear personal accounts of what the British were up to in Egypt, while for Oppenheim this direct access to the emperor was precisely the sort of privileged position that prejudiced officials at the German Foreign Office had tried to prevent.

This one-upmanship over his employers gave Oppenheim a new authority and independence that enabled him further to develop his contacts with the Egyptian nationalists, the Ottoman High Commission and the Khedive – in other words, with the main elements of anti-British sentiment. As German diplomats in Cairo generally had a long history of good personal relations with the British, it is not surprising that from this point onward Oppenheim gradually became something of an embarrassment to them.

In April 1905, Oppenheim travelled to Algiers to participate in a congress of international orientalists, and he used the trip to strengthen his relations with the Sanusi Brotherhood.[7] In fact, he already knew well one of the Sanusi's chief agents in Cairo, a merchant in Khan al-Khalili bazaar named Kahhal;[8] and for years he had been writing reports about the Sanusi, who were still fighting the French on Libya's southern frontier. But Oppenheim now began to cultivate the idea of the Sanusi playing a leading role in the Pan-Islamic struggle against the colonial powers in the Near East and North Africa.

Inevitably, Oppenheim's activities finally resulted in a diplomatic explosion, and, when it came, it involved the French and the Italians as well as the British. In the early spring of 1906 a crisis in Ottoman-British relations arose over the delineation of Egypt's eastern border. The "Taba crisis", named after the southern point of that boundary (between Egypt and Palestine) on the Gulf of Aqaba, was caused by Turkish agents knocking over the boundary posts and claiming that the real borderline was further to the west. Both parties strengthened their forces in the area, and briefly it seemed as if the issue might lead them to war.[9]

[6] Anecdote related to the author by head archivist Gabriele Teichmann, Sal. Oppenheim jr. & Cie, Cologne.

[7] Teichmann *et al.* (2001), p. 44.

[8] Typescript of unpublished autobiographical notes, pp. 59 and 67. Oppenheim Archives, Cologne. The Kahhal shop still operates in Khan al-Khalili.

[9] In May 1906 André von Dumreicher was ordered to Nakhl and then to the Gulf of Aqaba with one hundred men of the Coastguard Camel Corps, two Maxims and a mountain gun.

There followed a flurry of telegrams between Cairo and London on the subject of Oppenheim's involvement in this affair. The following one, containing a good summary of Britain's complaint, was sent by Lord Cromer to Sir Edward Grey, the Foreign Secretary:

> As you will have already observed from my telegrams on the subject of the Aqaba frontier incident, considerable activity is being displayed by Baron Oppenheim, the Oriental Secretary to the German Agency in Egypt.
>
> Since last summer, when he engineered the reception in Berlin of the notorious Mustapha Kamel Pasha,[10] Baron Oppenheim has been in constant communication with pan-Islamic agents both in Egypt and elsewhere. Articles which are known to be inspired by him have been constantly appearing in the Lewa and other Anglophobe and pan-Islamic journals. As has already been reported, the general purport of these articles is:-
>
> 1. that Islam is threatened with extinction by Europe;
> 2. that France and England are at the head of the anti-Islamic movement;
> 3. that the Sultan is the last hope of the faithful;
> 4. that Germany is the friend of the Sultan, and is therefore the only European nation which can be regarded by good Moslems as a friend.
>
> The object of these manoeuvres on the part of Baron Oppenheim can only be to stir up ill-feeling against England and against France in Algiers and Morocco, with a view to fishing in the troubled waters, should it appear to be in the interests of Germany to do so.
>
> A document has just been communicated to me in strict confidence by the First Secretary to the French Agency ... The pan-Islamic and anti-English and French tone is ... extremely marked. This appeal to Moslems to unite against Europe is signed by a certain Salah Bey, formerly a not too reputable employee of the French colonial government in Algeria, and who is now resident in Cairo, and in constant communication with Baron Oppenheim. It was sent to Paris to be printed in several thousand copies in Arabic, and the bill was to be sent to Baron Oppenheim. By some means, however ... it fell into the hands of the French authorities.

[10] The Egyptian nationalist, not to be confused with Mustafa Kemal (Atatürk).

There would be little use in my complaining to Baron Jenisch, the German Consul-General, of Baron Oppenheim's intrigues. He would certainly deny all knowledge of them, and I believe that Baron Oppenheim – like German Military Attachés – reports to Berlin direct, and not through the *Chef de Mission*. I think, however, that it might be advisable that His Majesty's Ambassador at Berlin should be informed of the intrigues in which Baron Oppenheim is engaged.[11]

Several weeks later the Italian newspaper *La Voce della Verità* claimed that "a certain Oppenheim living in Cairo" was disseminating German propaganda against the Italians in Libya;[12] and this was followed over the next few days by pieces in the French *Le Temps*, quoting the Italian article, but going on to claim that Oppenheim was also trying to undermine French colonial rule in Algeria and Morocco.

In April the British learned that Oppenheim was about to leave for Syria "on a scientific mission". Cromer suggested to the British Foreign Office that he be followed wherever he went,[13] and the British Ambassador in Constantinople cabled back that he had "taken the necessary action".[14] European newspaper articles were now calling Oppenheim one of the original promoters of the Baghdad–Berlin Railway, which was soon to reach northern Syria and which was already exciting British and French suspicions.[15] Nevertheless, one cannot help but suspect that the German Foreign Office had merely told Oppenheim to go on leave until the diplomatic storm had passed. In any case, Oppenheim already knew of the archaeological potential of Tell Halaf and really was planning an expedition there.

By June the Taba Crisis had passed. The German *chargé d'affaires* in London assured Sir Edward Grey personally that the German Foreign Office had ordered "a searching enquiry" into Oppenheim's conduct, and he repeatedly stressed "that Baron Oppenheim had no official position in Cairo", although he admitted that "he enjoyed diplomatic privileges there".[16] Count Metternich himself had already denied that Germany had

[11] FO 371/59, Cromer to Grey, 28 February 1906.
[12] FO 371/65, quoted in *Le Temps*, 23 March 1906.
[13] Ibid., Telegram Cromer to Constantinople, 12 April 1906.
[14] Ibid., HM's Representative in Constantinople, 12 April 1906.
[15] For example, FO 371/65, *Le Temps*, 23 March 1906.

given encouragement to the Turks in the recent crisis, but Grey now pointed out to the *chargé* that Oppenheim had at the time paid daily visits to Mukhtar Pasha, the Ottoman High Commissioner, and that this had caused Egyptians to think that Turkey was receiving the advice and support of Germany.

In fact, within a week of the meeting between Grey and the German *chargé*, the British in Egypt were plunged into a far more dangerous and tragic affair when British officers of the Army of Occupation, hunting pigeons in the Nile Delta, caused a local riot by shooting privately owned birds. When one British officer died, draconian punishment was meted out to a number of peasants. Four were hanged and many others were jailed or flogged. "Denishwai", the village where the incident occurred, immediately became the battle cry of the nationalists and is remembered even today as a symbol of colonial injustice. A consequence was that within months Cromer's long reign as British proconsul in Egypt came to an end. Oppenheim had been out of the country, but a few British soldiers had done his work for him.

Oppenheim's memorandum on the fostering of Islamic revolution in the East was submitted to the German Foreign Office in October 1914. Largely concerned with Egypt, the document took as its premise that "all Egypt is anti-English" and that German diplomacy had "successfully united Enver Pasha, the Khedive, and the Egyptian nationalists";[17] and that with these three elements working together there was a realistic possibility that the British in Egypt could be defeated.

Briefly, the scenario he sketched for military action and revolution was as follows. The VIII Corps of the Turkish 4th Army (20,000 men), supported by countless irregulars from "Syria, the Hijaz, Central Arabia and Mesopotamia, as well as the Kurds", should begin to cross Sinai in mid-November, led by the Khedive and a senior Turkish general. British warships in the Suez Canal were to be mined. When the Turks reached the

[16] FO 371/65, Grey to Sir F. Lascelles, quoting the German *Chargé d'Affaires*, who had called on the British Foreign Secretary on 31 May 1906.

[17] Oppenheim's Memorandum ("Denkschrift Oppenheim über Revolutionierung der Islamischen Gebiete unsere Feinde", written in autumn 1914, Politisches Archiv des Auswärtigen Amts, R26319, Schuldreferat 131). See also Fritz Fischer (1967), *Germany's Aims in the First World War*, p. 124.

[18] Oppenheim's Memorandum.   [19] Ibid.

Canal, Holy War would erupt in the Nile Valley. The people of Egypt would storm British arsenals and seize the weapons; British non-combatants would flee the country; and their soldiers would be massacred. In the Sudan, the British would "suffer the fate of Gordon Pasha".[18]

An important role in this macabre drama would be played by the Sanusi.

> [Although] the Sanusi are only sparsely represented in Egypt ... in the oases and desert region of eastern Libya they constitute a most powerful presence and have at their disposal countless armed Bedouin ... from whom an invasion across the Western Frontier must, to the English, be a cause for great concern ... and Enver Pasha has already told the Grand Sanusi to prepare for war against England.[19]

Oppenheim concluded that an attack by the Sanusi occurring at the same time as the Turkish attack on the Canal would be a critical element in bringing about the success of the endeavour.

In fact, the Political Department of the German Foreign Office had already placed an agent in Libya. His name was Otto Mannesmann, and he was already in Tripoli, seeking to contact Sayyid Ahmad al-Sanusi.

6

The Turks Attack the Suez Canal

ON THE DAY OF ROYLE'S frustrating first encounter with Sayyid Ahmad (17 November 1914), the SS *Beethoven* arrived at Alexandria bearing a skeleton three-man, three aircraft detachment of the Royal Flying Corps.[1] The group's commander was Captain Massy of the 29th Punjabis; with him were pilots, Captain Reilly and Second Lieutenant Cockerell. The aeroplanes, Maurice Farmans, were without armaments of any kind and were normally used for training and reconnaissance. Although they were 1913 and 1914 models, they looked disconcertingly like the Wright brothers' original "flying machine", but more of a problem than their match-stick appearance was the fact that only two engines had been supplied for the three aircraft. Nevertheless, General Maxwell quickly found a way to supplement this miniscule air force. There was an aviation club at Heliopolis, near Cairo, where two older Henri Farmans[2] were kept, and Maxwell requisitioned these for use by the RFC.[3] Ismailia, mid-way

---

[1] AIR 1/691/21/20/30, Diary No. 30 Squadron, RFC Detachment, Egypt; also WO 33/714 (No. 292 E) 17 November 1914.

[2] Frenchmen Henri Farman and his brother Maurice Farman were pioneers of early aviation, and their aeroplanes were popular among the allies for reconnaissance purposes.

[3] WO 33/714 (NO. 224 E) 1 November 1914 and (No. 1921 cipher) 2 November 1914. These refer to three Henri Farmans in good working order, but only two were requisitioned into RFC service.

between Port Said and Suez, was selected as the most appropriate location for monitoring the Turkish approach across Sinai, and an airfield was hastily constructed there with a couple of tent hangars and four sheds brought over from Heliopolis.

As Royle returned from Sollum and reported for duty the first aeroplane to be unpacked and re-assembled carried out an initial trial reconnaissance over northern Sinai.[4] The fifty-mile flight went over Qatiya (in the area where the Egyptian coastguards had recently gone missing) but only a few Bedouin were seen – there was no sign of the Turkish 4th Army. Royle made his first flight as an observer in this machine, flown by Lt. Cockerell, on 2 December. A few days later a second Maurice Farman was declared airworthy and took to the sky. Capt. Reilly took Royle up in this second Farman and the two spent nearly five hours flying to 'Ain al-Sudr in Sinai, south-east of Suez, and back. The maximum flying time of the aeroplane was three and three quarter hours, so they refuelled at a forward landing field and fuel depôt recently set up by the Bikanirs near the Mitla Pass.[5] This first week's flying must have been exhilarating for Royle. At last he was airborne, in a machine that weighed 2,000 pounds and flew sixty miles per hour. As he and Reilly reached 4,000 feet they could see Port Said at one end of the Canal and Suez at the other – and, of course, the entire 100-mile long waterway in between.

On 1 December, five French two-seater Nieuport seaplanes arrived at Port Said aboard the French carrier *Foudre* to provide additional air cover for Egypt. These particular machines had originally been manufactured for the Ottoman Government, but – like the two battleships built for the Turks on the Tyne – they ended up being used by the allies. The Nieuports, which took off and landed on water, were much superior to the machines at Ismailia and were soon being used to monitor the Mediterranean coast from Port Said to Syria.

During his first two weeks at Ismailia Royle participated in four reconnaissance flights as a trainee observer, but on 15 December his new flying career nearly ended in disaster. In bad weather conditions Cockerell and Royle crashed at Suez in one of the Maurice Farmans. Royle was badly bruised and not able to fly again for several months. Cockerell suffered a broken arm; three months later, before he could resume flying,

[4] AIR 1/691/21/20/30.
[5] Due east of Suez and on the way to 'Ain al-Sudr.

he contracted smallpox and died.[6]

On Boxing Day 1914, while Royle was recovering, his friend and fellow coastguard Roy Tweedie arrived at the Ismailia aerodrome. Lt. Tweedie was twenty-six – six years younger than Royle – and his first month as a trainee observer was full of excitement. On 17 January he flew with Captain Reilly and observed Turkish troop movements in the area of Bir al-'Abd on the main road from al-'Arish to Qantara in northern Sinai. They found over 700 infantry, 50 cavalry and 100 cavalry irregulars all advancing down the road to Qantara. The airplane was fired upon and hit, but they made it back safely to Ismailia.[7]

Three days later Tweedie was flown back to monitor the same area. This time he counted 1000 infantry and 200 cavalry and dropped two 20-pound bombs as the machine passed overhead. This exploit earned a brief mention in *The Egyptian Gazette*: "The English airman, who recently threw bombs on a Turkish column and inflicted serious losses upon the enemy, was Mr Tweedie, the son of the P&O agent at Port Said."[8] On the 25th, Tweedie went to Bir al-'Abd for the third time and very nearly did not make it back. The pilot had to make a forced landing on the Mediterranean coast due to engine trouble. While on the ground they were attacked by a 300-strong patrol of Turkish cavalry and only just managed to escape. The aeroplane was badly damaged by shrapnel.[9]

On 1 February 1915, as the Turks approached the Canal, Royle and Tweedie were told that they had qualified as RFC observers.[10]

Entrenched on both banks of the Suez Canal at this time were some 30,000 combat troops from around the British Empire. Most were from India: in addition to the Bikanirs there were Punjabis, Rajputs, Brahmans, Sikhs, Baluchis, and Gurkhas; but there were also Egyptians, New Zealanders and Australians. British soldiers were also there, of course, especially as officers in the Indian units and as yeomanry (that is, horse-mounted cavalry from the English counties). In military terms, the defenders comprised two infantry divisions, a brigade of assorted cavalry,

[6] AIR 1/691/21/20/30.   [7] Ibid.
[8] *EG*, 1 February 1915. Press clipping provided by Tweedie's son-in-law, Mr Rhoddy Macleod. Tweedie's father had succeeded George Royle as P&O agent at Port Said.
[9] AIR 1/691/21/20/30.
[10] AIR/1/1753/204/141/4, War Diary, 5th Wing RFC, cf R 45.

a camel corps, and nine batteries of artillery. To back up this main force, if needed, were two more divisions of infantry (not yet fully trained) and various additional brigades of light horse and yeomanry.[11] Finally, there was the heavy firepower provided by Royal Navy and French warships both within the Canal and offshore. Did General Maxwell believe that his defensive forces would see off the Turkish invaders? An anxious lady asked him this at a dinner party, to which he replied: "I don't really know … but I do know that if I am sent any more I shall have to lengthen the Canal."[12]

Ahmad Jemal Pasha – Young Turk, member with Enver and Talaat of the ruling triumvirate, former governor of Istanbul, Minister of the Navy, Turkish commander in Syria, and publicly (if prematurely) proclaimed "Saviour of Egypt" – arrived in Damascus on 6 December 1914. There preparations were well underway to assemble an expeditionary force to cross Sinai and attack the British at the Suez Canal. Already gathered were 25,000 men, including regulars from the Ottoman Army, Bedouin irregulars, and ten artillery batteries. A staff of German officers was also attached to the force, having been sent by Enver, and one of these, Colonel Kress von Kressenstein, was responsible for the expedition's overall organization. Once Jemal had arrived, preparations moved ahead quickly. Arrangements were made for the supply of water; some 5,000 pack camels were purchased; engineers ascertained that the track would be passable all the way from Beersheba (in southern Palestine) to the Canal. Much of the desert surface was, in von Kressenstein's words, "ready-made macadam",[13] although there were great stretches of deep sand that also had to be traversed, and through which the Turks patiently laid down a trail of crushed brushwood to facilitate passage.

In mid-January 1915, the Turkish expeditionary force marched out of Beersheba on a path that would lead it through the middle of the peninsula. The normal way across Sinai was an old coastal road through al-'Arish, but this was not an option due to patrolling by allied warships and aeroplanes. Eventually, to keep the British wondering about where the main attack would occur, Jemal split the Turkish force and sent one

[11] Sheffy (1998), *British Military Intelligence in the Palestine Campaign 1914–1918*, p. 48.
[12] Weldon (1926), *Hard Lying: Eastern Mediterranean 1914–1919*, p. 4.
[13] G. MacMunn and C. Falls (1928), *Military Operations: Egypt & Palestine*, Kressenstein's account quoted on p. 35.

diversionary column towards Qantara, at the northern end of the Canal (this being the column that was watched and harrassed by Roy Tweedie) and another in the direction of Suez, to the south. The main column, meanwhile, continued to move on Ismailia, in the centre.

It took nearly two weeks for the Turks to reach the Canal, and for most of this period the British were indeed uncertain where the principal attack would come. For one thing, British intelligence had long judged a large troop movement through central Sinai to be unfeasible because of the lack of water there. For another, the RFC aeroplanes assigned to reconnoitre east of the Canal had such a short range that unless there was an opportunity to refuel – and there was no fuel depôt directly east of Ismailia – they could only operate within a maximum seventy-five miles of the aerodrome, and this only under optimum conditions. As the Turks drew near conditions were far from optimum. Although both the RFC's land-based aeroplanes and the French seaplanes were monitoring the progress of the Turks' northern column, their main column in the centre proved elusive. Cloudy weather conditions and frequent sandstorms did not help, but in addition to bad weather technical problems led to flights being cancelled over central Sinai. In fact, in a crucial six-day period during the third and fourth week of January there were no flights at all over this sector. The Turks, meanwhile, did most of their marching by night and spent the daytime resting out of sight in whatever shade was afforded by the dry water courses and hills of Sinai.

It was not until the end of January – just a few days before the attack – that the British spotted the enemy main force, which left little time to redistribute the British defensive forces and strengthen the centre. Even then British generals found it difficult to believe that the main attack would occur there, more or less opposite Ismailia, and as late as 27 January they were still convinced that the attack would be in the north.

> Today the French seaplane flew over Katia and Bir el-Abd and reported nothing to be seen, but this information is hard to credit. One of our planes with good observers is being sent tomorrow morning to verify this. There is no doubt that the enemy takes steps to hide from aeroplanes, and this is fairly easy on the northern line owing to palm trees.[14]

But on 28 January an RFC reconnaissance flight was finally able to pinpoint three or four thousand Ottoman soldiers eight miles east of the Canal and four miles south of Ismailia; the next day that Turkish force had substantially increased, confirming that the enemy main column had at last been located.

If the organisation and execution of the march across Sinai had been brilliantly carried out, the actual attack when it came was a complete anticlimax. The Turks easily avoided the handful of guard posts on the eastern bank of the Canal, but there were many more of these on the western bank and they were all on the alert. On the night of 2–3 February the Turkish forward battalions, carrying German pontoons of galvanized iron, moved to the Canal just below Lake Timsah. The defenders' guard posts in that sector were manned by Punjabis. At 3.30 in the morning, the attackers slipped their pontoons into the water, but muffled sounds were heard by the Punjabi guards opposite. If the guards had any doubt that the enemy was on the move nearby, it was quickly dispelled when Arab and Bedouin irregulars gave away their location by screaming "*Allahu akbar!*" (God is great!). In absolute darkness a Punjabi machine gun unit began to rake the eastern bank with fire, when suddenly a full moon emerged from the clouds to illuminate the scene and reveal hundreds of men sliding down the Canal's eastern bank. The advantage was now with the defenders. The Turks rushed down to the water along a mile and a half-long front. Some pontoons managed to cross the Canal, but enemy soldiers who reached the west bank were all easily killed or captured.

The battle dragged on after daybreak, the Turks trying again and again to get across the Canal. The awful truth for the attackers was that the Suez Canal that day was the widest, most fortified moat in the world. As always the Turks fought bravely; and their artillery was effective, both against their entrenched opponents and against HMS *Hardinge*, which suffered considerable damage until it darted to safety in Lake Timsah. But Jemal must have realized early on that he was simply not going to succeed. In the northern sector his soldiers made half-hearted feints against Firdan and Qantara, but these proved equally futile. Late in the day, perhaps fearing that his army might be trapped now that its forward momentum had been stopped, Jemal ordered his force to retreat.

[14] Quoted by Sheffy (1998), p. 54: WO 95/4360, Brig.-Gen. Bingley, GSO, Canal Defences, 27 January 1915.

On 4 February the Turkish rearguard was still creating some excitement when one of Lawrence's Intelligence colleagues, Staff Officer George Lloyd, paid a visit to the front. A letter he wrote afterwards conveys the atmosphere of what it was like for the defenders towards the end of battle; it also gives the impression that the experience was an enjoyable, albeit rather noisy, day away from the office.

> General Maxwell … said I was to go to the outer lines and report, and come back by the midnight train. I went out by motor to the Canal Ferry, crossed over [to the east bank] with an ammunition column of mules, all of us blinded and choked with sand, and made my way up the hill to the first line of trenches held by the New Zealanders. They were all enjoying it immensely, it being the first action they have been in. I spied about and got the line, and then made my way out for one mile to the outer line of trenches and got in sight of the whole show. It was really rather remarkable. The outer line was held by Sikhs who behaved very well, and I got into a bastion with a young officer of the Sikhs, and watched what was going on. It reminded me of a grouse-drive: we were in a sand butt with trenches to the left and right. The Turks were attacking from our half-right … I enjoyed it quite immensely.[15]

Over the following week Jemal successfully removed most of his force to the relative safety of eastern Sinai. The fact that the British did not follow in pursuit rankled among some in the War Office and came back to haunt General Maxwell later on. The expedition cost the Turks some 200 killed and just over 700 lost as prisoners of war. The British lost 32 dead.

Was the Turkish invasion hopeless from the start? Max von Oppenheim had stressed that, in addition to the attack on the Canal, simultaneous action by the Sanusi and the nationalists were needed to break Britain's hold on Egypt. For several months General Maxwell had been reasonably certain that the Sanusi would not invade when the Turks reached the Canal – at least not in February 1915. The possibility of a nationalist uprising, however, had been on everyone's mind at this time. Replacing the professional soldiers of the Army of Occupation with inexperienced Territorials had made many in Egypt nervous. The British had friends

---

[15] C. F. Adam (1948), *The Life of Lord Lloyd*, p. 65.

there, both foreign and Egyptian, but the fact was that *most Egyptians* wanted the Occupation to end. The day that the Turks arrived at the Canal that most discerning of observers, T. E. Lawrence, wrote: "[T]he Egyptian townsmen do hate us so. I thought it was only a coldness … but it is a most burning dislike."[16] Similarly, his colleague at Military Intelligence, Aubrey Herbert, noted: "Many of the English thought that we were living on a sleeping volcano", and that "one used sometimes to get black looks in the bazaar and scowls from the class of Effendis".[17] This predominant disapproval of the Occupation among Arab Egyptians was why most of the Egyptian Army was kept in the Sudan – so that it would not pose a threat to the British. But even in the Sudan this simmering discontent of the average Egyptian soldier had to be watched. The Sirdar of the Egyptian Army, Reginald Wingate, admitted as much when he wrote: "[T]he internal situation in the Sudan is satisfactory … but I cannot say the same of the Egyptian officers and officials, who all seem to be tarred with Turco-German propaganda."[18] But it was not the propaganda, of course, that was the cause of their disaffection: it was the Occupation itself. Did Jemal Pasha really believe that the people of Egypt would help him by rising against the British? The German officer Kress von Kressenstein, in his account, reveals that Jemal did indeed hope that the Turks' arrival at the Canal would trigger a revolt.[19] But in that case the Turkish commander was sorely deceived. Nothing happened: there was no simultaneous uprising and no Sanusi invasion. Therefore, Jemal's promised "liberation" of Egypt failed.

After the battle on the Canal, General Maxwell asked Royle, who was still recovering from his injuries, to visit Sayyid Ahmad and tell him personally about the failure of the Turkish attack. The Sanusi received Royle and listened to his account of the battle with good grace, asking Royle to assure General Maxwell of his continuing friendship and esteem for the British.[20] There is no reason to doubt the sincerity of these words. Since

[16] D. Garnett (1938), *The Letters of T. E. Lawrence*, letter to Hogarth, 2 February 1915.
[17] Aubrey Herbert (n. d.), *Mons, Anzac & Kut*, pp. 88 and 90.
[18] PRO 30/57/47, Wingate to Fitzgerald, 24 February 1915.
[19] MacMunn and Falls (1928), p. 35.
[20] Sir John Maxwell Papers, Princeton University Library. Confirmed in letter from General Maxwell to Sayyid Ahmad, undated, but written shortly after Royle's return in February 1915.

Royle's last visit, Sayyid Ahmad had been so angered by Sulayman al-Baruni's constant arguing on behalf of the Turks that he had had him placed under arrest.

Sayyid Ahmad also mentioned to Royle that he was waiting for news about his cousin, Muhammad Idris, who had left Cyrenaica many months earlier to go on pilgrimage to Mecca and was now expected back. On returning to Cairo, Royle told Maxwell about this, and the General wrote to Sayyid Ahmad promising "to spare no pains" in welcoming Idris when he arrived in Egypt and in assisting his return to Libya.[21] In fact, Muhammad Idris and his party arrived in Egypt shortly thereafter, and as his visit would have significant after-effects at the end of the Sanusi War, it deserves at least brief consideration.

As noted earlier, Muhammad Idris was the eldest son of the second Grand Sanusi, but when the latter died, Idris being only twelve years old, the succession passed to his cousin Sayyid Ahmad. In April 1914 Muhammad Idris, now twenty-four, left Jaghbub to go on pilgrimage to Mecca with a few companions and servants. Travelling on horseback, with their supplies being carried on camels, the party reached the Mediterranean coast at Baqbaq, near Sollum.[22] They then turned east, calling at all the Sanusi *zawiya*s along the way. At al-Dab'a they were met by coastguard Muhammad Saleh Harb. They took the Khedive's personal train to Alexandria, where they stayed at Ras al-Tin Palace as guests of 'Abbas Hilmi II and eventually proceeded to Haifa by steamer. Muhammad Idris spent the rest of 1914 in the Hejaz, and he was at Madina when war broke out between Turkey and Great Britain.

Muhammad Idris and his party now wished to make the same journey in reverse. At Haifa in late February 1915 they found an Italian steamer about to sail for Port Said and Naples. Not knowing whether he would be welcome in Egypt, since the Sanusi were allies of the Turks, Idris was prepared to go on to Italy if necessary. However, he had no trouble at all in Egypt. He and his party were allowed to disembark at Port Said, where he sent telegrams to the new Egyptian Sultan and to Henry McMahon.

[21] Sir John Maxwell Papers, Manuscripts Division, Department of Rare Books and Special Collections, Princeton University Library.
[22] "There I saw the sea for the first time." (quoted in De Candole (1988), *The Life and Times of King Idris of Libya*, p. 20).
[23] De Candole (1988), p. 22.

He received friendly responses from both and so went to Cairo. He stayed with Sultan Husayn at Abdin Palace. He also met McMahon, Maxwell and Clayton, and discussed with each in turn Sanusi relations, not just with the British, but also with the Turks and the Italians. The three British officials stressed to Idris the importance, as they saw it, of the Grand Sanusi remaining strictly neutral in the European war and therefore breaking off relations with the Turks. Idris said that he understood the British position, but that he could not make any commitment without consulting Sayyid Ahmad. Nevertheless, he liked the British and was "favourably impressed by their friendly attitude and their military strength".[23]

Idris and his party then travelled by Egyptian Coastguard steamer to Sollum and returned to Cyrenaica. They had been away for nearly a year.

By March Royle was fully recovered and again flying over Sinai. The Turks had mostly pulled out of the peninsula, of course, but since the British had failed to follow their withdrawal, some Turkish troops remained in possession of the more important sites, especially the wells. One of these sites was al-Murra, near the Mediterranean coast, about 90 miles north-east of the Ismailia aerodrome. To reach al-Murra the RFC pilots would normally land at a makeshift runway and fuel depôt at Qatiya, 42 miles from the aerodrome; then, having refuelled, fly to al-Murra and back to the depôt in a single flight; then refuel again and return to base at Ismailia. The RFC now decided to try to reach al-Murra and return in a single non-stop flight. In December the detachment had received from a flying school in India a single BE2a biplane, which was a more modern machine than the Farmans and which lent itself more readily to modification. The flight engineers fitted to the BE2a an especially large fuel tank. With Captain Reilly as pilot and Royle as observer the aeroplane successfully covered the whole distance – 176 miles – without stopping, remaining airborne for three hours and twenty-eight minutes. They not only reached al-Murra; they also located the Turkish camp there, counted 207 tents and 300 infantrymen, dropped bombs on them, and then, with ground fire blazing away in their direction, flew back to base at Ismailia. This experimental flight was the longest made so far by the RFC in Egypt. Captain Reilly received a promotion to Brevet-Major, and Leo Royle was awarded the Military Cross.

7

Ottoman Missions to the Sanusi

Enver had returned to Constantinople from Cyrenaica in December of 1912 as the Ottoman army faced disaster in the Balkans. Its troops were falling back on all fronts before the forces of Bulgaria, Serbia, Montenegro and Greece. Before long Ottoman possessions in Europe were reduced to Constantinople itself, a few regional cities to the west, and the Gallipoli peninsula. The country was in turmoil, and some senior government officials, including the Grand Vizier, were considering conceding defeat and seeking peace terms.

This defeatism within the civilian government was abhorrent to the Young Turk officers who were responsible for the revolution of 1908, and they decided to overthrow the government. On 23 January 1913, a group led by Enver stormed into a cabinet meeting at the Sublime Porte. Amidst the shouting and general confusion a bodyguard of the Minister of War, Nazim Pasha, shot one of the intruders dead. One of Enver's men then shot and killed the Minister. The conspirators forced the Grand Vizier to resign, and in the reshuffled government the man whom Enver preferred to become Grand Vizier, Mahmud Shevket Pasha, was duly approved by the Sultan. When Mahmud Shevket was assassinated the following summer, the last vestiges of the Turks' five-year-old democracy were discarded in favour of military dictatorship: Enver, Talaat and Jemal assumed power.

One consequence of the *coup d'état* was that the Balkan War continued.

In fact, the Ottomans had a stroke of luck when the Balkan alliance against them began to fall apart, its member countries turning on each other. Thanks to this unexpected development the Ottoman army was able to rally and recapture some lost ground. A peace treaty was finally signed on 29 September 1913, and the Ottomans kept possession of eastern Thrace as well as some shreds of honour.

These events were followed with unease by Great Britain and France, for behind the scenes in Turkey German influence was growing. The Grand Vizier who had been forced to resign had been pro-British. But Enver was a Germanophile: he spoke German well and he had served for two years as the Ottoman military attaché in Berlin.

In mid-November 1913, a German Military Mission under General Liman von Sanders arrived in Constantinople to help rebuild the Ottoman army. The presence in the Ottoman capital of forty-two German officers raised a storm of protest by the British and French ambassadors. Six weeks later (in early January 1914) Enver became the Minister of War, and Germany's pre-eminent position in Ottoman military matters was firmly established. Enver was convinced that a European war was inevitable and that the Germans would win. By allying Turkey with a victorious Germany he hoped to provide a miraculous solution to the unremitting fragmentation of the Ottoman Empire.

On 2 August 1914 – as the first declarations of war were ringing out in Europe – the Ottoman government officially and secretly entered into a formal military alliance with Germany.[1] Among Ottoman obligations resulting from this alliance were the declaration of Holy War on Great Britain and her allies, the mounting of attacks upon British-occupied Egypt, and inciting the people of Egypt to rebel against their British occupiers – all steps recommended by Oppenheim.[2]

For three months Turkey was supposedly neutral in the conflict, but preparations for the country's eventual involvement progressed inexorably. One of the measures taken was the reorganisation and strengthening of a

[1] Great Britain and her allies were also busy drawing up secret agreements at this time. In one of them the Russians won the consent, first of the French (in August 1914) and then of the British (in October 1914), that Russia would decide the fate of Constantinople. In March 1915 they signed another secret treaty expressly promising that city to Russia after the war. See Ernest Jackh (1944), *The Rising Crescent*, p. 111.
[2] Stoddard (1963), pp. 16 and 63; see also Trumpener (1968), *Germany and the Ottoman Empire*, Ch. 2.

covert force which had existed for some years but which only recently (1913) had been given the official title of *Teshkilât-ı Mahsusa*, the Special Organization.[3]

The Special Organization was in essence Enver's personal army and secret service. It had been born out of the underground network of army officers who formed the Young Turk movement and was largely made up of patriotic militants who had worked with Enver in Libya. At the start of the First World War the Special Organization was officially incorporated into the Ministry of War, and it remained under Enver's direct control.[4] The notable benefit of this reorganisation was financial. In the past the force had always been under-funded; henceforth it would be financed out of the Ministry's own secret budget and from shipments of gold provided by the German Military Mission.[5]

One of the first missions undertaken by the reorganized Special Organization was that of Sulayman al-Baruni to Sayyid Ahmad al-Sharif al-Sanusi in September 1914 with the purpose of bringing about a Sanusi invasion of Egypt. As matters stood at the start of the war this was not an easy task. Sayyid Ahmad hated the French and the Italians with good reason, but having had negligible but amicable contact with the British he had no reason to want to fight them. Moreover, al-Baruni arrived at the Sanusi camp before Turkey was actually at war with Britain, and therefore also before the Sultan-Caliph's calls for Islamic solidarity and holy war. To Sayyid Ahmad it must have seemed as if Turkey was looking for trouble. Before the Turco-Italian War Sanusi relations with the Turks had often been cool; but when at the end of that war Turkey made a separate peace with Italy, leaving the Libyans to fight the Italians on their own, those relations became positively strained. If Enver was rash enough to want to take on the British Empire, why should the Sanusi Brotherhood get involved?

It is also possible that Enver chose the wrong man for the mission. In his mid-forties at the time and possessed of a tempestuous personality, Sulayman al-Baruni was from the Jebel Nafusa, on the far side of Libya by the Tunisian border. Like many Libyans he was a Berber. But he was also an Ibadite Muslim, that is, a member of a sect which in early Islam at least was considered unorthodox and fanatical. The extremism of the Ibadites was much diluted by the 20th century, but the fact is that the Sanusi were

[3] Stoddard (1963), p. 53.   [4] Ibid., p. 58.   [5] Ibid., p. 59.

strictly orthodox and tended to view the Ibadites with suspicion. Al-Baruni was a cultivated man. He had studied in Tunis and at Al-Azhar in Cairo, and – despite being a Berber – he spoke very polished Arabic. He was a poet, and he had been a publisher of Ibadite literature. But he also had a political agenda of his own. He had founded a newspaper which promoted the idea that the Ibadites of Jebel Nafusa should secede from Libya and establish their own imamate. Naturally, such sentiments were viewed as treasonable by the Ottoman government, but they were also deplored by non-Ibadite Libyans. During the Turco-Italian War, al-Baruni helped to organize the Arab resistance. When the Turks signed the peace treaty with Italy he continued to fight the Italians in the Jebel Nafusa, determined to realize his dream of an independent Ibadite imamate until (in March 1913) al-Baruni's Ibadite force was decisively defeated. Al-Baruni escaped to Constantinople, where he was hailed as a hero for his efforts against the Italians and awarded the rank of pasha.[6]

Evidently, al-Baruni impressed Enver. Cultured and debonair, al-Baruni had a strong personality and a good war record – and his Ibadite credentials would have meant nothing to Enver, who was more interested in politics than religion. Through the Special Organization Enver sent al-Baruni back to Libya and gave him a large sum of sum of money to be used to influence the Sanusi against the British. As we have seen, the mission failed. Sayyid Ahmad did not like al-Baruni, and he was definitely not then inclined to join any German-Turkish adventure against Egypt. Eventually Sayyid Ahmad heard that al-Baruni was spreading the word among the Sanusi brethren that their leader was shirking his responsibilities towards the Ottoman government. Worse, al-Baruni was found to be using forged documents to try to force Sayyid Ahmad's hand, and it was at this point that Enver's first agent to Cyrenaica was arrested and kept in isolation.

The failure of Sulayman al-Baruni's mission was a setback to German and Turkish war plans. The invasion of Egypt from the west was a crucial element in their scheme to overthrow the British in Egypt – and so Enver was determined to try again.

On 6 January 1915, as Jemal's expeditionary force prepared to cross Sinai

---

[6] See L. Veccia Vaglieri's article on al-Baruni, *Encyclopedia of Islam* (1960), vol. 1, pp. 1070–1.

in order to attack Egypt, two more Special Organization agents left Constantinople on their way to Libya. First, they travelled to Athens in the guise of diplomatic couriers. One was a small man, a Turk with delicate features and a moustache which only succeeded in making him look younger than his twenty-five years; the other was a twenty-nine-year-old Mesopotamian Arab, large in size and in personality. The Turk was Nuri Bey, Enver's younger brother, who had served with Enver in Libya in the 1911–12 war and then stayed on in Jaghbub when Enver had returned to Constantinople. The other was Ja'far al-'Askari, a Staff Officer in the Ottoman Army. He too was closely associated with Enver, having known him both as a military colleague and as a friend. The two secret agents carried documents to support their cover, and diplomatic bags containing a large amount of cash in gold coins.[7]

Upon arrival in Athens they were met by the Ottoman ambassador to Greece, Ghalib Bey, who used his local knowledge and influence to help them acquire the supplies they needed for the risky voyage across the Mediterranean. Through the ambassador's subordinate, the Ottoman consul at Piraeus, the agents came to an arrangement with a Beiruti gun-runner named Muhyi al-Din Shatila: for 3,000 Turkish gold lira they would buy a small steamer and Muhyi al-Din would run them through the Anglo-French blockade to the eastern coast of Libya. As incentive to carry this out successfully the smuggler would get to keep the boat.[8]

With these terms agreed, Nuri and Ja'far set about buying arms and ammunition – both abundantly and cheaply available on the Greek black market since the Balkan War. Then by night they loaded the steamer. Joining the party at this point were two volunteers: Muhammad Bey al-Jibani, a Libyan noble from Benghazi, who had fought with Enver and Nuri; and Kamel al-Bunduqi, a friend of Nuri Bey, whose large physical frame and passing resemblance to Ja'far would have curious consequences in the future. Towards the end of January they sailed out of Piraeus harbour.

In rough wintry conditions the five men sailed round to the south side of Crete, but they found the open sea too choppy and were forced to seek

---

[7] Ja'far al-'Askari (1988), *Mudhakkirāt Ja'far al-'Askari*, Ch. 4. The translations are the author's, but an excellent English edition of Ja'far's autobiography has recently appeared – *A Soldier's Story: The Memoirs of Jafar Pasha Al-Askari*, Arabian Publishing, London, 2003. [8] Ibid., Ch. 4.

shelter on a barren island near the Cretan coast. There they spent a week waiting for the waves to abate. Finally, they were able to continue on their way, making landfall (in Ja'far's words) "some twenty miles north-west of Sollum". There are several tiny inlets along that rocky coast but only one natural cove. Situated sixteen miles from Sollum, Bardia was already being used as a port by the Sanusi to land contraband of war, so it is likely that Muhyi al-Din Shatila chose that location for dropping off his passengers. In any case, he sailed off with the steamer that was now his own, while those who had disembarked were welcomed by Arabs of the Menefa tribe who were encamped in the area. The Menefa despatched a runner to the Grand Sanusi with the news that a new mission from Enver had arrived.

The newcomers were escorted to Bir Wa'r, the site of an old well, where the Turks already had their own camp and an arms depot. The Turkish camp was two miles south-west of Amsa'id, where Sayyid Ahmad's own tents were located and four miles from the Turkish-built fort on the Sollum heights, now occupied by the Egyptian Army.

On the day of their arrival Nuri and Ja'far settled in at the Turkish camp, and that night they were ushered into the presence of the Grand Sanusi. Nuri, of course, already knew Sayyid Ahmad, but Royle's account (1912) of Nuri's refusal to lower the Turkish flag at Jaghbub and Sayyid Ahmad's sending armed Sudanese soldiers to remove it suggests an uneasy relationship.[9] This first meeting with the Sanusi, while civil, was not promising for the mission: Sayyid Ahmad once again said outright that he wished to maintain good relations with the British. Nevertheless, Nuri and Ja'far were made welcome and given leave to stay at Bir Wa'r.

The arrival of the new Ottoman mission from Enver must have presented Sayyid Ahmad with a dilemma. This time the Turks were at war with Britain, and the Sultan-Caliph had declared holy war against Turkey's enemies. Not to receive the mission would look bad to his Sanusi followers. On the other hand, for Sayyid Ahmad openly to receive and support a military mission from Enver would jeopardize both his relations with the British and the supplies which they permitted across the border. But Sayyid Ahmad's real quandary was that, whereas the British allowed shipments of food, Nuri and Ja'far had brought gold and offers of military assistance. To accept these would be tantamount to committing to the Turkish cause; but to reject these enticements outright was to Sayyid

[9] See page 35.

Ahmad equally unthinkable. His solution, therefore, was to temporize. He instructed his visitors to keep a low profile and hoped that the British would not learn of their presence.

Throughout February and March 1915, Sayyid Ahmad continued to meet with Nuri and Ja'far, but the meetings were always at night and in secret. He listened politely to their arguments, but, no matter how compelling these were, he still refused to move against Egypt. When news came of the failed Turkish attack on the Canal, the mission's task seemed hopeless. It was a miserable omen: the best opportunity for a two-front attack on Egypt had been missed, and not only was Sayyid Ahmad refusing to join Turkey's side in the war – he would not even meet with Enver's representatives in the light of day. Meanwhile, Egyptian coastguards made regular visits to the Sanusi camp to ensure that no change occurred in the status quo. Later in the spring Snow and Royle went together to call on Sayyid Ahmad, Royle taking a few days from his RFC duties in order to introduce his uncle to the Sanusi leader.[10] There is no evidence at this stage that either they or any other coastguard was aware that Enver's own brother was there trying to incite the Sanusi against the British.

In the last half of March 1915 news arrived that finally tipped the scales of opposing arguments in favour of the Turks. The British and their allies had launched a naval attack on the Dardanelles. With the approaches to Constantinople now being assaulted Sayyid Ahmad suddenly agreed to accept Turkish financial and military assistance – but he continued to refuse to commit to an attack on Egypt. Nevertheless, it was possible that this was the breakthrough that Nuri and Ja'far were waiting for. As Jennings Bramly had pointed out to Cheetham,[11] the food that the British allowed to be delivered from Egypt was not supplied free of charge. If the Sanusi accepted gold, military equipment, and the training of his soldiers by Turkish officers, then it was much more likely that the Turks would win Sayyid Ahmad over in the end.

Nuri and Ja'far decided to inform Enver immediately of this development, since only the Ottoman government could determine the details of this new relationship with the Sanusi. They also agreed that Ja'far was the best person to try to get this news to Enver. But to attempt to sail directly to Constantinople was now too risky: the Mediterranean was

---

[10] FO 371/2353, pp. 286–7. Letter of 3 June 1915 mentions Sanusi having recently been visited by Royle and Snow "who were well-received".   [11] See p. 64.

teeming with allied warships because of the new offensive operations against Turkey. So how was Ja'far to proceed? The answer lay in the confusion reigning on Egypt's western frontier. Sayyid Ahmad gave Ja'far a document identifying him as a Libyan Sanusi bound for Mecca on pilgrimage. Ja'far then joined two Sanusi who really were going on pilgrimage. The obvious weakness in the proposed deception was Ja'far's eastern Arabic dialect. It was decided that, if spoken to by Egyptian or British officials, he should speak only in classical Arabic and pretend to be an Islamic scholar. But, as his command of classical Arabic was not good, Ja'far was not confident that he could be convincing in the role, and so he determined to keep quiet as much as possible.[12]

The three *hajji*s successfully crossed the frontier at Sollum and within a few days were in Alexandria, where they were met by a Sanusi representative named Muhammad al-Hani. Egypt was now under martial law, and the British were carefully monitoring all arrivals and departures. Consequently, Sanusi visitors from Libya were required to register with the police in Alexandria. The interview with Gordon Ingram Bey,[13] an Arabic-speaking officer with twelve years' experience in the Egyptian Police – and now a Staff Officer in Intelligence – caused Ja'far some tense moments.

> We stayed in Alexandria for ten days during which time we met the director of the Alexandria Police, Major Ingram. I could tell by the look on his face that he had some doubt about my identity, but our friend Muhammad al-Hani tried to reassure him by saying that I had never before left Kufra [in Libya], and that my work there was studying and teaching. I said as little as possible; and what I did say I tried to express in Classical Arabic, at least to the extent that I could. Fortunately my "dialect" was more than Major Ingram could handle as he only knew Egyptian colloquial Arabic. I indicated that I could not understand him, so he asked Muhammad al-Hani to explain to me what he was saying. The situation was very uncomfortable for me, but he finally signed the document that I was holding, which virtually amounted to a passport.[14]

[12] Ja'far al-'Askari's autobiography is virtually the only source for his extraordinary mission.

[13] See Thomas Russell (1949), as well as Gordon Ingram's obituary in *The Times*. Ingram died in Egypt of typhoid on 28 February 1929. See also *Who Was Who, 1929–1940*, p. 692.

The next step for the three men was to get out of Egypt and to reach Ottoman territory. This was not as difficult as one might expect. Despite the recent Turkish attack on Egypt and the battles currently raging at Gallipoli, ships were still sailing from Egypt to Palestine and Syria. Egypt was officially neutral; and Italy would not enter the war for another few weeks, the peace treaty she signed with the Ottomans in 1912 being still in effect.[15] The men were therefore able to find an Italian steamer that was about to sail from Alexandria to Jaffa.

While waiting to leave Egypt, Ja'far went to a studio in Alexandria and was photographed in his flowing Sanusi robes. The photo is dated 27 April 1915.

The voyage from Alexandria to Ottoman-ruled Palestine went smoothly and took only twenty-four hours. But as it was clearly impossible to get from Jaffa to Constantinople by sea, and as it would take too long to get there by land, Ja'far decided to contact the one member of Turkey's ruling triumvirate who was nearby: Jemal Pasha. Fortunately for Ja'far, Jemal happened to be in Jerusalem and not, as usual, at 4th Army headquarters in Damascus. So Ja'far went to Jerusalem, where he parted company with his two fellow-travellers, and then he went to call on Jemal.

Three months had passed since the abortive Turkish attack on the Suez Canal, and Jemal now seemed to have lost all interest in Egypt. He received Ja'far coolly and with complete indifference to the plan to entice the Sanusi onto Turkey's side in the war. Jemal also feigned surprise that Ja'far should think that the Turkish High Command was hoping for a Sanusi attack on Egypt. That country's western frontier was not his business, he said, and, besides, he was now involved in a campaign to rid Syria of anti-Turkish Arab Nationalists and other "traitors".

Jemal's excuses were of course disingenuous: as a member of the ruling triumvirate and as Minister of the Navy he knew, without doubt, about the plans for a two-front attack on Egypt. But the triumvirs were scarcely united on policy at the best of times. While Enver was overtly and consistently pro-German, Jemal and (Minister of the Interior) Talaat had, before the war, tended to be Francophile and, consequently, were reluctant comrades-in-arms with the Germans. Each triumvir jealously guarded his

[14] Ja'far al-'Askari (1988), Ch. 5.
[15] Italy declared war on Austro-Hungary on 23 May 1915, on Turkey, 21 August 1915, and on Germany a year later, in August 1916.

own powers and prerogatives. It is likely, therefore, that since Ja'far was one of Enver's men, Jemal did not feel inclined to be helpful. He did, however, finally agree to inform the Turkish High Command of Ja'far's presence in Jerusalem and to pass on his news about the Sanusi; and perhaps he was not as surprised as he pretended to be when two days later he received a telegram which stressed the importance of Ja'far's present mission and instructed him to provide all possible assistance. But when Ja'far said that guns, ammunition, equipment and money must urgently be sent to the Sanusi, Jemal laughed sarcastically and then exploded in anger. No one, he said, would be so mad as to undertake such a mission across the allied-controlled eastern Mediterranean. Ja'far explained in detail what he and Nuri had already accomplished, that they had already taken money and weapons across the Mediterranean from Greece, through the blockade, and that he – Ja'far – had come to Jerusalem by way of Sollum and Alexandria, right under the noses of the British, and that, furthermore, there was one man mad enough to undertake this further mission because he – Ja'far – would do it.

> [Jemal's] anger vanished as quickly as it had come and he cheerfully started issuing orders to help me: to Jalal Bey in Aleppo, to Bakr Sami Bey in Beirut, and to the officers in charge of stores and supplies. I was to get everything I wanted in the way of equipment, ammunition, transport, money ... So off I went to Aleppo, where I met the governor, who arranged for me to get a bill of exchange for part of the money from some local merchants that I would be able to redeem through other merchants in Alexandria. The rest of the money I carried with me and went to Beirut. There I met with Bakr Sami Bey ... He greatly facilitated things for me with the relevant offices in Beirut. I was able to buy a 250-ton sailing vessel ... Arms, ammunition and dried food was sent to us from Syria. Then we loaded everything onto the ship. Because British and Russian warships were patrolling the Syrian coast, we had to bide our time waiting for a favourable opportunity to leave Beirut harbour. Finally one night in the middle of June[16] ... we set sail. Accompanying me on the voyage were an officer and twenty men, all Arabs; the ship's crew included the captain and four seamen.[17]

---

[16] In fact, their departure must have been late June or early July 1915.

[17] Ja'far al-'Askari (1988), Ch. 5.　　[18] Ibid.

The vessel, the *Hafez al-Rahman*, headed north along the Syrian coastline. It took two days to reach the Anatolian coastal town of Alanya, where they stayed for several days more. They then sailed to the south-west "leaving Rhodes and Crete on our starboard side". Again the crossing was rough, although it was now summertime, and there was the further anxiety that whenever they saw a ship they had to strike the sail and wait, hoping that they had not themselves been seen. In this way, they managed to get within sight of the Libyan coast, when there occurred what Ja'far, with great understatement, calls "a strange incident".

> It happened about midnight, when we saw a ship coming in our direction. We immediately lowered the sail; then we took an empty water barrel and tied our money boxes to it. I gave orders that when the ship got within range and opened fire we were to scuttle our own vessel and take to the lifeboat with the barrel – and hope that the tide would take us ashore. In fact, one of the sailors, a man named Murad Tabalu, actually began to chop away at the hull. We lowered the lifeboat with the barrel in it. Then the ship we had seen suddenly stopped a quarter of a mile away. It waited for three or four minutes and then hurried off in the opposite direction as fast as it could. To this day I can only think that they must have thought that our vessel was a submarine.[18]

After this close call came another. As they approached shore just before dawn, Sanusi soldiers guarding the coast saw them and, thinking that they were Italians trying to land, opened fire. Ja'far's party waved a white flag and finally managed to come ashore safely.

8

German Missions to the Sanusi

WHILE JA'FAR WAS AWAY in the Levant, two German agents, travelling separately, arrived at the Sanusi camp at Amsa'id. The first was Baron Otto von Gumpenberg, a twenty-five-year-old soldier of fortune, now working for the German Foreign Ministry.

As was the case with Baron Max von Oppenheim, von Gumpenberg was known to the British authorities in Cairo. He had been in Egypt in December 1911, early in the Turco-Italian War, prior to joining the Turkish side in the conflict. After a few weeks of lavish living at Alexandria's Excelsior Hotel and at the Grand Continental in Cairo, von Gumpenberg had obtained a permit to go hunting near Lake Mariout. He had bought camels and horses, assumed the name of "Abdul Karim Bey", and then disappeared into the desert in the company of a German artillery officer called von Bentheim and an English adventurer named Smallwood.[1] Serving as *aide de camp* to Enver, von Gumpenberg had stayed in Libya until the Turks signed the peace treaty.[2] In late 1912 he had returned to Germany, again passing through Egypt. Before long – and in common with Aubrey Herbert – he became embroiled in a war in Albania. Von Gumpenberg appears to have had numerous English friends who admired

[1] One of the few English volunteers to join the Turks in Libya, Smallwood was killed in the fighting in Cyrenaica. See page 33.
[2] *EG*, 14 April 1915: article entitled "The German Spy: von Gunpenberg [*sic*] in Egypt".

his dashing and reckless life-style, with the result that, when the British press reported (on 27 April 1915) that one "Baron von Gunpenberg" [*sic*] was believed to be spying for Germany in Egypt, both the War Office and the press received a flood of information about him.[3]

Pretending to be a reporter for the *New York Herald* and carrying a forged American passport in the name of "Roeder",[4] von Gumpenberg had in the spring of 1915 travelled to Libya from Crete, where he had stopped to organize arms shipments to the Sanusi.[5] Once in the Sanusi camp, however, he clashed with Nuri, who feared German interference just as he seemed to be making progress with Sayyid Ahmad. Nuri complained to Enver that von Gumpenberg's presence had created a situation in which Sayyid Ahmad could play off Turks and Germans against each other. Enver took this complaint to German officials in Constantinople and von Gumpenberg was recalled.[6]

While the young adventurer was preparing to depart from Cyrenaica, on 11 July, a runner arrived at the Sanusi camp from the coast to say that Ja'far had returned in a vessel filled with weapons and ammunition. Camels were sent to Bardia to transport the cargo back to Amsa'id, and with them went Lieutenant von Gumpenberg. Getting the material ashore must have taken some considerable time for there were 250 crates of Mauser rifles, 100 of ammunition, and numerous crates of dynamite.[7] When it had all been off-loaded, von Gumpenberg sailed away aboard the *Hafez al-Rahman*.

Ja'far's memoirs mention his meeting the German agent:

> There [at Bardia on the day of my return to Libya] I met a German
> officer who had recently been in the service of the Sanusi, one von

---

[3] FO 371/2356, p. 111. Letter of 28 April from William Thompson to Sir George Arthur at the War Office. Thompson says that mention of von Gumpenberg occurred in "yesterday's papers", that is, of 27 April. The author was unable to find mention in *The Times* of that day, but there was wide coverage of von Gumpenberg's return to the Middle East in *The Egyptian Gazette*, e.g., 14 April 1915, and the item had obviously been picked up by some of the London papers.
[4] WO 33/714, Maxwell to Kitchener (No. 1531 E) 20 July 1915.
[5] McKale (1998), *War by Revolution*, p. 148.
[6] Ibid.
[7] FO 371/2356, p. 314. Western Desert Intelligence. Based on information received in early November, four months after the vessel's capture.

Gumpenberg. He asked me if he could leave with the boat as it returned to Syria, and then he boarded the vessel with the sailors, including one named Mustapha, and the two Tabalu brothers, Muhammad and Murad. They sailed away towards the north that same afternoon.[8]

In fact, just hours later on that day (11 July) the steamer was stopped by a British warship, HMS *Dufferin*. Von Gumpenberg's American passport fooled no one, and he was taken into custody. Interned at Alexandria, he was informed that he would be treated as a prisoner of war – that is, not shot as a spy – provided that he gave British Intelligence the full details of his mission to the Sanusi. Von Gumpenberg related a plausible story about having been sent to Libya in order to get Sayyid Ahmad to come to terms with the Italians, adding that because the Italians had now entered the war on the side of the allies, his mission had failed, and he was on his way to Greece or Turkey when captured. An exchange of telegrams between Maxwell and Kitchener reveals the former to have been the more gullible. "I believe his tale to be true," wrote Maxwell, "as it is in the main confirmed by what we already know."[9] Kitchener, however, appears not to have expected a captured German officer to give details of a secret mission quite so readily. "It is very important that the subject of his mission to Senoussi ... be exactly ascertained. His account of it is evidently made up. You should do your best to have him thoroughly pumped by a competent secret service agent."[10]

Von Gumpenberg stuck to his story and, since there was no way to disprove it, he was allowed to settle into life as a prisoner of war. He did not reveal the extent to which arms were being smuggled into Cyrenaica despite the allied blockade, nor the existence of a far more important German agent in the Sanusi camp, whose name was Otto Mannesmann.

Mannesmann arrived at Amsa'id in May 1915, a few weeks after von Gumpenberg. Although in the course of that month the Egyptian Coastguard's Arab agents finally reported the existence of "one or two

[8] Ja'far al-'Askari (1988), Ch. 5.
[9] WO 33/731, Maxwell to Kitchener (No. 1531 E) of 20 July 1915.
[10] Ibid., Kitchener to Maxwell (No. 6428 cipher) of 21 July 1915.
[11] Ibid., Maxwell to Kitchener (No. 1041 E) of 7 May 1915 and (No. 1113 E) of 19 May 1915. The latter telegram actually refers to three Germans staying at Amsa'id.

Germans"[11] with the Sanusi, Mannesmann's identity remained unknown to the British for nearly six months. Not until October 1915 was Sir Edward Grey informed that British Intelligence had "received confirmation from a most reliable source that Dr Otto Mannesmann is in fact with the Senoussi, and it is reported that he is assisting actively in a movement to raise an insurrection throughout North Africa."[12] Grey would have certainly recognized the name. Before the war European newspapers had given ample coverage to the Mannesmann family's commercial and political activities, especially in Morocco. Their clashes with French interests in that country had embarrassed the German Foreign Ministry, although the more aggressive and militarist segments of German opinion had been delighted. But more important to Grey, since the outbreak of war he had seen disturbing despatches about the political activities of the Mannesmann family in the United Kingdom itself, where their agents were suspected of running arms to Ireland,[13] and in Spain, where they had recently purchased three steamboats apparently with the aim of mining the Straits of Gibraltar.[14] But for the time being Grey did not know that Otto Mannesmann was with the Sanusi, and when in late October he did learn of the German's presence there, it was but a few days before the sinking of the *Tara*.

Otto Mannesmann was the youngest of six sons born to the German inventor and industrialist, Reinhard Mannesmann. To be the last-born in the family was, in the view of his brothers, a stroke of good fortune.

Whereas they had been brought up in relatively Spartan circumstances, by the time Otto was born (in 1874) the family was reaping the benefits of new wealth based on the manufacture of pipes and tubes. So Otto grew up in opulent surroundings. The family home in Remscheid was large, newly-built and stately; but something of that Spartan ethos seems to have survived in a family work ethic that demanded, first, educational excellence, preferably in chemistry and physics, and, then, single-minded

[12] FO 371/2354, letter from Sir Arthur Nicholson to Sir Edward Grey, 28 October 1915.
[13] FO 371/2202, document 47498, letter from A. Shipley of 24 August 1914 to HM's *Chargé d'Affaires*, Tangiers.
[14] FO 372/717, document 98579, *Note Verbale*, 19 Nov 1914, Arthur Hardinge to the Marquis of Lema in Madrid.

participation in the family enterprise. Whether or not he was more pampered in childhood than his brothers, Otto was definitely of the same mould. He studied physics at university, receiving his doctorate in 1897. His spare time throughout these years was devoted to scientific experiments carried out with his brothers, either in the laboratory located in the basement of their home, or in the more sophisticated facilities at university, but always in the service of the family business.[15] Another important and formative activity of this period was Otto's military training with the Uhlan Regiment at Ludwigsburg, near Stuttgart.[16]

In 1905 German foreign policy suddenly focused on Morocco, not so much with a view to challenging French influence in that country as to defy the recent *Entente Cordiale* between France and Britain. An important part of this historic agreement was the reciprocal acceptance by each of the two signatories of the other's interests in North Africa – that is, France would now accept the British occupation of Egypt; Britain would accept that Morocco was part of the French sphere of influence. The problem with this arrangement was that France had signed the Treaty of Madrid of 1880, which specifically prohibited the Great Powers from including Morocco in their African land grab. No sooner had France neutralized any possible objection by Britain, by means of the Entente, than she violated the earlier Treaty by demanding control over the Moroccan army and police. Needless to say, she did not consult Germany before doing this, and Germany, already outraged by the very existence of the Franco-British alliance, chose Morocco as being the best place to demonstrate how she felt about these developments. Kaiser Wilhelm II personally landed at Tangiers from a German warship and delivered a speech in favour of Moroccan independence. Germany then demanded a conference on Morocco's future. There was indeed a conference, but when it met in 1906 French claims in the country were supported, while German complaints were rebuffed.

In 1906, as the first Moroccan crisis was still simmering, the Mannesmann family began to develop its own business interests in Morocco, mainly to do with the exploitation of iron and gold. They

[15] His own successful invention, for which he took out a patent in 1900, was an inverted or hanging gas-lamp, which did not cast a shadow below the burner.
[16] André von Dumreicher served in the same regiment, also at Ludwigsburg, in the 1880s.

wanted concessions there, and they were in competition for them with industrialists from France, England and Spain. The governments of the various countries concerned jointly wished to organize the granting of rights according to a mining law that was then being drafted that would operate within the framework of an international syndicate. The Mannesmanns, interested neither in waiting for the mining law nor in the syndicate, seized the initiative by becoming involved with a rebel leader who was happy to take their money against a promise that Mannesmann business interests would be favoured over those of their competitors. In 1908 that rebel leader became Sultan and the Mannesmanns were granted the potentially lucrative concessions. This caused an international uproar, and the German Foreign Ministry refused to support the unscrupulous business methods employed by the family. The Mannesmanns, however, took the matter to the German public by waging an expensive propaganda campaign in the press against their own Foreign Ministry. The problem smouldered for several years, and those most disgruntled were the French, who of course considered Morocco to be their own sphere of influence.

In 1911 a second Moroccan crisis flared up when the German gunboat *Panther* went to Agadir to protect German interests. Again the crisis passed, although the involvement of the Mannesmann brothers was alleged by a French newspaper, who published a Mannesmann family photograph over the caption "Those for whom the *Panther* went to Agadir".[17]

Otto was in the forefront of his family's meddling in "French territory" and not above manufacturing incidents to force matters to a conclusion in their favour. For example, during the second crisis he was overheard planning to let himself be captured by Arabs in order to force the German government to land troops and rescue him.[18] His brother Reinhard confirmed that the family's affairs in the country were driving events, writing home that their situation was auspicious, and that the German Foreign Ministry "will not dare to leave us in the lurch".[19] Reinhard was overly optimistic, however, and the crisis soon passed with Germany gaining some token colonial possessions elsewhere in Africa. Nevertheless,

[17] Brandt-Mannesmann (1964), *Dokumente aus dem Leben der Erfinder*, p. 131.

[18] Neil Sherwood Lewis, "German Policy in Southern Morocco during the Agadir Crisis of 1911" (Ph.D thesis, University of Michigan, 1977). See especially p. 159, n. 15.

[19] Reinhard Mannesmann letter of 16 Aug 1911 quoted in Brandt-Mannesmann (1964), p. 131.

for France and Britain the two crises in Morocco were proof of a growing German menace, and the Mannesmanns' role in those and subsequent events was discussed at the highest levels in terms that portrayed the family as examples of the increasing aggressiveness and militancy of German society.[20]

In August 1914 Germany no longer had an interest in restraining Otto's bravado. Although he was a reserve officer in the Uhlans, he was referred to the Foreign Ministry as an experienced expert in North Africa. Before the month was out he was sent to the German Consulate in Tripoli, the Libyan capital. His initial orders were to continue subverting his old enemies, the French, in the neighbouring countries of Tunisia, Algeria, and Morocco. But with Max von Oppenheim already writing his Near Eastern masterplan and talking about the importance of winning over the Sanusi, the Political Department of the German Foreign Office decided to add to Otto Mannesmann's brief the subversion of British rule in Egypt. Headstrong and unsubtle, Otto responded by immediately sending a messenger to Sayyid Ahmad urging him to attack the British.[21] In fact, on 6 September 1914, Royle reported hearing that a messenger from the Germans was expected any day at Amsa'id, and this was almost certainly related to Mannesmann's activities.[22]

In December 1914 Otto Mannesmann's position at the Tripoli Consulate became vulnerable when another letter from him to Sayyid Ahmad, together with a quantity of printed circulars urging the Cyrenaican tribes to wage war against the British, fell into the hands of the Italians. Despite Germany's policy of not wanting to antagonize her then still wavering ally, the German Foreign Ministry refused Italian demands to have Mannesmann recalled.[23] But in March 1915 the Italians seized and impounded a shipment of arms hidden in beer barrels on a ship in Venice

---

[20] Brandt-Mannesmann (1964), p. 144, *cf.* letter from French General Lyautey in Morocco: "Je me propose d'adresser une plainte formelle à Tanger sur les relations étroites entretenues par Otto Mannesmann avec un caïd rebelle du Tiout."

[21] McKale (1998), p. 51.

[22] WO 157/687; and McKale (1998), p. 51.

[23] McKale (1998), p. 51.

[24] Ibid., p. 146.

[25] Brandt-Mannesmann (1964), p. 160.

[26] Ibid.

[27] McKale (1998), p. 148.

harbour. Mannesmann had arranged the shipment, which had been destined for Cyrenaica. Once again the Italians were outraged and this time Mannesmann was recalled to Germany.[24] His brief "diplomatic" career was over, but now he would pursue similar activities without diplomatic cover directly with the Sanusi. He made a quick visit to the family home at Remscheid. It was to be his last and one of his sisters-in-law recalled how, during a family gathering there, Otto nervously paced the floor, in anticipation of his coming mission.[25] Within weeks he was on his way back to Libya, ostensibly as a "salesman". Travelling by way of Crete he was smuggled into Cyrenaica and taken to Amsa'id.

Like the other visitors seeking to influence the Sanusi – Royle, Nuri and Ja'far, von Gumpenberg – Otto Mannesmann was received personally by Sayyid Ahmad and received from him a gift just like the one Sayyid Ahmad had given to Royle the previous November.

> From Sayyid Ahmad Herr Mannesmann received a holy robe lined with sable, such as only senior Sanussi sheikhs are allowed to wear ... The robe has been twice worn by the Grand Sanussi himself which makes it an especially significant gift.[26]

Mannesmann promised Sayyid Ahmad that the German government would look favourably upon a Sanusi sphere of influence and expansion to the south, where Sanusi activity had been curtailed by the French.

Mannesmann set up his headquarters on the coast north-west of the Sanusi camp.[27] There it was less likely that he would be spotted by Royle or the Egyptian Coastguard's Arab agents during their visits to Sayyid Ahmad, while he would also be well-positioned to help organize and receive shipments of money and arms. So far, these had arrived on whatever sailboats and steamers the experienced smugglers of the eastern Mediterranean could get through the blockade, but before long shipments would be arriving on German and Austrian U-boats. From this base Mannesmann would also find ample opportunity to disrupt the Sanusi's relations with the British.

9

Gallipoli and the Downturn in British–Sanusi Relations

IN LATE MARCH 1915 General Sir Ian Hamilton, commander of the expeditionary force being assembled to land at Gallipoli, arrived in Egypt. He had just spent a week observing allied naval operations which had failed to penetrate the Dardanelles. Since the Admiralty had confidently expected the naval attack to succeed, Hamilton was now uneasy about the task before him. On the heels of the Navy's failure in the straits could the Army succeed by land?

On the 28th Hamilton lunched with the Egyptian Sultan, Husayn Kamel Pasha, at Abdin Palace. Government ministers were in attendance, and the atmosphere was thoroughly convivial. Speaking French, the Sultan broached the subject of Gallipoli, telling Hamilton that Turkish defences there were "absolutely impregnable".[1] Hamilton struggled to remain sanguine in face of his host's comment, but he knew that allied intelligence about Turkish defences on Gallipoli was largely speculative and that, with German help, the Turks were even now improving their fortifications there. But one can easily believe that the Sultan's words bothered Hamilton more than he let on in his diary entry for the day: "The words 'absolute' and 'impregnable' don't impress me overmuch," he wrote. "They

---

[1] Ian Hamilton (1920), *Gallipoli Diary*, vol. 1, entry for 28 March.

are only human opinion used to gloss over flaws in human knowledge or will. Nothing is impregnable either – that's a sure thing."[2]

But before leaving Egypt, Hamilton was disconcerted again from another quarter. A few days after his lunch with the Sultan he came upon an article in *The Egyptian Gazette* that openly discussed the allies' plans for attacking Gallipoli. Hamilton protested to McMahon, the High Commissioner, but the latter answered that he was "not the keeper of *The Egyptian Gazette* and must not quarrel with it as Egypt is not at war".[3] Baffled by the lack of censorship, but apparently unable to do anything about it, the general could only hope that the Turks would not believe that the British would be so foolish as to announce their intentions in the newspaper and would see the leaks as attempted disinformation.

Reports in Egyptian newspapers are unlikely to have influenced the outcome at Gallipoli – the naval attacks had made the allies' intentions quite clear. All the same, starting in April 1915, five hundred thousand men were put ashore, only to spend the rest of the year on the peninsula's southern tip, with many living in, and fighting from, a catacomb of caves and dugouts on steep hillsides overlooking the sea whence they had come. Roughly half of the allied soldiers participating in the campaign entered the casualty lists as dead or wounded. By January 1916 it was over. The soldiers were evacuated, and the allied fleets did not reach Constantinople until two days after the Armistice in 1918. The very word "Gallipoli" became a byword for military disaster.

Throughout 1915 life in Egypt was profoundly affected by the operations on the other side of the eastern Mediterranean. Hundreds of thousands of troops entered the country through the port cities and then settled into large temporary camps that overflowed the usual confines of Cairo, Ismailia, and Alexandria. Alexandrians, especially, found themselves a minority in their own city, which gradually metamorphosed into one enormous hospital camp of sick and wounded. This, of course, affected the morale of those who lived in Egypt. Natives and non–natives doubtless reacted to the news differently, but surprisingly early in 1915, and despite a belated enthusiasm for censorship by the British authorities, it was soon common knowledge that the invasion of Turkey was going horribly wrong.

[2] Hamilton (1920), vol. 1, entry for 28 March.
[3] Ibid., entries for 31 March and 4 April 1915.

These events were watched closely by the Sanusi, and April marked a downturn in his relations with the British. At the end of the month Vice-Admiral Sir Richard Peirse, the Senior Naval Officer in Egypt, sent a message to the Admiralty indicating that recent optimism over the state of those relations may have been ill-founded, noting that Turkish agents were undermining Sayyid Ahmad's goodwill towards Egypt.[4] This is the first indication that Nuri's activities had at last been uncovered by the British. General Maxwell was certainly in possession of the same information as Vice-Admiral Peirse, but apparently he hesitated for two weeks before he could bring himself to discuss this important development with Kitchener, and by that time knowledge of the separate German mission in Cyrenaica had also reached Army Headquarters in Cairo. On 6 May Maxwell finally sent to Kitchener the following enigmatic message: "I have reason to believe that powerful influences are being brought to bear on Senoussi, and he may not be able to control the force. He may move west himself and leave his followers without control. We may then have trouble on the western border. Snow is on the spot watching."[5] Kitchener's concern was immediate. He responded that Maxwell's cable was "difficult to understand", and asked for clarification: "What powerful influences are at work, and why should Senoussi move west? It is important that you should keep me well informed about this in view of the position of Italy."[6]

At that time, Italy seemed to be on everyone's mind. Since 1882 she had been a member of the Triple Alliance with Germany and Austria-Hungary, but now Italy was quarrelling with Austria over issues relating to their common border and sending signals to Britain, France and Russia that she was on the verge of leaving the Alliance. Germany did what she could to keep the Alliance together, the Kaiser hurrying to visit Emperor Franz Josef to seek Austrian concessions that might save the situation. But it was to no avail. Italy had made up her mind, although she was still hesitating before openly announcing her intentions – possibly waiting to get a higher bid from Britain and her allies in return for changing sides. Britain and France redoubled their efforts to win Italy over, offering her "absolute supremacy in the Adriatic, without any political or territorial

[4] WO 33/731, (No. 399) C-in-C East Indies to Admiralty, 25 April 1915.
[5] Ibid., (No. 1033 E), of 6 May 1915.
[6] Ibid., (No. 4484 cipher) of 7 May 1915.
[7] *EG*, "Italy and the War", 15 April 1915.

limitations".[7] In Libya at this time the Sanusi army had the upper hand over the Italians, who were still failing to conquer the country, and Kitchener knew that any change in the status quo on Egypt's western frontier would be of strategic importance.

On 7 May Maxwell sent the following to explain the situation:

> Senoussi is still at Sollum busily collecting supplies and with a considerable number of armed followers. He expresses bitter hatred of the Italians, against whom he has scored considerable successes recently, but he still professes his friendship for us. The influences working against us are Enver at Constantinople, through his brother Nouri Bey, who is now with Senoussi. Several other Turkish officers, including Barouni, and one or two Germans are in Cyrenaica.
>
> It is obvious ... that hostilities between Senoussi and us would help the Italians, who are probably shutting their eyes to intrigues which may be going on through Egyptians, Germans and Turks in Rome.
>
> The Senoussists have doubtless heard the rumours which are current here to the effect that we are in difficulties in the Dardanelles. If Senoussi finds that the force is getting beyond his control he may go west, and thus be able to disown any rupture between his tribes and ours.
>
> Hunter is gone west and Snow is there.[8]

On 23 May 1915 the die was finally cast as Italy declared war on Austria. The Triple Alliance was now an "Austro-German Alliance" with Turkey as a military partner. Britain and her allies saw this as rare good news. Few stopped to wonder what price might have to be paid for welcoming the Sanusi's bitter enemy onto their side in the hostilities.

In the short term British–Sanusi relations seemed not to suffer, but several days after Italy's dramatic move an incident occurred which might under the circumstances have made the British very uncomfortable. An Italian prisoner escaped from the Sanusi and made his way to Sollum. At first Sayyid Ahmad demanded that the British hand him back. Sir Edward Grey quickly became involved, and the Italian was spirited out of Egypt and returned to Italy. Sayyid Ahmad was promised that in the future the man would serve against the Austrians and would never be seen again in Libya. Sayyid Ahmad's response to the British sleight of hand (addressed to

[8] WO 33/731, (No. 1041 E) of 7 May 1915.

Maxwell) is perhaps the only example of Sanusi irony ever recorded: "You say that the man is German. I am sure that's true. Thank you for taking him away and saving us the trouble of looking after him!"[9]

Sayyid Ahmad's magnanimity and humour concerning this issue may have been due to the fact that his forces had just won an astonishing victory over the Italians. On 29 April a column of 4,000 Italian soldiers under Colonel Miani had marched out of Misurata against the Sanusi Army and been virtually wiped out. From the scene of battle the Arabs had collected thousands of rifles, millions of rounds of ammunition, plus artillery, supplies and money.[10]

The significance of this further downturn in Italian fortunes in Libya was not grasped by everyone in Cairo. At the British Agency McMahon wrote to Kitchener in terms which, at least with hindsight, sound almost inane. "The Senoussi makes me a little anxious for the moment, but I have just sent him a nice letter … Italy joining us will doubtless make him think … The Germans [had] told him that Italy was joining them."[11] It seems quite amazing that the High Commissioner could not foresee that gaining the Italians as an ally just as the Sanusi was defeating them on the field of battle – together with the accumulation of bad news from Gallipoli – would inevitably lead Sayyid Ahmad to listen more attentively to the Turks and Germans.

Maxwell, at least, was attentive to the new dangers on the west, although one of his proposals for countering them was deemed by Kitchener and the War Office to be somewhat bizarre. "It is very necessary to prevent contraband from reaching the Turks," he wrote Kitchener, "and Turkish boats carrying emissaries from reaching their destinations, but this cannot be done without ships. The matter has assumed greater importance by the advent of submarines."[12] A few weeks later he began to develop a plan for confronting this new menace, suggesting that Britain should resort to using:

[9] WO 33/731, (No. 1192 E) 30 May 1915, in which Maxwell quotes to Kitchener an excerpt from the Sanusi's telegram.
[10] John Wright (1969), p. 135. Wright calls this defeat "the greatest blow of the war" for Italy.
[11] PRO 30/57/47, McMahon to Kitchener, letter of 24 May 1915.
[12] WO 33/731, (1138 E) 23 May 1915.
[13] Ibid., (1309 E) 19 June 1915.

the most influential and powerful Hashish smuggler and his organisation, paying a monthly subsidy for expenses and a heavy reward for the capture or destruction of a submarine or of benzine boats. The smuggler would have to use the whole of his workmen and organisation in his own way. We have the necessary man in our hands … If this scheme is sanctioned, the whole of the littoral and islands would be thoroughly searched by the aid of the smugglers' intelligence service, which is unique. [!!!] We should have to outbid the Germans, as there is no doubt that they are using a similar organisation.[13]

A few days later he came back to the idea of recruiting smugglers.

[A]s you will know they have a very efficient organisation but we would only pay by results, big money for big results! I think the Germans are using this organisation, so it would be a question of the highest bidder![14]

Kitchener apparently refrained from commenting on Maxwell's brainstorm, and one is left guessing whether this was because of the indignity or the cost of using the smuggler network.

Over the summer of 1915 there was no let up in the bad news from Gallipoli, while at the same time tension began to mount at Sollum. The capture of von Gumpenberg (11 July) was presented in encouraging headlines, but at British headquarters this good news was rather spoiled by the knowledge, kept strictly secret, that the *Hafez al-Rahman* had successfully landed an enormous quantity of arms and supplies a few hours before the capture. On 14 July a German submarine was reported to have been sighted near Sollum, and, whether or not there really was a U-boat there, it was assumed in Cairo that this would increasingly be their enemies' preferred method of delivering arms and men to the Sanusi camp.[15]

Early in August an enormous intelligence blunder came to Maxwell's attention. He learned that on 16 June (nearly two months earlier!) the French navy had captured a felucca on a special mission to the Sanusi. Called the *Olympia*, the boat was stopped near Crete with:

[14] PRO 30/57/47, Maxwell to Kitchener, 24 June 1915.
[15] WO 33/731, (1504 E) 16 July 1915. Maxwell told of the reported sighting by Vice-Admiral Peirse.

two Turkish officers and five non-commissioned officers together with costly presents, 5,000 lira of Turkish gold, decorations, ammunition, grenades and an autograph letter from the Sultan in which he acknowledges receipt of a letter from Senoussi. He confers on Senoussi the grade of Vezir and authorizes him to proclaim a Holy War against England, France and Russia; he makes no mention of Italy beyond giving congratulations on having been successful against the latter. He also informs Senoussi that the Turco-German forces will drive the Anglo-French at Gallipoli into the sea.[16]

Maxwell concluded his account of this event to Kitchener by adding, "[a]nxiety over the situation at the Dardanelles is increasing even among our best friends".

In mid-August there occurred the most serious incident on the western frontier to date, one which either side might have seen as a justification for war. Two British submarines were involved, the *B-6* and the *B-11*. The latter was a semi-obsolete craft of 1905 vintage, commanded by a twenty-seven year old lieutenant, Norman Douglas Holbrook. The previous December Holbrook had received the Royal Navy's first Victoria Cross of the war for taking his submarine under five rows of mines and successfully torpedoing a Turkish battleship in the Straits of Gallipoli, all in a single nine-hour dive.

The latest incident occurred on the morning of 16 August 1915, when the two submarines were cruising on the surface a few miles southeast of Ras Lakk between Sollum and Tobruk. They happened to pass near the camp set up by Otto Mannesmann for receiving arms shipments, and that morning Mannesmann was there as they came into view. The *B-11* was about a thousand yards from shore when look-outs on board spotted first one Bedouin, then others, and eventually a European. The latter began to wave a large white flag as if he wished to communicate with the submarine. Commander Holbrook lowered a boat and rowed alone towards the shore. As he approached, the European shouted "Are you English?" When Holbrook replied that he was, the European pointed to a sandy beach where he could land. At this point Holbrook appears suddenly to have realized the vulnerability of his situation, or, as he put it in his official report, he noticed that his interlocutor – who was of course

[16] WO 33/731, (No. 1628 E) 7 August 1915.

Mannesmann – "carried a large Mauser pistol", and so Holbrook turned about and began furiously to row back to the submarine. He made it back unmolested, but as he arrived the men on shore opened fire. The British returned fire with rifles and a Maxim gun, but before they could get out of range one British sailor was killed and two others wounded.[17]

Trying to explain the incident to Kitchener, Maxwell wrote

> There is no doubt that Nouri's party is in the ascendancy with Senoussi and this incident will precipitate matters. I have telegraphed to Senoussi our account of the incident and asked why his officers disobeyed his orders and fired on a British ship. I am awaiting his reply … I do not know the reason for the presence of submarines at Sollum or the orders they received. The incident is most unfortunate.[18]

Holbrook tried to explain the presence of the two submarines along the Libyan coast by saying that the seas had been particularly rough during the night of 15–16 August and that they were merely looking for calm water. Maxwell was restrained in his comments about the matter, but others were stingingly critical. McMahon referred to matters in the West being made worse due to "acts of naval stupidity";[19] while Reginald Wingate, the Sirdar, noted discrepancies in the various accounts of the incident and concluded that "there seems to be a bit of *suppressio veri* going on".[20]

With Snow at Sollum, meanwhile, were some seventy Egyptians, including the Egyptian Army detachment at the fort. For two days they waited to see if the incident would trigger hostile action against their outpost, as HMS *Minerva* stood by in the harbour in case they needed to be evacuated.[21]

On 18 August the tense situation was finally relieved when Maxwell received a conciliatory message from Sayyid Ahmad.

---

[17] WO 33/731, (No. 1700 E) 16 August 1915; and (No. 1703 E) 17 August 1915. Holbrook submitted his report on the incident to Snow at Sollum.
[18] Ibid., (No. 1703 E) 17 August 1915.
[19] PRO 30/57/47, letter from McMahon to Fitzgerald, 19 August 1915.
[20] Durham University, the Sudan Archive, Box 469/10, Wingate to Clayton, 27 August 1915.
[21] WO 33/731, (No. 1703 E) of 17 August 1915.
[22] Ibid., (No. 1716 E) of 18 August 1915.

You know that we have had posts all along the coast since the beginning of the war with Italy, and that Italian battleships often cruise off the coast and fire at our troops, and it was for this reason that I gave strict orders to all officers commanding the west coast to fire on the ships before they could do our men harm. It was not possible for our men to know that [they] were British.[22]

Before the month was out the safety of the Sollum outpost was again threatened. Snow reported that at 10.00pm on the night of the 28th about a hundred Sanusi soldiers "took up positions within a few yards of our fort".

[O]thers penetrated beyond our sentries, refusing to listen to their orders to return to their own territories, others lined the crest of the hills overlooking Sollum, also some forty armed men marched into our village; the whole of this force remained in position until early morning.[23]

Again Maxwell had been put into the position of having to protest to Sayyid Ahmad, but no sooner had he sent his latest complaint than he was shown a bundle of documents recently dispatched by the Sanusi to various Muslim notables. These had fallen into the hands of British intelligence and contained irrefutable evidence of the Sanusi's double-dealing with the British and his sympathy for Britain's enemies. Maxwell's telegram to Kitchener of the 30th reveals a new level of disillusionment.

Private and secret. The attitude of Senoussi is distinctly dangerous, and his people have been latterly executing night manoeuvres round our post at Sollum. When I asked that this should stop, he denied that they had taken place. Today, I ... got hold of a packet of letters from him to the Muslim potentates and journalists all over Arabia and India, inciting them to Jihad and informing them that he is the representative of the Caliph in North Africa ... I think we should be better prepared.[24]

---

[23] Sir George Arthur (1932), *General Sir John Maxwell*, pp. 216–17, quoting Snow's report of 29 August 1915.
[24] WO 33/731, (No. 1782 E) 30 August 1915.

But as this new conviction took hold of Maxwell, his chief was suddenly beset with uncharacteristic indecision. Defeat was looming at Gallipoli; on the Western Front there had just occurred disastrous battles at Neuve Chapelle and Ypres; and the allies were about to attack at Loos which might be (and indeed proved to be) just as costly in allied lives as the others. Perhaps Kitchener simply could not face the possibility of an attack against Egypt by thousands of tribesman intent upon Holy War. In any case, where would he find the troops to defend Egypt when he was already having difficulty finding men for his overstretched forces in France and Gallipoli? Therefore, in response to the latest crisis in Egypt Kitchener sent Maxwell a plain and simple message: that he should keep the Sanusi quiet at any price.

> It is hardly necessary, I know, for me to recommend the greatest caution to you and to those officers in touch with the situation in dealing with the Senoussi, whose friendship should be fostered in every way. In this respect Royle, as well as … the Senoussi agent in Cairo, might be useful.[25]

In fact, Maxwell had already taken the precaution of sending Royle back to Sollum after the Holbrook incident. In the past few months Royle's RFC career had been interrupted several times due to the situation in the west. First, the Italians wanted to use his influence to get Sayyid Ahmad to accept the creation of an autonomous "Sanusi zone" in Cyrenaica under joint Italian and British protection – an offer which was made, but which, being hardly attractive to a man who thought he had the Italians on the run, was rejected. Then, in May, when the British realized that Turkish and German agents were at Amsa'id trying to influence the Sanusi against them, Royle had been sent to visit Sayyid Ahmad in the company of Cecil Snow – and any hope that Royle may have entertained that by introducing his uncle to the Grand Sanusi he might free himself to get on with his RFC duties was soon dashed by the succession of bad news during the summer.

The other man referred to in Kitchener's telegram, "the Senoussi agent in Cairo", was Muhammad Idrisi,[26] who got along well with the English

---

[25] WO 33/731, (No. 7488 cipher) 31 August 1915.
[26] Not to be confused with Sayyid Muhammad Idris, Sayyid Ahmad's nephew and future head of the Brotherhood (and eventually King of Libya).

and whom Sayyid Ahmad had delegated to be his senior representative in the Egyptian capital. Maxwell took Kitchener's advice and immediately had an interview with Idrisi with the aim of restricting the right of free passage into and out of Egypt, which the Sanusi followers in Cyrenaica seemed to take for granted. Although Muhammad Idrisi agreed to forward the scheme to Sayyid Ahmad, it did not work. On the one hand, the Sanusi had never accepted that the Egyptian police and coastguards had a right to impede his people's movement across the frontier; on the other, recent history had proven that any tribesman with a knowledge of the passes could come and go at will, as they had when acting as guides for Turkish officers during the Turco-Italian War.

On 13 September, Kitchener again wrote to Maxwell that the situation in the west required very careful handling, adding:

> I should be glad if you would send me by early mail a report on the situation from either Snow or Royle … Please also let me have by telegraph a general short statement on the situation in Egypt as regards internal order and security.[27]

Maxwell instructed Snow to prepare a report for the Minister of War; he also ordered an analysis of the general security situation from his staff at Army Headquarters. The two reports were sent to London by mail in early October. The security statement concluded that there was "no material change" in the overall security situation "though the check at the Dardanelles has increased intrigue and unrest".[28] Cecil Snow's analysis reviewed developments in the west since the Grand Sanusi's arrival at Amsa'id nearly a year earlier. By the time Kitchener had read them he was preparing to leave for the eastern Mediterranean to discuss Gallipoli with his generals. His last telegram to Maxwell before his departure expressed the apprehensions of a man watching a nightmare come true. He said that he feared disastrous consequences for Egypt, which would "have to be secured on both its east and west frontiers if the Turks are prematurely released from being held up by the Dardanelles force".[29]

---

[27] WO 33/731, (No. 8196) 24 September 1915.
[28] Ibid., (No. 1928 E) 1 October 1915.
[29] Ibid., (No. 9450) 2 November 1915.

Interestingly, Snow's report[30] (dated 29 September) does not echo the foreboding that had begun to characterize Maxwell's own comments since the discovery of the Sanusi's duplicity. Perhaps Snow was not told about the captured bundle of letters calling for Holy War and therefore continued to believe in the Sanusi's goodwill. In any event, Snow's overall conclusion was that Sayyid Ahmad was still on the fence, but with "good intentions" and "friendly feelings" towards the British. Snow believed Nuri's influence with the Sanusi had grown because of Turkish gold – "32,000 Turkish lira" worth of it, which, handed out little by little, had enabled Sayyid Ahmad "to pay off very heavy debts to merchants in our village of Sollum". Snow's agents had told him that "on their arrival, Nouri and Jaafar were so disgruntled over their reception that they were on the point of returning to Stamboul". The Sanusi had originally ordered them to live at Bir Wa'r "but time and money are telling in favour of Nouri, who quite recently has been allowed to live at Amsa'id and is now in command of the troops quartered there". Nuri's ultimate aim, Snow wrote, was to provoke an incident "which would drive the Sanusi into war with Egypt". Snow describes two events by way of illustration (the first being taken from a report he had written in June):

> Last night Ahmad Haqqi Bey, of influence at [Amsa'id], together with another, assembled by bugle call a certain portion of the Senoussi forces … with the intention of a raid on Sollum. The Senoussi, hearing the disturbance, enquired into its origin and sent the men back to their quarters. Next morning the leaders were severely flogged and others sent west. Nouri denied complicity.
>
> On another occasion Nouri bribed a Bedouin to shoot both myself and Hunter Pasha when visiting the old Turkish barracks … [which only] failed by the Bedouin being a few seconds too late.[31]

Snow assessed the strength of the force assembled on the plateau to be 1,500 trained and uniformed soldiers (*Muhafizia*); 600 new levies undergoing training by the Turks at Bir Wa'r; and smaller bodies of troops at locations west and south of Amsa'id. The total force numbered between 2,500 and 3,500 "officers, NCOs, and men trained or in training and equipped", with Nuri in command and Ja'far as second-in-command, "all

[30] FO 371/2354.   [31] Ibid.

armed with either captured Italian rifles or the new short carbine of German make recently smuggled in, also many old Greek rifles".[32]

On the morning of 29 September, just as Snow was completing the report, a messenger arrived from Amsaʻid with an invitation for him to visit Sayyid Ahmad. The surprise of receiving this unexpected message was as nothing compared to that which awaited him when he arrived at the Sanusi camp at midday. His meeting with Sayyid Ahmad was deferred until later in the afternoon, but in the meantime he was invited to lunch by three members of the Sanusi's inner circle. The first was Hasan Bey al-Biseikli, a Libyan Turk; the second was Sayyid Harun, an Egyptian Sanusi sheikh; and the third was none other than Jaʻfar al-ʻAskari. Snow fully enjoyed several convivial hours in the company of these men. He was, of course, especially interested to meet Jaʻfar with whom he spoke in French.[33] Snow found Jaʻfar "intelligent" and "most communicative", and he was regaled with tales of Jaʻfar's two years with the German Army and of his service in the Balkan War. Jaʻfar also related an account he had heard of the defeat of Colonel Miani's column in April, how the battle had lasted "two whole days, when the Italians broke and ran leaving everything behind them". Jaʻfar's assessment of the tribesmen under his command was that "they do not … understand discipline as do European troops, but if treated quietly they are excellent and [could be] very clever in military movements".[34]

At five o'clock in the afternoon Snow was ushered into Sayyid Ahmad's tent. The Sanusi was ill with "a wracking cough" and the interview was short.

> He said he had much to talk to me about but was not able to do so just then being ordered by his doctor not to speak at all, that he had asked me to come and see him as he had so often put me off before. So beyond a few commonplace remarks nothing happened.[35]

As he walked around the camp Snow counted roughly 500 Bedouin

[32] FO 371/2354.

[33] That Snow and Jaʻfar should settle on French when everyone at the lunch spoke Arabic is not actually surprising. Like Gordan Ingram, Cecil Snow spoke Egyptian Arabic. Jaʻfar's Mesopotamian dialect was considerably different.

[34] FO 371/2354.   [35] Ibid.

tents and about fifty European tents like those used by the Egyptian Army. He also counted

> roughly 1,000 uniformed men, not more, some of these being little more than boys. At the time I counted them they were all out drilling, marching with a very slow imitation German step.[36]

The first few weeks of October 1915 were relatively quiet at Sollum. Several dozen sheikhs arrived at Amsa'id at the beginning of the month to take part, as it turned out, in a marriage feast: both Sayyid Ahmad and his nephew Muhammad Idris were taking additional wives. Some of the native Egyptian coastguards went from Sollum to attend. Nuri was there; and "a German", obviously Otto Mannesmann, who commanded some of the troops in a march past the brides and bridegrooms.[37]

On 7 October Snow reported two interesting items of news to the Military Intelligence Office in Cairo. The first was that al-Baruni had finally been released from confinement. The second was that

> Mannesmann is the name of the German who showed the white flag to induce Holbrook to land at Ras Likk. He is tall and broadly built, has blue eyes and a prominent nose.[38]

The French military mission in Cairo immediately provided some background information, explaining the intrigues of the Mannesmann brothers in Morocco, which "culminated ... in the Agadir incident and the Franco-German crisis of 1911". Their statement also claimed that one of the brothers had been executed by the French at the start of the war, although in fact this assertion was not correct.[39]

On 10 October word reached Sollum of another significant Arab victory over the Italians near Tripoli. It was said that two thousand prisoners had been captured along with thirty pieces of artillery, many rifles and eight thousand pounds in cash.[40]

On the 13th sensational news arrived, that Sayyid Ahmad's younger

[36] FO 371/2354.
[37] FO 371/2356, reports of 4 and 8 October 1915.   [38] Ibid., p. 279.
[39] Ibid., report of 12 October 1915, p. 285.
[40] Ibid., report of 10 October 1915, p. 282.

brother Hilal had "fled" the Sanusi camp and gone to Egypt. He arrived at
Sidi Barani (with his entourage) and asked the coastguards if he could
borrow a tent, which Snow authorized. Sayyid Ahmad was reported to be
very angry, and apparently he accused Nuri of instigating Hilal's departure.
The Sanusi sent a telegram to Sidi Barani ordering Hilal to return by the
start of the feast of Bairam, which that year fell on 19 October. Hilal wired
back cryptically that he would return "when he had finished pacifying the
Bedouin" at Sidi Barani. From Roy Tweedie at Sidi Barani Snow heard
that Hilal was busy "collecting tithes".[41] Sayyid Ahmad then sent another
telegram, to which Hilal replied,

> Have received your telegram but cannot leave before the Bairam, but will
> come soon by automobile. I have levied some money on our people here
> and will leave when I have collected it. Have finished pacifying the
> Bedouin.[42]

At the Coastguard station at Sidi Barani there was a Model T Ford. It is
possible that Hilal had never ridden in an automobile before and that
Tweedie had enticed him with the promise of this new experience to get
him to return to Amsa'id. Finally, on 18 October, Hilal was given dinner
at the station and then taken back to Sollum in the Ford accompanied by
Egyptian Coastguard officer Muhammad Saleh Harb (the same man who
had helped Enver to cross the frontier in 1911). They arrived at Sollum at
11pm and, leaving the Model T there, zigzagged back up the escarpment
path to Amsa'id at midnight, riding on horseback for the final two miles.[43]

The following morning at Sidi Barani a large squad of *Muhafizia*[44] with
their officers – part of Hilal's entourage – arrived at the Coastguard
barracks and asked Tweedie what they should do since Hilal had gone back
to Amsa'id. Tweedie told them that they would have to march back to the
Sanusi camp, a distance of over sixty miles, and this they proceeded to do,
tramping westwards in the dust in ragged formation.[45]

---

[41] Tweedie, like Royle, had now been recalled to the Western Desert.

[42] FO 371/2356, p. 295, telegram from Snow of 18 October; Hilal's "flight" reported
in Military Intelligence summaries of 15, 19, 21 October 1915.

[43] FO 371/2356, 3 November; also 21 and 26 October.

[44] Uniformed and trained Sanusi regulars.

[45] FO 371/2356, p. 301, 26 October.

PART II

10

Arrival and Disappearance of HMS Tara

O N 23 OCTOBER 1915 HMS *Tara* arrived at Alexandria, where the
port authorities opened the newly erected anti-submarine boom to
allow her into the Western Harbour. The *Tara* had sailed from Devonport
sixteen days earlier and, despite anxieties about enemy U-boats, had
reached Egypt without mishap. As she passed the breakwater and moved
into position in front of Ras al-Tin Palace, her arrival excited particular
interest among the men of HMS *Scotia*, already at anchor inside the
harbour. The *Scotia* had arrived several months earlier and had since been
patrolling along Egypt's northern coast. In fact, on 16 August the *Scotia* had
been in the general area of Ras Lakk when the *B-6* and *B-11* were
attacked offshore there, and she had escorted the two British submarines
to Sollum. Now her entire crew were on deck waving and cheering the
Tara – for the *Scotia* and the *Tara* were sister-ships, virtually identical, both
built for the London and North-Western Railway at the turn of the
century. Both, prior to requisition by the Admiralty, had been employed
sailing back and forth across the Irish channel between Holyhead (in north
Wales) and Dublin. But the real reason for the present excitement was that
the two crews were predominantly men from Holyhead. That evening
there were over two hundred Welshmen, almost all friends and relations,
celebrating the reunion in the already teeming restaurants and bars of
Alexandria.

The next day the *Tara* took over the north coast patrol to Sollum, and the *Scotia* was transferred to the Red Sea. Before the *Tara* sailed out on her first patrol an interpreter was brought on board and introduced to the crew. A lively and efficient man of Egyptian-Greek background, he handed out cards printed in French identifying himself as Basil Lambrinidis and his normal place of "business" as the Bar Mishmish, number 11 Bawaki St., Cairo. With this new, 104th member of the ship's complement now aboard, the *Tara* steamed out of the harbour.

The *Tara*'s first patrol lasted a week and was uneventful. She stopped and searched all vessels coming within sight – with Basil doing most of the talking – but they were few in number, mostly native fishing boats. When she was in the general vicinity of Sollum, the *Tara* made daily runs into the little harbour. Crew members would wander up and down the beach or visit the little bazaar and the Greek grocery in the village, while Captain Gwatkin-Williams would meet with Lt.-Col. Snow to discuss the security situation and the need for various provisions.

At the end of the week the *Tara* sailed back to Alexandria. She spent a full day taking on supplies for Sollum and, on 3 November, headed west again on her second patrol.

Several months after the seizure of the *Olympia* by the French torpedo boat *Mousqueton*, Enver Pasha asked his German allies if one of their U-boats could be used to deliver to Sayyid Ahmad al-Sanusi a consignment of arms, valuable gifts, and a personal letter from the Sultan – in other words, a shipment similar to the one seized by the French in June. The Germans chose a large submarine, the *U-35*, which had arrived in the Mediterranean in August, and which was commanded by Kapitänleutnant Waldemar Kophamel. Based in the Adriatic at Cattaro, on the Montenegrin coast, the *U-35* sailed from that port on 12 October, heading for the Gulf of Salonica. Britain and her allies had just declared war on Bulgaria and were now busy sending ships with troops and munitions into the area. Attacking such targets was one objective of the *U-35*'s present mission. On the 18th, for example, she sank a small Italian steamer, the *Scilla* – presumably while pretending to be an Austrian U-boat, since Germany and Italy were not yet at war.[1] And on the 23rd (the day the *Tara*

---

[1] The use of "false flags" by German U-boats was one of the reasons Italy finally declared war on Germany in August 1916.

crew were boisterously welcomed to Alexandria) the *U-35* sank a 7,000-ton British troopship called the *Marquette*. After this second attack Kophamel noticed that enemy ships were taking the precaution of moving only at night. As the weather conditions did not favour night attacks, and as several other U-boats were in the area anyway, he decided to focus immediately on the mission's second objective, that of helping the Turks to supply their mission to the Sanusi.

The *U-35* called first at a German signal station in the Gulf of Xeros to the west of Gallipoli — passing close to the British and French fleets — to receive his latest instructions regarding "the Turkish-Arab mission".[2] Kophamel then headed for Orak Island, near Bodrum in southwest Turkey. Arriving there on 31 October the *U-35* loaded munitions and other supplies destined for Libya, including huge quantities of cartridges, machine-gun ammunition, and money. In all, thirteen and a half tons of crated supplies were distributed all over the U-boat. In addition, place had to be found on board for a group of ten Ottoman officers (referred to in Kophamel's orders as a "revolutionary committee") and these men were accommodated among the crates, in the forward torpedo room, and in the officers' quarters. To provide further reinforcements for the Sanusi two large sailboats loaded with more munitions and 120 more Ottoman soldiers were to sail from Orak at the same time as the *U-35*. Kophamel agreed that the *U-35* would try to tow these two boats so long as the weather was good and the sea was clear of enemy ships.

On 1 November, under cover of night, the U-boat embarked on the risky voyage to Libya, sailing on the surface into the Aegean Sea with the sailboats trailing behind in tow. That first night the tow rope broke four times, but even when the line held this unlikely flotilla was able to move at only 5 knots — roughly a third of the U-boat's normal surface speed.[3] At midday on 2 November Kophamel set the boats loose, the wind now being favourable, but later the wind dropped again, and the U-boat came to the aid of the slower of the two boats and towed it for a few hours more. That night they were back in the usual shipping lanes, and as vessels were normally blacked out and visibility was poor anyway the towing experiment perforce came to an end. The *U-35* had assisted the Turkish boats over a distance of 110 sea miles; it now set itself free and headed

---

[2] *U-35* logbook entry for 25 October 1915, Bundesarchiv, Freiburg.
[3] The *U-35* was capable of 16.4 knots on the surface and 9.7 knots under water.

alone for the African coast.

Once unhampered by the extra weight and able to dive, the *U-35* was again in a position to hunt enemy ships. South of Crete on the morning of 3 November, she came upon an English steamer, the *Woolwich*, which was carrying phosphate and tin from Port Sudan to Plymouth. This ship was either unarmed or simply not disposed to put up a fight when challenged. Her crew were allowed to man the lifeboats and the ship was sunk. Another opportunity to attack came on the afternoon of the same day. The U-boat dived in order to stalk a large steamer that had come into view, but the first torpedo missed and the steamer ran off at 13 knots. The *U-35* followed in pursuit for an hour, finally giving up in order to get back on course for Libya.

At dawn on the next day (4 November) the African coastline was already in sight. The Turkish ensign was raised, and the U-boat sailed into Bardia cove. The voyage from Bodrum had taken only two and a half days, but it had entailed some uncustomary problems. The towing had been a minor and temporary hindrance, but the presence of ten Ottoman officers and their supplies had completely upset normal routines onboard and caused wide-spread inconvenience. Normal movement was hampered by the crates of munitions piled high in the passages. The ventilator had to be permanently on maximum, which strained the power system and pushed the temperature up until it was scarcely endurable. Worse still, the Turks were seasick, and to get away from the stench some of the German officers had to be moved to the Deck Officers' Room. In short, it was two and a half days of misery for everyone on board.

Awaiting the U-boat as it glided into Bardia cove was a small party of Turkish soldiers together with a large band of armed Arabs. The Germans were surprised to find that this Libyan "port" had no facilities whatsoever, not even boats for offloading the cargo. Kophamel's only option was to use his vessel's own dinghy, so he dropped anchor as close to the rocky shore as he could, while his men rigged up a line between the Arabs standing among the boulders at the water's edge and the *U-35*.[4] They then proceeded to unload the tons of cargo by pulling the dinghy back and forth along the rope-line, and it took five hours to get it all ashore.

---

[4] In two slightly out-of-focus photos inserted into this section of the *U-35*'s logbook one can just make out the shore party among the rocks, the ravine rising steeply behind them.

Positioned among the high rocks on both sides of the entrance to the inlet were Arab sentries watching for approaching vessels. Around mid-afternoon, when the off-loading was finished, one of the sentries raised the alarm, and the Germans hastily prepared to depart. Once underway and out of the cove, however, they found this to have been a false alarm. Nevertheless, Kophamel was pleased to have the opportunity to run a few tests and confirm that the *U-35* was still in good running order after the exertions of the previous three days. They dropped anchor in the open sea near the inlet and made plans for the next day. One of the Turks at Bardia had informed Kophamel that in Sollum harbour, thirteen miles to the south, there were two British ships at anchor, and this intelligence made Kophamel impatient to attack Sollum, which he resolved to do early on the following morning.

The morning of 5 November was crisp and clear with a light breeze blowing from the northwest. Kophamel had apparently been up much of the night – at 3.20am he was describing the day's events in the ship's log, mentioning also his intention to attack Sollum and destroy the two cruisers there. But this early morning strike was unexpectedly curtailed. Shortly after dawn the *U-35* dived and made straight for Sollum, where the Coastguard cruisers were at anchor in shallow water close to shore. Having at this point no idea of Sollum's defences Kophamel preferred to execute his attack submerged and with torpedoes, but he now judged that to be unfeasible because of the shallows. While he considered his options he ordered the U-boat to turn, still submerged, and it stole away unnoticed. When the *U-35* surfaced at 9am, the two stacks of HMS *Tara* were spotted on the north-east horizon. The Germans dived again and waited.

Captain Gwatkin-Williams and Commander Kophamel both noted the precise time the torpedo struck the starboard side of the *Tara's* engine room. The Welshman wrote:

> For a second my surprise was so great that I was speechless ... my tongue and my limbs were frozen, immovable. Then ... I found I was gazing at my wrist-watch; it was 10.10 am.[5]

The German's timepiece gave the same information, except that it was

[5] Gwatkin-Williams (1919), p. 15.

permanently set to German time, one hour back. His entry in the log reads:

9.10 am. Fired. Hit the engine room. Ship immediately begins to list.[6]

Following the explosion Kophamel watched the scene for several minutes through his periscope. Eventually someone onboard the *Tara* spotted the spray thrown off by this device, whereupon seaman gunner Millward, standing behind a Hotchkiss six-pounder, fired eight rounds, forcing the U-boat to descend to ten metres.

It took ten minutes for the *Tara* to sink. Her stern went first, throwing her bows up perpendicular to the sea. When the *U-35* finally re-surfaced, where the ship had been there were now three lifeboats and a lot of men still in the water. Some of the German crew were on the deck of the approaching U-boat, as Gwatkin-Williams put it, "armed to the teeth".

The survivors who could not find room in the lifeboats were taken aboard the submarine. The dead body of the ship's cook, Walter Jackson, was also recovered, as well as a live terrier, the ship's mascot. Among the ninety-two survivors one man was badly wounded, the *Tara's* quartermaster, William Thomas, who had got into a lifeboat which had capsized while still hooked to a davit; as the boat was thrown about he suffered a compound leg fracture and, though hauled out of the water still conscious, he was badly hurt.

Kophamel was convinced that his attack on HMS *Tara* had been heard and maybe even observed from Sollum; in his logbook he expressed surprise that no one there made any effort to rescue the British crew, adding that "therefore, they shall have to be delivered to Bardia as prisoners of war".

Gwatkin-Williams was among the *Tara's* crew members now onboard the *U-35*, and he was taken to meet Kophamel. The German commander informed him that the prisoners would be handed over to the Turks at Bardia. Gwatkin-Williams asked if they could be allowed to row to Sollum instead, but this was denied.

The U-boat prepared the tow-line. Soon she was again approaching the cliff-lined shore of Cyrenaica, the three lifeboats following behind, and again the German flag was replaced with the Ottoman star and crescent.

[6] *U-35* logbook entry for 5 November 1915.

This time a larger party of Turks and Arabs was waiting at Bardia. Kophamel used one of the *Tara* lifeboats to go ashore, where Nuri Pasha and Otto Mannesmann stepped forward and introduced themselves. The three men consulted for twenty minutes, making arrangements for the prisoners to be placed in the custody of the Turks under Nuri's authority. Returning to the *U-35* Kophamel informed Gwatkin-Williams of these arrangements, adding that he, Gwatkin-Williams, would be kept on the U-boat and delivered into relatively more comfortable captivity in Austria. However, Gwatkin-Williams asked to be allowed to stay with his men whatever the discomforts, and Kophamel did not insist.

The *U-35* remained at Bardia for several hours. The prisoners were disembarked onto the nearest rocks and made to gather on a sandy beach at the head of the cove, where they were watched by armed Sanusi. Kophamel, meanwhile, continued his consultations with the Turkish general and the German consul and secret agent, later recording their conversations in some detail. Nuri and Mannesmann both emphasized the importance of having the U-boat remain in the area to help find the two missing Turkish sailboats; they also urged Kophamel to attack the British at Sollum, assuring him that the harbour defences there were minimal. Regarding the first request Kophamel promised to look for the boats, although he made it clear that he had to get back to Cattaro soon. The attack on Sollum he promised to carry out that very afternoon.

Mannesmann handed over a telegram to be sent to the German Foreign Office. It contains impressive evidence of Enver's commitment to attacking the British through Egypt's western frontier; and of Sayyid Ahmad's readiness to participate in that plan if the price were right.

> Please forward to General Staff, Department 36. U-35 has brought 300,000 cartridges, 80 belts of machine gun ammunition, and 120,000 francs. Whether two sailboats will arrive with 120 Turkish soldiers and 300,000 more cartridges is doubtful. In Marmaris harbour, just west of Bodrum, are 700 Turkish soldiers; also 6 cannons, 2 machine guns and [more ammunition] that Major Djemal Bey will try to bring here. Nouri requests U-boat from Pola[7] be sent to Marmaris with Major Djemal in order to escort boats [delivering above reinforcements and munitions] to

[7] On the Adriatic, near Trieste.
[8] Telegram in *U-35* logbook, 5 November 1915.

Bardia. Major Djemal will wait at Consulate in Pola for answer by wire. STOP. Nouri requests one million francs for Ahmad and that funding of move [against Egypt] be delivered by U-boat; also 1000 carbines, each with 300 cartridges, and 2 million percussion caps … Ahmad's attack immediately upon receipt [of above] is assured. Please also send 400,000 francs for Algiers. Mannesmann.[8]

Towards mid-afternoon Nuri and Mannesmann made a brief tour of the U-boat, and Major Jemal Bey went on board for the trip to Pola. Then shortly before 4 o'clock the *U-35* again left Bardia, bound for Sollum. At 5.15 she surfaced just outside the harbour there and proceeded to spend the next 45 minutes pounding the harbour facilities, the two coastguard cruisers, and every sign and symbol of British occupation with her 7.5 cm deck-gun. But was it really Otto Mannesmann whom Cecil Snow saw watching this spectacle from the cliffs above? One can well imagine how much Mannesmann, after having spoken with Kophamel, would have wanted to witness the attack in person. If he had left Bardia on horseback before 4pm, there was certainly time for him to reach Sollum before the attack ended at 6pm. In short, if Snow was right that the man on the plateau was European, then he was certainly Mannesmann. But the matter of Mannesmann's presence during the attack is an unimportant detail. The crowning success of his mission would come when Sayyid Ahmad led his army into Egypt.

11

November 1915: The Sanusi Invade Egypt

THE ATTACK ON SOLLUM triggered immediate efforts by the British to strengthen their defences in the west. Arrangements were made (in the first instance) to send an "emergency squadron", mainly of armoured cars belonging to the Royal Naval Armoured Car Division (RNACD), to protect the outposts along the coast; and (thereafter) to assemble a full "Western Frontier Force" sufficient to defend the Western Desert from invasion.

The Emergency Squadron was sent by train to the railhead at al-Dab'a, between Alexandria and Mersa Matruh. On 9 November the man appointed to lead the squadron, Lieutenant-Commander Charles Lister, arrived and assumed command. Lister had served with the RNACD in Gallipoli, where he had been wounded, and had only recently been released from hospital.[1] Also arriving at al-Dab'a that day was George Purvis, Deputy Director-General of the Egyptian Coastguard Administration, who was to accompany the squadron as Political Officer. "Purvis Bey" was fifty-six years old, and, in addition to nineteen years with the Coastguard, had been a serving junior officer in 1882 at the British naval bombardment of Alexandria. By the time the two men arrived at al-

---

[1] Not to be confused with another and better-known officer of the same name (a son of Lord Ribblesdale and member of the Rupert Brooke set), who had recently died at Gallipoli.

Dab'a the RNACD had removed their vehicles and equipment from the train and were in the process of establishing their forward base nearby.

Making up the Emergency Squadron were six Rolls Royce armoured cars, about a dozen Model T Fords, two wireless vehicles, an ambulance, and assorted motorcycles and Talbot wagons.[2] In addition to providing immediate reinforcement of British/Egyptian authority on the frontier, the Squadron was also supposed to guarantee communications in the event that the telegraph were cut (or otherwise not functioning) and to ensure the safety of the Coastguard stations along the coast – al-Dab'a, Mersa Matruh, Sidi Barani, Baqbaq, and Sollum.

There were problems from the outset. A minor one was that two of the vehicles broke down and had to be left at al-Dab'a; a more serious obstacle was that two wireless sets were not enough to cover the distance between al-Dab'a and Sollum. The plan was made, nevertheless, to leave one wireless car at Mersa Matruh and the other at Sollum, for there was a possibility that two more wireless cars would soon be available, in which case communications would be ensured over the entire stretch. The convoy was supposed to leave al-Dab'a at first light on 10 November but, during the evening of the 9th, word came that the necessary third and fourth wireless vehicles would not be available after all. The fall-back plan was to rely on the telegraph between Mersa Matruh and al-Dab'a, and to hope (despite prevailing pessimism on the matter) that the distance between Mersa Matruh and Sollum was not too great for the two wireless sets they already had.[3]

The convoy of armoured cars, Model T Fords, Talbot wagons, wireless cars and motorcycles departed westwards down the dusty Khedivial Road[4] just after 8am[5] and arrived at Mersa Matruh six hours later. That evening two telegrams arrived for Purvis: one from Snow advising that the situation at Sollum was now critical and requesting that at least some of the Emergency Squadron try to arrive there no later than the following

---

[2] The numbers and types of vehicles available to the Squadron changed constantly over several days from 8 November. The author's assessment of the "final" figures is based on the entry of 14 November, 1.05am, in the WFF War Diary (WO 95/4437).
[3] WFF War Diary, WO 95/4437, entries 9 to 13 November.
[4] This rather grand name referred to the dirt track from al-Dab'a to Sollum, prepared before the war by Egyptian coastguards and named after Khedive 'Abbas Hilmi II.
[5] The total force was divided between al-Dab'a, Matruh, Sidi Barani and Sollum. Reinforcements remained at al-Dab'a.

day, the 11th; the other from Cairo asking Purvis to arrange transport for Sanusi agent Muhammad Idrisi, who was travelling with six companions on an important political mission to Sayyid Ahmad. The next morning Purvis sent several cars back to the railhead at al-Dab'a to collect Muhammad Idrisi and his party. Then, leaving one wireless car and two Model T's at Matruh, the remaining vehicles left for Sidi Barani. They arrived there at midday, again dropped off men and vehicles, and the much diminished convoy proceeded on the last leg to Sollum. All went well until the cars were approaching Baqbaq, when the wireless car broke down. Despite strenuous efforts to get it running again, it had to be left where it was on the rutted track. In fact, the patches of soft sand had been so churned up that it was impossible to get any of the heavier vehicles through to Sollum. The armoured cars, therefore, were sent back to Sidi Barani, and only the light cars continued. Finally, at 5.30pm (11 November), with headlamps on against the gathering darkness, the remnants of the RNACD convoy – five Model T's and two motorcycles – arrived at Sollum. In addition to Lister and Purvis, the arriving party included a surgeon and a medical attendant (RAMC); five men for operating and maintaining the wireless, now left in the sand near Baqbaq; and seventeen assorted drivers and soldiers. Apart from side-arms and rifles the only weaponry they had brought were two Maxims, although two 9 cm Krupp guns were expected by sea shortly with another Egyptian Army detachment of twenty-one men.[6]

The convoy arrived amidst some excitement. The Italian ship *Misurata* had that day picked up thirty-four survivors – mostly Indian Lancers and lascars – from a torpedoed animal transport called *Moorina*, and had dropped them off at Sollum. But Snow was clearly relieved that the convoy had arrived.

Early the next day some of the Model T's were sent the twenty miles back to Baqbaq to dismount the wireless from the broken-down vehicle and bring it to Sollum. When it arrived the wireless men made wooden foundations for it and had it working by 4pm.[7] Unfortunately (but as expected) the distance to Mersa Matruh was too great and communication could not be established. A telegram was sent to

[6] WO 95/4437. Also, Purvis' second report to Hunter of 18 November, 131/6/6–8, Sudan Archives, Durham University.

[7] Purvis' second report of 18 November, see above.

Alexandria requesting at least one more wireless set and complaining that the Talbot wagons were useless – and that the "roads [were] only suitable for Fords. Should like more [Model T Fords] in place of waggons".[8]

Lister, meanwhile, was informed via the telegraph that he and the Emergency Squadron were under the orders of Cecil Snow, OC Sollum. Here was another anomaly which was typical of British rule in Egypt. Snow, as a lieutenant-colonel in the Egyptian Coastguard, received his salary from the Egyptian Government; Charles Lister was a lieutenant commander in the Royal Naval Air Service (Armoured Cars) and received his from the British Government. But since 1911, when Kitchener arrived as British Agent and Consul-General, the British officers of the Coastguard – from George Hunter on down – had reported to the British Agency. It was an arrangement about which the Khedive had complained in vain, but by the second year of the war it was simply a fact of life.

On 13 November Snow, Purvis and Lister decided to try to solve the communications problem by using just the two wireless sets. They agreed to try moving the wireless in Mersa Matruh to Sidi Barani and then, between those two locations, to run messages overland via the Fords and motorcycles. This was done but, frustratingly, the set that was moved to Barani still could not communicate with Sollum. Another frantic cable was sent to Alexandria – "Agitate for third wireless set. Cannot get Sollum from here sixty miles"[9] – but then the next morning contact was in fact established between the two sets. Ford and motorcycle patrols began to operate to the east of Barani, and a provisional communication system was finally up and running.

On the same day, the Coastguard cruiser *Rasheed* arrived at Sollum with two old Krupp field guns and the Egyptian Army unit to man them. But if the situation seemed to be improving, this was not to last. At 2am on 15 November two Egyptian Army sentries, on guard half way up the escarpment path to the plateau

> were rushed by some ten armed Senoussi soldiers, knocked down by rifle butts and their rifles taken; one man was knocked insensible and at 5pm the same day, he was hardly conscious and was pretty bad … the other sentry told his companions that he was going to get his rifle back from

[8] WO 95/4437, entry of 13 November (12.10pm).
[9] Ibid., (11.30pm).

the Senoussi as he would be court-martialled for losing it ... He went off and nothing [has been heard of him since] ... I [Purvis] understand that both sentries before being assaulted, challenged, blew their whistles, and one fired two rounds in the air ... The same evening one of the Egyptian sentries going on guard dropped his clothes in a bundle through a window of the barracks and later on ... took his bundle and deserted to the Senoussi.[10]

According to Purvis' report the following night was scarcely better.

At 2.30am on the 16th I was awakened by sharp rifle fire not far from my tent. Going outside I could see no flashes, but I heard the bullets striking the water pretty close to me. I judged the firing to be about three or four hundred yards from us as the reports were very sharp. All hands manned the defences and remained there till daylight. About forty shots were fired altogether. No one was hit, but Snow informed me that bullets pitched in the convicts' camp, which was about one hundred yards from my tent.[11]

In the morning it was found that the telegraph line had been cut in four places over a stretch of six miles to the east of Sollum. The line was repaired within a few hours, but in any case the wireless was still working.[12]

Later in the day, Snow was informed by the wireless operator at Sidi Barani that a band of mounted Sanusi regulars had just killed "two friendly Bedouin" there,[13] but nothing could be done about this from Sollum. Despite the deteriorating situation, Purvis had to leave. His orders were to complete his inspection of the situation at Sollum by the 16th, immediately to get back to Cairo, and to write a detailed report on conditions in the west for Gilbert Clayton. On his way east he passed through Sidi Barani, where he briefed Roy Tweedie on the latest events at Sollum.

[10] Report on the situation at Sollum, Sudan Archives, Durham University, 131/6/3–5, 18 November.
[11] Ibid.
[12] FO 371/2356 (p. 332), reported by Director of Egyptian State Telegraphs on 16 November.
[13] WO 33/731, Maxwell to War Office, 18 November. Also, FO 371/2356, p. 337.

The next day (17 November) there was another disturbing message
from the operator at Barani. This time he reported that 300 Sanusi regulars
had seized the *zawiya* there and turned out its Sheikh and the inhabitants.[14]
This was a considerable overestimation of the actual number of regulars
involved – there were about fifty – and the expulsion was only temporary.
Nevertheless, the local Arabs were now talking about an imminent attack
on the Barani Coastguard barracks, and tension was still high that night
when a Sanusi soldier rode up to the *zawiya* and again ordered everyone
to leave as (he said) a U-boat was about to attack the barracks.[15]

The submarine attack did not happen, but at 10pm on 18 November
Tweedie reported that Sidi Barani was under attack by the Sanusi. A few
hours later he again contacted Sollum, this time reporting that the attack
was now "intermittent" and under control.[16] The attackers were the same
group of *muhafizia* who had caused the disturbance at the *zawiya*. They
had fired on the Coastguard station and barracks from three directions,
then stormed into the village, looting shops as they went. After a respite of
several hours they returned at 3am, again firing and looting. After the
second attack Tweedie sent out an armoured car, whereupon the attackers
fled back to the confines of the *zawiya*. A private in the Coastguard Camel
Corps was killed in the attack on the barracks as well as five camels.

Upon receiving Tweedie's first message Snow immediately reported the
incident to Sayyid Ahmad, who professed surprise and anger. He used his
own telegraph to contact the officer commanding his soldiers at Sidi
Barani, and Snow's signallers were able to monitor the Sanusi's telegram,
which was sent at 11.45pm.

> I am informed that the *muhafizia* under your orders have been making a
> disturbance [at Sidi Barani] and that they tried to attack the market and
> have expelled the sheikh of the *zawiya* there. I am astonished that your
> men are making trouble between [me] and the Government. Inform me
> of the truth of this matter and prevent any recurrence … I await your
> urgent reply.[17]

In the morning Sayyid Ahmad still seemed inclined to be helpful. He
sent Ja'far al-'Askari to call on Snow and to hand over a personal letter. Its
contents are not known, although Snow described the Sanusi's message as

[14] FO 371/2356, p. 338.   [15] Ibid., p. 339.   [16] Ibid., p. 339.   [17] Ibid., p. 339.

"sympathetic". But more significant is the fact that Snow's encounter with Ja'far at this time resulted in a most curious arrangement for assisting Tweedie at Sidi Barani. Snow was just about to send Royle to Sidi Barani with a couple of the Fords. Ja'far said that he had been ordered by Sayyid Ahmad to go there also, and as Ja'far's presence would likely carry more authority with the rebellious *muhafizia*, Snow agreed that Ja'far and Royle could go together.

Ja'far must have found his present situation to be absurd. He was now in command of the regular forces of the Sanusi Army and under orders to help precipitate an attack on Egypt as early as possible – and now he was being sent to Sidi Barani as peacemaker! Ja'far's memoirs give an interesting account of the reasons for the trouble at Sidi Barani:

> Nuri had had the idea of attacking the fort on the plateau above Sollum and making war between the Sanusi and the British a *fait accompli*. Nuri was unsuccessful, however, because the Sanusi was always right near Sollum and this prevented the tribesmen and soldiers from making such an attack. Finally, Nuri was able to convince a Tripolitanian officer named Ahmad Mukhtar and another man named Abu-l-Qasim bin Sayyid al-'Isawi, who was head of the *zawiya* at Benghazi, very close to Sayyid Ahmad and a member of his Executive Council. In addition to these two there were fifty volunteers. They crossed the border and attacked Sidi Barani ... east of Sollum. The English protested against this incursion, and the Sanusi became very angry with both Nuri and me, since I was now commanding his regular forces. Nuri pretended to know nothing about the incident and said that the responsibility fell on Abu-l-Qasim and Lieutenant Ahmad Mukhtar. In a move to defuse the situation the Sanusi sent me to get Abu-l-Qasim and his men to withdraw from Egyptian territory.[18]

So at 9.15am on 19 November Royle and Ja'far (and the latter's *aide-de-camp*) took two of the Fords and went to Sidi Barani,[19] covering the sixty miles over rough track in three hours. There they learned from Tweedie that thirty-five of the attackers were still at the *zawiya*. Tweedie assembled

[18] Ja'far al-'Askari (1988), Ch. 6.
[19] Royle's report to Snow, 21 November, Sudan Archives, Durham University, 131/6/24-26.

a small force of one armoured car and thirty-five camel-mounted coastguards, and joining Royle, Ja'far, and the ADC, they all went to the *zawiya*. The mounted coastguards were divided into three sections, one of which took up position a thousand yards west of the building; a second was sent to a point a similar distance to the east; the third, together with the armoured car, advanced with Royle, Ja'far and the ADC. They cautiously approached the building only to find one old man there. But suddenly the second section of coastguards, which was not yet in position, was fired upon from a ridge directly in front of it. The men quickly retired but, unable to see their attackers, they did not return fire.[20]

In describing what happened next Ja'far was uncharacteristically reticent:

> I asked Bimbashi Royle to stay about half a mile back while I went to talk to Abu-l-Qasim. I told the latter how serious the situation was and that he had to go back, but not to go to the camp as the Sanusi was extremely angry at both him and Ahmad Mukhtar ... He agreed to do as I asked and said he would return with his men that same day.[21]

Royle's account of the incident, suggesting that Ja'far had qualms about approaching the attackers, rings true. Nuri had instigated this incident; now here was Ja'far driving around with the enemy trying to stop it. Could Ja'far be sure in these circumstances that he would not be shot by his own men?

> I urged Jaafar to walk over to them with me ... and to talk to his soldiers who were firing on us. He said he would when I had retired my men so that nothing was visible and firing had ceased. [But] then he would not go and talk to them, saying they were savages and would shoot ... Then, I suggested, the only thing to be done was for me to deal with them.
>   Fortunately, at that time, up rode the Bedouin Omdah[22] of Barrani and another man from the West, and Jaafar agreed to go with them ... on the condition that I not come, saying if he wanted me or help he would wave

[20] Sudan Archives, Durham University, 131/6/24-26, 21 November.
[21] Ja'far al-'Askari (1988), Ch. 6.
[22] Village chief.

his hat. I let him go some 400 yards and followed him ... [having myself] first signalled back for two mounted men and a camel for me [to approach].

When he reached them, the *muhafizia* and bedouins who had been firing got up and went to him. Then I saw some twenty to twenty-five horsemen gallop away to the southwest ... and at the same time he waved his hat. I signalled for the armoured car – containing besides the driver, Lieutenant Yeo RNVR and Lieutenant Tweedie – to come to me. I told them to try to cut off the horsemen and to fire on them if they would not stop or resisted.

The car went about 500 yards and was fired on by the horsemen, who had dismounted ... [Those in the armoured car] stopped and brought their machine gun into action at a range of about 800 yards.[23]

Ja'far and the *'umda* galloped up to Royle in a state of great agitation. They pleaded with him to signal the car to cease firing, arguing that they had already convinced the Sanusi band to return to the Libyan side of the frontier, and that to shoot at them while they were doing this was unfair. Royle ordered the gunner to cease fire; then Ja'far remounted and went after his men. Although again fired at initially, Ja'far was, for the second time, allowed to approach and talk to them. When he returned, he assured Royle that "they would all return to Amsa'id at once and take their punishment when they got there",[24] but he added without elaboration that there were still some two hundred other *muhafizia* somewhere in the vicinity. On the way back to the barracks Ja'far repeatedly complained of the humiliation of having his soldiers refusing to obey him – and even firing at him![25]

That evening the two Ottoman officers joined the British officers for dinner at the Barani Coastguard barracks. Ja'far and his ADC happily indulged in cigarettes, beer and port – all strictly forbidden at the Sanusi camp. When the meal was over, Ja'far surprised the others by suddenly

[23] Royle's report to Snow, 21 November, Sudan Archives, Durham University, 131/6/24-26.
[24] Ibid.
[25] However great Ja'far's discomfort that day the leaders of the mutinous Sanusi force paid a far higher price. As Abu-l-Qasim and Ahmad Mukhtar led their men back to Amsa'id, they were met by another Sanusi force sent by Sayyid Ahmad to end the rebellion. Ahmad Mukhtar was shot outright and Abu-l-Qasim fled for his life.

insisting, despite the late hour, that he now wanted to search for the second group of *muhafizia*. The Coastguard officers lent him some camels and, together with the ADC, the *'umda* and one coastguard private (!), Ja'far left the barracks. What Ja'far did not tell his hosts was that he himself had ordered the second and larger force to Sidi Barani. Indeed, they had left the Sanusi camp with Ja'far, but while their commander had gone to call on Snow, they had taken a different path into Egypt. Ja'far's midnight excursion lasted until three in the morning, when he and his companions returned to the barracks. Neither Royle's report nor Ja'far's account in his memoirs mentions whether or not the nocturnal excursion was successful, but as nothing more was heard of this force it presumably returned to Amsa'id.

At the conclusion of this day's strange adventures Royle did not hold Ja'far in very high esteem. He was irritated that Ja'far had stopped him from preventing the attackers' escape back to Libya. He also felt that Ja'far, though personable, "told the most extraordinary lies".[26] But under the circumstances, there was not much "truth" that Ja'far could have shared with Royle. Better than most, Ja'far knew that he and Nuri were close to enticing the Sanusi into war against the British. He also knew the whereabouts of the *Tara* survivors – in fact, he had already been to visit them.

On 18 November, two days after leaving Sollum and the day before the above events, Purvis was back at Coastguard headquarters near Cairo's Bab al-Luq station.[27] George Hunter was there to welcome him and to hear in person the results of the trip. Hunter discussed with Purvis the points that needed to be made in the report for Military Intelligence. They agreed to stress that the status quo at Sollum was no longer tenable and that the policy of temporizing with the Sanusi should now be scrapped. The report's conclusion shows that Purvis felt that Sayyid Ahmad (like the Italians earlier in the year) was now selling himself to the highest bidder.

> Altogether I consider that the present situation is impossible; it is not right that men should be placed in a position where they are knocked about, and shot at, without being allowed to retaliate. Our influence in

[26] Sudan Archives, Durham University, 131/6/24-26.
[27] At Sharia al-Qased, near the house and gardens rented by Oppenheim until 1910.

that vicinity has vanished, and farther east is rapidly disappearing; the Senoussi soldiers are all over our part of the Western Desert – and what can the native think when he sees they are allowed to do what they like but that we are afraid or powerless to prevent them. To put an end to the present situation the Senoussi should be bought by offering a sum which the Turks and Germans could not hope to outbid; and [we should] place Sollum in a proper state of defence, moving the Senoussi back some two miles from the crest of the hills, which our sentries should hold. If this cannot be done, then Sollum should be properly garrisoned and the Senoussi informed that force would be used to repel force.

Alternatively, Sollum should be abandoned.[28]

Hunter wrote a covering letter which strongly reinforced the report's conclusions:

I think it is my duty to put on record my opinion that the time has arrived for the adoption of a more decided policy towards Sidi Ahmed el Sherif el-Senussi. The situation both in the Senussi camp and on the Western Desert is clear and needs no comment, and as regards Sollum it is only a matter of time before some action on our part will lead to reprisals from the muhafizia, which can only end in the abandonment of the place and consequent loss of life to our detachment. Therefore I would suggest that either of the following proposals be adopted:

(i) to buy the good will of the Senussi outright not by driblets of insignificant sums, but a sum of money as would make all hope of competition on the part of any German or Turkish agent ... hopeless;

(ii) If no. 1 fails, [that] the post at Sollum be adequately defended and all Senussi outposts in its neighbourhood retired west of the Senussi camp at [Amsa'id];

(iii) If nos. 1 and 2 are not adopted, that the post at Sollum be abandoned at once ... We already have lost all influence and practically all prestige in the Western Desert and by continuing our present policy we will not only lose the latter altogether, but in addition most of the detachment now at Sollum.[29]

[28] Purvis' first report to Hunter of 18 November, Sudan Archives, Durham University, 131/6/3-5.
[29] Courtesy of Mr Archie Hunter: family papers.

When Clayton received the Coastguard's recommendations, General Maxwell was still with Kitchener. Nevertheless, a constant stream of information flowed from Egypt to Mudros to keep Maxwell abreast of political and military developments, including those on the Western Frontier; in any case, he too now accepted that the policy of keeping the Sanusi friendly at any price was pointless, that whatever Sayyid Ahmad decided to do, his army – trained and led by Nuri and Ja'far, and supplied with the help of Mannesmann and German U-boats – was now champing to invade Egypt. The meetings at Mudros may have been mainly about Gallipoli, but Egyptian security and the Sanusi situation were also high on the agenda.

But Kitchener's own influence in military matters was no longer going unchallenged in London, where politicians now sensed that Britain was in danger of losing the war. Unprecedented casualty figures, repeated failure on the Western Front, and now the looming failure at Gallipoli, led those in power to look for military men with new ideas who could do better – and for scapegoats. The effect was felt in Mudros and in Cairo. The so-called "Alexandretta scheme" for a second allied attempt to block the Turks, proposed by the Military Intelligence Office in Cairo and endorsed by Kitchener, was meeting stiff resistance by the General Staff at the War Office and would be rejected within days. That same General Staff – men who wanted to concentrate British attentions and resources on the Western Front – were insisting upon defending Egypt at the Suez Canal instead of keeping the Turks occupied at Alexandretta (ie, those Turks who were about to be freed from the fighting at Gallipoli). Kitchener's waning influence was one thing, but now men in Whitehall were trying to tell him how to defend Egypt. He could scarcely contain his anger as he cabled Prime Minister Asquith from Mudros on 13 November.

> McMahon, Maxwell and myself must be admitted to know the difficulties of defence in Egypt, and we are unanimously of opinion that your plan for carrying this out on the Canal is doomed to failure, while involving much greater commitments in men and resources than the plan we advocate. In Egypt we should have to face certain hostility all along the Western frontier, which would extend to Tunis, Algiers and Morocco; serious unrest and disturbances throughout Egypt and the Sudan, endangering our internal communications as well as the closing of the

Canal for a prolonged period. Reliance on the defence of Egypt in Egypt foreshadows, in our opinion, a withdrawal from it and the Sudan within a measurable time, with results so far-reaching both for ourselves and France as possibly to allow the Germans to attain their object and thus jeopardize the campaign in Europe by the withdrawal of larger forces than can be afforded.[30]

Oppenheim would have been delighted to learn that he and the British Minister of War now foresaw the same future for Egypt and North Africa.

On 24 November Kitchener departed Mudros for London (against the wishes of many in government who wanted him to stay away) and Maxwell returned to Egypt. The two men had been military colleagues since the darkest days of the Sudanese war against the Mahdi, and they would never see each other again.

The crises at Sollum and Sidi Barani had taken their toll upon Cecil Snow. For weeks he had had little sleep, being up much of the night sending and receiving messages. Royle and Ja'far returned to Sollum on the morning of 20 November, but Snow spent most of that day in discussions with Muhammad Idrisi, the Sanusi agent. Idrisi now feared the worst. Sayyid Ahmad knew that he was losing control of his followers and he was – according to Idrisi – planning to leave for Jaghbub. Idrisi also confirmed that Coastguard and Egyptian Army officers and men, including Muhammad Saleh Harb,[31] were being won over by the Nuri faction at the Sanusi camp. Was this information about Muhammad Saleh Harb conveyed at the time to Coastguard headquarters? If so, subsequent events indicate that no action was taken concerning his possible defection. Snow and Idrisi also discussed the current state of negotiations between the British and Sayyid Ahmad. Snow cabled Maxwell that the Sanusi was

> willing to dismiss Germans but not Nouri immediately as it would injure
> him in eyes of Muslim world. In addition to sum mentioned requires a

[30] WO 33/747, Kitchener to Asquith, 13 November 1915.
[31] WFF War Diary, WO 95/4437. "Coastguards, EA officers, Hamed Sileh [Muhammad Saleh] have been won over by Nouri. Sileh promises to raise Matruh Bedouins." Entry is not dated but another source (FO 371/2356, p. 342) confirms the interview took place on 20 November.

guarantee of one million pounds paid in instalments, also a supply of rifles. First sum should be forthcoming before Sanussi leaves for Jaghbub. He says we must act quickly. Germans have promised unlimited supplies.[32]

Unfortunately the first "sum mentioned" is not specified in this or other sources, but the whole package, with the £1,000,000 guarantee and the rifles, would have been a powerful inducement to Sayyid Ahmad not to join the Turks and Germans, the latter of whom had offered Sayyid Ahmad "one million francs" to march against Egypt.[33] But Maxwell now had no intention of agreeing to the bribe. He telegraphed back to Snow:

> Sidi Ahmad trying to fool us … [He] has little intention of keeping his promises. Temporise [!] with him. Coastguard and Egyptian officers can be changed if necessary. Withdraw Girba patrol to Matruh. Force ready for Matruh when negotiations fail.[34]

That night (20 November) Sanusi soldiers laid a telephone wire down the escarpment to the house of a pro-Sanusi resident of Sollum village. Bazley-White went with some Egyptian soldiers from the fort and destroyed it. When the next day the telephone line was repaired, Snow asked for instructions. Clayton replied to him directly instructing him not to take further action concerning the telephone line. Clayton may have feared that Bazley-White's action might trigger the invasion. Or else that they might put the evacuation of the outpost at risk. But if evacuation was imminent, Snow apparently did not know it. Several hours after midnight, on 22 November, he again cabled in obvious distress:[35]

> Situation … very critical. Shall lose Sollum if not reinforced. This would cause the whole country to Alexandria and Fayoum to rise. Our efforts to strengthen our posts have caused derision amongst Bedouins. Nouri Bey determined to force Senoussi's hand and is collecting at Bir Waer a force of which latter has no knowledge in hope Bedouins may insist on

---

[32] Quoted in WFF War Diary and cited as 'Telegram 6613'.
[33] See Mannesmann's telegram to the German Foreign Office on pp. 131–2.
[34] WFF War Diary, WO 95/4437 (entry 20 November, time not given).
[35] Ibid., (entries 21 November).

marching on Egypt. Very difficult for Senoussi to keep his followers quiet when we only have a handful of men. Attack may take place tonight or next.[36]

Uncertainty about German U-boats was also preying on Snow's mind. He believed that the November 5 attack on Sollum had been carried out by two of them. His own Arab agents had reported six in the vicinity, and this gloomy assessment was apparently reinforced by the fact that a British linesman for the Egyptian State Telegraph had reported seeing a U-boat near Sidi Barani on 15 November, and three more on the following day. Then a private in the Coastguard reported that he too had seen one. In fact, since the *U-35* had returned to Cattaro, there were no U-boats in the area at all.[37]

Since the skirmishes at Sidi Barani, British and colonial troops had been on their way to Mersa Matruh. The first units to move were the 15th Sikhs and the Nottinghamshire Battery of the Royal Horse Artillery, both of which were being sent from the Suez Canal to al-Dab'a by train, and from there to Matruh by means of three trawlers on loan from Vice-Admiral Peirse. Following receipt of Snow's message that an attack was imminent, Army HQ in Cairo finally gave orders for Sollum to be evacuated. The trawlers were to land their first load of Sikhs at Matruh and then to proceed immediately to Sollum, which they would probably reach late on 24 November.[38]

During the night of 22 November the Coastguard station at Sidi Barani was again fired upon. In the morning, with the evacuation now reported to be imminent, Snow ordered Tweedie and Lister to withdraw to Mersa Matruh. Tweedie left at midday with the large Barani detachment of the Coastguard Camel Corps, together with a crowd of women and children from the village; shortly afterwards Lister drove past them with the armoured cars and Model T Fords. When Lister arrived at Matruh at 9pm he sent back two armoured cars and eight Fords for the women and children. It was fortunate that he did, because by the time they arrived

[36] WO 95/4437 (entry 22 November, 2.16am). Also FO 371/2356, p. 343.
[37] After the Bedouin agent reported Nuri saying there were six U-boats in the area (FO 371/2356, 29 October), and after the attacks by *U-35*, sightings were reported in WFF War Diary, entries 15 and 16 November; and also in FO 371/2356 pages 332, 334, 339 and 357.
[38] WFF War Diary, WO 95/4437, entry midnight, 23 November.

most of the native coastguards had deserted – fourteen Egyptian officers, including Muhammad Saleh Harb, and 120 rank and file had gone over to the Sanusi, taking 176 camels plus their arms and equipment. The slowly moving band of refugees left behind with Tweedie had been left mainly unarmed and vulnerable to attack.[39]

Then, early on the 23rd, Snow learned that another trusted coastguard officer, Mahmoud Labib, OC of the Baqbaq district, had also deserted and taken the outpost's last eight baggage camels with him.[40]

These mass defections were yet another calamity for the British officers of the Egyptian Coastguard, who over forty years had often been tried by misfortune: the killing of their first "Inspector-General" in the Sudan; the numerous deaths of colleagues by disease and smuggler violence; the incident in Sinai with Captain Chope and the Bikanirs. With these latest events the era of Egypt's British-led coastguard service was in effect over.

Meanwhile at Sollum the entire native population now seemed to be decamping to the enemy. All morning the village merchants and the local Bedouin were to be seen loading their goods and personal effects onto camels and taking them up the escarpment to Amsa'id.

When, later that morning (23 November) the Coastguard cruiser *Rasheed* sailed into Sollum harbour, Snow seized the opportunity to get the garrison away, fearing that to wait any longer for the trawlers to arrive would be to risk being captured – or worse, they might be killed by the increasingly out-of-control soldiers of Sayyid Ahmad. As the embarkation got underway, the RNACD men hurriedly dismantled the wireless from the wooden foundation they had made on arrival and took it onboard the cruiser. Most of the store of ammunition was also transported to the vessel, together with Government documents and cash. But not everything was transportable. The two Krupp guns, brought by the same cruiser the previous week, were left behind, although the breech locks and sights were removed and thrown into the sea. Also disabled and abandoned were three RNACD Fords.[41]

[39] Letter from Snow to General Wallace of 24 Nov, Sudan Archives, Durham University, 131/6/27-29. The figures given for the number of deserters are those printed in General Maxwell's official version of events, *Supplement to the London Gazette*, 21 June 1916.
[40] Snow's letter to Wallace of 24 November, Sudan Archives, Durham University, 131/6/27-29. [41] Ibid.

While the preparations for departure were going on, a large number of *muhafizia* suddenly arrived at the village.

> [A]t first [they] appeared to make an attempt to keep order amongst the Bedouins, who were out to loot. They, however, began to help themselves and by the time the embarkation was completed the place was over-run by them all. I refrained from firing on them, for fear of drawing their fire upon the boatloads of men passing to the ship.[42]

The heavily-laden *Rasheed* sailed at 2.30pm, 23 November. Towed behind were the two lifeboats "left by the shipwrecked crew of SS *Moorina*, in case of being torpedoed on our way".[43] That night, as they sailed passed Sidi Barani, Snow and Royle stood at the rails and watched flames rising from the Coastguard station and barracks. At dawn on the following day they arrived at Mersa Matruh.

With the British now gone from Sollum the Sanusi army swarmed across the frontier into Egypt. Ja'far, however, was aghast at the lack of self-control shown by the Bedouin when they entered Sollum village.

> I was extremely upset when I saw what these rampaging tribesmen had done to the garrison pharmacy. There were drugs and medicines enough to supply our needs for a long time, but unfortunately they had broken all the jars and mixed all the medicines to the point where they were useless.[44]

Nevertheless, the Sanusi were overwhelmingly exultant as their army descended from the plateau and advanced towards Sidi Barani, arriving at the burnt-out shell of the Coastguard station at the end of the second day's march.

> At Sidi Barani we found some automobiles; these we turned over to Yousbashi Ghalib Bey for him to repair so that they could be used to run messages back and forth between the Sanusi camp and our military headquarters.[45]

---

[42] Sudan Archives, Durham University, 131/6/27-29.   [43] Ibid.
[44] Ja'far al-'Askari (1988), Ch. 6.   [45] Ibid.

Ja'far spent two days gathering his forces at Sidi Barani. While he was there Turkish-Sanusi morale received another boost. The Egyptian Coastguards who had deserted returned to Sidi Barani to a rapturous welcome. One hundred and thirty-four trained and uniformed Egyptians on white Bishareen camels[46] must have been a very welcome sight for the Sanusi soldiers.

> They were commanded by Bimbashi Muhammad Saleh [Harb] Bey, and there were other officers with him: Yousbashi Adeeb Effendi, Lieutenant Abu Zeid ... The tribesmen were jubilant at this development, and morale among our forces was very high.
>
> After welcoming this detachment and its leader we sent them off to join Sayyid Ahmad, because it did not seem appropriate to use them in the front line [i.e., against their former colleagues] ... There was another reason why I did not want the Coastguard detachment to stay with us. That was because there was very little discipline and control in our army, and I feared that this beautiful and well-organised unit would fall victim to our chaotic ways. In any case, circumstances did not really allow for us to feed and care for them as necessary, which would have meant their gradual destruction and loss.[47]

As for Otto Mannesmann, he was ecstatic. For months he had worked in virtual seclusion, but now he seemed to be everywhere, camera in hand, taking snapshots of Sollum fort, the ruined village, the Sanusi Army marching towards Baqbaq. Even Sayyid Ahmad posed for shots as he majestically crossed into Egypt.

On the afternoon of the day following the Sanusi army's arrival at Baqbaq, Muhammad Idrisi was sitting in a tent waiting for tea. With him were Muhammad Saleh and some of the other Egyptian coastguards, when suddenly Mannesmann entered the tent with an interpreter. Introducing himself to Idrisi, the German began to talk about the attack that would soon take place on the Suez Canal. He said that the Germans and Turks had only been waiting to finish with the Russians, from whom they had

---

[46] See von Dumreicher (1931), *Trackers and Smugglers*; also Janet Starkey "Perceptions of the Ababda and Bisharin in the Atbai", paper presented to the Fifth International Conference on Sudan Studies, Durham University, 31 August–1 September 2000.

[47] Ja'far al-'Askari (1988), Ch. 6.

seized many thousands of guns and taken half a million prisoners; and that the British were now powerless, as was clear from the fact that not a single warship had been sent to stop the Sanusi invasion. During this conversation someone asked about Oppenheim. Mannesmann said that Oppenheim would be accompanying the new expedition invading Egypt from the east, and that with him would come a host of German scholars specializing in the region. The Kaiser's wish, he said, was to help the Islamic countries of the world so that in the future there would be one united Islamic *ummah* (nation) and one large German Empire. Other countries would be insignificant by comparison.[48]

His mission over, Mannesmann bade farewell to Sayyid Ahmad at Baqbaq. His new assignment, he said, was to return to the Maghreb to help the Arabs there to fight the French.

Over the next few days the Sanusi and Turkish forces consolidated at Sidi Barani, and then they began their march eastward towards Mersa Matruh.

Was the precipitate evacuation of Sollum necessary? In his report to General Wallace, commander of the new Western Frontier Force, Cecil Snow justified his decision to leave before the arrival of the trawlers.

> Having ... received trustworthy information that we were to be attacked by four submarines at the same time as the land attack – to be made by a specially prepared force under Nouri Bey and a German officer – I was not surprised to receive conclusive information on the morning of the 23rd that the combined attack was due to take place that afternoon or the next morning.
>
> The nature of our position was such as to make it impossible to resist an attack, the submarine fire alone being sufficient to wipe us out.[49]

As we have seen, there were no German submarines in the area; and Snow's intelligence-gathering was always – indeed, could scarcely have been anything but – a process of sifting through rumours, many of them

[48] Sir John Maxwell Papers, Princeton University Library. See 8-page debriefing of Muhammad Idrisi.

[49] Snow's letter to Wallace of 24 November, Sudan Archives, Durham University, 131/6/27-29.

baseless, brought by paid native agents from the Sanusi camp. What the "trustworthy" and "conclusive" information was, the archives do not reveal. But there can be little doubt that during his last days and nights at Sollum Snow was overwrought, perhaps even suffering a nervous crisis. On the other hand, it is equally certain that the Turkish faction was now in control among the Sanusi and that the fall of the British outpost was inevitable sooner or later.

On the day that the *Rasheed* arrived at Mersa Matruh with the garrison General Maxwell, while returning by ship from Mudros, cabled the War Office: "Last night the Sollum garrison was withdrawn by sea and the Barani garrison by land. The former arrived complete and safe this morning at Matruh, the latter is still on the way."[50] Maxwell did not know it yet, but his statement was inaccurate. He arrived back at Cairo to learn that some of the native Egyptian Army soldiers based at Sollum fort had been left behind there.

At first this abandonment of Egyptian soldiers at Sollum seems to have been ignored, it being assumed that any Egyptians who had not left on the *Rasheed* had deserted to the Sanusi. Then, about ten days after Sollum was abandoned, something entirely unexpected happened near Mersa Matruh. Out of a cloud of dust to the west of the camp there came marching an Egyptian Army officer and thirteen men, all loyal native Egyptians, who had been left behind while manning their posts in the heights over Sollum.

Equally embarrassing for the British was a report supplied a few days later by Sanusi agent Muhammad Idrisi when he returned to Egypt from Amsa'id, where he had been still trying to negotiate peace even after the evacuation of Sollum. On that fateful day of the evacuation, Sayyid Ahmad had sent Muhammad Idrisi to see Snow to assure him that despite the skirmishes at Sidi Barani there was no hostile intent on his part, that the perpetrators of the mutiny would be punished, and that "everything would be arranged satisfactorily".[51] But when Idrisi reached the fort prior to descending the escarpment he found there the Egyptian officer and his men standing at the edge of the cliff, greatly perturbed, gesticulating to the departing cruiser to return. Then, as they were telling Idrisi that they

---

[50] WO 33/731, Maxwell to War Office (No. 2267 E) 24 November 1915.
[51] Sudan Archives, Durham University, 131/6/91-99, "Information obtained from Mohamed Sherif el-Idrisi" 17 December 1915.

wanted to be evacuated also, Nuri arrived with Sanusi soldiers who took them prisoner. One of the Egyptians tried to escape and was shot dead. The others were then taken to Sayyid Ahmad, who decided to let them go. Nuri protested, saying that they were prisoners of war. Mahmoud Labib, the coastguard deserter who had commanded at Baqbaq, said it would look bad to send them back simply because they did not want to serve with the Sanusi. But Sayyid Ahmad had made up his mind to release them. They marched with the Sanusi Army to Sidi Barani, where they were given two rifles to protect themselves on the road, and some money, two dollars for each of the men and four dollars for their officer. From there they marched the ninety miles to Mersa Matruh.[52]

Bazley-White, the British officer commanding the Egyptian Army detachment, was ordered to explain how this debacle could have occurred. He submitted a report, but he had apparently been so distressed while writing it that it is barely coherent. It does, however, contain a vivid description of the scene at the village:

> Enemy cavalry were riding in and out of the houses looting and driving people up the hill at point of bayonet. My guards remained as long as possible at their posts.[53]

General Maxwell was, understandably, very displeased with this abandonment of part of the Sollum Garrison, and he ordered an inquiry.[54] Six months later, in the euphoria of having waged a successful campaign against the Sanusi, Maxwell made a brief allusion to the incident in his official account of the war.

> In the evacuation it was unfortunately found necessary ... to abandon an outlying post of one Egyptian officer and fourteen other ranks which failed to reach the beach in time to embark.[55]

Before the narrative shifts to events at Mersa Matruh there remains one other interesting matter to consider: the visit of T. E. Lawrence to Sollum

[52] Sudan Archives, Durham University, 131/6/91-99.
[53] Ibid., 131/6/88-90.
[54] The results of the inquiry are not known.
[55] *Supplement to the London Gazette*, 21 June 1916.

just before the evacuation.

On 8 November, Army headquarters issued "Western Frontier Force Operational Order No. 1" providing for the creation of the Emergency Squadron to secure communications with Sollum, and in it reference was made to the need for a new cipher for use in the Western Desert.[56] Turkish and Sanusi soldiers had been tampering with the telegraph line that ran from Alexandria to Sollum, parallel to the coastline. Given that the Turks at Amsa'id had communications specialists adept in telegraphy and wireless, tapping onto the line would have been almost as easy as cutting it. Although breaking the British cipher would have been much more difficult, the Turks might have managed this with help from the Germans. Furthermore, the Egyptian State Telegraph was an integral part of the British military communication system even after the wireless sets were in place, and among its employees were many Egyptians any of whom might have nationalist tendencies. In other words, the old cipher might have been compromised, and the Western Frontier Force needed a new one.

At Army headquarters in Cairo there was a special group involved in ciphering. In June 1915 T. E. Lawrence wrote in a letter home:

> Newcombe, one Macdonnell and myself are Intelligence; Captain Cosens, Lord Anglesey, Lord Hartington & Prince Alexander of Battenburg do the ciphering & deciphering with us.[57]

By November 1915 Lawrence was exercising levels of authority and independence almost unimaginable for a 2nd lieutenant. Despite his having exasperated many professional soldiers, who bristled at his unmilitary bearing, his infringement of the military dress code, and even on occasion his insolence, within headquarters his brilliance was recognized and he was allowed to become something of a key player. His Oxford mentor and fellow Intelligence officer, D. G. Hogarth, confirmed this:

> T. E. Lawrence, whose power of initiative, reasoned audacity, compelling personality, and singular persuasiveness I had often had reason to confess

---

[56] Sudan Archives, Durham University, 131/6/9–11.
[57] Lawrence, M. R. (1954) (ed.), *The Home Letters of T. E. Lawrence and his Brothers*, letter of 23 June 1915.

in past years, was still a second lieutenant in the Cairo military intelligence, but with a purpose more clearly foreseen than perhaps that of anyone else, he was already pulling the wires.[58]

Anyway, it was Lawrence who compiled the new code; and it was he who took it to Cecil Snow shortly before the evacuation of Sollum.

A brief description of Lawrence at work on the code was given by E. M. Dowson, Director of the Survey of Egypt:

> Thus one morning he [Lawrence] came to the Press and asked if he could sit there for a couple of hours as he could not be quiet at the Arab Bureau. He explained that the forces operating against the Sanussi in the Western Desert were using a code which was known to the Turks, and that he wanted to compile a new one. He completed this the same morning and the code he made appears to have continued in use until the end of these operations.[59]

The so-called Arab Bureau was not set up until the spring of 1916; and the assertion that the Turks had broken the previous code was almost certainly an overstatement – either this was a minor lapse in memory on Dowson's part, or, more likely, the result of an exaggeration of the facts by Lawrence. Despite these two inaccuracies, Dowson's description obviously refers to the code – the only code! – compiled at this time for the Western Frontier Force.

Lawrence's trip to the Western Desert is confirmed by both Liddell Hart and Robert Graves in their respective biographies. Lawrence told both authors that he had gone there; and both books merely mention that fact with no elaboration of why or when. Neither book mentions specifically that Lawrence had visited Sollum – only that he had gone to "the Western Desert". One might assume that Lawrence could have chosen to drop the code off at al-Dab'a, where Captain Hay was at RNACD headquarters. But the code was urgently needed at Sollum and the Khedivial Road was by then virtually closed to traffic. A further courier either by land or by

[58] Jeremy Wilson (1989), *Lawrence of Arabia*, p. 213.
[59] Lawrence, A. W. (1937) (ed.), *T. E. Lawrence by his Friends*, p. 142.
[60] WO 95/4437, WFF War Diary, 21 November.
[61] Ibid., Matruh, 24 November.

sea would have been required to get the new code to Sollum; and if Lawrence was going to use a courier, he could have used one from Cairo. In any case, the Western Desert War Diary for the month of November, in an entry for the 21st (a message from Cairo HQ), reads: "Code books to hand. Officer gone to Sollum."[60] And that officer was T. E. Lawrence.

Determining when Lawrence went to Sollum is not that difficult. It is certain that Snow received the new code before the evacuation on 23 November. When Snow arrived at Mersa Matruh the following morning he inadvertently left the code on board the cruiser – another entry in the War Diary specifically says "Snow left new code on *Rasheed*. (Dewhurst brought it off ship later)".[61] In fact, Lawrence must have seen Snow by the 20th, because on that day Snow compiled a detailed Intelligence report in a very structured format that was in sharp contrast to his previous reports. But – more importantly – from that day the new reports were addressed as follows:

> To:-
> Intrusive,
> Intelligence, War Office,
> Cairo.

"Intrusive" was the specific call sign for Lawrence's office. The new formatting of the reports and their being addressed to "Intrusive", inevitably suggest the influence of Lawrence.

Lawrence's contribution was a small one in the sense that any of the other cipher specialists might have compiled the new code; and any trustworthy courier could have delivered it to Sollum. Nevertheless, his few days work and travel to the Western Desert were obviously appreciated by General Maxwell, who in his official account of the Western Desert campaign (in *The London Gazette*) listed Lawrence among those performing exemplary service.

12

Wadi Senab

AN HOUR BEFORE SUNSET on 23 November Lt.-Col. John Gordon arrived at the quay of Alexandria's Western Harbour. As commander of the 15th Sikhs, Gordon had just been briefed by General Wallace and Chief of Staff George Hunter at WFF headquarters[1] and had then returned to "Camp A" at Gabbari, south of the port, to order half of his men to prepare to leave immediately. As he, and they, arrived at the quay, the Naval Transport Officer signalled three trawlers to pull up alongside, and in no time three hundred men were clambering aboard with rifles, packs, and equipment.

At an average height of six feet, with rolled beards and enormous puggaree turbans, the Sikhs were an impressive sight. These superb soldiers, the pride of their British officers, had already seen fierce action in France and had only been withdrawn from that country because defences in Egypt were below strength. They would be in Egypt for only two months, but for that period they would be the mainstay of the Western Frontier Force.

The three vessels, weighed-down and overflowing with soldiers, were North Sea fishing trawlers. Like the *Tara*, the *Scotia*, and numerous other civilian craft, the trawlers had been sent to the Mediterranean in case they were needed at Gallipoli. Each had a single deck which split into two

[1] At the Attarine Caracol (police station) near Muhammad Ali Square.

narrow passages that ran either side of the wheelhouse, rising steeply in the bow, where they came together again. Under normal conditions the stern would have accommodated the most passengers, but now it was largely taken up by a three-pounder gun mounted there.

When the three boats sailed out of the harbour, Colonel Gordon returned to camp, knowing that he would have to repeat the whole process – three more trawlers and another three hundred men – on the following day.[2]

Mersa Matruh is on Egypt's northern coast, 175 miles west of Alexandria and 125 miles east of Sollum. There are ancient ruins in the area, and today's tourist industry encourages the legend that Cleopatra had a seaside villa there where she disported with Antony. The current town, by a beautiful natural lagoon, was begun early in the twentieth century by the Egyptian Coastguard under the supervision of Royle's mentor, André von Dumreicher. A few Italians and Greeks had previously visited the lagoon for a few months every year, camping on the beach and eking out a living fishing for sponges, but with the Government wishing to encourage more permanent settlement, von Dumreicher built a village of white-washed houses, a bazaar, a mosque, and even an Orthodox church.

The oval lagoon measures roughly 3,000 yards east to west and 1,000 yards north to south. The south side of the oval is the main beach. If you stand there at mid-point and look out to sea, the northern side begins as a spit of land to your right and continues in the middle as submerged reef. The spit, separating the lagoon from the open sea, creates a sheltered bay on the eastern side of the oval, and there visiting vessels used to anchor. On the spit itself stood a crenellated fort which was the Coastguard station. The only opening through the reef is 1,000 yards west of the fort, and this was guarded by two old Krupp field guns (identical to those abandoned at Sollum) positioned in front of the fort.

In the mid-afternoon of 24 November the three trawlers bearing the first half of the Sikh regiment negotiated the narrow passage through the reef and entered the lagoon. It had taken twenty-two hours to get there and the trip had not been pleasant. A strong head wind had tossed the trawlers about and drenched the men with heavy spray – and nearly all of them were seasick. Already at anchor in the bay was the *Rasheed*, which

[2] WO 95/4428, War Diary 15th Sikhs.

had arrived that morning bearing Snow, Royle and the other evacuees from Sollum.

The landing stage was a moored raft that allowed vessels with 18 ft of draft to draw alongside. One at a time the trawlers tied up to it and gradually three hundred queasy soldiers disembarked and were rowed to *terra firma*.

Already at Mersa Matruh were most of the men and vehicles of the RNACD Emergency Squadron. A few hundred yards south of the beach the Khedivial Road passed right through the heart of von Dumreicher's settlement, and drawn up on the hard gravel there were the six armoured Rolls Royces mounted with machine guns as well as those Fords which had not been disabled and abandoned at Sollum and Sidi Barani. The squadron had about one hundred officers and men in Matruh by now. From other units there were 140 men, including those who had arrived aboard the *Rasheed* that morning. These were mostly Egyptian Army regulars, including the artillery detachment. But there were also assorted coastguards, among them those native Egyptians who had not deserted to the Sanusi, but who now had to suffer the indignity of the widely-held belief that they might still bolt if not carefully watched. Temporarily in command of all the elements of this motley force was Cecil Snow. (Colonel Gordon would take over command when he arrived the following day.) There was also a small population of Awlad 'Ali which mainly resided around a few wells a mile to the east. The Greeks and Italians, the usual residents of the houses, had all been evacuated to Alexandria.

The Sikhs set up camp on the beach just east of the Matruh settlement, that is, opposite the anchorage and the Coastguard station, and spent the next few hours manhandling supplies and equipment over the deep sand, or were sent as pickets to man a ridge of hills running parallel to the coastline about a mile to the south.

On 25 November Colonel Gordon arrived with the second half of his regiment. Thereafter and for the next few months, trawlers and old steamers continued to make regular trips between Alexandria and Mersa Matruh, and the relentless unpleasantness of sailing on them is a recurring theme in the soldiers' accounts of the campaign.

The 15th Sikhs were part of the WFF's "Composite Infantry Brigade", while the rest would be elements of the Royal Scots and the Middlesex

Regiment. Cavalry would be gathered from assorted English county yeomanry (including the Dorset Yeomanry) and the Australian Light Horse Regiment, and the artillery units would come from the Nottinghamshire (or Notts) Battery of the Royal Horse Artillery (RHA). The number of men arriving daily averaged less than two hundred. By 3 December, for example, there were about 1,400 soldiers at Matruh camp.

While the WFF was taking shape, the soldiers already in Matruh were employed digging trenches, piling sand bags, and generally preparing the fortifications of the camp. The projected defensive perimeter extended for three and a half miles, so this involved considerable work, in addition to which pickets had to be posted at night around the entire periphery.

Although there was no sign of the enemy at Mersa Matruh, on 27 November Leo Royle, now working as an intelligence officer for the WFF, received word that the Sanusi were beginning to gather about 25 miles to the south-west, and a few days later there were "rumours of [an] impending attack on Mersa Matruh in considerable strength".[3] Nevertheless, apart from a brief incident when some shots were fired by nervous pickets near the west end of the beach there were no anxious moments.

For the first week the real enemy was the weather. Dust storms alternated with squalls of rain making it impossible for the men to stay clean or for the cooks to prepare sand-free food. This, on top of the effects of the sea journey and the hard labour required to put the camp in order, made many men ill. The weather finally changed for the better on 2 December, and a few days of glorious sunshine were enough to raise spirits and cure many cases of illness. Then the work progressed faster. Colonel Gordon's adjutant noted in the regimental diary: "Nothing better than the present climate could possibly be wished for";[4] and "Tents of the supply and ordnance services, British and Indian Field Hospitals, headquarters, etc., appear to grow daily out of the sand".[5]

On 30 November the generals began to arrive. Major-General Wallace came by automobile down the rutted and muddy road from al-Dab'a, and with him was Colonel Hunter, his Chief-of-Staff. They stayed one night,

---

[3] WO 33/714, GOC Egypt to WO (No. 2345 E), 3 December 1915; and WO 95/4428, entry for 27 November 1915.
[4] WO 95/4428, War Diary 15th Sikhs, entry for 5 December 1915.
[5] Ibid.

made an inspection of the defensive arrangements, and left the following morning. A week later they returned with the full Western Frontier Force staff, sailing into the lagoon aboard the new Royal Navy submarine monitor, HMS *Clematis*. In the meantime Brigadier-General Lord Lucan had arrived to take over command of the Composite Infantry Brigade from Colonel Gordon, which freed the latter to return to the command of his regiment.

Much interest and excitement were generated by the arrival of two BE2c biplanes which flew in and landed on Matruh beach on 4 December. Developed by Geoffrey de Havilland before the war, the BE2 was used mainly for reconnaissance and light bombing, and by late 1915 the "c" version was one of the most up-to-date machines in the RFC airfleet. More stable than versions "a" and "b", and supplied with a machine-gun for use by the observer, it had been developed specifically to cope with the superior German Fokker D-VII. The two BE2c's belonged to No. 14 Squadron, 5th Wing, which had left England on 9 November and, by dint of using rail transport to Marseilles, had made the trip to Alexandria in just ten days. They had been sent by train to al-Dab'a, unpacked, and assembled there – the only two aeroplanes earmarked for the Western Frontier Force. The rest of the Squadron's machines (with those of No. 17 Squadron) were based at Ismailia on the Canal.

Reconnaissance flights began immediately. By 5 December Maxwell was able to cable to the War Office that the Sanusi were gathering "southeast, south, and west of Matruh in parties of 100 to 500; total strength 2,500".[6] But there was another use for the BE2c's, even more vital than that of finding and counting parties of Sanusi: it was hoped that when the fighting started the observers, from above the battlefield, would be able to pinpoint Sanusi positions and movements so that the land force, together with the two 4-inch guns of HMS *Clematis*, could operate more efficiently.

Royle must have been delighted at the possibility of having his various roles – RFC observer, Western Desert specialist and intelligence officer – finally merge. It would have been uncharacteristic of him to force himself upon the other RFC airmen, but his unique qualifications for the job at

---

[6] WO 33/714, GOC Egypt to WO (No. 2374 E), 5 December. Presumably, the figure of 2,500 refers to total Sanusi and Turkish in Egypt, i.e., spread all along the coast from Mersa Matruh to Sollum.

hand were obvious and before long he would in fact be flying with them.

Gradually the Western Frontier Force prepared to go on the offensive against the Sanusi. On 9 December, Gordon and the other unit commanders were summoned to Wallace's headquarters to discuss the first operations outside the camp's perimeter. For the less experienced officers meeting Wallace must have been a bizarre, if not daunting, experience. He was an old warhorse, who had learned his trade in India and Afghanistan in the 1870s and '80s, and he was clearly an anachronism in the new world of aeroplanes and armoured cars. He had been badly wounded more than once, and now, at fifty-seven, with a wooden leg, he had arrived in the Western Desert to wage war one last time.

As his headquarters Wallace had taken over one of the houses of the original settlement. Inside, standing by a map on the wall, he outlined his plan for the imminent reconnaissance that he expected would result in an encounter with the Sanusi. He would personally, he said, lead a force of cavalry, infantry and guns that would march to the west for two days; reconnoitre on the third day; and march back to Mersa Matruh, returning at the end of the fifth day. As they would be following a rough coastal track, transport facilities were to be the old-fashioned kind: sixty mules and eleven wagons, each carrying 2,000 pounds of kit, equipment and rations. Meanwhile, the RNACD cars would deploy on the Khedivial Road, which ran roughly parallel to the coast, several miles inland.

But the next day more precise information arrived about the Sanusi force in the area, and Wallace substantially changed this plan. Twenty-five miles west of Matruh, air reconnaissance had spotted a group of 400 Sanusi, who were thought to be *muhafizia*. In the revised plan the British would forgo the land reconnaissance and simply go after those Sanusi regulars. Wallace increased the number of infantry in the expedition, while the cavalry would now form a second column, which would follow the Khedivial Road with the armoured cars and a section of Royal Horse Artillery, and which would try to sweep the enemy force toward the infantry. Wallace would now remain behind in Matruh and attempt to stay in touch (via telegraph line, heliograph and the aeroplanes) from there. The number of days out was decreased to three. And, finally, HMS *Clematis* and a trawler would lie offshore in case they were needed to evacuate the wounded.

At 7am on 11 December the British columns moved out of Mersa

Matruh. The main infantry, under Colonel Gordon, consisted of 350 men of the 15th Sikhs, plus support troops. They headed for a village called Umm al-Rakhm, 12 miles west, where they expected to camp for the night. The second column (taking the road) was commanded by cavalry officer Major Wigan (Berks Yeomanry) and with him rode Cecil Snow in his capacity of Political Officer (ie, local expert). Royle was away in al-Dab'a.

As Sayyid Ahmad's army moved into Egypt it occupied successively Baqbaq, Sidi Barani and Unjeila (mid-way between Barani and Matruh). Its commander, Ja'far al-'Askari, then moved from Unjeila eastwards with a force of about a thousand *muhafizia;*[7] three tribal battalions (the Menefa, the 'Awaqir, and the Awlad 'Ali) of approximately 300 men each; one company of cavalry, two mountain guns and four machine guns.[8] As it moved east the Sanusi army had several times seen the British aeroplanes and hidden itself as best it could; once, however, in the Wadi Majid, part of the force – presumably the large band of *muhafizia* that the British column was now looking for – had been caught in the open and made to scatter.

On the morning of 11 December the Awlad 'Ali battalion was carrying out a reconnaissance of its own to the west of Mersa Matruh, when the tribesmen saw the British cavalry heading towards them down the Khedivial Road. They took up positions in the broken terrain on the north side of the road and waited.

The approaching column, now nine miles from Mersa Matruh, was moving fast, but it was longer and more dispersed than it should have been. The Arabs waited until the advance guard and the armoured cars had

---

[7] The *Muhafizia* Battalion, in being a mixed force of Sanusi soldiers and Turkish officers, was to that extent comparable to the 15th Sikhs, with their Sikh rank and file and British officers.

[8] Ja'far al-'Askari (1988), Ch. 6. In 1928 MacMunn and Falls, in *Military Operations, Egypt & Palestine,* p. 113, quote Ja'far (who was then in London) as saying he had "three battalions of *Muhafizia* of 300 men each … [while] another battalion … had been sent by him on the 21st towards Dabaa to interrupt communications with Alexandria". The English authors apparently misunderstood regarding the composition of the battalions since in his memoirs Ja'far makes it quite clear that of the four battalions there was one which was large, comprising about 1,000 regulars (*Muhafizia*), and three others of the Menefa, 'Awaqir, and Awlad 'Ali tribes, each of about 300 men. Before the invasion of Egypt the *Muhafizia* had camped with the Turks at Bir Wa'r, while the tribal battalions had lived at the Sanusi camp at Amsa'id (source: Ja 'far's memoirs).

passed and then opened fire upon the right flank of the main body of cavalry. Hearing gunfire behind him, Major Wigan tried to turn the advance guard and the cars back upon the attackers, but already the fire was so intense that the movement failed. Eventually, some of the cavalry managed to leave the road and began to manoeuvre to get around the Arabs' left flank, while the RHA section brought its two guns into action at the rear of the column.

Colonel Gordon and the 15th Sikhs were six miles away to the north. They could hear the gunfire but could see nothing due to the uneven ground in that direction. As most of his own column was on foot, Gordon reasoned that if Wigan needed reinforcements, he would be better off getting them from Matruh. The infantry therefore continued to march towards Umm al-Rakhm.

While Gordon was able to maintain telephone contact with Matruh by having his signallers tap onto the telegraph lines overhead, the column under attack was virtually incommunicado. A means of one-way communication was quickly established, however. As soon as firing was heard at Matruh, one of the biplanes was sent (at 12.20pm) to find out what was happening. While the pilot flew back and forth between the action and Matruh, the observer made notes which he dropped in canisters to keep headquarters informed. By these means, Wallace soon knew that the cavalry was held up near Wadi Senab; that the armoured cars were two miles in front, also in action; and that the column's two artillery pieces were firing at the rear.

The fighting continued for much of the afternoon, with the Awlad 'Ali gradually withdrawing and descending into a network of intersecting *wadis*. The armoured cars were unable to manoeuvre in these rocky, steep-sided, dry riverbeds, and so they had to stay above near the road, and they eventually withdrew with the wounded back to Matruh. The cavalry found a way down, however, and worked its way north along Wadi Senab chasing an enemy that would disappear into caves, or else pretend to be dead and then jump up and shoot at close range – tactics which clearly rattled their pursuers. At one point early in the skirmish a squadron of Berkshire Yeomanry operating above the *wadi* charged some retreating Arabs with disastrous results. The terrain looked flat and unbroken, but it hid an unseen thirty-foot gully into which sixteen riders tumbled, several of whom broke their necks. Towards the end of the fighting 120 men of the Australian Light Horse arrived from Matruh, but by then the enemy had disappeared. The pursuit was finally abandoned at 3pm.

British casualties in this first encounter between the Western Frontier Force and the Sanusi Army were sixteen killed and seventeen wounded, while Sanusi losses (according to British estimates) were eighty killed and seven taken prisoner. Among the Arab dead was the sheikh of the *zawiya* at nearby Unjeila, and, according to Ja'far, this man's death so upset the Awlad 'Ali that they were now set upon exacting revenge.[9] But for the coastguards, and especially for Leo Royle, the day was tragic – for among those killed was Cecil Snow.

Riding with Wigan, Snow had passed the concealed Awlad 'Ali before they opened fire on the cavalry. But later, when the fighting moved into the *wadi*, he and Wigan were watching from above when they saw a Bedouin hiding behind a large boulder at the mouth of a cave. According to Wigan's account Snow said that he wanted to talk the man into surrendering. He proposed trying to approach the Bedouin unseen from above, telling Wigan to stay where he was and to signal when he (Snow) was near the man. Wigan agreed, but he told Snow to stay out of the Bedouin's sight until he could get two men to help. Snow then moved off until Wigan signalled that he was standing above the Bedouin. To Wigan's alarm he then saw Snow, still alone, walk up to the edge of the gully, put his head over, and shout to the Bedouin in Arabic, presumably telling him to give himself up. The man raised his rifle and shot Snow at a distance of just two yards.

Being of the Awlad 'Ali, the Bedouin would have certainly known Snow. But did he have time to recognize him? Perhaps he recognized him too late, for after firing he shouted "Snow Bey!", as if suddenly realizing what he had done. But it was now too late for both of them. Snow fell, shot in the side of the hip; the Bedouin was killed on the spot by arriving British soldiers. Snow was carried to one of the armoured cars and driven back to Mersa Matruh with a medic (an RAMC[10] major) in attendance, but he died that evening due to loss of blood.

The column of Sikh infantry, meanwhile, eventually arrived at a point just east of Umm al-Rakhm, where they set up camp for the night and posted pickets around the camp perimeter. Procuring water for the horses and

---

[9] Ja'far al-'Askari (1988), Ch. 6.   [10] Royal Army Medical Corps.

mules of the transport train presented a risk since the wells were outside the perimeter, south of the village *zawiya*, but in fact nothing happened. At 6pm the squadron of Australian Light Horse arrived out of the darkness; an hour and a half later the rest of the cavalry rode in. There were no tents. Each man had been told to carry a blanket and waterproof sheet instead.

Also that evening Gordon telephoned Wallace to discuss the day's events and future course of action. Wallace said that in the morning he would send an aeroplane to reconnoitre Sanusi positions, and the results would be dropped at Umm al-Rakhm.

Contrary to what the soldiers expected, that first night at the camp passed without any sniping.

At 9.30 the next morning one of the BE2c's appeared, returning from its reconnaissance, but no message was dropped. The RFC observer, Major Ross, had in fact spotted some 200 tents at Duwwar Husayn (in Wadi Husheifiyat) four miles from the coast and seven miles south-west of the British camp at Umm al-Rakhm. At noon Gordon finally received this information from Wallace by telephone, but by then the day was so far advanced that Wallace decided to defer the next move against the enemy until the following day. The general told Gordon that he should stay near the coast and continue marching to the west as far as he could while returning to camp at Umm al-Rakhm. Gordon sensibly pointed out that to go west for ten miles, for example, when the enemy was seven miles to the south-west would be to expose his flank. He made a counter-suggestion that he should go west as far as Wadi Husheifiyat, and then proceed up the *wadi* to Duwwar Husayn to meet the enemy head on. Wallace agreed that this was a better idea and promised to send four armoured cars back down the Khedivial Road to block any Sanusi retreat to the south.

With offensive action temporarily postponed, cavalry patrols went in the afternoon to reconnoitre in Wadi Senab, site of most of the previous day's fighting. The caves in the area were searched, and this yielded an impressive amount of grain, which was confiscated – one cave alone containing two wagon loads of barley. In addition, the patrols rounded up some camels, sheep and cows. Some Arabs were "captured", but these were simply a few Arab men (all but one unarmed) who had been hiding in the caves with their women and children. According to a Dorset Yeomanry account, "every imaginable kind of rifle was picked up on the field – old muzzle loaders, elephant guns, shotguns firing lead bullets, and some new rifles of Italian manufacture obviously captured in Libya".[11]

The soldiers were back at camp by 7pm. An hour later the first of the reinforcements arrived for the next day's advance on Duwwar Husayn. These 548 men of the Royal Scots had left Matruh at 1pm but had been delayed by the convoy of wheeled transport carrying supplies. In fact, the rumble and creaking of arriving wagons continued until nearly midnight.

At 8.30am on 13 December, the British column marched out of camp to confront the Sanusi at Wadi Husheifiyat. The cavalry rode ahead; behind it marched No. 2 Company 15th Sikhs as advance guard; 600 yards behind them were a machine gun section (also 15th Sikhs), half a battalion of Royal Scots, British and Indian field ambulances, pack mules loaded with reserve ammunition and water, and – bringing up the rear – one further platoon of Royal Scots. In other words, it was a long, slow-moving formation. As soon as Umm al-Rakhm village had been passed Gordon ordered two platoons of Royal Scots to march parallel to the main body to reduce the exposure of its left flank.

During the fighting at Wadi Senab on the 11th, Ja'far al-'Askari had been two days' march to the west, but now – because of Wallace's postponement of the offensive operation (from 12 to 13 December) – he was with the Sanusi force at Wadi Husheifiyat.[12] At 9am some of the Awlad 'Ali brought news that the column was approaching from the east. Ja'far ordered the *muhafizia* hurriedly to clamber up the east side of the wadi and deploy on the north-facing hills and slopes. The British were close, and before the *muhafizia* could get into position, the Sanusi 'Awaqir Battalion, already on the high ground facing the middle of the two-mile-long British column, opened fire on the Royal Scots. The time was 9.25am.

Colonel Gordon was riding with his regiment behind the cavalry. As

[11] C.W. Thompson, *Records of the Dorset Yeomanry, Queen's Own, 1914–1919*, pp. 39 ff.
[12] Sources disagree over the size of the Sanusi force collected there. General Maxwell's official account in *Supplement to the London Gazette* of 21 June 1916 gives a figure of three battalions, artillery, and a cavalry detachment: perhaps 1,200 men. In *The History of the Great War, Military Operations, Egypt & Palestine*, authors MacMunn and Falls estimate the number of Sanusi at Wadi Husheifiyat as 1,000–1,500 regulars plus the auxiliaries (tribal battalions), which would mean a total of between 1,900 and 2,500 men (excluding the Sanusi cavalry, which evidently did not take part in this battle). In fact, some of the *muhafizia* were with Sayyid Ahmad and Nuri at Unjeila.

soon as he heard gunfire he ordered a halt, galloped onto high ground, and looked back. What he saw, or thought he saw, was at first inexplicable. He could clearly make out the left flank guard of the Royal Scots fleeing helter-skelter toward the beaches, making "no attempt at delaying the advance of what appeared to be a similar party of some fifty men dressed alike in khaki, who were in pursuit". As the attackers were in well-ordered and extended formation, the absurd thought crossed his mind that these were two groups of Royal Scots, one firing on the other.

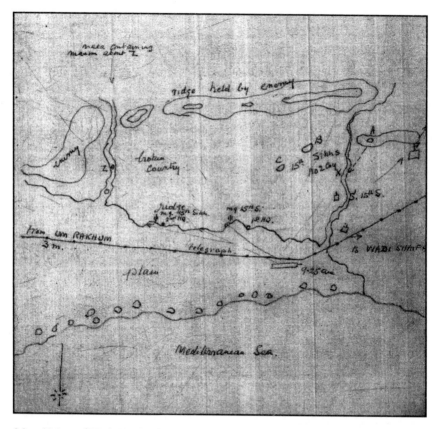

Map 4 Map of Wadi Husheifiyat on 13 December 1915, sketched on the spot by an officer of the Sikh regiment.

But a careful look through glasses disclosed this difference – that the second party were not carrying sacks and that they wore different headgear, while one Arab in Bedouin clothing soon proved that it was the enemy that had been encountered ... Meanwhile the left flank guard had gone clean away down the slope onto the plain and it was only the machine guns of the Regiment that stayed the enemy's further advance.[13]

Gordon sent his adjutant off with orders (firstly) to the main body of Royal Scots to advance to the ridge; (secondly) to Captain Hughes, commanding No. 2 Company 15th Sikhs, to turn and try to get behind the enemy; and (lastly) to the cavalry to sweep around to their left and similarly try to take the enemy from behind. He also told his signallers to send a message by heliograph[14] back to the camp (three to four miles away), the substance of which was that the perimeter should be lined immediately in preparation for a possible attack.

Although Ja'far's troops had opened fire prematurely, the element of surprise – as well as the high ground – was theirs. But the terrain between the British and their attackers was dominated by several mounds which the latter had not had time to secure. A company of Sikhs led by Captain Hughes, by turning and engaging the enemy immediately, was able to seize these crucial mounds. Hughes' men were in a position, therefore, to hold the enemy and simultaneously to provide some protection to the column, which had been left exposed by the fleeing Royal Scots. It was impossible, however, for the rest of the column to move up and support the Sikhs at the mounds. The nearest conceivable assistance would have come from the main body of Royal Scots, but it too was unable to move to the ridge. As for the mounted troops, they were more than a mile away and Gordon's order took some time even to reach them. When they did attempt to wheel to the left, a fresh body of Ja'far's troops attacked their front, and they were to spend the next few hours fighting right where they had been when the battle started.

Shortly before 10 o'clock Turkish artillerymen opened fire with mountain guns, but their aiming was erratic, with some shells landing hundreds of yards out to sea. The Turkish machine guns were more effective, however, one result being the Royal Scots' inability to line the ridge.

---

[13] WO 95/4428, War Diary 15th Sikhs, entry for 13 December.
[14] A portable signalling device using a mirror and sunlight to flash messages in code.

The signallers having again tapped the telegraph line, at 10.10am Gordon sent a message to Wallace in Matruh: "Enemy heavily attacking my force with guns four miles west of camp. Send out trawlers with guns or artillery." Thirty-five minutes later he sent another stressing the urgency of the situation: "Please send out total force you can spare. Enemy in considerable force but cannot estimate strength. Occupying very extended position. Enemy Senoussi's trained soldiers."[15]

In the meantime, the position of Captain Hughes and the Sikhs holding the mounds was precarious. The large gap between them and the column's main body meant they were receiving inadequate cover from behind, while in front an enemy in much greater numbers was closing on them. At 10.15 Hughes was ordered to rejoin the column but, as his men began to withdraw from behind the mounds, Sanusi and Turkish soldiers moved forward ready to seize the positions as soon as they were vacated. The Sikhs had several wounded who could not be moved due to the heavy fire, and, anyway, withdrawal was impossible. They would be exposed if they pulled back from the mounds; the enemy would seize their positions and pose an even greater threat to the column; and the wounded would have to be abandoned. So despite orders they stayed where they were.

At 10.55 Gordon sent another heliograph message to Captain Cates, in charge at Umm al-Rakhm camp, telling him to send reinforcements – every available man he could spare – as well as the Royal Scots' machine gun section, which had been left behind. Worried that the camp itself would be attacked, Gordon also ordered Cates to increase the pickets on the hill to the south of the camp to fifty men.

Cates sent 180 men, seventy-five of whom were Australians, to join the column. As the reinforcements approached the scene of battle, however, they came under fire from a machine gun positioned in a *wadi* to the east of the Royal Scots' main body. For the second time that day the Royal Scots – this time their machine gun section – broke and ran for cover in the sand dunes of the beach, but at least they took their carriage-mounted guns with them. The Australians stayed and joined the main body of the column.

For the next four hours the two sides were in deadlock. Eventually, the Royal Horse Artillery managed to position two guns near the beach between the rear of the column and the camp. From 5,500 yards they

[15] WO 95/4428, War Diary 15th Sikhs, entry for 13 December.

began firing over the column at enemy positions on the ridge, which they did with greater accuracy than the Turkish gunners had managed. HMS *Clematis*, lying offshore, was now also firing at Sanusi positions with her 4-inch shells. The Sanusi gradually retired. Finally, the Royal Scots succeeded in moving to the ridge, although Hughes and his men were no longer in danger.

The Sanusi army withdrew in safety towards the south, while a Turkish mountain gun, positioned near the Khedivial Road and deliberately held back by Ja'far, kept the armoured cars at bay.

It took much of the night to find and remove the British dead and wounded from the battlefield. They had to be carried half a mile or more across the sand dunes, loaded onto dinghies and rowed out to the trawlers. But their casualties were surprisingly light in the circumstances: nine killed and fifty-six wounded.

The Sanusi and Turkish soldiers took most of their casualties with them as they withdrew, making their losses difficult to estimate. Recalling the battle years later, Ja'far described their casualties as being "relatively light, two or three killed and a few wounded".[16] If this assessment is at first hard to credit, it is nevertheless supported by the 15th Sikh diarist, who reported that his men had been able to confirm no more than three enemy dead. In any case, it is beyond question that the Sanusi army fought well on 13 December. But for the British the day had nearly been a disaster. If Ja'far had had a few more minutes to get his *muhafizia* into position, their losses might have been much heavier.

What had gone wrong? Gordon had been aware of the risk to his left flank – indeed he had pointed out that risk to Wallace the evening before the battle. No doubt Gordon had erred in choosing two platoons from the Royal Scots to guard the flank, clearly overestimating the fighting capabilities of that regiment. But the Scots were not Regular Army – they were part of the Territorial Force. And although the Territorials were (since the start of the war, at least) no longer just part-time soldiers for home defence, they were nevertheless not as experienced and battle-hardened as the Regulars. In other words, Gordon should have used his Sikhs to guard the flank, but not even they could have prevented the ambush. The fact is that the British were moving slowly in the open with the sea on one side and a rocky ridge, perfect for a surprise attack, on the other; the Sanusi

[16] Ja'far al-'Askari (1988), Ch. 6.

held the ridge, and the British were caught without cover.

The night of 13–14 December was not a good one for Gordon's men, who were bivouacking near the battlefield. At 3.30am Turkish gunners reappeared and began firing again. Nevertheless, the British, Sikhs and Australians, most of whom were trying to sleep, were more annoyed by all the noise than threatened by shells fired in the dark. In the morning the column's cavalry and combat troops provided cover for the supply train and the support troops, and they all returned to Matruh.

After the battle Ja'far met with his officers and the tribal leaders. It was suggested that they should move the force to Wadi Majid, where the terrain would provide greater security. The Awlad 'Ali said that they had stored food in some caves there, and that there were wells nearby. A few men were sent to carry out a reconnaissance.

> They came back five hours later with the news that there was no one there, so I ordered us to move on to Wadi Majid, where we arrived at dawn. To us the wadi seemed as impregnable as the citadel at Verdun for the simple reason that the armoured cars could not manoeuvre there. You cannot imagine how much the tribesmen feared the armoured cars![17]

Two days after the move to Wadi Majid, Nuri arrived with the news that the Grand Sanusi was elated at the turn of events. Apparently, a rumour had reached Sayyid Ahmad at Sidi Barani that his army had been annihilated by the British, and then had come the reliable news that his men had in fact acquitted themselves well and that the British had withdrawn to lick their wounds.

Ja'far had a long talk with Nuri, telling him that Mersa Matruh was now too well fortified to attack; that "the best we could do was to harry the enemy, to disrupt his lines of communication, and generally to impede his freedom of movement".[18] But it was apparently Ja'far who decided the next move. Al-Dab'a was reported to be less well defended than Matruh, so he sent several hundred of the *muhafizia* with one mountain gun to seize or destroy British munitions and supplies at the railhead. With hindsight this decision seems to have been reckless. Without doubt, Ja'far was ebullient after the action near Wadi Husheifiyat, and he must have

---

[17] Ja'far al-'Askari (1988), Ch. 6.   [18] Ibid.

wanted to strike another blow before the British could be further reinforced. But in sending off some of his best troops at this point, Ja'far took a great risk. He evidently intended for the *muhafizia* to make the raid on the railhead and then to return as soon as possible. That is not what happened, however. It would be several weeks before the party of *muhafizia* was heard from again, and by then Fortune would be favouring the other side.

Captain Royle returned to Mersa Matruh on 12 December, too late to see his uncle alive. Snow had died of loss of blood during the evening of the 11th, the day he was shot. Royle was there, however, when Snow was buried in the camp's temporary graveyard.[19] For fifteen years Cecil Snow had been Leo's most accessible relative. Leo's two paternal uncles in Egypt, Charles Royle and George Royle, had both died before the war, and there had been no home leave since the war had started. It was with a heavy heart that he returned to work.

But Royle's immediate problem was *where* to work. He was now the principal intelligence officer at Matruh, and he needed a place where he could interview prisoners in peace and quiet.[20] Those conditions were not easily provided in a military camp with 1,500 soldiers and thousands of transport animals – not to mention the two aeroplanes constantly taking off and landing on the beach. There was no room for him in the house which served as WFF headquarters, but the problem was solved by George Hunter, who arranged for Royle to be provided with a spacious tent in which he could interview Arabs and write his reports for INTRUSIVE. On 16 December the WFF intelligence unit, now called INTELLIGENCE WESTFORCE, cabled INTRUSIVE that the Sanusi had managed to recover the breech blocks for the two Krupp guns which the British had abandoned at Sollum. These had been fished out of the harbour, and the guns – now fully operational – had been moved to north-facing positions behind Snow's house, where they could command the

---

[19] Snow and others killed during these operations were subsequently moved to Chatby Cemetery in Alexandria.

[20] Intelligence documents imply that Royle was not working alone in "INTELLIGENCE WESTFORCE" at this time, but give no clue how many others may have been assisting. It is possible that James Hay was with Royle now. Hay had signed the Intelligence Diary at the end of November and had therefore presumably moved from al-Dab'a to Mersa Matruh.

harbour and defend Sollum against any British approach by sea. The unit also confirmed that Ja'far, like Colonel Gordon, was using a field telephone which could be tapped onto the telegraph wires, and that he was thus in touch with Sanusi units at Sidi Barani and Sollum.

During that same week of mid–December INTRUSIVE, along with the rest of GHQ, was moving from the Army of Occupation building to the luxurious Savoy Hotel, a few hundred yards further up Cairo's Qasr el-Nil Street, in Midan Suleiman Pasha. The Section was also being reorganized and increased. In a letter written shortly after the move, T. E. Lawrence lists seventeen intelligence officers by name and special area (although four or five of those listed did not actually work at GHQ Cairo – ie, at the Savoy).[21] Only one man on the list was directly concerned with Sanusi matters, and that was the Irishman Mervyn Macdonnell. Thirty-five years old, Macdonnell had worked as a civil servant in the Sudan and Egypt before the war, and it was he who had now replaced James Hay[22] at GHQ

---

[21] Lawrence, M. R. (1954) (ed.), *The Home Letters of T. E. Lawrence and His Brothers*. The letter is dated "January, 1916".
The seventeen are:
Colonel Clayton – Chief
Capt. Deedes – Suspects
Capt. Cornwallis – S. W. Arabia
Capt. Macdonnell – Tripolitania
Capt. Graves – Turkish Army
Major [Engleton or Engledon] – Censor
Capt. Beaumont – Censor
Major Hennessy – Suspects
Woolley – French Fleet
Major Garvice – Alexandria
Major Barlow – Suez
Colonel Jennings-Bramly – Ismailia
Armbruster – Enemy trading
Rider – Enemy trading
Capt. Hadkinson – French Fleet
Capt. Stirling – Port Said
Myself – Maps
Lawrence also says cryptically at the end of the list, "There are a lot of others". In any case, the Intelligence Section at GHQ had evolved considerably in the six months since Lawrence had written (in June 1915) "Newcombe, one Macdonnell and myself are Intelligence".

and who was receiving the reports from INTELLIGENCE WESTFORCE.[23]

As for Lawrence, barely three weeks had passed since his visit to Sollum, and he was now living at the Savoy as well as working there. At the start of 1916 he was still a 2nd lieutenant; still preparing maps and intelligence summaries. But soon he would be helping to set up the Arab Bureau, right there in the Savoy, and the summaries would evolve into the more formal "Arab Bulletin". In the spring he would be in Iraq with his Intelligence colleague Aubrey Herbert, trying to bribe the Turks to lift the siege at Kut, where a British army was in trouble;[24] and by the year's end he would be in Arabia, about to become a legend.

---

[22] Hay subsequently moved from the Intelligence Department to the Military Police. At the war's end he was the Assistant Provost Marshal at GHQ Cairo. He died in Egypt in 1919.

[23] As a result of the move and reorganisation the Intelligence Section was in chaos throughout the second half of December and well into 1916. On 28 December Lawrence described this in another letter home: "We are just in the midst of changing our office for the third time: horrible din, & deadly confusion of papers." Two months later (21 February 1916) things were not much better: "We are changing office tonight, so that everything is in a royal disorder. Each time we change we get more and more rooms: here in the Savoy Hotel, which is Headquarters at present, we now have 15 rooms, not counting little rooms."

[24] The mission failed, and British General Townshend was forced to surrender ignominiously.

13

Captivity: 5–26 November 1915

A S THE *U-35* LEFT BARDIA cove to attack Sollum on the afternoon of
5 November, the *Tara's* ninety-two surviving crew members were
herded several hundred yards inland to the mouth of a ravine. Many were
barefoot and had hurt their feet coming ashore on the rocky side of the
beach, but William Thomas, the quartermaster, with his fractured tibia, was
suffering dreadfully. The sun was hot, and everyone was thirsty.[1]

Some Sanusi eventually brought several goatskins of foul-tasting,
reddish well-water, and one hard biscuit was given to each man. Later, they
came back with a live goat as "dinner", but as none of the crew knew how
to kill an animal, a guard summarily dispatched it with a bayonet.
Inexpertly cooked over the fire, the carcass provided one small piece of
meat for each man.

The crew had carried the body of the ship's cook, Walter Jackson, from
the beach to the ravine, and that evening they buried him in the sand.
Edward Tanner, the ship's master, led an impromptu burial service. The

---

[1] Chapters 13, 15 and 18, describing the British prisoners' captivity in Libya, are based
mainly on the following sources: Captain Gwatkin-Williams account "Brief Record
of Proceedings of Survivors of HMS *Tara* ..." (WO 106/1543); the diary of David
John Davies, Engineer of HMS *Tara* (Anglesey County Record Office); the diary of
Sub-Lt. Albert Marsh (Department of Documents, Imperial War Museum, London).
For a fuller account of their captivity see Gwatkin-Williams, R. S. (1919), *Prisoners of
the Red Desert*.

grave was covered with stones, and a cross was made from one of the lifeboat oars and placed at its head.

The prisoners then sat in the open until two tattered Arab tents were finally erected to shelter them. But the night was bitterly cold, and they were uncomfortable, hungry and full of foreboding for the future.

Three men were spared the hardships of their shipmates on that first night. Nuri invited Captain Gwatkin-Williams, Edward Tanner, and Basil Lambrinidis (the interpreter) to dine with him in his tent. Also of the party were two Turkish officers, called Fevzi and Husni. The meal was sufficient, if not copious, and at least the meat was properly cooked and served with rice. In Gwatkin-Williams' account of that evening there is an interesting description of Enver's younger brother.

> General Nouri Bey is a dark-eyed gentle-looking man, somewhat slightly built, and with a straggling black beard; he is an ardent antiquarian and naturalist, and spoke much of the ancient ruins of the interior. These, he said, he would put the *Tara's* men to excavate, and hearing that I was fond of sketching he said he would provide me with materials to illustrate this work, only that I must give him half the pictures …
>
> Two other Turkish officers were also in the tent, Fevzi and Husni … They were both kind and compassionate. One of the two, who had but just arrived from Turkey in the submarine, supplied me with soap and cigarettes. They had both been prisoners of the Bulgarians in the last Balkan War, and their sympathy was obviously heartfelt and genuine.[2]

The conversation was in French, which Nuri spoke reasonably well and of which Gwatkin-Williams had a smattering; the others relied on Basil to help them out. Nuri gave the impression of not being religious, but he quoted the Koran's injunction that prisoners must be well-treated. For the prisoner-invitees it was an unexpectedly convivial evening. They even spent the night in Nuri's tent.

The next morning the three rejoined the other prisoners, and all were moved to a cultivated patch of land further up the ravine, where there were two wells and a few withered fig trees. All day long they watched the Sanusi loading their camels with the supplies and ammunition brought by the U-boat, and then leading them along the steep path to the plateau. In

[2] Gwatkin-Williams (1919), p. 26.

the afternoon the men were permitted to return under guard to the beach for a wash and a swim. However, their cash, rings and other valuables were taken from them; and the food ration for the day was very meagre: one biscuit per man and some rice.

On Sunday morning (7 November) the prisoners were told to haul the lifeboats out of the water. They moved two of the boats to a corner of the beach, but the third, being damaged, they left on the rocks. Sheets of paper were distributed for letter-writing, and the men were assured that every effort would be made to have their letters delivered. Later, in the charge of Fevzi and Husni, the prisoners were moved again. They were led up the path to the plateau; then they walked several miles to the west. Most of the men had no shoes, and walking on the rocky, pebbly desert surface was a painful ordeal. The men who did have shoes or boots carried the wounded on stretchers made from oars and sails.

They eventually arrived at a place in a shallow valley where there were ancient ruins on one side and two small caves on the other, and there they would stay for a week. The food ration, issued shortly after their arrival, was marginally better than before: boiled rice and a piece of goat meat each. The prisoners were expected to sleep in the caves, but as these were cramped and fetid, having been used by animals, some chose to sleep outside in the cold.

On Monday (8 November) camels arrived with supplies for the prisoners. These included some Arab clothing – the *jalabiyya* (a long, shirt-like garment), the shirwal (a loose trouser-like undergarment), the *burnous* (a hooded outer cloak), and leather sandals – but there was not enough for everyone. There was also an assortment of cooking gear – pots, pans, basins and spoons, but no plates. Each of the prisoners received one and a half pounds of rice, one biscuit, one ounce of goat meat, and a small amount of tea, sugar and salt. They were also given the option of exchanging rice for flour, if they preferred. Some Arab girls delivered more skinfuls of reddish water from a nearby well. (The strange colour and taste of the water was in fact due to the Bedouin custom of treating their goatskins with saffron and red-pepper.)

As food and supplies were being distributed, Ja'far al-'Askari arrived in jovial mood. The prisoners were encouraged to put on their Arab garments, which they did with much laughing and joking. Ja'far had a camera and they gathered together for a picture. He also handed out more slips of paper for letters and asked the prisoners to write that they were being treated well.

On Tuesday (9 November) Fevzi and Husni departed, and the prisoners were left in the charge of a Turkish doctor named Béchie Fuad. Physically, the new "commandant" was heavy and unprepossessing, but he proved to be kind-hearted.[3] Like Nuri and many of the other Turks, he spoke French.

Béchie Fuad also had a taste for Scotch whisky. During the week's stay at "the caves", a whole case of Black and White scotch arrived from Nuri as a present for the British officers. This naturally had to be kept out of sight, the Sanusi being quite fanatical on the subject of alcohol. It was therefore kept in the doctor's tent, where he and the other Turkish officers, with Gwatkin-Williams, Tanner and Lambrinidis, sat around for much of the day playing cards, smoking (also strictly forbidden), and drinking "alternate tumblers … of sweet brewed Arab tea and of neat whisky."[4] His guests' enjoyment of this routine was somewhat spoiled when he informed them that the Sanusi penalty for drinking alcohol was amputation of the culprit's hand.

On Wednesday (10 November) Béchie Fuad mentioned the *U-35*'s attack on Sollum, the first time the prisoners heard this news. He also revealed that the U-boat, as it sailed away to the north, had sunk two more ships. These revelations were made in the context of a rumour having reached the camp that a boatload of shipwrecked survivors had been spotted offshore near Bardia. For reasons that were not readily apparent to the prisoners, the doctor told four of them, men who still had their uniforms, to go to investigate. Dressed again as British sailors, these men were escorted several miles to a point on the plateau that overlooked the sea. There they observed a ship and a boat approaching her. The men in the boat were apparently returning to their ship, which was about to sail off. Inexplicably, the four prisoners were then told that they were no longer needed. They stayed long enough to drink some tea with a hospitable Arab and were then escorted back to "the caves". For the prisoners the incident was an utter mystery.

In fact, the ship was almost certainly HMS *Jonquil* under Commander G. P. Bevan. The *Jonquil* was cruising near Crete when she intercepted a

---

[3] "To look at him, he was not beautiful, but he had the kindest of hearts for us whom he made his guests." Gwatkin-Williams (1919), p. 29.   [4] Ibid., p. 29.

signal reporting that the *Tara* had been torpedoed. She rushed to Sollum, arriving there on the morning of 10 November. After Bevan had spoken with Cecil Snow the *Jonquil* went to Bardia to look for the *Tara* crew. A boat was launched which entered the cove and spotted the broken lifeboat left on the rocks, but its men did not land on the beach.[5]

Another strange incident occurred that day at "the caves". A Sanusi nobleman, said to be related to the Grand Sanusi, arrived to see for himself the spectacle of British prisoners on their way to internment. Béchie Fuad hastily hid the whisky and cigarette stubs in his tent, but the visitor chose to sit outside shooting at rocks with his rifle and threatening to use his whip on any Sanusi not showing sufficient deference towards him. When he finally left, the Turks all openly expressed their dislike of this man.[6]

The next day (11 November) marked the end of the prisoners' first week in captivity. The prisoners' money and valuables were returned them, raising hopes that their release was being negotiated. Another rumour circulated: that a boat-load of Indians with three European officers had been picked up on the coast nearby.

On Friday, 12 November, the prisoners were much amused by an example of Turkish military discipline. Béchie Fuad caught two Turkish soldiers quarrelling. He called one of the men over, slapped his face, and knocked him down; he then summoned the other man and gave him the same treatment. This done, he made them kiss and make up. The two soldiers then walked off arm-in-arm.

By now the prisoners were all being troubled by bugs and fleas. A few

---

[5] Gwatkin-Williams offered a different theory. In *Prisoners of the Red Desert* (p. 35) he refers to an article in the *Daily Mail* of 31 January 1916, which says the following: "that not long after the sinking of the 'Tara,' a British officer who was in the vicinity landed a small force. A friendly native potentate came down to the sea-side and advised them to leave, else they would be exterminated by thousands of Arabs. The landing party 'wirelessed' for orders, and were instructed to withdraw." Gwatkin-Williams then (p. 46) refers to the visit to Bardia by the *Jonquil* as a separate event which, he says, occurred on 14 December. This date is wrong by more than a month. The *Jonquil* definitely reached Sollum on 10 November, the same day the four prisoners watched from the top of the escarpment as the boat returned to the ship. The information in the *Daily Mail* article may be basically correct, but it refers to the *Jonquil's* visit. FO/371/2356 Western Desert Intelligence, 10 November 1915, confirms that the *Jonquil* reached Sollum on 10 November.

[6] According to the diary of David John Davies, the nobleman's visit occurred the next day, 11 November.

pieces of soap were handed out, also an extra pint of water per man, with which to wash. The day's food ration included both meat and tomatoes.

On Saturday, 13 November, Gwatkin-Williams prepared both a letter and a telegram for Vice-Admiral Peirse, the Senior Naval Officer at Port Said, reporting the loss of the *Tara* and naming the eleven crew members who had been killed. Béchie Fuad promised to try to have them delivered.

Later that day, however, another crew member's name was added to the list of fatalities. In the afternoon Béchie Fuad inspected the broken leg of William Thomas and found it to be gangrenous and infected with maggots. He decided to amputate the limb immediately but had neither surgical instruments nor anaesthetic. With two of Thomas' messmates holding his hands and the ship's medic (medical student J. Arthur) assisting, the doctor cut the leg off below the knee, using a pair of scissors and a stone. When the operation was over, the doctor promised to send Thomas to Sollum in the morning. Thomas died of shock shortly before midnight.

At 8.30am, Sunday, 14 November, the prisoners buried William Thomas. Edward Tanner again led the burial service, and the prisoners, many of them weeping, sang one verse of "A day's march nearer home".

Later that morning a man arrived who looked European, spoke English well, and claimed that his name was 'Uthman Bey. As he appeared to speak neither Turkish nor Arabic the prisoners assumed he was German. 'Uthman Bey pressed Gwatkin-Williams into giving his word of honour, in writing, that he would not try to escape, saying that otherwise he would be sent to a different Sanusi camp where Italian prisoners were kept, implying that the consequences of such a move would be dire. Gwatkin-Williams agreed, but only on the condition that he could give seven days notice that he was ending the agreement. In return 'Uthman Bey promised that the prisoners would not be moved until transport and tents were provided for continuing the journey. No one else was asked to promise not to escape. When he left, this man took the letters with him, and in fact they arrived in England and Wales in February. 'Uthman Bey was, of course, Otto Mannesmann.

On Monday, 15 November, the prisoners were placed in the charge of a new commandant, and, to the regret of them all, Béchie Fuad left. They were told that the new man in charge was called Captain Ahmad Mansur, that he used to work for the Egyptian Coastguard, and that he had recently arrived by U-boat from Constantinople. An Egyptian Copt and nationalist, Captain Ahmad Mansur was indeed a former member of the Coastguard, although he was not a deserter. He had been dismissed from the service, and this, he evidently felt, was one more reason for him to hate the British. The other coastguards knew him as Ahmad Abu 'Ali, and he had been recognized in the bazaar at Sollum just six days before he took over command of the prisoners. Cecil Snow was informed of this sighting and also of the rumour that Ahmad Mansur had just landed by U-boat.[7] At 9am – contrary to the promise of "'Uthman Bey" that transport would be provided – the prisoners were mustered and the order given to move camp. All had now been issued Arab clothing and sandals, so at least they were better off than the last time they had to walk. With each man carrying his own gear, they marched about twelve miles, until 4.15pm, when a halt was called in a narrow gully with steep sides. The ground was rocky there, and they would be sleeping in the open. This location the prisoners dubbed "the dry dock".

In the evening four more prisoners arrived, led by a Turkish officer. They were from the horse transport SS *Moorina*: Lieutenant T. S. Apcar (Indian Lancers); Chief Officer, Mr Coalstead; Mr Richardson, an engineer; and the ship's African cook, known only as Joe. The *Tara* crew gave a loud cheer as they arrived. The *Moorina* had been sunk by the *U-35* on 7 November, and all hands had got off safely. Thirty-six others, all Indians, had from the start been kept apart from these four. Mr Coalstead immediately made friends by sharing a tin of Traveller Tobacco with some of the *Tara* crew. Two goats were killed for dinner after dark, but the men decided to keep the meat for the next day.

The night was cold and rainy, and the next day (16 November) Lt. Apcar came down with fever. Much of the meat which the prisoners had been saving was stolen by the Bedouin guards in the night. However, the day's rations were better than usual. Two more goats were killed; and there was more rice and plenty of good drinking water. Captain Ahmad ordered the prisoners' money, watches and rings to be collected again, and everything was carefully inventoried before being handed over.

At 4pm the prisoners, including the newcomers, left "the dry dock" and walked north-west. At dusk they stopped for an hour to rest (by a tent serving as a "telephone station") and then continued across flat terrain until 11pm. The sailors were not good walkers, and most of them were

---

[7] FO 371/2356, Western Desert Intelligence, 10 November 1915.

carrying extra clothes, sleeping mats, and cooking utensils. They camped in a village of half a dozen houses. At first all ninety-six men were herded into a small and dirty yard area, but on protesting they were allowed to sleep in the open. Again the night was cold.

The morning of 17 November the prisoners were given water with which to wash, and to do this they used the pots and pans. The midday food ration was two goats and some rice. The day's trek began at 3pm and continued until 8.30pm, when they arrived at a large camp of Bedouin tents. Despite now having sandals most of the men were severely footsore and in a state of near collapse. To make matters worse, there was no evening meal as supplies of food and water arrived too late. The officers, petty officers, and some of the men slept in tents. The rest tried to sleep in the open, but the night was again cold.

The next morning the prisoners breakfasted on a small amount of boiled rice and then began marching at 8am. Ninety minutes later a halt was called. They were given a biscuit and more rice and told they would be allowed six hours' rest. From this place, near Ras Lakk, the sea was visible, and at one point the men could see a ship on a zigzag course as if avoiding U-boats. In the late afternoon and evening they marched again for several hours. Again there was no evening meal, just some green tea. Lt. Apcar was now very sick and thought to be dying.

On Friday, 19 November, the men began the day with more boiled rice and green tea. Then they marched from 8am until midday, when they stopped to await the arrival of more food and water. Roughly a mile away there was an Arab camp on a hillside. Some villagers eventually turned up and asked if there was a doctor available to treat a sick woman. The medic, young Mr Arthur, went off with Basil, and they were away all day. In fact, the lady's "illness" consisted merely of a boil on her posterior. Once this was treated, the medic and his interpreter were regaled with a fine lunch, returning late in the afternoon. Camels finally arrived with food and water shortly after dark. Two goats were killed and the meat stewed; and there was also boiled rice. The men then slept on the hard ground in heavy fog.

During the night a young coal trimmer named Thomas Owen disappeared. Fearful of what might befall the youth on his own, Gwatkin-Williams informed Captain Ahmad, who sent guards off in all directions to look for the fugitive. The night sentries were then beaten by their sergeant. Owen's disappearance put Captain Ahmad in a foul mood. The prisoners were made to march all day on nothing more than a biscuit and a drink of water, and that night they camped in the open, suffering extremely of hunger, thirst, and exhaustion.

The next day (Sunday, 21 November) the prisoners were made to march from 8am until noon; and again from 3pm until 7pm. They had no food, just a water ration early in the morning and another during the midday halt. During the afternoon march three men collapsed – Mr Dutton (the paymaster), Mr Thomas (the 3rd mate), and Mr Cox (the boilermaker) – and had to be mounted on animals. The Sanusi second-in-command, Muhammad Effendi Zoueh, was sympathetic and humane. He dismounted from his horse, helped Mr Cox to get on the animal, and then he walked alongside. He also shared his water-bottle with the prisoners who were suffering most. Muhammad Effendi was from Benghazi. He had left that city to fight the Italians, but his wife and family were still there.

The punishment finally ended Monday morning. Thanks mainly to the interceding of Muhammad Effendi, Captain Ahmad finally relented and allowed a larger than usual food ration. Rice and sugar were handed out in the morning. The prisoners then marched until noon, when they ate rice and rested. (In desperation the men had begun to collect snails, which they cooked in the fire and ate, and this practice continued throughout their captivity.) In the afternoon they again marched, finally stopping near a well called Bir al-Zibla, south-west of Tobruk. Flour was distributed from which Arab bread was made. The prisoners were weak and exhausted, but at least they were less hungry than they had been since Thomas Owen's disappearance.

The next morning (23 November) the prisoners were allowed to wash at the well, but by now all were infested with lice and fleas, and the water and scrubbing provided only temporary relief. Captain Ahmad declared a day's rest and then disappeared for several hours. Rice and flour were issued. That evening a searchlight was visible to the north. (This was the day that the British evacuated Sollum and the Sanusi army invaded Egypt.) While the prisoners were at Bir al-Zibla, Captain Ahmad announced that a state of war now existed between the Sanusi and the British.

The night was cold and the dew heavy with the result that few were able to sleep. Mr Cook, the electrician, became ill due to a chill. Mr Cox, meanwhile, was continuing to suffer, his principal ailment being stricture of the urethra. His shipmates tried to bring him relief with a hot water wash, but this did not help much. A two-day ration of flour was made for cooking bread for the coming journey. The next stage of the march was to the south. They began at 4pm and continued until 9pm. After dark conditions became very difficult due to the rocky ground, and the ill and the lame feared being left behind. Captain Ahmad threatened to have stragglers flogged. Finally, the moon rose and conditions improved.

Thursday, 25 November, was the last full day of walking. The men ate some of the rice and Arabic bread, which they had prepared the previous day, and set off at 8am. They walked until early afternoon, with many eating all the food they were supposed to be carrying for the whole journey. After the rest they marched again from 3.30 to 9, and at one point they crossed the Enveria Road, which ran westwards from Sollum.

On the following day, Friday, 26 November, the prisoners were awakened before dawn. They marched for six hours over flat and utterly barren desert, and at midday they arrived at their final destination – Bir Hakim.

14

Christmas 1915 and the Battle of
Wadi Majid

FOLLOWING THE FIGHTING at Wadi Senab and Wadi Husheifiyat the Western Frontier Force faced two weeks of onerous preparations for its next encounter with the Sanusi. The enemy had shown that he could fight, and so the defences of Matruh camp had to be strengthened. For the soldiers that meant more daytime fatigues building up the long perimeter wall with sandbags and stone, while their nights were often disturbed by sniping. The tense atmosphere is well captured in the War Diary of the 15th Sikhs.

18 December. The whole place seething with activity, every available man being employed on fatigues connected with the defence.

19 December. ... Last night a certain amount of firing was heard about No. 7 picket. Some enemy snipers had apparently crept up to some houses 3/4 of a mile south and sniped into camp from there. Fatigues and bustle as usual. Oh for a rest!

20 December. ... burst of firing ... put everyone on the *qui vive*. It transpired later that a few snipers had worked along the strip of land [enclosing the lagoon] to see what they could do.

21 December. Fatigues as usual on the perimeter. The enemy last night tried our perimeter and sniped the camp from half a mile off. Fortunately

no damage was done although several of the bullets fell in camp. These nightly disturbances are becoming troublesome, as each one brings one out of bed. Prospects are quite bright of another little expedition shortly which, it is to be hoped, will end in a good round up. The enemy have been observed building *sangars*[1] on a position about seven miles away ... the enemy are there in some strength, anything from 2,000 to 3,000 men.[2]

On 16 December an Australian Light Horse patrol was reconnoitring near Jebel Medwa, six miles south-west of Matruh, when it ran into a band of Sanusi. Upon hearing gunfire Wallace sent out the armoured cars, ambulances and a section of the Royal Horse Artillery (RHA), but the Australians were already on their way back when the reinforcements reached them. The aeroplanes confirmed that the main concentration of Sanusi was now near the place where the Australians had been fired upon.

On 23 December General Wallace briefed his officers on a plan to attack the Sanusi on Christmas morning. He said he wanted to turn the tables on the Sanusi and take *them* by surprise: to do this the approach to Jebel Medwa would be made before dawn. Colonel Gordon would again command the right column, with infantry (15th Sikhs and New Zealand Rifle Brigade), some cavalry (Royal Bucks Hussars), and a section of the Notts Battery Royal Horse Artillery. They would march south-west straight down the road to Jebel Medwa. Brigadier-General Tyndale-Biscoe would command the left column with the rest of the cavalry and the second section of the Notts Battery RHA.[3] Wallace hoped that the second column would provide an additional element of surprise by leaving Matruh heading east, turning south down a riverbed called Wadi Tuweiwia, and gradually moving westward in a large arc – in theory reaching the Khedivial Road behind the Sanusi, where it would be in a position to block their retreat. General Wallace, as GOC, would follow behind the first column with reserves of infantry, cavalry, artillery, field

[1] A Hindu word denoting a stone breastwork built by Indian hill-tribes.
[2] WO 95/4428, War Diary 15th Sikhs.
[3] Five armoured cars of the RNACD had originally been designated to move with the cavalry, but Wadi Tuweiwia was too rocky and uneven for them to get through and they returned to Mersa Matruh.

ambulances and the supply train, while HMS *Clematis* would wait offshore to assist with her guns. The whole British force would number about 3,000 men.

On 24 December a strong westerly wind rose, buffeting the north coast with sand and dust and threatening the next day's expedition. Gordon called on Wallace to say that he would prefer to command the 15th Sikhs and relinquish overall command of the first column. Wallace rejected that proposal, and the plan stayed as it was. The Sikhs would be commanded by an officer named Major Evans.

On Christmas morning reveille was at 3am. It was bitterly cold, with the wind still blowing from the west. The men of the second column paraded at 4am and set off forty-five minutes later via the town's eastern exit, as if heading for Alexandria. They rode past the Coastguard barracks and the hospital tents, and after two miles they turned south off the road and began their great circular movement round to the west.

Gordon's column left Matruh from the opposite (west) side of town at 5am and marched straight down the road. There was no moon, and the stars gave only enough light to enable the men to keep to the road. But the glimmer of starlight was sufficient for the Sanusi sentries to see what was coming. The column had been gone barely an hour when a large bonfire appeared atop a hill to the front right, signalling the British approach. The notion of completely surprising the Sanusi had failed.

At 7am the column stopped on the east side of a wide depression called Wadi Raml, while two troops[4] of Royal Bucks Hussars rode off to reconnoitre in the direction of the fire. The Hussars soon found themselves targeted by artillery and machine guns positioned to the south of Jebel Medwa, and they returned to the column, which continued its advance across the *wadi*. Gradually, with increasing daylight, there came into view large numbers of Sanusi soldiers moving to the south-east, roughly towards the British column. Realising that on the right the Sanusi had not occupied Jebel Medwa, the dominant feature of the landscape, Gordon ordered Major Evans (at 7.30) to deploy one of two companies of Sikhs forming the advance guard (No. 3 company) on the *jebel* in order to protect the column's right flank. The remaining company of the Sikh advance guard (No. 4) continued to advance until, at 8.15, it was fired upon by a Turkish mountain gun. By riding onto high ground, Gordon

[4] About 40 riders.

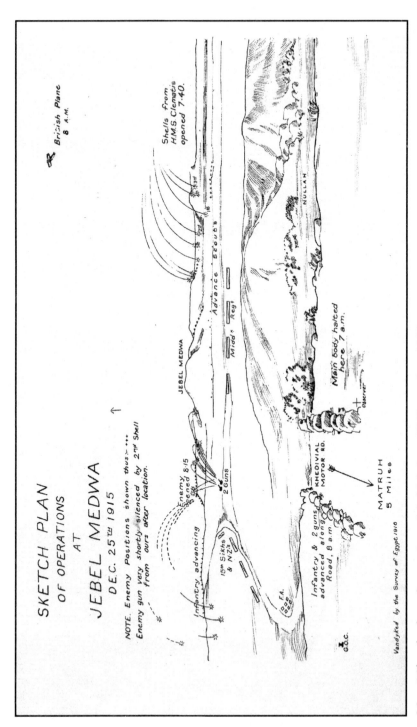

Map 5 Sketch plan of operations, Jebel Medwa, 25 December 1915.

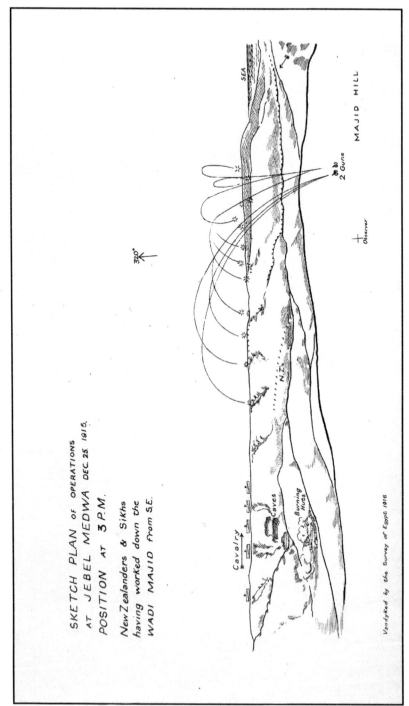

Map 6 Sketch plan of operations, Jebel Medwa, 3pm, 25 December 1915.

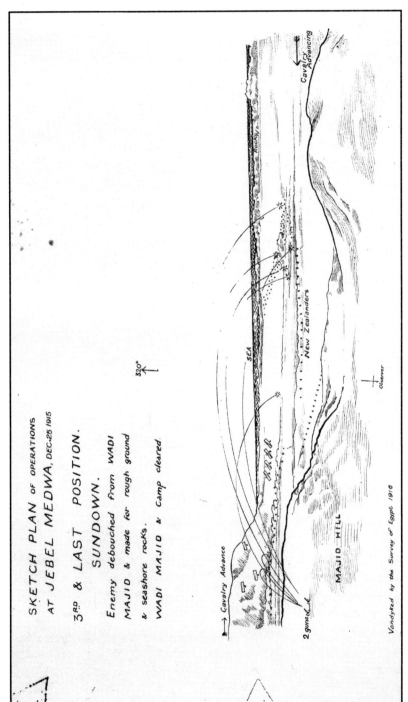

Map 7 Sketch plan of operations, Jebel Medwa, sundown, 25 December 1915.

was able to spot the enemy gun, and the Notts RHA section, firing their two guns from a point 2,000 yards east of Jebel Medwa, quickly forced the Turkish gun team to retire. By this time the guns of HMS *Clematis* were also firing, laying shells to the west and north of Jebel Medwa, while a BE2c flew overhead pinpointing targets.

At 8.45 Gordon ordered Major Evans to prepare to attack what appeared to be the main Sanusi position atop a ridge south-west of Jebel Medwa. Evans deployed Sikh No. 4 Company forward as the main firing line with a frontage of 200 yards. No. 1 Company, with the Sikh machine gun section, took up position three hundred yards behind, and a further four hundred yards to the rear was No. 2 Company. Simultaneously, the Royal Bucks Hussars and the 2/8th Middlesex (Territorials), keeping to the north-east of the *jebel*, prepared to move on the Sanusi left flank.

Shortly after the attack began Gordon ordered two companies of the New Zealand Rifle Brigade (1st Battalion) to back up the Sikhs, and another of the 2/8th Middlesex to relieve the Sikh No. 3 Company holding Jebel Medwa. He hoped that the latter would then be able to take part in the attack, but due to some garbled signalling No. 3 Company was slow in rejoining their regiment. There were further delays in getting the New Zealanders into position behind the Sikhs and in moving the RHA section forward, and, as a result, at 9.30 the Sikhs had to stop and wait. During this hiatus the Turkish artillery team returned to their gun and got it away.

As soon as the RHA guns had been moved forward and the New Zealanders had closed up behind the Sikhs, the attack was resumed. It went surprisingly quickly – by 10.15 the main group of Sanusi had broken and fled, and the ridge was taken.[5]

Behind the abandoned position was a plateau that ran north for nearly a mile. As the Sanusi withdrew across it towards the north-west, they kept up heavy fire behind them, and then dropped out of sight into Wadi Majid, which runs north towards the sea. Other Sanusi units could be seen retiring to the north and west on the plateau west of Wadi Majid, and these were now targeted by the two guns of the RHA section. At 11 o'clock the Sikhs and the New Zealand Rifles reached the edge of Wadi Majid.

With the Sanusi now in retreat, the second column was supposed to come into action, but it was nowhere to be seen. Gordon again climbed

[5] No. 3 Company 15th Sikhs had only arrived from Jebel Medwa at 10am.

to high ground, and looking to the south with his telescope, he could see the British cavalry about two miles away. He ordered the signallers to try to establish contact with the other column, but they received no answer. He then thought of contacting the reserve yeomanry regiment with General Wallace far to the rear, but the reserves were hidden in the folds of the terrain, and communication in that direction proved equally impossible.[6]

Having stopped to regroup on the edge of Wadi Majid, the Sikhs and New Zealanders now descended into the riverbed and continued the pursuit. They spent the next few hours clearing the caves and tributary gullies of Sanusi soldiers who had chosen to hide.

The two guns of the Notts RHA section, positioned just east of the *wadi*, were still firing at targets beyond the depression to the west, and a member of the section described their shooting skills:

> A camel was seen to appear as if from the ground, followed by a second. It was then realized that a hidden gully was being used as a place of concealment. Shells were dropped into it and men and animals fled in all directions. Over a hundred dead were later counted there.[7]

At 12.45pm Gordon finally received an answer from the second column. He signalled them to move northwards immediately, but, to his frustration, he then saw them continue to manoeuvre to the west for the next half hour. In the meantime, he sent off a motorcyclist to pass on the message in person. At 1.15pm he sent another signal with the heliograph: "[a]ssistance urgently required!", and at 2.30pm he tried again: "Move NE and round up enemy in front of infantry".[8] But it was of no use: the cavalry were not going to arrive in time.

Tyndale-Biscoe's left column had had its own problems, not least with the rough terrain south of Matruh.

---

[6] There were four signallers with the 15th Sikhs, but Gordon had sent two of them to Wallace at Wadi Raml to help with communications at that end. Nevertheless, neither Wallace nor Tyndale-Biscoe responded to the signals.
[7] Capt. M.T. Butt and Alec R. Cury (n. d.), *Mersa Matruh: How to See It*, p. 34.
[8] WO 95/4428, War Diary 15th Sikhs.
[9] Personal diary of Douglas Newbold, entry of 25 December 1915, Sudan Archive, Durham University.

> Five miles out in the Wadi Tuweiwia the Horse Artillery got stuck and
> the guns had to be man-handled with drag-ropes up the rocky sides. This
> delayed us three-quarters of an hour.[9]

Another hindrance had occurred four miles south of Jebel Medwa, when
the left column suddenly ran into Sanusi mounted troops, both cavalry and
camelry. This caused another hour's delay, until British machine guns forced
those Sanusi to pull back. Finally, there was the series of communication
problems, with signallers unable to read each other's messages.

Twenty-one year old Lieutenant Douglas Newbold was with the 17th
Machine Gun Squadron (assigned to the Dorset Yeomanry) and riding
with Tyndale-Biscoe's column. His diary plainly states that the message
received from Gordon at 11am (which the left column signallers
apparently failed to answer) was understood to mean that the cavalry
should go west, not north, to meet the retreating enemy, and succeeding
messages merely compounded the confusion.

> The cavalry were then sent along the end of the Taref Scarp to cut off
> the large body of Arabs that was escaping west along the shore. After a
> six-mile trot and gallop over very stony ground in an extended column
> of squadrons, the brigade wheeled to the right and made straight for the
> sea, hoping to bar their flight any further. But just then a motorcyclist
> arrived with a message saying the infantry wanted help. Half the
> mounted troops returned three miles to be met with a message cancelling
> the first. The delay gave a welcome rest to my pack-horses, which were
> done up, but prevented us overtaking the enemy.[10]

Meanwhile, the New Zealanders and Sikhs followed the Sanusi rear
guard northwards to the mouth of Wadi Majid, where some of the day's
heaviest fighting was underway. The Sanusi camp was located at the
northern end of the *wadi*, and the New Zealanders burnt all the tents as
they passed. They also captured the personal belongings and papers of
Ja'far al-'Askari.

There were some harrowing scenes when some Bedouin again
pretended to be dead or wounded and then suddenly fired at close range.
This so enraged the Sikhs that some of them picked up Bedouin who had

[10] Diary of Douglas Newbold, entry of 25 December.

done this and "threw them alive onto the bonfires of tents and bedding in their evacuated camp".[11]

At 4pm Ja'far was with 150 men of his rearguard, fighting at the northern end of Wadi Majid. As darkness fell they succeeded in crossing the narrow plain to the shore, which opposite the *wadi* is rocky. The cavalry from the two British columns had now reunited, but they could not follow onto the rocks, and so the battle was over.

The British cavalry returned that evening to Mersa Matruh, among them Douglas Newbold, who felt he had contributed little for all the day's effort. He also found conditions back at Matruh not to be ideal for a much needed rest.

> I only fired about a belt in the whole action. We did roughly forty miles in all and got into camp at 7pm after fourteen hours in the saddle, dead-tired. When we got in we found that we had to sleep in the inner, wired perimeter. Horselines, watering places, etc., had all been changed. Everybody was too tired to find his own unit in the chaos that followed in the darkness. We tied our horses up anywhere and slept in the sand where we were. Rained all night![12]

Similar sentiments were expressed by Major Hamilton of the City of London Yeomanry, part of the Composite Yeomanry Brigade, who had also ridden with the second column.

> I clicked for escorting the ambulances into camp, so it was after nine before I got to our bivouac inside the wire and had my Christmas dinner of bully and biscuits. To add to delights, it poured with rain all night.[13]

The lot of the foot-soldiers was, as usual, even more unenviable. They spent the bitterly cold night bivouacking by Jebel Medwa. They were so uncomfortable that when at 4am the order came to move they actually welcomed it. The walk back to Mersa Matruh, mostly in the dark, took them two and a half hours.

---

[11] Diary of Douglas Newbold, entry of 25 December.
[12] Ibid.
[13] Diary of Major A. S. Hamilton, City of London Yeomanry, Department of Documents, Imperial War Museum, London.

The Battle of Wadi Majid, despite delays, missing cavalry, and communication problems, was a clear victory for the British; for the Sanusi it was an ill omen for the battles to come. The various sources that give casualty figures are, for once, relatively consistent: British losses thirteen killed, fifty-one wounded, and one New Zealander taken prisoner; the Sanusi lost between 300 and 400 killed (including a number of Coastguard deserters still in their old uniforms) and more than 80 prisoners taken. One unexpected development during the day-long battle was the sudden appearance of an officer and eleven sepoys from the torpedoed ship *Moorina*. Having been employed by the Sanusi as camel drivers, they had managed to escape in the confusion of the battle.

Ja'far's account of the battle reflects the despair which had seized him and others in his army after the battle.

> At dawn on the [25th] of December 1915 we were surprised by an attack from the east where the road came from Mersa Matruh. The battle began there. At that location we had one piece of artillery, two machine guns, and a single company from the Menefa Battalion. The rest of us immediately set off in that direction from our headquarters which were located near the mouth of Wadi Majid. In fact, the *wadi* is about three miles long, and before I could get to where the picket was I saw soldiers already falling back – it became more of a rout than a retreat. I ordered the cavalry detachment off to the right to distract the attackers and to gain sufficient time to stop the panic. I saw Hajji Kamel Bey al-Bunduqi barefoot and bare-headed in full flight. Kamel Bey was a trusted friend of Nuri Pasha, but he was, in fact, a great inciter of discord between the Arab and Turkish officers. Unfortunately, he looked like me, large and with a black beard, and the rumour spread that Ja'far Pasha himself was fleeing the battlefield. With great difficulty I finally managed to stop the Menefa tribesmen from panicking by directing them to a position behind their company [already engaged with the enemy]. It was on high ground, overlooking the surrounding terrain in all directions. Once the sun came up I could see that we were completely surrounded by enemy troops.
>
> I could see two battalions of infantry advancing toward us from the [east]. There was a large mounted force to the right about one and a half miles from our cavalry in addition to the long column moving along the road towards ... Wadi Majid. And, to top it all, there was a warship lying

offshore, raking us with heavy gunfire. It was a terrifying scenario, but with great difficulty I managed to convince our men to hold their positions. The fighting continued into the afternoon without our situation getting a lot worse. But at 3pm – two hours before sunset – the attackers were able to tighten their grip and then, unbeknownst to me, many of our tribesmen left the field, taking all their baggage, in the direction of Bir 'Abdiya. I stayed with the 'Awaqir at the mouth of the *wadi* and we fought in a most frenzied manner. The New Zealand soldiers, meanwhile, seized our headquarters and all my personal effects, documents, and everything else that I had been carrying around with me fell into their hands. To this day I do not know what became of my possessions and documents ... I also had a number of maps showing the location of wells and cisterns ... which had been given to me by the German, Mannesmann.

When the sun set we withdrew, leaving our dead and wounded to the care of the enemy. All our equipment and supplies had been used up or lost. I rode my wretched mare that had been hit in the muzzle by a bullet and our broken column moved off in the direction of Bir 'Abdiya.[14]

Although the Sanusi had been roundly defeated, their casualties were small by the gory standards of the First World War. They had lost some ten per cent of their men, but they were still an army and able to fight again. The crisis among them was one of morale. The Bedouin auxiliaries who were such a large part of the Sanusi army began to understand that there was little hope of defeating the world's largest imperial power. Success in Egypt had always depended on factors that were not in the control of Ja'far, or Nuri, or Mannesmann – of even of the Grand Sanusi. There had been no uprising in the Nile Valley; the Turks had not crossed the Canal – indeed, they had not even made a second attempt after their failure in February. Therefore, after the Battle of Wadi Majid the Bedouin gradually began to trickle away from the army that had seemed invincible when a month earlier, and in their thousands, Sanusi soldiers had poured into the abandoned outposts of Sollum and Sidi Barani.

On 25 December Sayyid Ahmad and Nuri had been at Unjeila, midway between Mersa Matruh and Sidi Barani. On hearing of the army's defeat they quickly decamped to a place known as Halazin, south-east of

[14] Ja'far al-'Askari (1988), Ch. 7.   [15] Ibid.

Unjeila and away from the coast, out of the range of British naval bombardment. Surrounded by deep drifting sand, it was also a place which the armoured cars could not easily penetrate. The rest of the Sanusi army followed them there. The last to arrive were Ja'far and the 'Awaqir tribesmen who had also been the last to withdraw from Wadi Majid.

Ja'far's ill-humour turned to anger against Nuri and Sayyid Ahmad for failing to show up during the battle.

> I had hoped that Nuri would come to our assistance with the [the rest of the] Bir Wa'r Battalion [i.e. the rest of the *muhafizia*] and the two fast-firing mountain guns recently delivered by submarine. If only that had happened! It would have been of great benefit between 1 and 3 o'clock. But unfortunately the disgraceful behaviour of Kamel al-Bunduqi had broken the morale of tribesmen and soldiers and adversely affected even Sayyid Ahmad and Nuri. Instead of rushing to help us when they heard the gunfire, they ran away, not stopping for two days. There can be no doubt that ever since we had advanced to [Wadi] Majid, Nuri had become envious of me. He could not bear to see me taking the lead in the Ottoman military mission.[15]

It is true that from Unjeila Sayyid Ahmad and Nuri would have been able to hear the guns, especially those of HMS *Clematis*. But Unjeila is thirty miles west of Wadi Majid, and if they had left as soon as the first artillery was fired, around 6.30am, they could scarcely have arrived with more artillery in time to help. The horse-mounted troops were already with Ja'far. In any case, Sayyid Ahmad and Nuri would have had no way of knowing that Ja'far was in trouble. After all, he had done well with the troops at his disposal in the previous battle, at Wadi Husheifiyat. The truth was that he was at odds with the world, and probably mad at himself for having sent so many of his *muhafizia* to al-Dab'a.

A day or two after Ja'far arrived at Halazin that missing party of *muhafizia* suddenly returned – they had lost their way and spent a week wandering in the desert!

15

Arrival at Bir Hakim

THE BRITISH PRISONERS were stunned by their first glimpse of the "oasis" known as Bir Hakim. If they had imagined it to be a place of palm trees and pools of fresh water, what they now found was a desert well situated between two gravelly mounds, a small stone blockhouse, a few tower-shaped kilns, a single tent, and an ancient graveyard. The tent was inhabited by a bearded old man and his family. Otherwise, the only visible living creatures were a few donkeys, goats and a couple of dogs. There was not a palm tree in sight. Stretching to the horizon on all sides of this one-family commune was nothing but empty, stony, wind-swept desert.

Captain Ahmad went straight to the blockhouse and pitched his tent beside it. On the ground some distance away were tents for the prisoners, but the poles and ropes for erecting them had not arrived. Inevitably depressed at the prospect of spending the rest of the war in such a spot, the men rested and wrote letters home. Later there was a generous issue of rations — twelve ounces of rice and eight ounces of flour to each man — and this made everyone somewhat more cheerful. But in the evening a cold wind swept through the camp bearing sand and shrub. The prisoners set about collecting large stones and building low walls, and in the lee of these they used the tents as blankets and tried to sleep.

Week 4 of captivity (27 November to 3 December)

Early in the week Gwatkin-Williams was informed that Thomas Owen had been recaptured.

The prisoners were being guarded (at this point) by twenty Sanusi guards. Most of these had their women and children with them, which considerably increased the Arab population of the community. The guards turned out to be friendly, even occasionally inviting the prisoners to their tents. But the prisoners found their rations to be boring and insufficient to quell their hunger. Gwatkin-Williams, who kept a daily journal, wrote:

> Rice has been our only food for some time now, and we gradually get thinner. No grain of it is ever wasted. We wait eagerly until it is cooked and have half of it at a time. It is levelled into the iron wash basin and carefully divided into sectors clockwise, so that all may share exactly equally. Hunger makes us extremely jealous and watchful of any infringement of this. We squat round the basin in the dust and eat our portion like wolves as soon as it is cool enough. The infinitesimal tea ration is kept for the evenings and is impatiently awaited. The nights are very long and we have no lights and must lay shivering on the hard ground for fourteen hours.[1]

With the help of the natives the prisoners were at least able to improve their rice cooking method so that the rice was dry when cooked and not like porridge. The tea was their only luxury. After it was drunk the leaves were dried in the sun and smoked in lieu of tobacco.

Gradually the tents were set up. The prisoners were divided into five messes of about eighteen men each. Each mess had its own enamel saucepan and basin; each man had his own spoon and tea glass. Work parties were organized and everyone went (under armed escort) to gather firewood; or else they walked two miles north to a disused well and set about clearing it of rocks and debris as the rainy season was about to begin. During one of the outings some of the men discovered wheel tracks in the sand a mile to the south of Bir Hakim. The Turks had a few motor vehicles during the Turco-Italian War and the Italians had many of them, so the tracks were probably three or four years old.

[1] WO 106/1543.

On 2 December a caravan of sixty camels arrived from the Egyptian frontier to collect water. By talking with the visiting Arabs Basil learned that Sollum was about four or five days distant.

During the afternoon of the following day there was great excitement among the Arabs when a sheep was found to have been killed by a wolf. Most of the carcass was given to the prisoners, thus providing them with their first meat in a fortnight. But diarrhoea and dysentery were now common ailments among them.

Week 5 (4 to 10 December)

During this week the food situation improved, at least temporarily. On the 4th the ration again included flour as well as rice. This, together with the meat provided on the previous day, made the evening meal more copious than usual. The men were told that a herd of goats was on its way and that in the future meat would be available more often. In the meantime another fortuitous event provided everyone with meat for two days. A young camel fell down the well and drowned. Gwatkin-Williams had himself lowered down, and he put a rope around the carcass so that it could be pulled to the surface. Mr Rowlands, the Quarter-Master, volunteered his services as "butcher" and the animal was skinned and cut into pieces for cooking.

Sunday, 5 December, marked the end of the first month of captivity. The prisoners were given Sundays off as a holiday – that is, there were no work details. They began the habit, which continued throughout their captivity, of having a Sunday evening church service. This was put into jeopardy early on, however, when Captain Ahmad heard them singing "God save the King". He threatened that if they sang that again there would be no more church services.

One of the guards managed to shoot and kill the wolf.

Week 6 (11 to 17 December)

Early in the week Captain Ahmad, who seemed to relish revealing news which the British would consider bad, boasted about the defection of the Egyptian coastguards to the Turks. Gwatkin-Williams wrote a letter to Nuri Pasha asking if there was any possibility of a prisoner exchange. On

15 December Captain Ahmad collected all the prisoners' letters and left for Sollum with forty camels. He said that he would bring back special foods for Christmas, including eggs, chickens, and other such luxuries. He also promised to talk to Nuri on the prisoners' behalf about such matters as inadequate rations and the possibility of a prisoner exchange.

The nights remained cold with heavy fog, but there was still little rain. Nevertheless, the Arabs were certain that the winter rains would begin soon, and so work on clearing the disused well was accelerated.

The ragged state of the prisoners' clothes now made them look like ninety-four Robinson Crusoes. Someone managed to make a needle out of a piece of bone, and thread was pulled from some canvas that was once a sail for one of the *Tara's* lifeboats. The rice and flour bags were in great demand for making clothes.

At the end of the week (17 December) Thomas Owen was brought back after a month's absence. His punishment was relatively light; in fact, some of his shipmates thought it was too light considering how much they had been made to suffer after his disappearance. Muhammad Effendi smacked his face and had him confined within a dry cistern for a few hours. Owen was reluctant to talk, but he was apparently well-treated as in his pockets were soap and matches. When he was recaptured he was taken to Sollum before being brought to Bir Hakim. The journey by camel from Sollum to the prisoner camp took five days.

On the day of Owen's return Gwatkin-Williams was told that Captain Ahmad would not be coming back. But the good news that the prisoners would now be in the charge of Muhammad Effendi was offset by the likelihood that if Captain Ahmad was not coming back, the food and supplies that he had promised to bring them would not arrive either.

Week 7 (18 to 24 December)

This week there was new concern that rations were becoming short. There was no longer any sugar, and there had not been any tea for some days. The diet was rice and, every other day, a bit of meat. Nine men went out foraging and returned with seven hundred snails. These helped to diminish hunger but were not in the least palatable. Finally, on 22 December, nine camels arrived from the east bringing rice and flour – but not the tea, biscuits, and clothes that the men had been hoping for.

The prisoners had been without soap for weeks and were now verminous despite boiling their clothes and then drying them in the sun. All were covered with sores from scratching.

On 23 December it rained from 10am until 3pm, and water poured into the tents making everyone wet, cold, and miserable. The next day the officers built a 3ft stone wall round their tent – something the rest of the men had already done for their own tents. While they were doing this a Turkish officer called Lieutenant Mustafa arrived on his way to Sollum. He was amiable to the prisoners and offered to talk to Nuri on their behalf. Gwatkin-Williams then wrote another letter to Nuri listing the ninety-four prisoners by name and including a copy of the inventory of the money and valuables taken by Captain Ahmad. Other prisoners also wrote letters, and Lt. Mustafa said he would try to get them delivered to the British.

Christmas, 1915

The day was clear and cold. The men carrying out the well-works were given the day off on the understanding that they would work the next day (a Sunday) instead. The prisoners spent the day reminiscing about home and focusing on the preparation of the special food that was to be their Christmas dinner, and for which everyone had contributed part of his daily food ration for the past week. The three senior officers (Captain Gwatkin-Williams, Lieutenant Apcar, and Edward Tanner) made an "official" call on Muhammad Effendi, who responded cordially, offering Arabic bread and sugar, plus a quantity of white beans to put into the day's soup. Gwatkin-Williams and Tanner then visited the men in their tents. Celebrations began with a rice breakfast at 7am. At midday there was soup made out of a pound of goats' bones thickened with rice and the donated beans. In the mid-afternoon there was a special "pudding" that had been prepared by Mr Richardson, the Engineer from the SS *Moorina*. This was an amazing concoction of flour, rice, and sugar, the whole being boiled for five hours in the ample – now much too ample – trousers of Edward Tanner. Finally, in the evening, there was Arabic bread cooked in the ashes of the campfires. Gwatkin-Williams later wrote of this formidable day-long feast: "[I]t will long remain in our minds as the most enjoyable meal

[2] WO 106/1543, entry for 25 December 1915.

we have ever eaten!"[2] Later the men gathered round a fire and sang Christmas carols and then went to bed with the strange sensation of having full stomachs.

During the night a messenger arrived with news of the Battle of Wadi Majid, and then the Arab women began to wail.

16

Halazin

THE WESTERN FRONTIER FORCE spent Boxing Day resting at Mersa Matruh. The foot-soldiers tramped into camp just after daylight, when the cavalry – who, finding the horselines moved the previous evening, had tied up their animals anywhere they could and then slept in the sand – were just beginning to stir and look for their proper quarters. When Douglas Newbold, shattered from fatigue, finally got back to his bunk and kitbag in the morning, he found that his revolver and his camera had been stolen.

General Wallace knew that the campaign's momentum was now in his favour, and he had no intention of letting up the pressure on the Sanusi. On 27 December he informed his officers that another expedition was to be sent out the next day under Brigadier-General Lord Lucan. The objective this time was a large Bedouin camp at Jerawla, twelve miles to the south-east. So on the afternoon of the 28th another large British force left Matruh – six squadrons of Yeomanry and Australian Light Horse, two sections of artillery, two armoured cars, and infantry from the Sikh and New Zealand regiments. It searched for the Sanusi for three days but could not find them: the Bedouin stayed out of sight and the column had be to content with the destruction of eighty Arab tents and the rounding up of more sheep and camels.

In the meantime, British soldiers made a grisly find near the site of the recent battle:

a white man's body, stripped, on the eastern end of the southern edge of
the gully. [He was] one bruise from head to foot, evidently flogged to
death – probably the New Zealander left in their hands on Christmas
Day.[1]

Perhaps this was Bedouin revenge for the killing of the sheikh from the
Unjeila *zawiya*. Or retaliation for the Sikhs' burning Arabs alive in Wadi
Majid. Despite the fact that the New Zealander's death was the only
incident of its kind, it was enough to instil the idea that the enemy killed
prisoners and mutilated their bodies.

There was no further excitement until New Year's Eve when the Royal
Scots began celebrating hogmanay. They marched through the various
regimental camps playing their bagpipes and cadging drinks from obliging
officers. As their spirits rose the skirling grew wilder until, in the early
hours, sheer exhaustion finally got the upper hand of Scottish high spirits.
After the sun rose on the first morning of 1916, yeomanry officer Major
Hamilton went to get water and found an impressively large drummer
asleep with his instrument in some bushes near the beach.

On New Year's Day two Model T Fords went out to repair breaks in the
telegraph line east of Matruh. An aeroplane providing cover spotted
another Arab camp – eighty more tents – at Jebel Howeimil, thirty-five
miles to the south-east. Another column formed to deal with it – this time
under Tyndale-Biscoe – but then the weather turned. Days of torrential
rain followed, changing the desert into a quagmire and making further
operations impossible for nearly two weeks. Finally, on the 13th, the
terrain was dry enough for the column to move. It marched along the
coast to al-Baqqush, where camp was made, and the next day it turned
south. The cavalry, going ahead, destroyed the tents but again there was
little sign of the Sanusi. A troop of the Australian Light Horse brought in
one old man who had apparently been ill-treated by his fellow Bedouin.
Royle, who was with the column as intelligence officer, interviewed him
and learned that "two Turkish officers with eight men and two camels
loaded with dynamite were on their way to blow up the railway line east
of Dabaa".[2] The cavalry had also seen an alarm beacon to the west.
According to the Arab, if the cavalry had advanced in the direction of the

---

[1] Diary of Douglas Newbold, entry for 29 December.
[2] WO 95/4428, War Diary 15th Sikhs, entry for 14 January 1916.

26. *Above*: HMS *Tara*, formerly SS *Hibernia* of the London and North Western Railway Company. British–Sanusi relations quickly broke down when the *Tara* was torpedoed by the *U-35* and her crew handed over to Enver's brother, Nuri Bey.

27. *Below*: The *U-35* off the Adriatic port of Cattaro. Photograph courtesy of the Imperial War Museum, London: Q24049.

28. Kapitänleutnant Waldemar Kophamel, commander of the German submarine *U-35*. Photograph courtesy of the Imperial War Museum, London: HU53919.

29. View from the Western Frontier Force camp at Mersa Matruh, looking north towards the lagoon. The Coastguard fort can just be made out in the centre background.

30. The Egyptian Coastguard fort at Mersa Matruh. (Photo taken by Cecil Snow in 1911.)

31. View from the Western Frontier Force camp at Mersa Matruh, looking south towards the desert.

32. The Dorset Yeomanry resting at Umm al-Rakhm after the Battle of Wadi Majid, Christmas Day 1915.

33. Column of cavalry moving down Umm al-Rakhm hill towards Mersa Matruh late on Christmas Day 1915, after the Battle of Wadi Majid.

34. Ja'far al-'Askari, wounded and taken prisoner by the British, arrives at Sidi Barani after the Battle of al-'Aqaqir.

35. The burnt-out Coastguard station at Sidi Barani as it appeared when the WFF arrived on 28 February 1916

36. Supplies arriving by ship at Sidi Barani (late February or early March 1916).

37. The WFF's two BE2c biplanes at Sidi Barani after the Battle of al-'Aqaqir (late February or early March 1916). Note the hangar being erected in the background.

38. An Arab guide with the Western Frontier Force.

39. Two Armoured Cars in the Libyan Desert, shortly before the rescue of the *Tara* crew.

40. An Armoured Car in the Libyan Desert. The man is Arthur Jenkins, who drove one of the supply vehicles during the rescue expedition.

41. Interrogating Sanusi prisoners in March 1916. Captain Mervyn Macdonnell, Lawrence's Intelligence colleague at GHQ in Cairo, is the man in the centre with the coat over his arm. Leaning forward, fourth from the right, is Captain Royle. The location is likely to be Bir Wa'r.

42. Captured Turkish machine guns and ammunition at Bir Wa'r.

43 and 44. Scenes of the rescue at Bir Hakim, 17 March 1916.

45. Brigadier-General Laycock with *Tara* Captain Gwatkin-Williams at Bir Hakim, 17 March 1916.

46. The Duke of Westminster at Bir Hakim, 17 March 1916.

47. *Above*: Sir Hugh Richard Arthur Grosvenor, the Duke of Westminster, at a fancy dress party in Cairo in 1912. (The Duke is the top figure in the back row.)

48. *Opposite, above*: Claud H. Williams at the wheel of a Model T Ford. A New Zealander, Williams was the commander of Light Car Patrol No. 5 during the skirmish at Qirba, 3 February 1917.

49. *Opposite, below*: The citadel at Siwa, taken on the day the British expeditionary force entered the town, 5 February 1917. Photograph courtesy of the Imperial War Museum, London: Q58072.

50. Sayyid Ahmad al-Sharif al-Sanusi (seated) and ex-Coastguard officer Muhammad Saleh Harb (on the right). This picture was taken after the two men had left Libya in a German U-boat.

beacon, they would have come upon the missing residents of the Howeimil encampment.[3] Royle was more interested in the Turkish party planning to blow up the railway. He suggested that he should himself go with twenty men on camels in pursuit, but Tyndale-Biscoe rejected the idea as being too dangerous.

Most of the column marched back to Mersa Matruh on 16 January, although several units, including two squadrons of Australian Light Horse, continued to ride east to al-Dab'a for redeployment elsewhere. The expedition had been difficult, with the cavalry sometimes covering as much as fifty miles in a day, while the foot-soldiers had to cope with long marches on ground which alternated between deep mud and jagged rock.

The whereabouts of the Sanusi army was finally revealed on 18 January. On that day Royle was with a cavalry patrol that brought in four men from the convict camp at Sollum. They had been captured by the Sanusi and, having escaped, had been picked up by the patrol. They told Royle that the Sanusi camp was located twelve miles beyond Bir Shola (or twenty-four miles south-west of Matruh). According to the convicts Sayyid Ahmad was there, but he was now preparing to leave for Siwa. Ja'far and Nuri were also there with an army of about 3,000 men.

General Wallace again wanted to move quickly but first he wanted confirmation of the convicts' report. He sent Royle with one of the RFC pilots to reconnoitre the area by air. This was Royle's first flight with the WFF, and it was a particularly important one. With Lt. Rowden at the controls of the BE2c they took off from Matruh beach early on 19 January, the rising sun veiled in clouds behind them. Scattered everywhere across the desert were pools of water, especially around Bir Shola. Further on, in a hollow area amid ridges to both east and west, was the Arab camp. Royle estimated the number of tents to be 350; of these about a hundred were white, single-poled Egyptian Army tents left at Sollum and Sidi Barani by the British, the rest being Bedouin tents. Clearly visible at the south-west edge of the camp were the two tents of Sayyid Ahmad himself. Royle also counted some 300 camels, some of which were white Coastguard thoroughbreds, and confirmed the number of men at the camp to be about 3,000.

---

[3] In the 1920s Ja'far told George MacMunn that this was the camp of the *muhafizia* sent before the battle on Christmas Day to attack al-Dab'a, but this seems implausible. Why would trained soldiers leave their tents behind, even if they were lost?

The only defences visible from the air were four empty gun emplacements to the east of the camp, but large pools of water were around the site in every direction and this could only benefit the defenders. On his map Royle pin-pointed the camp's location at a place called Halazin.

In the meantime, Ja'far watched the reconnaissance flight from below.

> When we had been at Bir Tunis [Halazin] for four or five days a British aeroplane flew overhead to view our positions. We, meanwhile, were sending patrols to Bir 'Abdiya [on the coast] and Wadi Majid to watch their movements.[4]

At 10.30am Rowden and Royle were back at Matruh beach. The flight had lasted an hour and three quarters, and now the weather was turning bad again. There followed two hours of heavy rain, and the next day's operations had to be postponed. There was a positive side to the delay, however, as more South African infantry were expected imminently. In the afternoon the sun reappeared, and the skies were clear through the night.

On 20 January the weather seemed to be holding. In the morning the first troops of the 2nd South African Infantry began to arrive by sea. In the afternoon, however, there was a near disaster when one of the aeroplanes took off from the beach and immediately had engine trouble. In the time it took the pilot to turn around, the beach had become crowded with soldiers, and he was forced to ditch in the lagoon. Fortunately, neither he nor the observer (who was not Royle) was injured; they were quickly picked up by a boat and their machine was salvaged.

That evening the officers were told that the next move against the Sanusi would be on the 22nd. This time the force would leave in the afternoon for Bir Shola, where it would camp for the night, and the next morning it would attack the Sanusi at Halazin. Four weeks had passed since the encounter at Wadi Majid, and the whole period had been spent in preparation for the coming operation. Some men ventured to speculate that this time they would crush the Sanusi army once and for all. Others were more cautious, believing that the changeable weather could be an important factor on the day.

On 22 January an early air reconnaissance confirmed that the Sanusi

[4] Ja'far al-'Askari (1988), Ch. 7.

position had not changed. In the afternoon the force left Matruh, first the cavalry and then, at 4pm, the main force commanded by General Wallace personally. The twelve miles to Bir Shola were covered without mishap, although the night's bivouac there was predictably uncomfortable. Fires were not allowed and, in the face of all British hopes, it rained.

After what was for many a sleepless night, the usual two columns formed before dawn (6am) in the best approximation of silence that thousands of men with horses and camels could manage. On the right the infantry moved on a compass bearing which was based on Royle's map reference of several days earlier. The cavalry rode in echelon formation to the left, slightly in front of the infantry. Seven miles were covered in this manner, when (at 8.30am) the quasi silence was broken by distant artillery. The cavalry was already being fired on by Turkish gunners, who were two miles away towards the south-west.

Ja'far and his army had also suffered from the rain and the cold of the preceding night: "We were extremely uncomfortable and grumbled that the heavens were angry with us."[5] An hour before dawn his cavalry commander, 'Uthman al-Arna'uti, galloped into camp with the news that a long British column was heading their way.

Ja'far was satisfied that his present position, eight miles south of the road, with mud and water pools encircling the entire Sanusi camp, were to his army's advantage. Indeed the site had been chosen to ensure that the armoured cars would be virtually useless to the British. Moreover, for the first time the whole Turco-Sanusi force was going to fight together. Sayyid Ahmad and Nuri had arrived with the tribal battalions that had previously been kept back in Sidi Barani, and the *muhafizia* were back together again.

At first light Ja'far sent the *muhafizia* to take up defensive positions on a slight rise half a mile to the east of the campsite, that is, in the direction of the approaching British force. The eastern sky then cleared, and the battle started just as the sun broke the horizon.

Colonel Gordon, who was now again in command of the infantry,[6] rode forward to confer with Tyndale-Biscoe, whose guns had begun to return the Turkish fire. The brigadier told Gordon that he wanted the infantry to make a frontal attack while the cavalry kept back and attempted to work around the Sanusi flanks.

[5] Ja'far al-'Askari (1988), Ch. 7.
[6] General Wallace was now far to the rear with the supply train and ambulances.

Returning to the infantry column Gordon placed the Sikhs in forward attack formation with the South African and New Zealand battalions to the rear in support. Half a mile further back a small combined reserve of yeomanry and infantry would await the call to reinforce the attackers where needed. At the start of the action the Sanusi had the advantage of the light. Looking into the dawn, they could easily see the British force. The latter, however, had trouble seeing the Sanusi, and so a stone cairn, lying due west and representing the correct bearing, was given as the objective.

> The ground ... was absolutely flat, covered with small stones and small scraggy bushes about one foot high; and it was totally devoid of any cover ... further, the continual effect of mirage was most disconcerting, concealing the movements of the enemy and rendering effective artillery support exceedingly difficult.[7]

The Sanusi army had formed a crescent-shaped front about a mile and a half long. At 10am the Sikhs began to advance on the crescent's centre, which at that point was a mile away, while the South Africans and the New Zealanders followed behind. Initially, the attackers moved quickly, but the Turks had five machine guns – two in the centre directly ahead of the Sikhs, two to the right of centre, and another on the left (or southern) side of the formation – and facing so much firepower, the forward line eventually stalled. The Sikhs were using two machine guns (one of which jammed off and on throughout the day), and these were backed up by the four guns (two sections) of the Notts Battery RHA, which opened fire at 1,200 yards. At roughly midday, the British observed parties of Sanusi trying to move around both of their flanks. The Sanusi move on the right, 2,000 yards away, was led by Nuri, who had taken a Turkish machine gun section from the centre of his line, mounted the two guns onto camels, and was racing to the north to extend the crescent's arc and threaten the Sikhs from that side. A simultaneous attempt by the Sanusi to extend the

---

[7] WO 95/4428, War Diary 15th Sikhs.
[8] Several hours into the battle Ja'far told Sayyid Ahmad that he should escape while he could but to leave behind the force that usually guarded him, including the "Student Battalion". Sayyid Ahmad headed south, further into the desert, with only a small entourage.

opposite (left) side of the crescent was led by Ja'far, with the Sanusi cavalry and the so-called "Student Battalion", which was normally assigned to protect the Grand Sanusi.[8] In an attempt to counter Nuri's move to the north, Gordon sent two companies of South Africans to cover the flank, but as they moved, they were quickly checked by Nuri's machine guns. Gordon then sent a company of New Zealanders with machine guns to reinforce the South Africans, but Nuri's men continued to outflank them. A company of Royal Scots was then sent to the right also. These moves and counter-moves on the right greatly extended the Sanusi front, but the threat to Gordon's right column was eventually blocked.

On the left, meanwhile, Ja'far's men were posing an even greater threat to the attackers. At first the British cavalry was merely unable to advance, but by early afternoon it was being forced to the centre of the field behind the Sikhs, while the Sanusi cavalry made penetrating attacks in the same direction. Reinforcements from the reserve were unable to stop the left flank from being driven in; and, to make matters worse for the British, the Turks were now using their artillery on this side as well. At this point, the New Zealand Rifle Brigade played a crucial role in the battle. Gordon had sent one company from this unit to the right, and another to the front line immediately left of the Sikhs. He now sent the remaining two companies to bolster Tyndale-Biscoe's left flank, and with their support the situation on the left was brought back under control.

Throughout the difficulties on the British flanks the fighting in the centre was intense, with the Sikh and New Zealand front line gradually advancing, and the Sanusi line slowly withdrawing. Just before 2pm the attackers could see the Sanusi camp 800 yards directly ahead; it also became clear that the objective of the withdrawing Sanusi was to reach their entrenchments just behind the camp. Both sides fought with courage and determination for an hour, until the South Africans (those had been sent to the right flank) were able to join the Sikh front line. Then Sikhs, New Zealanders and South Africans were able to work their way through the Sanusi camp and beyond, eventually reaching the final line of trenches. By the time they got there most of the Sanusi army was nearly a mile to the west in full retreat.

It was mid-afternoon and a crucial battle was over. The Sanusi army had given the WFF some anxious moments, but they had been forced from the

---

[9] Ja'far al-'Askari (1988), Ch. 7.

field in the end. Although British respect for Ja'far's training and handling of the Sanusi army was mounting, this would have been small consolation for Ja'far, who knew that his soldiers would not be able to keep this up indefinitely. The British reported about 200 Sanusi and Turkish dead that day, and estimated a further 500 wounded. Their own, more precise, casualties were thirty–one dead and 291 wounded.

Ja'far's analysis of why his army lost at Halazin reflects an increasing strain in his relations with Nuri.

> By 3 o'clock in the afternoon our front extended for over five miles. Nuri had withdrawn towards the west with his machine guns instead of coordinating with the other sections of our front. The resulting breakdown in communications meant a loss of central command, with each unit having to act on its own until, finally, the enemy were able to push into our empty camp with its few tents and bits of baggage, all of which they burnt.[9]

The defeated Sanusi moved twenty miles west, where there was another well belonging to the Awlad 'Ali. The British cavalry, both men and animals, were simply too exhausted to pursue them.

The cavalries of both armies had churned up mud everywhere, making the battlefield look like a scene from the Western Front. The Sikh Regiment marched back across it in extended order through a rear guard of New Zealanders and Royal Scots, stopping here and there to pick up the wounded. In the process the Sikhs' British officers humorously greeted one of their own, Lieutenant Barstow, who that day had arrived at Matruh, having been in hospital in Alexandria, and had "borrowed" a car only to arrive just as the battle was ending. Typical of the Western Desert campaign was the sheer misery of that night when, carrying stretchers of wounded, the soldiers finally reached their bivouac at Bir Shola in the dark. The supply train – with medicines, food, water, and blankets – was somewhere in the distance still stuck in the mud. It rained at intervals through the night, and a torrential downpour began just before sunrise. It took two days for the whole force to get back to Mersa Matruh.

17

The Battle of al-'Aqaqir

FEBRUARY BEGAN WITH a miracle. The days became bright and sunny. The mud dried and gave way to flowers that burst forth in a dazzling display of colour.

> Everywhere were great fields of asphodel growing waist high, and in favoured spots were great yellow globes of ranunculus, scarlet anemones and purple iris.[1]

In another sign of change great flocks of birds arrived heading north. The men of both armies felt their spirits lifted by the arrival of spring.

Ja'far's soldiers needed this boost to their morale more than their opponents. The Sanusi army was now reduced to about 1,600 men, and only 400 of these were *muhafizia*.[2] Their heavy weapons were one quick-

---

[1] Anonymous, 'In the Western Desert of Egypt', *Blackwood's Edinburgh Magazine*, February 1917, p. 215.

[2] This figure for the *muhafizia* seems low given that the battalion had numbered 1,000 men at the start of the campaign. Nevertheless, Ja'far says explicitly in his memoirs (Ch. 7) that at al-'Aqaqir "there were only 400 regulars left, and about the same number in the Menefa Battalion, plus a small section of Awlad 'Ali". Unless the soldiers were deserting from this battalion as well as the tribal ones, which seems unlikely, this implies that 60% of the *muhafizia* had been lost at Wadi Majid and Halazin!

firing (QF) gun and three machine guns,[3] and these they hauled around sandy desert and rugged *wadis* where armoured cars – a constant threat now that the mud had dried – could not manoeuvre. But their greatest trial was the erratic supply of food from Bir Wa'r. At one point Ja'far's men were waiting for a supply caravan to arrive, when food ran out completely. The local Bedouin had to point out which of the desert plants were edible – and this was all their soldiers had to eat for several days.

After their defeat at Halazin, the Sanusi army stayed near the coast where Ja'far and his scouts could keep an eye on British movements. Ja'far personally reconnoitred as far as the outskirts of Umm al-Rakhm and once observed a British patrol near the shore. He also came upon the tyre tracks of a British biplane that had landed in the same area. In fact, it was not long before an RFC observer spotted the Sanusi army, and then there were regular reconnaissance flights overhead. With the British informed of their whereabouts, the Sanusi were liable to be attacked at any time, so Ja'far and Nuri decided to withdraw to an area of dunes called al-'Aqaqir, south of the Khedivial Road, fifteen miles from Sidi Barani. The Sanusi army assembled there and waited.

But what were they waiting for? It must have been obvious to the Turks and Arabs that another battle would destroy them as a fighting force. They knew that the British were receiving reinforcements and more supplies with each passing day. In contrast, their own army was diminishing. The soldiers were weak with hunger and demoralized by their defeat in the two previous battles; and the Bedouin were continuing to leave. Ja'far would write that he argued strongly with Nuri in favour of withdrawing back to the Libyan plateau where their supplies were secure and where they could be in direct contact with the German submarines.[4] Nevertheless, they decided first to wait for another caravan of food and supplies and then to withdraw. But the caravan did not arrive. The soldiers were starving. And their next encounter with the British would be right there in the dunes of al-'Aqaqir.

Amazingly, even with the Sanusi in this desperate situation, occasional volunteers managed to avoid British patrols and to arrive at al-'Aqaqir. 'Abd al-Rahman 'Azzam was a young Egyptian nationalist who had studied in London before the war. His memoirs provide a fascinating

---

[3] Jafar Pasha Al-Askari (2003), *A Soldier's Story*, p. 86.
[4] Ibid., p. 88.

picture of the Sanusi camp at this time.[5] 'Azzam had left his home-town of Cairo and gone to a village near Alexandria, where he had an introduction to two Bedouin guides. The three men then dodged British patrols and managed to cross the Western Desert in eight days. 'Azzam recalled the warm reception he received from Nuri, to whom he handed over correspondence and maps from the Egyptian nationalists. He was very favourably impressed by Nuri, with whom he ate on that first evening – perhaps the usual meagre rations being supplemented by 'Azzam's own supplies – and they had a long conversation that ranged over nationalist politics, the war and the military situation there in the desert. 'Azzam admitted that he needed military training, and Nuri presented him with a new gun, assigning another volunteer, a deserter from the British-led Egyptian Army, to provide the necessary instruction.[6]

'Azzam was amazed to find at al-'Aqaqir someone whom he had known in London, a certain Sayyid al-Dasuqi, who told of his own adventures in joining the Sanusi. An Egyptian doctor, al-Dasuqi had left England at the start of the war and made his way from there to Turkey, where he had taken passage on a smugglers' boat bringing weapons to the Sanusi.[7]

After the warm receptions given to him by Nuri and al-Dasuqi, 'Azzam was inclined to overlook the desperate predicament which the Sanusi were in. He found the atmosphere of their desert camp irresistibly romantic – the stories of battle, the Arabic songs and poetry around evening campfires, the beauty of the desert in early spring, all of which combined to enchant the young Egyptian volunteer.

But during the last week of February came the inevitable news that the British were again on the march. Ja'far rushed to the northern side of the dunes with the Menefa Battalion, taking the quick-firing mountain gun, and two of the machine guns. They had barely reached the northern edge of al-'Aqaqir when they spotted the British force moving along the shore just two miles away, preparing to camp for the night. It was too late in the day to fight a battle, but there was at least time to surprise the British with a few shells from the mountain gun.

---

[5] See Ralph M. Coury (1998), *The Making of an Egyptian Nationalist: The Early Years of Azzam Pasha.*
[6] Ibid., pp. 101–4.   [7] Ibid., p. 104.

At Mersa Matruh great changes had taken place in the formation of the Western Frontier Force. The 15th Sikhs had been recalled at the end of January for redeployment in India, and they were replaced by the 1st and 3rd Battalions of the South African Infantry. (The 2nd Battalion had already arrived and fought at Halazin.) Lieutenant-Commander Lister's detachment of Royal Navy armoured cars, the forward unit of the original Emergency Squadron, was also recalled. The six RNACD Rolls Royces returned to Alexandria and were replaced by a Light Armoured Car Brigade of twelve vehicles, also Rolls Royces, under the command of Hugh Richard Arthur Grosvenor, the Duke of Westminster.

Other steps were taken to improve the WFF's mobility and supply lines. By mid-February two thousand camels had been allocated to the force. Before, the columns had been hampered by a limited "radius of action" – that is, a maximum force of three battalions of infantry and six squadrons of cavalry could operate out of Matruh for only five days at a time. By using camel transport for the supply train (in place of horse-drawn wagons) the columns would be completely mobile and not have to return to base after every action.

Another significant change occurred when General Maxwell visited Mersa Matruh early in the month. General Wallace asked Maxwell to relieve him of his command "on the ground of age" (he was fifty-seven). A week later (10 February) Major-General William Peyton arrived as the new GOC. Forty-nine years old and 6ft 6in tall, Peyton cut an impressive figure, and he had the military record to match. He had fought with Kitchener in the Sudan (where he had been dangerously wounded and had his horse speared beneath him); he had served in the South African War; and in the present war he had commanded a mounted division at Gallipoli. Peyton was determined to conclude the campaign quickly and successfully. However, he had only been at Matruh a day when air reconnaissance reported that five hundred Sanusi soldiers had invaded the oasis of Bahariyya (near Fayum) and were in striking distance of the Nile Valley.

This unexpected move by the Sanusi was headed by Muhammad Saleh Harb. British aeroplanes tried to drop bombs on this force, but the Sanusi soldiers countered by mingling with the oasis' six thousand local inhabitants, who welcomed them. Other oases within easy reach of the Nile – Dakhla, Kharga and Farafra – were also threatened and likely to fall to (or to welcome) the invaders, so General Maxwell was now obliged to create a whole new command, the Southern Force, under Major-General John Adye, who hurriedly deployed some 25,000 men at points between Wadi Natrun (north-west of Cairo) and Aswan in order to protect the Nile Valley from invasion.

For the normally imperturbable Maxwell this new Sanusi offensive came as a blow. He was scheduled to leave Egypt within weeks. The campaign had seemed to be entering its final phase and he had hoped to see off the Sanusi threat before his departure. Suddenly he was again facing the possibility that German and Turkish schemes for undermining the British occupation of Egypt would become a reality. He wired the War Office that he was worried about the fact that Sayyid Ahmad still had three thousand warriors at Siwa, enough to occupy the other oases near the Nile, and that if this happened "five hundred miles of Nile Valley" would be threatened. He added that "it would take but little enemy pressure [to incite the local inhabitants to Holy War] which when started would spread rapidly" – just as von Oppenheim had planned. Despite this new source of worry, Maxwell decided to complete the defeat of the remnants of the Sanusi force in the north and to take only defensive action in the south.

Meanwhile, at WFF headquarters Peyton had orders to reoccupy Sollum as soon as possible. His first move, therefore, was to set up a supply depot at Unjeila (thirty miles west of Matruh) and to that aim a column of 800 camels carrying twenty-eight days' rations for 1,400 men (plus fodder for the animals themselves) left Matruh on 13 February. Accompanying this "British caravan" was a small force with two of the new armoured cars. Within three days the depot was established, and on 20 February a column (under Brig.-Gen. Lukin) left Matruh with orders to take back Sidi Barani. Its infantry (2,000 men) were mainly the newly arrived South Africans; and the cavalry, about 330 "sabres", consisted of three squadrons of The Queen's Own Dorset Yeomanry plus another of the Royal Bucks Hussars. They reached Unjeila on the 22nd, but when they arrived there was news that they would be in battle sooner than expected. The occupation of Barani would have to wait because air reconnaissance had found the Sanusi camp at al-'Aqaqir.

Lukin acted quickly. He left the New Zealanders and Royal Scots to guard the supplies at Unjeila, and with the rest of the column he marched twelve miles on the 23rd and a further sixteen miles on the 24th to a point

where a riverbed called Wadi Maqtila opened out onto the beach a few
miles north of al-'Aqaqir. Friday, 25 February, was declared a rest day for
the men to recover from the two day's march. Then, Lukin hoped, another
silent approach by night would catch the Sanusi off-guard at dawn on the
26th.

The day's rest on the beach was much appreciated:

> Our camp was on the shores of a beautiful little bay, entirely sheltered
> from inland by lime and sandstone mounds. The troops bathed
> sumptuously all day, as the weather was warm, and only those detailed for
> water-duty underwent the unpleasantness of being industriously sniped
> at on their way to and from the wells which were in an uncovered
> position.[8]

The presence of enemy snipers at Wadi Maqtila seems strangely
inconsistent with Lukin's plan for a stealthy night approach and a surprise
attack at dawn. Nevertheless, preparations continued for the night march
until, at 5.30pm, with the sun on the horizon, it was the British column
which was taken by surprise.

> All was ready to move off at night-fall when a distant boom was heard
> followed immediately by the whining of a shell, and plump it came into
> the middle of the horse lines ... Then they came hot and fast ... it was
> ... alarming to see the little gun-team drivers attempting to saddle up
> their massive pairs of horses amidst the crash of falling shells and the
> showers of sand and clouds of dust which they threw up ... Our guardian
> angel was at hand, however, for some such providential influence caused
> the enemy battery commander to increase his range. Thereafter, for two
> hours, we watched his shells falling harmlessly into the sea about 10 yards
> from the beach. Only one poor man was killed and by a shell which
> dropped amidst a group of 14 but did not explode. With 4,000 men and
> horses congregated in the little basin-like cove ... it can be imagined
> what loss we should have sustained had our opponent's judgement of the
> range been 50 yards more accurate.[9]

The force had been observed not just by enemy snipers, of course. Ja'far

[8] Capt M. T. Butt and Alec R. Cury (n. d.), p. 39.   [9] Ibid., pp. 39–40.

himself was only a mile or two away with the Menefa battalion, and that same afternoon he had watched the British pickets and tried to guess the precise position of the British camp.

> We waited until shortly before sunset … and opened fire with our mountain gun, aiming for that part of the shoreline where we thought most of the force would be concentrated. The enemy then replied with his own guns, but it was soon dark making it impossible to continue fighting.[10]

The British lost one soldier dead and another wounded, and the night march was abandoned.

In the dark Jaʿfar rushed back to al-ʿAqaqir knowing that the salvos of artillery had created more noise than damage and done little to change the course of the coming confrontation.

> When we got back … I told Nuri that we had better get away [from al-ʿAqaqir] and move west as fast as possible. Without doubt, the British would attack us the next day with many more men than we could muster and with much better equipment. Unfortunately, we did not leave right away as we should have done. Instead, we spent the night right where we were, intending to move off before dawn. The next morning, before we were ready to decamp, one of our patrols arrived from the coast with the news that the enemy was already on the move, and that, in fact, our patrols had already exchanged fire with the British cavalry. The reality was worse than that – the British were already entering the dunes on the north side of al-ʿAqaqir.[11]

In this passage from his memoirs Jaʿfar implies that Nuri was responsible for waiting until morning to try to get away. Certainly, Nuri outranked Jaʿfar, although the latter was still responsible for the Sanusi army. Whoever made the final decision for the army to spend that night at al-ʿAqaqir, the next day no one actually gave the order for the army to move before dawn. Indeed, it had still not moved at 11am. Perhaps Nuri had second thoughts about risking being caught on the move by the armoured cars, preferring instead to fight from entrenched positions in the dunes.

[10] Jaʿfar al-ʿAskari (1988), Ch. 7.   [11] Ibid.

At first light on 26 February the British yeomanry moved south to reconnoitre in the area where Ja'far had been hiding the previous day. They confirmed that the Sanusi were no longer there, and later an aeroplane ascertained that the enemy was back at his camp at al-'Aqaqir. With the exception of two patrols that continued the reconnaissance, the yeomanry halted where they were and waited for the infantry to move up.[12]

After receiving the reconnaissance report, Lukin led the infantry out of camp (9.30am) and rejoined the yeomanry. They moved quickly because at 11 o'clock the head of the column was five and a half miles south of their own camp and had reached the Khedivial Road. There they found six armoured cars and the motor ambulances waiting, and looking south they could see the al-'Aqaqir dunes in the distance. Just beyond the road there was a mound which offered an unimpaired view of the Sanusi position, and Lukin chose this location as his headquarters. Among the officers gathered there to watch the coming battle were Leo Royle, George Hunter, and Richard Bazley-White. Second Lieutenant J. H. Blaksley of the Dorset Yeomanry, was also there shortly before the battle:

> You must imagine a slightly undulating plain of firm sand with low tufts of scrub ... In front of us were some low sand hills of broken country, and this was where the Senussi had made their camp ... From the beginning we could see them (through our glasses) loading up their camels and slowly moving away. They had a great many camels – altogether it is estimated that they spread out over a mile of ground by 300 or 400 yards wide.[13]

There by the road Lukin deployed his force and the attack began. The yeomanry (less one squadron) and two armoured cars went off to the right. In the centre this time were the 3rd South Africans, advancing in line formation two paces apart with machine guns on the flanks. The remaining squadron of yeomanry was sent to the left with two more armoured cars, which were to support both left and centre. To the rear the

[12] "Then [we] halted two hours while the infantry came up. Yeatman and Bulteel took two strong officers' patrols to locate the enemy. Both found him and got back safely. Bulteel got right behind his camp and got the MC for it" (diary of Douglas Newbold).

[13] J. H. Blaksley, "Charge of the Dorset Yeomanry at Agagia". Proof copy of a published letter held by the National Army Museum, London (Acc. No. 8201-23).

Notts Battery prepared to harass the Turkish gun positions. The 1st South Africans and the last two armoured cars were kept out of sight behind the mound in reserve.

By 11.20am the advancing centre came under fire, but since the Sanusi were still a thousand yards distant this was not yet a threat. The yeomanry, however, had a difficult three mile stretch to cross to get into position on the British right flank, which from the start was within the range of Sanusi machine guns. They were observed by Lt. Blaksley:

> They were at once shelled and fired on by the machine guns, but they lost very little. They had perhaps three miles to cross before they were again in safety, and it was a magnificent sight to watch them galloping round, all extended so as not to make too easy a target. Half an hour later I followed over the same ground with my twenty men, but the Senussi did not think it worthwhile to shell so small a force.[14]

Once in position the yeomanry dismounted – though still being fired at by the Sanusi left – and waited for the first signs of a Sanusi withdrawal. When that moment came the yeomanry would be called upon to cut off the Sanusi retreat.

Meanwhile, two Sanusi battalions (the Menefa and the *muhafizia*) were hidden in the dunes and firing upon the advancing South Africans. As the gap between the two front lines closed, the South Africans began to suffer casualties.

Ja'far realized that the weakest point on the British front was its left, and so tried a swift outflanking movement on that side. Lukin sent a company of 1st South Africans from his reserve to reinforce the weak flank and the Sanusi movement failed. Ja'far then had an inexplicable problem with his own centre, where the *muhafizia* suddenly withdrew to the rear ninety minutes into the battle. Ja'far hurriedly replaced them with what was left of his battalion of Awlad 'Ali tribesmen, but his front line was now considerably weaker.

Perhaps the armoured cars had something to do with this precipitate withdrawal of the *muhafizia*. For a while the two cars supporting the 3rd South Africans manoeuvred without much difficulty, advancing right up to the edge of the dunes where the Sanusi gun emplacements were. They

[14] Blaksley, J. H. (n. d.).

finally killed a Turkish machine gunner, whereupon some of the other gunners abandoned their positions. The two cars (in one of which was the Duke of Westminster) then tried to enter the area of dunes and got stuck.[15]

When the 3rd South Africans were five hundred yards from the Sanusi front Lukin threw his remaining reserves into the fight, including the last two armoured cars. He also sent a staff officer to tell Colonel Souter (commanding the Dorsets on the right) that the time had come for the yeomanry to move.

> About 1pm I received a message from the GOC saying that he wished me to pursue and to cut off the enemy if possible. It was my intention to let the enemy get clear of the sandhills, where there might have been wire or trenches, and then to attack him in the open. I therefore pursued on a line parallel to, and about 1000 yards west of, the line of retreat, attacking with dismounted fire wherever the horses [needed a rest].[16]

Ja'far watched in increasing desperation as his army disintegrated:

> That was our situation as there I was, watching the enemy infantry approach in a slow jog with two armoured cars behind them and the artillery raining fire down on us, especially on our mountain gun and machine guns. After about an hour I saw a detachment of cavalry trying to envelop our left flank. The fighting continued until the enemy occupied our forward positions – where our battalion of *muhafizia* had fought from early morning until they withdrew. From these positions the enemy infantry then began to fire on our gun and machine guns. I ordered the artillery officer to move the mountain gun to the rear. I then received a brief message from Nuri Pasha saying that he was going south to prevent the supply caravan from falling into the hands of the British and that he was taking the *muhafizia* with him.
>
> Here was a perfect example of the disorganized way in which we wage war. We start out by sharing responsibility and making our plan of

[15] The two armoured cars supporting the yeomanry also had trouble manoeuvring on the desert surface. Both got stuck in sand, but one of them was close enough to the enemy to be of assistance nonetheless. The vehicle's gunner dismounted the Maxim and took it forward to a point where it was used with some effect.

[16] Souter's report, quoted in *Supplement to the London Gazette*, 21 June 1916, p. 25.

campaign. Then we drop it all and leave matters to fate as soon as the going gets rough.

So the *muhafizia* withdrew with Nuri Pasha and with them went no small number of tribal heads, officers from headquarters and cavalry. Those of us who were left stayed in our positions until the enemy was just two or three hundred yards away, when I was finally forced to give the order to retreat.[17]

The last of the Sanusi withdrew through the dunes trying to cover their backs as the South Africans pursued them with bayonets now fixed. When the South Africans reached the southern edge of the sand-hills they halted, it being nearly 3pm. In front of them, heading south across the plain, was a caravan over a mile long. At its front the Bedouin irregulars were escorting their camels, many of these hastily loaded with what remained of their food, baggage and supplies. At the back were the *muhafizia* and Turks, their Maxim guns guarding their rear and flanks. Now began one of the most dramatic events of the entire campaign. The Dorsets' time had come and Lt. Blaksley was at the very heart of the action.[18]

All the Dorsets were together except one troop. We probably numbered about 180 ... Then the led horses were whistled up, we were ordered to 'mount' and 'form line'. Then and not till then we knew what was coming ... We were spread out in two ranks, eight yards roughly between each man of the front rank and four yards in the second. This was how we galloped for well over half-a-mile straight into their fire. The amazing thing is that when we reached them not one man in ten was down. At first they fired very fast and you saw the bullets knocking up the sand in front of you, as the machine guns pumped them out. But as we kept getting nearer, they began to lose their nerve and (I expect) forgot to lower their sights. Anyhow the bullets began going over us, and we saw them firing wildly and beginning to run; but some of them – I expect the Turkish officers – kept the machine guns playing on us. We were within thirty yards of the line when down came my mare ... stone dead ... The line swept past me and I was almost alone, but the next moment

---

[17] Ja'far al-'Askari (1988), Ch. 7.
[18] The squadron of Royal Bucks Hussars were off chasing some Sanusi who had broken away from their column.

I saw a spare horse; I snatched it and galloped on after my troop; but within 100 yards down he fell like the mare. Then I had a very narrow escape; the second horse was not quite dead and was plunging; it took me a moment to get clear of him on the ground. I had barely done so when I saw a Senussi aiming his rifle at about 20 yards. I at once let fly with my revolver and over he rolled, but still on the ground he tried to get a shot at me so I sent another shot after the first, which settled him. There was no other horse to get and I was alone, then a strange thing happened. Six or seven men had, I suppose, recognized me as an officer. Anyhow they rushed up to me and in abject terror began begging for their lives. I saw they were men of consequence, but that was all I knew. The chief one was covered with blood, with a sword-thrust through his arm. I stood over them as best I could with my revolver, and signed to them that if they stopped their men from shooting at me, I would not shoot them.[19]

Douglas Newbold, with his Machine Gun section, was also there at this crucial moment:

As soon as I saw swords drawn, I raced to the left flank and got the guns into action, but the left squadron masked my fire at once. I mounted again and plugged on after the Regiment, which had gone clean through the enemy leaving behind 30 killed and 30 wounded out of 150 sabres. The wounded all got away pillion or otherwise. I saw C Squadron reforming on the left and so made for it through the demoralized left Senussi flank. A sniper left behind shot at me from behind a bush at 40 yards and killed the gun-pack leader who was riding just behind.[20]

Newbold rode on "for half a mile" when he suddenly heard Colonel Souter shouting. Souter was now with Blaksley, and like the latter had had his horse shot from under him. But Souter had recognized the "Turkish officer" with the wounded arm as being none other than Ja'far, and so he too now had his revolver in Ja'far's face. But with Ja'far's men already rushing to rescue him, the situation was grim. Blaksley, meanwhile, glimpsed the scene of horror unfolding around them:

[19] Blaksley, J. H. (n. d.).
[20] Diary of Douglas Newbold.

The Senussi were running in all directions, shrieking and yelling and throwing away their arms and belongings; the Yeomen after them, sticking them through the backs and slashing right and left with their swords.[21]

Finally, Ja'far himself waved his men back. At this point Newbold arrived:

> Souter[,] ... Blaksley and [Private W.] Brown ... were trying to get away Gaafar Pasha and his staff. Gaafar had been stuck in the arm and surrendered to Blaksley but his two Turkish staff officers were trying to get men up to rescue him. I sent the pack-horses off and took in 10 gunners with drawn swords, put Gaafar on a horse and by pricking his staff behind with swords got them to double away from the field before any Bedouin arrived. Took Gaafar's revolver and map and glasses and the Section pinched the rest of his equipment. He had with him a motley staff, a Turkish machine gun officer, Nehud Bey, a Turkish Sergeant-Major, one of our Coastguard deserters, a huge orderly about 6' 4" high, several Senussi regulars and half a dozen ragged Bedouin with muzzle-loaders. Took the lot to Observation Hill [i.e., field headquarters] and handed them over to the South Africans who had just arrived.[22]

Ja'far was barely conscious as he was hurried from the battlefield. At Lukin's HQ, which was now crowded with excited soldiers, Souter personally tended to Ja'far's wound.

> The next thing I knew an English officer was binding my wound and standing beside him was someone whom I immediately recognized. It was Captain Royle, who had been at Sollum with Colonel Snow. Royle told me that the man dressing my wound was Colonel Souter, the commander of the Dorset Yeomanry ... General Lukin gathered his soldiers around him and delivered a speech. I did not speak English then and the only thing I understood was the "hurrah!" at the end. It was late in the day, half an hour before sunset, the 26th of February 1916.[23]

[21] Blaksley, J. H. (n. d.).
[22] Diary of Douglas Newbold.
[23] Ja'far al-'Askari (1988), Ch. 7.

After the battle there was some confusion about what had happened to Nuri. The rumour spread among the victors that he had been killed. Blaksley's account says that he was "ridden down, whether killed or wounded or only knocked over we do not know". Sam Rolls, one of the armoured car drivers, claimed to have seen him "galloping towards the horizon on a beautiful piebald horse".[24] In any case, Maxwell was informed that Nuri had been killed and he reported this to the War Office; within a few days this information had to be amended: Nuri had got away, slightly wounded.

The Dorsets suffered heavily in the charge. Thirty-two of their men were killed; twenty-six more were wounded. Blaksley's own squadron suffered the worst casualties:

> In the charge, the squadron I belong to, "B" Squadron, was on the right, and my troop on the extreme right of the whole line; it happened that we came in for it more heavily than the left. Of the four officers in the squadron two were killed and one was wounded, and I was the fourth. I led 17 men (being my troop) into the charge, of whom 11 were killed and one got back wounded ... I had a bullet through the case of my field glasses, and another through the pocket of my tunic; so my tunic is quite a relic, with the bullet hole on one side and old Gaafar's blood on the other! Altogether ... I have a lot to be thankful for in getting through untouched.[25]

The WFF's other casualties, mainly South Africans, were 15 killed, 111 wounded.

The Sanusi army, once again, had come off much worse. Maxwell originally reported their losses to be "more than 200 killed and wounded".[26] Blaksley estimated their casualties to be 300 to 500 killed and

---

[24] S. C. Rolls (1937), *Steel Chariots in the Desert*, p. 31.   [25] Blaksley, J. H. (n. d.).
[26] WO 33/750, Maxwell to CIGS, 28 February 1916.
[27] MacMunn and Falls (1928), p. 128.
[28] For example, a recent history of that event is entitled *The Last Charge: The 21st Lancers and the Battle of Omdurman* (by Terry Brighton, published in 2000 by Crowood Press, UK).
[29] "It was magnificent, but it wasn't playing by the rules!" Jaʿfar was jokingly adapting the famous comment by Maréchal Bosquet, who was present at the charge of the Light Brigade: "C'est magnifique, mais ce n'est pas la guerre!"

wounded. The "official" figure was then fixed at 500.[27]

It is often said that the last cavalry charge by the British Army was that of the 21st Lancers at the Battle of Omdurman in 1898.[28] One might suppose, therefore, that the charge at al-'Aqaqir eighteen years later by the Queen's Own Dorset Yeomanry is a better candidate for that honour. In fact, according to the National Army Museum in London, the title properly applies to a charge by the Royal Buckinghamshire Hussars at the Battle of al-Mughar, near Jerusalem, on 13 November 1917. For the Bucks Regiment to have this honour is a nice irony, since their squadron missed the *dénouement* at al-'Aqaqir. In any event, the charge at al-'Aqaqir was indisputably one of the last. That form of warfare was disappearing forever.

Perhaps the last word on al-'Aqaqir should be given to Ja'far. The day after the battle Colonel Souter went to see him. Speaking of the cavalry charge, Ja'far said: "*C'est magnifique, mais ce n'est pas selon les règles!*"[29]

18

Facing Starvation

ON BOXING DAY at Bir Hakim there was much discussion of the previous day's battle at Wadi Majid. There was no way to determine what had really happened, and the men mulled over wild rumours concerning the number of dead. The Sanusi claimed to have killed three thousand British and taken nine hundred prisoners; their own losses were said to be a thousand dead. One of the wives of Holy Joe (the prisoners' name for the old Arab who was at Bir Hakim when they arrived) was mourning her brother, who was killed in the battle. On the 27th the sound of heavy guns could be heard from the north-east. The prisoners assumed that British warships were pounding Sollum, and the Sanusi were clearly anxious about this sudden proximity of the war.

Week 8 (from 26 to 31 December)

With the Christmas feasting over the prisoners returned to their usual routines: clearing the dry well, collecting firewood, improving the stone walls by their tents. Rations were now being delivered on a weekly basis – three bags of rice and one of flour for ninety-four men. Some olive oil was also distributed, which the men mixed with their rice. Someone discovered wild garlic growing in the desert, and soon everyone was looking for it. On New Year's Eve the prisoners were given a sheep.

Twenty men now had dysentery. Muhammad Effendi was concerned about this and ordered all sick men to be put in one tent. This upset the men who were not sick since it disrupted the crew's system of separate messes.

Week 9 (1 to 7 January)

New Year's Day was mostly sunny and warm, but a heavy rain fell in the late afternoon. Since the rations were not bad that week – rice, flour and, on alternating days, either an ounce of meat or a spoonful of oil – the prisoners celebrated the first day of 1916 with a supplementary tea-time meal of boiled flour and meat pudding.

It rained quite often that week, and one day there was not just rain, but hailstones as well. The various ditches and walls that the men had built to protect their tents against the winter weather were found to be ineffective, and everyone was wet and cold. Nevertheless, their spirits were raised when Basil constructed a hive-shaped clay oven for the baking of bread, which proved to be a great success.

The number of men with dysentery fell to twelve, but another six had hernia problems of one sort or another. Two men were seriously ill: Mr Hodgson of dysentery and Mr Cox of uric acid poisoning. On 5 January, the day of the hailstorm, Mr Cox died. His body was sewn up in sacking and buried several hundred yards to the south of camp. Among the hymns which the men sang at the funeral service were "Abide with Me", "A day's march nearer home" and others in Welsh.

Week 10 (8 to 14 January)

There was less rain this week, but the weather was still cold and unpleasant. Food was always on the men's minds, and the messes competed to produce the best fare. One of them once managed to produce a separate pudding course of its own, boiling flour, sugar and water in a pair of *shirwal*. The popularity of Lieutenant Apcar, who was no longer sick, reached new heights when he showed his fellow-prisoners how to cook pilaus and kebabs with the daily rations.

A baking pan was provided for the prisoners to boil their clothes. There was no soap, but at least this helped to get rid of the lice and fleas. This washing could only be done on a warm day as the men had nothing else to wear while their clothes were drying.

On Sunday, the 9th, evening hymns were sung as usual. Sub-Lieutenant Marsh, an Englishman, noted in his diary that the Welsh in the next tent had beautiful voices.[1]

The next day Mr Hodgson died. He was buried next to Mr Cox. There were now ninety-two prisoners, of whom twenty-five were listed as sick. Muhammad Effendi tried to cheer everyone up by telling them that Greece had joined the allies' side in the war!

On 12 January a Sanusi cook named Muhammad left Bir Hakim, supposedly to procure medicine and supplies.

Week 11 (15 to 21 January)

There were good rations this week. On the 15th, for example, the prisoners ate rice for breakfast; mutton soup, rice and dumplings for lunch; more rice and a sweet pudding for dinner. Gwatkin-Williams wrote that for once everyone went to bed full and slept soundly.[2]

On the 17th gunfire could be heard in the morning. In the afternoon two more Indian prisoners arrived, shipmates of the three men from the SS *Moorina*.

The following morning Muhammad Effendi left for Sollum to argue the case for more supplies and medicines for the prisoners. Gwatkin-Williams gave him a letter he had written to Nuri, giving seven days' notice of the withdrawal of his promise not to try to escape. His justification for this was that Nuri had promised that the prisoners would be held in better conditions than those at Bir Hakim. In charge of the prisoners during Muhammad Effendi's absence was Salim Effendi. He was of dark complexion, with yellow teeth and a black moustache. He too was kind, and through Basil he said that he believed that the Sanusi would soon make peace with the British, perhaps even be taken under their protection. Evidently, he was not a great supporter of the Turks.

At the end of the week three men were very sick: chief engineer Robert Williams, fireman Owen Roberts, and quartermaster Robert Abbit.

[1] Diary of Sub-Lt. Marsh, Department of Documents, Imperial War Museum.
[2] WO 106/1543, Gwatkin-Williams, entry for 15 January 1916.

Week 12 (22 to 28 January)

The weather was now mostly cold but dry. The firewood gatherers were having to go farther afield to find wood. As most were barefoot and the ground was covered in stones, this was difficult work. On the positive side, since the rains a lot of wild garlic had sprouted in the desert, and this was collected for adding to the food.

On the 23rd camels arrived bearing twelve more sacks of rice. Rations now consisted of rice and salt, with meat on alternate days.

On the 24th Salim Effendi told Basil that he had heard that an armistice was being arranged between the Sanusi and the British. The prisoners became very excited about this "news" and when the next day numerous stray Arabs arrived from the battlefields near Mersa Matruh heading west, they assumed that this was evidence that the fighting had indeed ended. But the Arabs passing through the camp were mostly hungry and unarmed – they had simply had enough of the war and were going home.

On the last day of the week Mr Williams died.

Week 13 (29 January to 4 February)

Rations were short again this week, and there was concern all around that the food might actually run out before new supplies arrived. Salim Effendi invited Gwatkin-Williams to his tent and offered him soured camel's milk. He expressed confidence that the prisoners would be released before long; also that a caravan would arrive soon with the promised food, medicine and supplies. He said once again that the Grand Sanusi was negotiating a cease-fire, and as if he thought the Turks were the only obstacle to this, he claimed there were not many of them left with the Sanusi army. On the 31st, Salim told Gwatkin-Williams that a foot-messenger was leaving that evening for Sollum and would take the prisoners' mail. Gwatkin-Williams wrote letters to Tariq Bey (commander at Sollum), Muhammad Effendi, Captain Ahmad, the Grand Sanusi, and even addressed one to "the officer commanding the British forces". In all of them he stressed the desperate plight of the prisoners.

One afternoon eight Sanusi dignitaries visited the camp and called on Salim Effendi. This occasion was the source of an amusing example of culture-shock for the prisoners, who were still unaccustomed to the ways of the East. Walsh wrote in his diary: "The meeting between them and our Commandant, Salim Effendi, was worth seeing. Salim Effendi plunged at each one alternately hugging …, kissing faces, both cheeks and hands, and going at it like fury … I'm thunderstruck yet!"[3] The visitors were very friendly and, with Basil interpreting, they told the prisoners that the war was over and that they would be going home soon. However, when Salim, following Arab custom, generously had a sheep killed and then sat with the visitors to eat, the prisoners grumbled that that feast would mean less food for them.

The weather was mostly dry and cold, but there was often a strong easterly wind which made it necessary to cook inside the tents.

Week 14 (5 to 11 February)

Sunday, 6 February, was a beautiful warm day. Everyone stripped down and washed with his bit of soap. Unfortunately, the only food now was a small amount of rice. One day a sheep drowned in the well. The happy result was that the prisoners got to eat a bit of meat with their short ration of rice. But by week's end the quality of the rice was no longer good – just the broken grains and rice flour from the bottom of the sacks. This "turned to glue" as soon as it was cooked, but such as it was, there was still too little of it.

The Sanusi were still expressing optimism about the political situation, and even Holy Joe had begun to talk about the prisoners' imminent release.

As if affected by this optimism, the desert suddenly seemed more cheerful – after the recent rains it suddenly turned green. When the wind blew from the north, there were butterflies; and numerous hares were also in evidence, although they were practically impossible to kill.

On 8 February two Sanusi arrived at midday, bringing a small amount of medicine for dysentery. Salim Effendi told Gwatkin-Williams to write Nuri Pasha another letter specifying what the men needed in the way of boots, clothes and additional food. Gwatkin-Williams reflected solemnly on the logic of the inference that Nuri was still in charge, which seemed to conflict with the claim that the Sanusi were making a separate peace with the British.

[3] Diary of Sub-Lt. Marsh, entry for 1 February 1916.

On 11 February a letter arrived for Captain Gwatkin-Williams from Tariq Bey, Commander at Sollum. It was in French and dated the previous day, 10 February:

Dear Colonel [*sic*],

I have received the letter which you sent to His Excellency General Nuri Pasha, and I will forward it to him immediately. I have read it and understand it. I hope you and your men will be repatriated in two or three months as [we hope] the world war will be over by this summer. As soon as the General approves your list of requirements, I shall send the supplies to you wherever you are. The General is at Mersa Matruh. I am going to see him and will take the necessary steps when I return.

Respectfully yours,
Commandant Tariq[4]

There were no work parties for several days. In any case, the prisoners were not at the moment allowed to walk towards the north, which led them to assume that there was some movement of troops beyond the rise to that side of camp.

Week 15 (12 to 18 February)

Muhammad the cook returned on the 12th and announced that Muhammad Effendi would be back in a few days. Gwatkin-Williams wrote another letter specifying what the prisoners needed in the hope that Muhammad Effendi would bring the supplies with him.

On the 15th Holy Joe and Muhammad the cook went north saying they would try to get shoes for the prisoners. They returned a few days later without them. But it was the food shortage that was becoming critical. The prisoners were eating snails in whatever quantities they could gather them, and "their white shells lay in heaps outside each tent door".[5] More than a thousand snails were collected. The prisoners had several methods of cooking them. One was to boil them for five minutes, shell

[4] WO 106/1543, entry for 11 February 1916.
[5] Ibid., entry for 14 February 1916.

them, and then simmer them for another twenty minutes with rice flour, which made a thick soup; another was simply to cook them for ten minutes in salted water.

Then, mid-week, a caravan finally arrived with ten sacks of dates and barley, enough for a few days at least. Salim said that the Sanusi army was virtually surviving on dates. The prisoners found them "delicious beyond belief". Nevertheless, at week's end a delegation of all the officers confronted Salim about the food shortage and the fact that every week the prisoners were left wondering if they were going to starve to death. Salim responded by saying that if sufficient food supplies did not arrive within five days, he would march the prisoners back to Sollum himself. Shortly afterwards shepherds arrived with a flock of sheep; it was not clear whether Salim now felt he was "off the hook" concerning his promise.

It rained several times that week and the water level in the main well rose by two feet.

Week 16 (19 to 25 February)

On the morning of Saturday, 19 February, Owen Roberts died. He was buried that afternoon, the fourth to be laid to rest in the prisoners' graveyard.

With dates now part of the food ration the prisoners discovered that boiling them made a delicious sweet tea; also that the date pits could be roasted, ground and brewed into "a wonderful imitation of coffee".[6]

On 20 February Gwatkin-Williams announced to the officers that he was going to try to escape. He wanted to go alone, he said, and would make his move that evening before the rising of the moon, walking by night and resting during the day. The men in his mess gave him a share of their rice, dates and bits of meat, and that night he left as planned, unnoticed by the guards. The distance from Bir Hakim to Sollum is about eighty miles as the crow flies.

The next day the Sanusi remained unaware of the captain's absence. But on the following day Holy Joe called on Basil, who was unwell, and asked where Gwatkin-Williams was. The alarm was raised, the prisoners all saying they had no idea where their captain was and that he must have left that morning. Salim Effendi was very upset.

---

[6] WO 106/1543, entry for 19 February 1916.

There was now glorious early spring weather. But food was again desperately short. Everyone who could walk regularly went out hunting for snails. One day an (unidentified) sailor, called "the Snail King", and one of his shipmates, ate a thousand snails between them!

Week 17 (26 February to 3 March)

On the 26th word came that Gwatkin-Williams had been recaptured, and Salim Effendi went off to bring him back. Later that day Mr Tanner and several officers went to the blockhouse to discuss the rations with the Sanusi sergeant left in charge. While they were talking, some other prisoners approached the blockhouse, and the guards suddenly got excited as if fearing a mutiny, and shots were fired. The prisoners quietly returned to their tents, while the sergeant threw stones at his men for having fired their guns without orders. The sergeant promised to provide one animal each day, but said that he could only give half the usual amount of rice and dates. Walsh acknowledged in his diary that the man clearly "wants to do his best for us, but has not got the food to give us".[7]

The next day the Sanusi sergeant had another discipline problem with his men, when they began to fight over the head of a sheep just slaughtered for the prisoners. To restore order the sergeant again gave his men a sound beating.

In the late afternoon of the 29th there was sudden excitement over the firing of guns to the north. It turned out to be Salim Effendi and his party escorting Captain Gwatkin-Williams back to camp. The whole garrison ran to meet them, followed by the women and children. Holy Joe gave the Captain a few hefty blows with the handle of his whip. Then a soldier slapped his face, while the women made a show of pelting him with stones. The fugitive was then sent to the sheep-pen, where four armed sentries were made to stand guard. This public humiliation of Gwatkin-Williams having been accomplished, as soon as it was dark, he was brought dates, water and "a huge bowl of rice", which Gwatkin-Williams took to be Salim's own supper. "The sentry himself also gave me a cigarette to smoke and a large fire burned all night to keep me warm. Such is the Arab character."[8]

[7] Diary of Sub-Lt. Marsh, entry for 26 February 1916.
[8] WO 106/1543, entry for 29 February 1916.

In the morning Gwatkin-Williams was returned to the officers' mess. He told everyone that he had been well-treated by all and sundry since his recapture. The men listened politely, but they did not believe him.[9]

Week 18 (4 to 10 March)

Not much happened this week. The prisoners were so debilitated that they now found it difficult to walk beyond the camp. Some tried to continue gathering firewood, but it was exhausting work. There was no more rice, and the remains of the date supply were bad (although the men continued to make "coffee" from the pits). The anxiety over the food supply was now affecting prisoners and Arabs alike. At the end of the week Marsh wrote in his diary:

> Excitement in Arab camp in forenoon. Some of the guards had stolen a sheep and hid it in their tent. It was killed and divided amongst them. They are beginning to feel hungry, I suppose, but apparently can live on less food than we can. Only one or two days rations, excluding meat, left in camp, and so matters look very serious.[10]

On the 8th Salim Effendi again went away, leaving the sergeant in charge.

Week 19 (11 to 17 March)

At the start of the week the sergeant promised that the food caravan would arrive the next day. No one believed him, but the next afternoon a herd of twenty-two animals did reach Bir Hakim. The men were then issued a quarter pound of meat per day, but nothing else. Most of them were now unable to walk and felt dizzy when they tried. Another messenger arrived on the 14th and announced that a caravan with rice and barley would arrive the next day.

Although the caravan did not arrive as announced, in the early morning of the 15th the sergeant awakened the prisoners to say that the Chief

---

[9] For Gwatkin-Williams' amusing first-hand account of his picaresque adventures on the run, written for British Intelligence at Ras al-Tin Hospital, see Appendix 1.
[10] Diary of Sub-Lt. Marsh, entry for 10 March 1916.

Officer, Sub-Lieutenant Leslie Dudgeon, and Basil Lambrinidis, were to return to al-Zibla at once, taking lists of such food and supplies as would enable all the prisoners to make a journey. Where they would all be going and how long the journey would take was not specified. Nevertheless, this was seen as a positive development. The lists were prepared, and at 10am the two men departed, heading north with two soldiers and a camel.

In the evening of that day Holy Joe and his family suddenly packed up their tent and left, but none of the prisoners knew why.

19

Sollum Reoccupied

TWO DAYS AFTER their victory at al-ʿAqaqir the Western Frontier Force occupied Sidi Barani without opposition. To the surprise of many, the place was nothing but the charred ruins of the Coastguard station – the same one that Royle and Snow, standing at the rail of the SS *Rasheed*, had watched burning in the night back in November. There was no village at Sidi Barani, and even worse in the eyes of the soldiers, there was very little beach, the coast there being mostly rocky and dangerous.[1] There was, however, a small cove with a makeshift jetty where supplies could be landed by sea, and supply ships began to arrive with food, ammunition and equipment. By 8 March the whole force had assembled at Sidi Barani in preparation for the advance on Sollum.

As February turned to March the *khamsin* began to blow, and from this hot, southerly wind there was no escape. It made life in the open plain a misery.

> One evening we were sitting at dinner when … a terrific squall of sand-laden wind drove across the camp taking everything loose with it. Small

---

[1] Two British soldiers drowned there in the rough sea, the second trying to rescue the first.

[2] Anon. (1917), "In the Western Desert of Egypt", *Blackwood's Edinburgh Magazine*, p. 217.   [3] Hunter family archives.

articles such as towels, socks, helmets, and mugs went careering off down the wind, and great was the searching and sorting out of stray articles that went on next morning.[2]

The wind was no respecter of rank, and the soldiers were much amused when, one evening, General Peyton was dining with his staff and his tent blew down on top of them.

On 8 March several of the armoured cars went to reconnoitre in the vicinity of Baqbaq, half way between Sidi Barani and Sollum. As they approached the Coastguard station there (once again a small, solitary building in an otherwise empty plain) two Turks walked out into the open bearing a white flag. One of them carried a letter in French from Nuri, identifying the bearer, Pertev Tewfik, as his secretary and "plenipotentiary" with the authority to deal with the British in the matter of supplying food and clothing to the prisoners being held in the Libyan Desert. The letter went on to explain that the prisoners had dysentery and, generally, were in a bad condition. The two Turks were immediately driven to Sidi Barani.

General Peyton was interested in this development, but he felt that he was not in a position both to negotiate with the Turks and, at the same time, to advance on Sollum to push them out of Egypt – for Nuri had retreated with the remnants of his army to their camp at Bir Wa'r, two miles from Sollum. Another potential complication was that Tewfik happened to mention in conversation that he was also empowered to negotiate an exchange of Turkish prisoners for British prisoners. Therefore, Peyton sent Tewfik to Mersa Matruh (by trawler that afternoon) and cabled Cairo to send a negotiator immediately. To the other (unnamed) Turk he handed the following message in French to be conveyed back to Nuri:

To Lieutenant-General Nouri Pasha,

In response to your letter sent via your secretary Pertev Tewfik Bey, I have the honour to inform you that I shall send a message to the GOC of the English Army in Cairo on the matter of food and clothing for the English prisoners now in your hands in Tripoli. At the same time I shall raise the issue of an exchange of Turkish prisoners in Egypt for your English prisoners.

[Major-General W. E. Peyton][3]

That being done, Peyton was able to turn his attention once again to planning for the reoccupation of Sollum. His main concern in this next, and hopefully last, phase of the campaign was that Nuri might by now have received reinforcements from Cyrenaica. In any case, the only way to take and hold Sollum safely was to secure a defensible section of the plateau above. Clearly the WFF could not simply march into Sollum while Nuri's force was holding the surrounding escarpment. Peyton's only option was to find a way to get his army onto the plateau, preferably undetected, and to attack Nuri at Bir Wa'r.

From Sollum the escarpment runs inland toward the south-east, and there are several passes in the first twenty-mile stretch of it. All of them – Halfaya, al-'Araqib, Augerin, Medean – were well-known to Leo Royle, who must have accompanied the armoured car and two Fords that made a reconnaissance of these passes on 9 March. This patrol reported that the passes were usable for the infantry and the mounted troops but not for the vehicles, and that these would have a better chance of reaching the plateau if they used a pass known as 'Alam al-Rabiya further down the escarpment. But, in principle, the inland approach was possible. Peyton initially planned for a column of infantry under General Lukin to reach the plateau using the Medean Pass; for a column of mounted troops under Brig.-Gen. Hampden to climb the nearer Augerin Pass; for the armoured cars to use 'Alam al-Rabiya; and for them all to come together at Augerin ready to attack the Sanusi at Bir Wa'r, Amsa'id, and Sollum. To make the plan work Peyton needed to assure an adequate supply of water for thousands of men and animals marching in the desert for several days. Intelligence reported the existence of wells at Augerin and a cistern at Medean, all on the plain below the escarpment, and of another cistern at Siwiat on the plateau above. But the rains had stopped five weeks earlier: would there still be water in the cisterns? On 10 March Peyton sent a Staff officer, a colonel in the Royal Engineers named Griffiths, with an armoured car escort, to find out.

In fact, having decided that approaching Sollum by the coast alone would be too costly if the Sanusi put up a spirited fight from the cliffs, Peyton was already gambling that there would be enough water at the wells and cisterns for an inland approach, or that, if there was not enough, the problem was not insurmountable. Lukin's infantry column (four battalions) left Sidi Barani on the 9th. On the 11th the armoured cars left for 'Alam al-Rabiya, while the infantry bivouacked at Baqbaq, expecting to reach the Medean Pass the next day. But later, also on the 11th, Colonel Griffiths returned to say that the cisterns were empty and that the well-water was insufficient and of bad quality.

Forced to amend his original plan, Peyton now ordered Lukin to proceed to Medean with just two of his four South African battalions and a company of Australian Camel Corps bearing water. This reduced column would move against the Sanusi from above in concert with the armoured cars. Hampden's cavalry, meanwhile, was now ordered to stay below and move towards Sollum along the coast. Lukin's remaining two battalions of infantry were sent back to Baqbaq to become a third column, under Peyton's personal command, and it would also take the coastal track. The three columns would re-unite at Halfaya Pass, three miles south-east of Sollum.

Getting the armoured cars up the pass at 'Alam al-Rabiya and along the escarpment to the rendezvous with Lukin's infantry was painfully slow work. The Duke of Westminster wanted the cars to climb at night[4] in the hope that the Sanusi, unaware of their presence on the plateau, would be caught by surprise. 'Alam al-Rabiya was twenty-five miles beyond the Medean Pass.[5] Having slowly picked their way across the uneven and rocky terrain to get there on 11 March, the vehicles then had to climb a winding rock-strewn camel track in the dark. At the cost of a few tyres and a lot of pushing from behind, the cars all made it onto the plateau. There the brigade camped for the rest of the night. "Guards were posted, with machine guns mounted on tripods, and the signallers were ready throughout the night with their flash lamps to answer any message signalled from the plain below."[6]

At 7.30am (on the 12th) they started for the rendezvous. Sam Rolls recalled driving

as close as possible to the edge of the precipice, picking my way between the great stones, and stopping frequently when further movement was made impossible by the obstructions. Then men from the other cars would run forward and remove some of the stones, until a passage had been opened large enough to drive through.

[4] Protheroe report, Cheshire County Council, HMS Tara Archives, Ref. PP 19/284.
[5] That is, to the south-east of Medean Pass. [6] S.C. Rolls (1937), p. 35.

> When we had gone fourteen miles on this nerve-racking journey a
> halt was called, and I received the order to drive as close as possible to the
> edge ... so that the signaller whom I carried might set up his heliograph
> and try to get into communication with the troops advancing across the
> plain below ... Our eyes, straining to catch an answering flash, at last
> distinguished an intermittent glitter far away in the distant haze. All
> crowded round while the signaller repeated ... "This is General Lukin.
> Left Bakbak early this morning. General Peyton then at point four miles
> east. Wells here [Augerin] almost dry. Searching for water. Position
> serious." ... We could only signal back that we had as yet discovered no
> water on the plateau.[7]

Evidently, the logistical problem of loading the camels with water and
getting them to the infantry took a perilously long time.

The armoured cars proceeded to the Medean Pass, arriving there just as
the first of the South Africans reached the plateau.[8] The latter were in a
bad way when they got there, however, dehydrated and gasping for water.
The armoured car brigade shared what they had, but they too were short
of water by now, their twelve-gallon *fantasses* having mostly been boiled
away by the car engines.

Relief finally came on the next day, 13 March. First, one of the
armoured cars that had stayed behind to escort the convoy arrived with
supplies and as much water as one car could carry. Then, the Australian
Camel Corps finally arrived at the foot of the pass. The whole day was
spent getting men, supplies, water, and camels up onto the plateau. Late in
the afternoon the column on the plateau finally moved to Bir Siwiat (half-
way between Medean and Sollum), where they set up camp for the night.
On the plain below Peyton's infantry column was nineteen miles east of
Sollum, at a point known as 'Alam Tajdid, where there was water; and
General Hampden's column of cavalry was at nearby Baqbaq. For the first
time in several days Peyton was now in signalling communication with his
whole force. At 5.30 pm all three columns witnessed an interesting
phenomenon to the west: "[A]n immense cloud of smoke rose into the still

---

[7] S.C. Rolls (1937), pp. 35–36.
[8] Most of the South African Infantry stayed below on 12 March, only climbing the
escarpment after water arrived on the 13th.
[9] Anon. (1917), *Blackwood's Magazine*, p. 219.

air, like an enormous mushroom."[9] They heard no explosion, but for several minutes black smoke hung in the air high over the plateau.

For three days the WFF had manoeuvred into this position despite severe logistical problems and erratic communications. But where were the enemy? Did they know the British force was closing in both on the plateau and on the plain? And what was the cause of the explosion? In fact, Peyton already had the answers. The Sanusi, dispersed between Bir Wa'r, Amsa'id, and Sollum, were using the telephone wires to communicate with each other. Throughout the 12th and 13th British signallers had a tap on the line and, using an Egyptian who spoke both Arabic and Turkish, were intercepting Sanusi and Turkish communications.[10]

The picture that emerges from the transcripts was of a broken army desperately trying to gather transport camels at Bir Wa'r in order to get ammunition and supplies away as fast as possible. They knew that a British column was on the plateau, but they had no inkling that the armoured cars were there as well. The WFF columns on the plain had not been sighted. To organize the Sanusi retreat into Libya, Nuri was darting here and there on his white charger chivvying his men and shouting orders. The late afternoon explosion on the 13th was the destruction of all the ammunition that Nuri's men could not move west.

As dawn broke on 14 March it was obvious that this would be an eventful day. The cavalry left Baqbaq at 4am. A few hours later it united with Peyton's infantry at 'Alam Tajdid and the merged force moved down the Khedivial Road. First they had to make their rendezvous at Halfaya Pass, where they would remain below and Lukin's column above. Then the

---

[10] WO 95/4438. The English transcripts that resulted from this operation are sometimes incomprehensible:

> – Is there any guns?
> – Pasha has taken the 61. Is there any news from the camels?
> – Do you think they could come today? How far it must be?
> – Ten hours.

sometimes moving:

> – Where we were [al-'Aqaqir] there was a little grass and here [Sollum] we have nothing but dirt. Send us food, food, food!

and sometimes comical:

> ... the man [on the line] was furious and said:
> – If you are not good [for anything] you may leave the telephone.
> – Go on. We may bring men to work.
> – Oh miserable, miserables. I am waiting one hour. Miserables.

two columns would march the remaining three miles to Sollum.

The convergence of the force took place at mid-morning as planned. At about the same time aeroplane reconnaissance reported that the Sanusi had evacuated their positions at Bir Wa'r and Sollum and were hurriedly moving west. Peyton moved his cavalry up Halfaya Pass, where they would be in a position to support the armoured cars if needed. The cars, however, were ordered to proceed immediately to Bir Wa'r, and the cavalry were soon left far behind.

From Halfaya Pass it was seven miles to the enemy camp at Bir Wa'r. Once again the ground was uneven and rocky, so it took an hour for the cars to get there. Bir Wa'r was empty except for a few Arabs found milling about the abandoned stores and equipment. One of them − a straggler or perhaps merely a scavenger − was quite content to talk. Nuri had left the previous evening with 150 to 200 of his *muhafizia*. The Arab indicated the direction which they had taken. In fact, Nuri had headed for the Tobruk road (which the Turks and Arabs called the Enveria Road, after his brother).

The Duke of Westminster had been given leave to pursue Nuri and the *muhafizia* with "reasonable boldness". He had thirty-two men and ten vehicles − nine of the brigade's armoured cars, each with driver, gunner, and officer; plus one Model T Ford (with a machine gun in the back) carrying the remaining personnel. With the Arab's help the road was found and the cars headed into Libya.[11] The Enveria Road was simply a dirt track like the Khedivial Road that they were used to in Egypt. But this one did not have the ruts and potholes of the other, caused by overuse in all weather since the previous November. The surface was good and the cars travelled west at thirty miles per hour, and sometimes more. In the desert on either side of the road were hundreds of armed camel-mounted Bedouin hurrying in the same direction. Clearly they had been in the tribal units of the Sanusi army, fighting against the British. Nevertheless, the Bedouin were ignored, for Nuri and his remaining regulars were the better prize.

When they had travelled this way for about twenty miles, they came upon a broken-down automobile − one of the Coastguard Fords abandoned in November − which four men were trying to repair. Shots

---

[11] The British had asked the Italians in advance for permission to pursue the Sanusi into Libya and this had been granted.

were exchanged, but again the column just passed by. Before long, they came to a well known as Bir 'Aziz, and there, where there was a bend in the road, they found what they were looking for. About a mile off the road to the south was Nuri's camp – for evidently his force had trekked late into the night and was only now, at midday, getting ready to move again. The skirmish on the roadside had alerted everyone; men were running in all directions; camels bearing great loads were being hurried off; and on the near side of the camp a ten-pounder gun was already firing at the column. As shells fell around them, the Duke deployed the armoured cars in a single line abreast, and they charged straight for the guns – and by now several Turkish machine guns were also firing. Although it was only mid-March the sun was blazing down as if it were summer, and Sams Rolls' account of the action stresses the great heat inside the cars:

> There were three of us in [my car] and, our movements being hampered by this overcrowding, we soon began to get irritable ... The reek of burnt cordite, blending with the stench of our hot, sweating bodies, made us gasp for fresh air, but with the armour lid closed down there was little chance of getting any. The heat, a combination of that given out by the racing engine and that of the sun on the steel cylinder, added to the din of the stuttering gun and the clatter of the ammunition belts, made the conditions nerve-shattering. Hot, empty cartridge-cases frequently fell on my bare neck, and into my shirt, stinging my flesh; and the general sensation ... was infernal.[12]

The Turkish gunners stood their ground and were all killed; and the rest of the Sanusi were still dispersing. But they had been caught in the open, and the fight was hopelessly unequal. Of the Turkish and Sanusi *muhafizia* regulars fifty were killed; forty threw down their arms and surrendered. The rest, however, managed to reach fissured and rocky terrain where the cars could not go. Among the escapees once again was Nuri, nimble and elusive on his white horse. Moving less quickly were the supply camels, which were being hurried into this impenetrable zone. A number of these were targeted while they were still within range, sometimes with extraordinary results: when the unfortunate animals were carrying ammunition or fuel, they simply exploded when hit.

[12] S. C. Rolls (1937), p. 40.

The armoured cars had left the Bir Siwiat camp at 7am. They had been at Halfaya when the force merged; been to the Turkish camp at Bir Wa'r; driven twenty-five miles into Libya; fought a battle – and it was now only one o'clock in the afternoon. In December each army had pitted its infantry and cavalry against that of the other and fought to roughly stalemated conclusions in what were essentially 19th century battles – the armoured cars had scarcely participated, the aeroplanes had mainly been for observing. The Dorsets' charge at al-'Aqaqir may have been decisive but it was completely, almost absurdly, anachronistic. The rout at Bir 'Aziz was a milestone in desert warfare: it was the 20th century being summarily triumphant over the past.

While the men of the armoured car brigade destroyed Sanusi weapons and guarded prisoners, the Duke himself hurried back to Egypt to tell General Peyton the news. (And with him went the unit's only casualty, a man slightly wounded by a splintered bullet.)

Back at Bir Wa'r the yeomanry and the camel corps had finally arrived and were busy sorting, stacking, and burning the enemy's abandoned supplies and equipment. Below the escarpment, meanwhile, General Lukin's infantry had walking into Sollum without opposition, led by a band of South African Scots playing bagpipes.

The main objectives of the WFF campaign had been achieved: the Sanusi had been defeated along the coast and Sollum had been re-occupied. Of course, Sayyid Ahmad was still at Siwa with thousands of armed supporters; and Muhammad Saleh Harb and his men were still uncomfortably close to the Nile, although they had been contained in the main oases there, and the Nile Valley appeared to be secure. The WFF's only urgent unfinished business was the matter of the British prisoners in Libya.

20

The Rescue

A WEEK HAD NOW passed since the Turkish delegation from Nuri had arrived in Egypt to obtain food and clothing for the prisoners at Bir Hakim. General Maxwell wanted to accept Nuri's proposal, and the British Agency in Cairo was already opening channels to the Turks and the Sanusi through the Italians in Libya. Meanwhile, Pertev Tewfik was waiting aboard HMS *Humber*, anchored off Matruh.

But at Sollum something happened that suggested the possibility of another solution to the problem of the prisoners. After the action at Bir 'Aziz on 14 March one of the Armoured Car Brigade's officers, Captain Amphlett, stopped to search the broken-down Ford near the battlefield. In it were some "empty petrol tins and a heap of rubbish",[1] but on further inspection Amphlett also found a letter from Captain Gwatkin-Williams addressed to the Turkish commander at Sollum, Tariq Bey, and dated "Bir Hakkim Abbyat, February 1st, 1916".[2] He put the letter into his pocket and forgot about it until the next day, when he gave it to the intelligence officers – that is, to Royle and Lawrence's colleague, Mervyn Macdonnell, who had come to Mersa Matruh to interrogate Ja'far and then had stayed with the WFF.[3]

Other letters from the British prisoners were found at Bir Wa'r, but the one found by Capt. Amphlett was the only one that mentioned Bir

---

[1] Gwatkin-Williams (1919), p. 285. [2] Ibid.

Hakim. Royle and Macdonnell had no idea where the place was, but two
months earlier Royle, while questioning a prisoner at Mersa Matruh, had
been told that the *Tara* crew were being held at a location known as
"Akeim [which was] five or six days south of Derna".[4] No such place
could be found on maps of the Libyan interior, either with or without the
initial "H", and so the information seemed to lead nowhere – until now.
Gwatkin-Williams' letter confirmed the exact name of the place, but
where exactly was Bir Hakim and were the prisoners still there? Derna
was on the Libyan coast west of Tobruk, about one hundred and sixty
miles from Sollum. Five or six days by camel from Derna to the south
would be about the same distance again, so clearly more precise
information was needed if a rescue party were not to get lost in the Libyan
Desert, which was also home to the enemy. Royle, whose Arabic was
better than Macdonnell's, set to work interrogating the Arab and Turkish
prisoners taken at Bir 'Aziz. Two Bedouin were found who had heard of
Bir Hakim and were willing to help. One was an old man who said that
he had grazed his camels there in his youth and thought he knew roughly
where the place was. The other claimed to know the Libyan Desert well,
but he had no precise knowledge of Bir Hakim itself. Royle told Peyton
that he was convinced the two Arabs were telling the truth, but that they
had only the vaguest concept of the distances involved to get there. But
based on the Arabs' statements he estimated that the prisoners were
probably being held about seventy-five miles south-west of Sollum.[5]
Peyton went to consult with the Duke of Westminster, who had already
been twenty-five miles west of Sollum and knew at least what the terrain
was like in that area. They discussed the various uncertainties: distance,
direction, and likely driving conditions beyond Bir 'Aziz. The Duke then
volunteered to lead a rescue attempt with the Light Armoured Car
Brigade. Peyton was tempted, but first he had to consider the risks
involved in such a gamble.

[3] The various archives contain different versions of how and where the precise
reference to Bir Hakim was found in prisoner correspondence. Gwatkin-Williams'
own version is more or less substantiated by a report written on 26 March 1916 by
Temp. Capt. A. H. Protheroe, ASC, who was at Bir 'Aziz with Capt. Amphlett. See
Protheroe, Cheshire County Council, HMS *Tara* Archives PP 19/284.
[4] ADM 137/334.
[5] Peyton's Report of 18 March, Cheshire Country Council, HMS *Tara* Archives, PP
19/284.

I gave his offer careful consideration. Our information was scanty and conflicting; the country to be traversed practically unknown and unmapped; the distance most uncertain; and the fact of our prisoners being at the spot by no means established; finally it was more than possible that reinforcing enemy in strength might be met with, coming from the west. However, encouraged by the Duke of Westminster's quiet confidence and having still fresh in my mind his brilliant leadership of March 14th, and greatly influenced by the misery to which our fellow countrymen are being exposed and to the still greater misery to which they would be indefinitely condemned unless a rescue was effected, I decided to accept the Duke's offer.[6]

Sir Hugh Richard Arthur Grosvenor, the second Duke and fourth Marquess of Westminster, may have been an exemplary soldier, but he was certainly not a run-of-the-mill one. He was one of the richest men in England when England was the richest country on earth; and he was also a man of character, since no less a figure than Winston Churchill called him "fearless, gay, and delightful".[7]

Grosvenor was known to his close friends as "Bend Or", a racy school-boy sobriquet from his days at Eton in the 1890s. He had no career other than the management of his estates. His overriding interest was sport, and in that domain he was a keen player of polo, an excellent shot, and had a passion for automobiles. During the Boer War he enlisted in the Army and served on Lord Roberts' staff.

In 1912 Grosvenor "wintered" in Egypt, that is to say, he arrived with a stud of polo ponies and reserved a luxurious suite of rooms at Cairo's Gezireh Palace Hotel. For the next few months he was to be found playing polo by day, and enjoying the city's glittering social life by night. Dining and dancing at the Savoy; fancy-dress parties; gala evenings at villas, palaces, consulates, and hotels – it was all followed with great admiration by *The Egyptian Gazette*'s social correspondent.

On the outbreak of the First World War Grosvenor again became a staff officer, this time for Britain's senior general on the Western Front, John French, and he took with him a Rolls-Royce touring car with a Hotchkiss machine gun stowed in the back "in case of need". He moved in a circle

---

[6] Peyton's Report of 18 March, Cheshire Country Council, PP 19/284.
[7] Obituary in *The Times*, 21 July 1953.

that was interested in armour-plating automobiles for military use, and as the idea had the support of the First Lord of the Admiralty, Winston Churchill, it was quickly implemented. In November 1914 Grosvenor was posted to the Royal Naval Air Service Armoured Car Division at Wormwood Scrubs in London. He was given the command of No. 2 Squadron (out of twenty-one) consisting from the outset of twelve Rolls-Royces. Cars, guns and equipment were financed by Grosvenor; running expenses and the salaries of his men were paid by the Admiralty.

By March 1915 Grosvenor was back in France, but this time with his squadron. The Battle of Neuve Chapelle was about to begin, but in a muddy landscape of trenches and shell holes there was not much use for armoured cars. Months passed with the squadron doing little more than providing transportation for staff officers in areas where it was unsafe to use non-armoured cars. Later in the year, the unit was sent back to England and transferred to the Army. During Christmas week 1915, they were sent by train across France to the port of Marseilles, where they embarked for Egypt.

General Peyton, with his staff and senior officers, spent the entire day of 16 March working out the details of the rescue attempt, while others were busy getting all available automobiles up the escarpment at Sollum. The ten cars that had been to Bir 'Aziz were still on the plateau, but now, with much pushing and pulling, thirty-one[8] additional vehicles were helped to the top, including ten motorized ambulances, all Fords and Studebakers; two more Fords with Maxims (there being one on the plateau already); eleven Ford trucks ("tenders"); one Wolseley; and, among the remaining automobiles, five normally assigned to convey Peyton's staff officers – and the Duke of Westminster's Rolls-Royce touring car. The column was supplied with petrol for a journey of three hundred miles and food and water for three days. Finally, a forward base camp was prepared at Bir 'Aziz by the Berkshire Yeomanry and the Australian Camel Corps. This, it was

---

[8] Sources do not agree on the exact number of cars used in the rescue: some say 41, others 42, 43, and 45. Assuming that the sources with the greatest detail are more likely to be correct, the author has concluded that a total of 41 cars is the most likely to be the correct figure. See especially 4-page typed diary from Light Armoured Car Brigade, entry 17 March, Cheshire County Council HMS *Tara* Archives. Otherwise: S. C. Rolls says there were 45 cars; Sub-Lt. Marsh 41; Protheroe 42; Laycock 42; Gwatkin-Williams 43 – and they were all there!

thought, would be useful whatever the outcome of the expedition – either for facilitating the arrival of reinforcements if necessary, or for receiving the liberated prisoners if all went well.

By evening the tableland immediately above Sollum had begun to look like a dusty racing circuit. The Duke, who had walked up the escarpment track with a party of fellow officers, dined with them under a tarpaulin stretched between two vehicles. Then, as the expedition was to move off at 3am, everyone but the sentries tried to rest, although excitement and bitter cold kept many from sleeping. Sam Rolls recalled their early departure the next morning:

> In the earliest hour of the 17th … we were roused by the sentries, and at once the courtyard began to hum with voices and the movements of men. Light was supplied by the dimmed lamps of some of the cars, and by bits of candle. I had thrown a tarpaulin over my engine to protect it from the cold dew and so avoid difficulty in starting.[9]

The column set off under strict orders to keep all headlamps turned off. By moonlight they passed Bir Wa'r, where some Bedouin families were surprised scavenging among the litter, and then proceeded to the base camp at Bir 'Aziz. The moon had now set and the column had to wait an hour till daybreak.

> A halt was called for breakfast, and the bully beef and biscuits, and the hot tea tasted good after our drive in the cold air. There had been no mishap so far, and the column had kept well together. Drawn up behind the armoured cars were the light Fords, loaded with petrol, water and provisions, and behind these again the ambulances were strung out in a long line. Two armoured cars brought up the rear.
>
> Our halt was short, and soon we were on the move again, following the [Tobruk] road and putting on speed wherever the going was firm and smooth enough to allow it. Nothing broke the monotony of the undulating plain but hills of sand or rock, grim and bare under the rays of the sun.[10]

The Duke's touring car stayed at the head of the column. In it sat the

[9] S. C. Rolls (1937), p. 48. [10] Ibid., p. 49.

Duke himself, Leo Royle, the two Bedouin (now acting as guides), and a Lieutenant-Colonel Laycock.[11]

At about 10 o'clock, when they had travelled forty miles, the column spotted five horse-mounted men off in the distance. One of the armoured cars left the road in pursuit, but two of the riders galloped into a stony tract and got away. The other three were questioned and released.[12] The only other sign of life was the occasional herd of camels and the few nomads tending them.

The column also came upon a derelict Talbot car which, Laycock assumed,

> our people must have left when the Senussi drove them out in November. A new tyre had been cleverly improvised from rubber, in the shape of mats; we ourselves had found tons of this rubber strewn along the beach, part of an immense cargo consigned to America.[13]

When the column had travelled eighty-five miles it turned off the road and headed south into the open wilderness

> After we left the main road we struck one of the most desolate pieces of country I have ever seen and what the guides steered by I have no conception – as a matter of fact I was getting very pessimistic by this time as every time we came to a ridge the guides would say "The well is over this ridge" … This happened about five times each ridge being four or five miles beyond the last. When the guides themselves began quarrelling we thought it was up with us when lo and behold! we pulled up and the guides said they could see the well. We had then been 130 miles across unmapped, unknown country.[14]

---

[11] Laycock was the commander of the Nottinghamshire Battery, RHA. Since his unit was not assigned to the expedition, one may assume he was along for the ride.

[12] One of the three to be questioned and released was Dr Béchie Fuad (See *Prisoners of the Red Desert*, p. 289).

[13] Narrative of Lt.-Col. J. F. Laycock, Cheshire County Council, HMS *Tara* Archives PP 19/284. Gwatkin-Williams says it was the British Naval Wireless Telegraphy Wolseley car which had fallen into the enemy's hands four months previously. The author could find no other reference to this "lost Wolseley" and assumes that Laycock was correct since he was there and Gwatkin-Williams was not.

[14] Protheroe Report of 26 March 1916, Cheshire County Council, PP 19/284.

At first, none of the British could see what the guides were pointing at, even with field glasses.

> But off charged the cars with the Duke at their head and [us] following a couple of hundred yards behind. We could see a mound in the desert with a large number of figures silhouetted against the sky line. I shouted "it must be them" as they made no attempt to run away but stood like statues. When they got over the first shock of seeing us they started to beckon us with their arms and wave their clothes.[15]

It was 3 o'clock in the afternoon of Friday, 17 March. It was also St. Patrick's Day, although the prisoners had not the heart to want to celebrate it. Their captivity had begun nineteen weeks ago to the day, and neither Gwatkin-Williams nor anyone else in camp dared to think that the nightmare might soon be over.

> I had just put on our supper to cook and was starting to write my diary, when someone came running into the tent and said the soldiers were very excited, had all gone off for their rifles and run up the mound. I hoped it was the long-expected caravan and went on writing. Suddenly someone shouted there was a motor-car coming, and we all ran out to see, not daring to believe our eyes and fearful of disappointment. But there it was right enough, its khaki body coming rapidly round the bend of the incline to the east-north-east ... [T]his must be a British envoy allowed to come and see us and arrange our release at last. But there was no flag... Suddenly more cars appeared, and more and more, all tearing towards us over the stones. On sighting us they seemed to check for a moment, and then fly forward again. We were certain now. We went mad. We yelled ourselves hoarse. We could see now that some were armoured cars and others ambulances. The latter drew up at our tattered tents and, in a moment, we were tearing [at] bully-beef, bread and tinned chicken, and drinking condensed milk out of tins. We tore our food like famished wolves, with tears in our eyes ... An officer approached and asked if I was Captain Williams, and a second or two later I was shaking hands with the Duke of Westminster.[16]

---

[15] Protheroe, Cheshire County Council, PP 19/284.
[16] WO 106/1543.

Still stunned by this unexpected, unexplained and apparently miraculous event Gwatkin-Williams scarcely comprehended the implications of the question when the Duke asked where the Sanusi guards were. His mouth full of food he merely pointed to the scrub-covered plain to the west of the camp, and the armoured cars dashed off round the mound in that direction.

> Almost immediately, while the Duke was questioning me as to our treatment, I heard the Maxims splutter. I shouted "Save them. They have been kind to us" and dashed up the mound for the last time, the Duke with me. But we were too late ... the garrison (I suppose nine soldiers) had been wiped out in a few seconds, and I could see only prostrate forms lying among the desert scrub.[17]

There is a haunting image in one of the undelivered letters found at Bir Wa'r. The *Tara*'s civilian captain, Edward Tanner, had written to his twelve-year-old son: "I used sometimes to draw water at the well for Senussi women and children, until I became too weak to do so. It used to delight them whenever I would take out my artificial teeth for them. They would clap their hands and laugh and dance around and look into my mouth to see how the teeth were secured."[18] There were, in fact, many women and children living at the camp, and they had run off together with their men at the approach of the cars. With mind-numbing indiscrimination the British gunners killed them all.

Sam Rolls claimed that what had happened was the natural result of seeing his fellow-countrymen in such a miserable state, "a throng of living skeletons" as he put it.

> [T]here was no room left in us for compassion. The guards were running with their women and children ... We did not look to see who or what they were.[19]

But it was pointless slaughter. The nine armoured cars could easily have corralled the fleeing Sanusi and taken them prisoner, and the unnecessary

[17] WO 106/1543.
[18] Cheshire Country Council, HMS *Tara* Archives, PP 19/284
[19] S. C. Rolls (1937), p. 55.

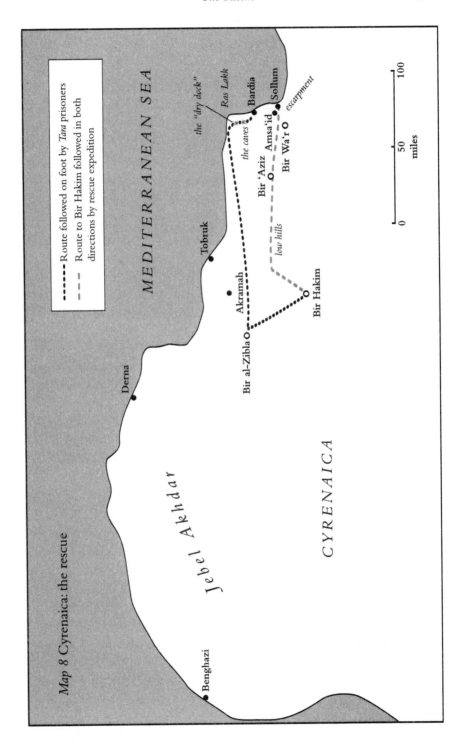

Map 8 Cyrenaica: the rescue

········ Route followed on foot by *Tara* prisoners

– – – Route to Bir Hakim followed in both
directions by rescue expedition

MEDITERRANEAN SEA

CYRENAICA

Jebel Akhdar

Benghazi

Derna

Tobruk

Akramah

Bir al-Zibla

Bir Hakim

Ras Lakk

the "dry dock"

the caves

Bardia

Sollum

Bir 'Aziz

Amsa'id

Bir Wa'r

low hills

escarpment

0   50   100

miles

and brutal killing of the guards and their families brought no credit to the Armoured Car Brigade and stained an otherwise faultlessly-executed expedition.

The dead were left where they lay. Back at the prisoners' tents blue hospital suits were being handed out to the liberated men. The latter quickly gathered their belongings and were distributed among the cars, the sickest and weakest being helped to the ambulances. According to Gwatkin-Williams barely half an hour elapsed from the first sighting of the cars to their setting off again on the return trip.

> On leaving [Bir Hakim] we headed north-east making fifteen miles an hour. [We were] soon on the Sollum Road, where we tore along at from twenty to twenty-five miles an hour … The yellow dust was blinding, but we could smell the … sea and the cars appeared the height of luxury in a land where we had marched in pain and weariness and suffered so much. We flew past the numerous twin mounds of ancient Roman wells. Past the signs of recent battle, where dead camels and men lay beside the road and the ravens were already beginning to gather. Past a smashed Turkish motor-car, and a solitary Bedouin or two, who stared dumbfounded at us, and neither attempted to flee nor to take cover.[20]

The sun set at 6pm; with a full moon and headlamps on this time, all the cars safely reached base camp at Bir 'Aziz by 1am.

> There we … were again fed with hot milk, spirits, meat, bread and jam. The cosiest of quarters for the night in tents and ambulances with soft warm rugs to cover us. We were all far too excited to sleep … and after talking all night, rose at earliest dawn to continue … eating. Then breakfast with *real* tea, and at 8am on the 18th of March we started on the last stage to Sollum over a [road now obliterated and obscured by a] nearly impenetrable sandstorm. On, till we came to the old British [sic] fort which crowns the heights and looks down on the sea, and where we saw the old flag flying for the first time. The kindest of greetings from General and private alike, and we were descending on camels the 500 feet of rocky slope leading down to the Mediterranean, never more beautiful

[20] WO 106/1543, Gwatkin-Williams, p. 31.

and inviting than now, with the shipping curvetting and dancing to the fresh north-westerly breeze, a picture of blue [sea] and golden sand I shall never forget.[21]

While the WFF's campaign was coming to a sudden and successful conclusion, behind the scene negotiations were continuing between British, Turkish, Sanusi Arab, and Italian diplomatic channels to get food, medicine and other supplies to the prisoners at Bir Hakim. On 15 March a messenger had arrived at Bir Hakim with the news that the supplies were on a ship in an Italian port. The cargo would be released when the British Consul in Libya had proof that it would indeed reach the prisoners. Therefore, Sub-Lieutenant Leslie Dudgeon and the interpreter, Basil Lambrinidis, were sent to meet with the appropriate authorities and return with the supplies.

Travelling by camel the two men were escorted north for two days and then east. They stayed in Arab and Turkish military camps, and it soon became clear that the port they were approaching was Tobruk. Finally, they were handed over to a Turkish officer named 'Abdi Bey, who was to escort them into Tobruk. They were treated kindly throughout the trek, but especially so by 'Abdi Bey, who, Dudgeon wrote later, "treated us with the greatest kindness, entertaining us most hospitably and doing everything to make us comfortable".[22] By now Dudgeon and Lambrinidis had been away from Bir Hakim for three or four days and the rescue of the other prisoners had already taken place. 'Abdi Bey knew this, but he simply handed the two men over to the Italian authorities. It is possible that they were handed over to the Italians in exchange for the much-needed supplies. Even so, the important thing was that they were now free.

By any standard, the operation to rescue the prisoners was risky and its chances of success dubious. General Peyton had known this. He did not

[21] WO 106/1543, p. 31.

[22] FO 383/238, letter from Leslie Dudgeon to Marquis Santasilia, Naval Commandant at Tobruk.

[23] See page 273.

[24] This was unusual insofar as this was not the case with his colleagues in the Coastguard Administration, whose names – Hunter, von Dumreicher, Snow, Tweedie, Armstrong, Gärtner and dozens of others – appeared regularly in *The Egyptian Gazette*.

agree to allow the operation to go ahead simply because the Duke of Westminster had courageously volunteered to undertake it. He agreed because Royle said that he could find Bir Hakim. The key to success was good intelligence, and Royle provided it. Indeed, General Maxwell actually said that it was mainly due to Royle that the operation succeeded.[23]

The importance of Royle's contribution to the rescue effort, and indeed to the whole campaign, was not always obvious. For example, he is not mentioned by name in the two best-known books to come out of the Sanusi War: Gwatkin-Williams' *Prisoners of the Red Desert* and S. C. Rolls' *Steel Chariots in the Desert*. It is interesting to reflect that before the war, Royle, who had been at the forefront of the Egyptian Government's campaign against the smugglers, had been known to almost everyone in the Western Desert – that is, to the sparse Bedouin population and to those who worked in public security there; but that he had been virtually unknown in the social and political world of Cairo and Alexandria, except to Kitchener, Maxwell and a few senior officials who worked with them.[24] The role he played in the Sanusi campaign was different in that he was usually far from the action, a member of the General Staff who interviewed prisoners and advised generals on the lay of the land and the customs of the enemy, but he remained almost as unknown to the soldiers of the WFF as he had been to Cairo society. To the extent that he came to their attention at all – for example, when he made reconnaissance flights or advised the Duke of Westminster during the rescue – he was simply "the Intelligence Officer". There is no paradox here. Royle was self-sufficient and solitary by nature. He shunned the limelight. And while circumstances may have thrown him into the noisy, crowded world of British soldiers on campaign, the very fact that he could stand apart no doubt made it easier for him to continue to work with the Bedouin even in wartime. His long desert experience and his rapport with the Bedouin were crucial to the success of the rescue.

21

The Long Road to Akramah

THE *TARA* SURVIVORS were sent to Alexandria to recover in hospital and most were soon home in Holyhead.

For the vast majority of the British and Colonial soldiers who had been involved in the campaign to push the Sanusi army out of Egypt, the "Sanusi War" was over.[1] Many were sent to France, as were General Lukin and the South African Infantry, and the Brigade suffered horrific losses on the Somme that July. General Peyton also went to France, with an appointment to General Haig's headquarters.

General Maxwell handed over the command of Egypt to General Sir Archibald Murray on 19 March. Maxwell's next appointment was as commander of British forces in Ireland. It was the year of the Easter uprising in Dublin, and ever since his name has been associated with the execution of Irish rebels.

But, of course, the Sanusi War was not over. Sollum was again in the hands of the British, but the Sanusi had not been defeated so much as scattered. In the chain of oases in the centre of Egypt between Siwa and the Nile there were still several thousand Sanusi ready to carry on fighting, not to mention that in Libya Nuri was still in command of the Turkish contingent there and a powerful influence among pro-war Libyan Arabs.

---

[1] The final entry of the WFF War Diary (General Staff) reads "28 March. WFF ceased to exist." (WO 95/4437).

At Sollum the long overdue strengthening of defences was carried out. A 4.7-inch gun was mounted near the harbour to protect the new military camp there from further attacks by submarines, and an aeroplane landing field was established on the plateau within sight of the former Sanusi camp. The Armoured Car Brigade was still active there, although later in the year Major L. V. Owston replaced the Duke of Westminster as its commander. The British had asked for, and received, Italian permission to pursue the remnants of the Sanusi force that were across the border in Libya. In April they participated in four raids in which great quantities of arms and ammunition were either destroyed or brought back to Sollum. In May Italian troops occupied Bardia. In June the British and the Italians agreed to work together in the area, and thereafter the raids on the Libyan side of the border were often joint operations.

In April 1916 Sayyid Ahmad surprised everyone by leaving Siwa, not for Jaghbub or some other haven in Libya, but for the Egyptian Oasis of Dakhla. Considering the difficulties which his army in Egypt now faced, this was a bold move. The Sanusi force in central Egypt posed far less of a threat to the British than had the army under Ja'far's command in the north of the country, so one can only assume that he went to Dakhla fearing loss of his authority if he withdrew to Libya.

British Intelligence assessed Sanusi strength in the Western Desert at about 3,000 men. To attack that force so deep in the desert, where the Sanusi were in their native environment, was perceived to be unnecessarily risky, so the British decided to contain the enemy where they were, away from populated areas. Nevertheless, they soon had an opportunity to reoccupy Kharga, the central oasis nearest to the Nile Valley.[2] In mid-April aerial reconnaissance and local agents reported that oasis to be clear of Sanusi, and the British rushed a force of 1,600 men there by means of an already existing light railway. Their engineers were soon at work extending that rail line westwards, towards Dakhla. A few hundred miles to the north, they began to lay tracks for a new light railway from the Nile Valley to Bahariyya Oasis, and to build a parallel line of defensive blockhouses just to the south of the projected new rail line.

While these various engineering projects were underway, long-range reconnaissance was carried out by two new formations: the Light Car Patrols (LCPs) and the Imperial Camel Corps (ICC), both of which were

---

[2] 195 miles west of Luxor.

manned primarily by Australians and New Zealanders.

During the WFF's campaign along the coast the relative strengths and weaknesses of Rolls-Royces and Model T Fords for desert use had been clearly demonstrated. The armoured Rolls-Royce had excelled as an attack vehicle, and the Ford had been used mainly in supporting roles. But in the present stage of operations mobility was more important than armour. The Ford had good ground clearance, was light-weight and easy to maintain, and it quickly became the vehicle of choice for long-distance desert raids and reconnaissance patrols. In May 1916 there were six Light Car Patrols, each consisting of six Fords (five of which had a mounted Lewis gun, the sixth being a supply tender).[3]

As for the Imperial Camel Corps, four companies were initially formed in January 1916 (mainly from men of the 14th Australian Light Horse) and placed under the command of Lieutenant-Colonel C. L. Smith, VC.[4] A detachment of this force had served with General Peyton, having arrived just in time to participate in the reoccupation of Sollum.

In the late spring and early summer of 1916 the main focus of LCP and ICC patrolling was from Kharga to the west (towards Dakhla) and to the south for about fifty miles. But there was also extensive coverage of the area between Kharga and the Nile Valley; of the environs of Farafra and Bahariyya; and, in the far north, of the area around Moghara (south of el-Alamein) and Wadi Natrun (between Alexandria and Fayum). There were numerous small successes by both the Light Cars and the camel patrols, when they intercepted either small bands of Sanusi soldiers or caravans bearing supplies, arms or mail. There were no significant developments, however, until October.

Muhammad Saleh Harb, who was now a general (*lewa*) in the Sanusi army, had come to the central oases hoping to be able to trigger a rise of his fellow countrymen against the British. He successfully established contact with certain important sheikhs in Minya, Asyut, and Fayum, but the sheikhs now considered the Sanusi military campaign in Egypt to be

---

[3] G. E. Badcock (1925*), A History of the Transport Services of the Egyptian Expeditionary Force, 1916–1917–1918*, pp. 241–3. Twenty-one men were assigned to each patrol: two officers, two sergeants, two corporals, and fifteen additional men of various ranks who were the drivers and machine gunners.

[4] The Imperial Camel Corps would later grow into a brigade of four battalions for use principally in the Egyptian Expeditionary Force moving on Palestine.

hopeless and their responses were not encouraging. During the summer the Sanusi in the oases suffered badly due to sickness and to a severe shortage of food, and for several months they had virtually nothing to eat but dates. The British were slowly but inexorably approaching, morale was low, and so Sayyid Ahmad and Saleh Harb decided to withdraw back to the west before it was too late. Saleh Harb tried to cover the retreat by feigning an attack against the British in the north, near the Fayum Oasis. In September he sent a small force with the task of creating the impression that the whole Sanusi army was about to attack. There was, in fact, an exchange of fire, but to the British this was just another small skirmish among many, and they were not taken in by the feint. Sayyid Ahmad, meanwhile, was reported to have moved from Dakhla to Bahariyya (120 miles to the north). In October the British heard from their agents that over the three days, from 8 to 10 October, Sayyid Ahmad and most of the Sanusi army had departed for Siwa. The new British commander in the Western Desert, Major-General William Watson, ordered an immediate attack, hoping to cut off the Sanusi retreat.[5] All the Light Cars in the sector gathered near Bahariyya and raced westwards. But it was too late – the Sanusi force reached the Great Sand Sea and escaped to Siwa.

Between 17 and 19 October mobile columns of the Imperial Camel Corps occupied Bahariyya. To the south a small force of Sanusi were reported to be still in Dakhla, however, so Watson sent a motorised column from Kharga, followed by one company of the Imperial Camel Corps. The column[6] entered Dakhla also on the 17th, and the Camel Corps arrived two days later. About 135 Sanusi soldiers were captured without resistance as well as a number of local Sanusi sympathisers. Four weeks later, on 19 November 1916, Farafra too was occupied by the British.

The only major Egyptian oasis still in the hands of the Sanusi was Siwa.

On 20 January 1917 a General Staff Officer at GHQ Cairo named Alan Dawnay wrote to General Watson about discussions then taking place at headquarters concerning an imminent raid against Siwa.[7] The purpose of the operation, Dawnay said, was "to clear up the situation in the Western Desert before all our energies are ... turned back to the Eastern front [ie,

---

[5] General Watson was appointed 4 October 1916.
[6] One Rolls-Royce armoured car, six Fords with Lewis guns, one supply tender and twelve motorcycles!

for an attack against the Turks in Palestine]". A conference was scheduled at the Savoy on the 22nd to discuss this further, and Watson, as overall commander in the Western Desert, was asked to attend. Broadly, the plan under consideration was to send a force of camel corps (both Imperial and Bikanir) together with "as many armoured cars as we can concentrate for the purpose" in an attempt finally to defeat the Sanusi in Egypt. Brigadier-General Henry Hodgson would probably be appointed as commander of the operation. Dawnay also mentioned that Royle would be available to deal with intelligence matters.[8]

The conference was duly held, but in addition to confirming the details outlined in Dawnay's letter, it produced a curious consequence for Royle. Working closely with General Watson was a certain staff officer named Major Charles W. Maclean, who was forty years old and had a long record of service in Egypt, including seven years with the Egyptian Army before the war. He was also married to Leo Royle's cousin, Gladys Royle. Again Royle was to work in the Western Desert with a relative, albeit this time one by marriage.

As expected, General Hodgson was appointed to command the raid, but several days after the conference "reliable information" arrived from Sollum necessitating a change in the arrangements.[9] Part of the Sanusi force had already left Siwa, and Sayyid Ahmad himself was said to be about to leave for Jaghbub. For the British to organise the various companies of camel corps and get them to Siwa would take weeks, and that was no longer feasible as one of the principal objectives of the plan was "to capture Sayyid Ahmad".[10] As speed was essential, the use of animals was dropped from the scheme and preparations made instead to assemble a large mechanised mobile column at Mersa Matruh. Eleven Rolls Royces of the Light Armoured Car Brigade under Major Owston, together with Light Car Patrols numbers 4, 5 and 6, were to be the attack element of the force, that is, twenty-nine vehicles; but also going were an additional eighty-two touring cars, vans and lorries for Headquarters Staff, the medics, the signallers, not to mention the supplies of food, water, and

---

[7] Alan Dawnay, was a friend and colleague of T. E. Lawrence, who later wrote: "Dawnay was Allenby's greatest gift to us – greater than thousands of baggage camels. As a professional officer, he had the class-touch" (*Seven Pillars of Wisdom*, Ch. XCII).
[8] WO 95/4438, letter from A. C. Dawnay to General Watson, 20 January 1917.
[9] WO 95/4438. See 2-page annex to the War Diaries entitled "Scheme".
[10] Ibid.

petrol necessary for the expedition – this time the total number of cars was 111!

Royle was telegraphed to assemble the Bedouin guides and to meet Hodgson and his Staff at Alexandria for departure by train to Mersa Matruh on 29 January. The intention had been for the column to start for Siwa on the 31st, but then a sandstorm caused a day's delay by preventing the heavy supply lorries from arriving in time from al-Dab'a.

The column finally left Mersa Matruh early on 1 February. It covered 121 miles over the hard, mostly flat plateau until, late in the day, a halt was called for the night, and the signallers used their wireless to inform Matruh of the day's progress. The next day the vehicles continued for another sixty miles, when at midday they arrived at a place twelve miles north of the Shaqqah Pass (leading into the Siwa/Qirba depression) a point dubbed in the operational plan "the Point of Concentration". That afternoon Royle guided a patrol in two of the LCP Fords in a reconnaissance of the pass down the escarpment. Royle found the pass to be undefended and usable by the cars, so Hodgson issued orders for the next day's attack. Since part of the Sanusi force was known to be at Qirba, in the northern part of the depression, the main part of the column would move against that location first. Six armoured cars under Major Owston would lead, followed by – in order – Headquarters and the Signals detachment; two Light Car Patrols (Nos. 4 and 5) plus two more armoured cars, all of which would comprise the reserve, and a small fleet of RAMC ambulances. While that force was thus occupied, a smaller one (three armoured cars, No. 6 Light Car Patrol, and one Ford ambulance) under the command of Captain Mangles would leave the Point of Concentration and proceed westward to block the pass at Munassib, on the main track to Jaghbub. Any Sanusi retreating from the Siwa depression to Jaghbub would, it was thought, have to get back onto the plateau and redescend into the Qeiqab depression at Munassib.[11] Thus, by holding the pass, Mangles' detachment would (in theory, at least) be in a position to foil any attempted Sanusi retreat into Libya.

All vehicles not assigned to one or other of these two forces were to remain at the Point of Concentration.

The two forces left the Point of Concentration at 6.30am on 3

[11] The way from Siwa to Jaghbub, via Munassib Pass and 'Ain Qeiqab, was first described to Royle by the Egyptian coastguard who went to Jaghbub after Sayyid Ahmad's first contact with the British in 1912 (see Ch. 1, page 34).

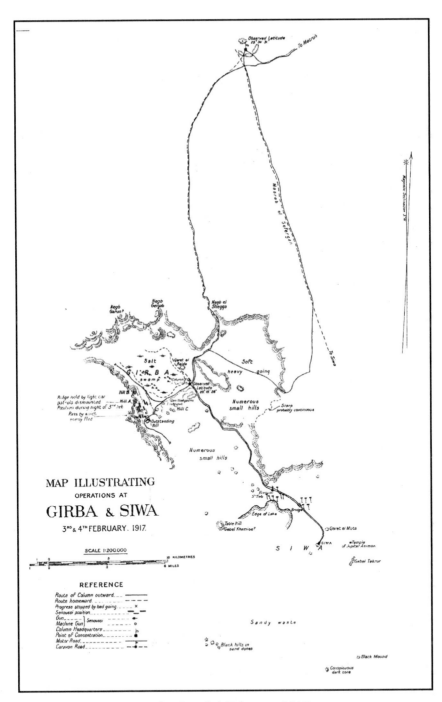

Map 9 Operations at Qirba, 3 and 4 February 1917.

February. The main one reached the top of the Shaqqah Pass, where Hodgson again went through the plan of attack with the unit commanders, and then the drivers gingerly drove their vehicles down to the depression floor. The descent took several hours, but by 9.30 all had reached the bottom of the escarpment. From there a dirt track led west to a large, roughly square pan-like area boxed in on three sides by the escarpment and on the fourth (southern) side by low rocky hills. The dirt track continued south through the hills to Siwa itself. Much of the pan was a salty swamp, although this was not evident at first, as a thin crust had formed across its surface. The pan was roughly nine square miles, and somewhere along its inner periphery were the Sanusi. Royle knew of three camp sites in the area used by the Siwans. But which one would the Sanusi be using? Hodgson's solution was to divide the six armoured cars into three pairs, each with an Arab guide. Each pair was assigned one of three likely campsites.

The cars reached the eastern side of the pan without any problems, but as they began to cross it two of the cars went through the crust and got stuck, while two others were delayed trying to get across. The third pair of armoured cars, with Major Owston, successfully negotiated the crossing of the swamp crust and came upon the Sanusi force at what was known as the "winter camp" on a ridge below the escarpment on the west side of the pan.

> We finally came in sight of the Senoussi Camp, which consisted of tents and stone huts grouped on a flat ledge of rock with a semicircle of steep rugged cliffs frowning down upon it. The rocky ledge broke away in a low but precipitous bank in front of the camp and formed a very excellent protection against car attack.[12]

The Sanusi, who had had virtually no encounter with the British in over three months, were taken completely unawares. They scrambled on to the rocks and cliffs behind their camp and opened fire on the two armoured cars, the time being 10.15am. Another pair of armoured cars soon arrived at the area of the shooting, while Hodgson, hearing the gunfire, sent forward the two he had been holding in reserve, replacing them with the two cars which had been stuck in the marsh but which

---

[12] Williams, Claud H. (n. d.), "Light Car Patrols in the Libyan Desert", p. 19.

were now free. He also sent Light Car Patrols Nos. 4 and 5 forward to assist in the attack.

At 11am the Sanusi began firing two mountain guns and two machine guns. The armoured cars and the LCP Fords were operating at about 1,000 yards east of the Sanusi position, and the rough ground made it impossible to manoeuvre the vehicles any closer. Some of the LCP men managed to advance on foot carrying four Lewis Guns to within about 800 yards of the enemy, but "accurate machine gun fire"[13] prevented them from getting any closer. The Sanusi were also handling their mountain guns effectively, and shells "[forced] the cars to keep changing position and many of them narrowly escaped direct hits".[14]

Column headquarters had been set up near the point where the road passed through the hills to Siwa, although Hodgson managed to reach a look-out position about 2,000 yards from the battle. At these rear positions the British came in touch (about midday) with some Arabs, or "stray deserters" as Hodgson called them in his report, who said that the Sanusi strength at Qirba was 850 men, and that 400 to 500 additional Sanusi soldiers were at Siwa.[15] In fact, although the British did not know this, Sayyid Ahmad and Mohammad Saleh Harb had both been in Siwa at the start of the action. When the first shots were fired, Saleh Harb hurried to Qirba to take command, while Sayyid Ahmad made off to the west, hoping to escape to Jaghbub. Hodgson had anticipated that Sayyid Ahmad would attempt to cross into Libya, but not knowing where Saleh Harb was, he was anxious that the latter might lead the Sanusi force in Siwa through the hills and attack the British left flank and rear. The Light Car Patrols were therefore withdrawn from the battle (2.30pm); LCP No. 5 was sent to watch the Shaqqah Pass; No. 4 was sent to guard the southern approaches to Qirba; and all unnecessary support vehicles were sent back up to the plateau.

Late in the day (4.00pm) Royle and Maclean, in two armoured cars under Major Owston, moved to a position on the Sanusi right flank. This time the cars managed to get to within 300 yards of the enemy camp. One of the enemy mountain guns had by this time been put out of action by an armoured car, but in any case their gunfire was now dying down. Owston's men continued to fire into the camp through the night. The

[13] WO 95/4438, Hodgson's report of 9 February 1917, pp. 4–5.
[14] Ibid. [15] Ibid.

Sanusi responded with some sniping and occasional bursts from their machine guns.

At 5.00am the next morning (4 February) the Sanusi fired four final rounds from the mountain guns and a few more bursts from the machine guns. Then all was quiet. It was still nearly dark, but the British could see fires behind the camp and some movement of men and camels. By break of day the site of the battle was empty: the Sanusi had all escaped with their animals over a pass behind their camp.

The firing had gone on for nearly twenty hours. Claud Williams, the New Zealander commanding Light Car Patrol No. 5, wrote that the battle at Qirba was "a regular 'opera bouffe' affair: an immense amount of noise and very little blood-shed".[16] Three British officers had been wounded. Sanusi casualties were not immediately apparent – no burial sites were found in the area and the Sanusi had taken their wounded with them.

Early on the 5th the British force at Qirba left for nearby Siwa. Sam Rolls, still driving with the Armoured Car Brigade, described what happened next:

> We had not descended far into the valley when a man dressed in a white
> robe and waving a white flag was seen coming towards us. A halt was
> called and the envoy beckoned to us to come near ... [T]hrough the
> interpreter [Royle], we learnt that the Senusite leader and the remainder
> of his followers had fled towards the west the day before. Our new friend,
> one of the notables of Siwa, had come to welcome us to the place in the

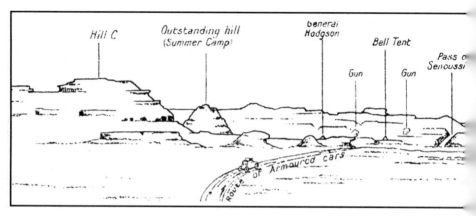

Map 10 Profile sketch of enemy position at Qirba.

name of the local sheikhs ... We asked him to ride in with us in one of the cars, and he mounted to a seat on a rifle-box of one of them, and there remained in motionless dignity. The road [passed] between avenues of trees, heavily laden with limes, figs, olives, pomegranates, oranges, lemons, and other fruits; and the rows of date palms extended for miles about us. We drove across quaint little wooden bridges which spanned the irrigation channels of cool clear water, and passed several lakes bordered by green fields and more orchards ... I was almost awed by the richness of the scene into which we had come.[17]

The newcomers were equally amazed by Siwa town. Rolls called it "the queerest town that I have ever seen ... [It was] built of mud, and on its decayed walls tier above tier of little wood-and-mud houses were stuck like swallows' nests".[18]

We now halted the cars, and the guide got down and requested our commander to follow him into the town. This he did, accompanied by his staff, and they were met by some more of the chief men of the place as they approached. We watched them conferring together, and the rest of the inhabitants, most of whom had retreated into their hovels, eyed our cars from their windows and doorways ... At last our officers returned, and we received the order to drive into the town in single file ... [Finally,] we drew up in front of a long, low building.[19]

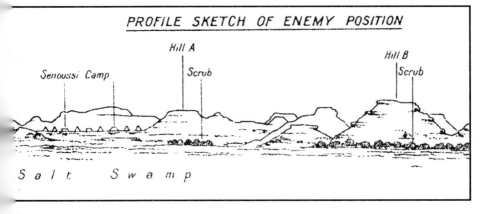

PROFILE SKETCH OF ENEMY POSITION

Hill A

Hill B

Senoussi Camp

Scrub

Scrub

Salt   Swamp

This was the *markaz*, the Government administration building, which, however, had been unused by Egyptian Government officials since November 1915. Royle and the Siwan sheikh who had ridden into town with the column spread the word that all the other sheikhs were to assemble outside the *markaz* to listen to a speech by General Hodgson. When these were present, Hodgon spoke, while Royle interpreted. He explained what had happened at Qirba; that the Sanusi army had now been defeated and had withdrawn to Libya; and he told the sheikhs to have all arms collected and delivered to the British, and to see that all passes into the Oasis were opened. The sheikhs agreed. The atmosphere was surprisingly friendly. A nine-gun salute was fired; and Hodgson even escorted the assembled notables on an inspection tour of the cars, which for this purpose were drawn up in a single line with the crews standing at attention. While this was going on a British Army cameraman cranked away behind his tripod, filming the event for posterity.

The Siwans then offered the British hospitality, culminating (on the following day) with an invitation by one Siwan sheikh to all the British and Colonial soldiers in the Oasis to his home for lunch!

But while British–Siwan relations were flourishing in the Oasis, Captain Mangles' detachment was still at Munassib Pass. He and his men had been only partially successful. They had had great difficulty, despite the presence of Bedouin guides, finding their way to the Pass. Moreover, when the track was finally found, the going was too rough for the three Rolls Royce armoured cars, and these had to be left on the plateau eighteen miles from their destination. No. 6 Light Car Patrol (in other words, the Fords) carried on and made it to the edge of the escarpment in the early evening (7pm on 3 February). The next morning, with great difficulty, the LCP cars made it down the Munassib Pass and took up positions to intercept any Sanusi coming from either direction. On that day a twenty-camel caravan carrying supplies and mail for Siwa arrived from the west, and this was captured and the supplies destroyed. On the next day (the 5th) an advance party of Sanusi retreating from the fight at Qirba were ambushed descending the pass. Seven Sanusi were killed; the rest scrambled back up to the plateau and disappeared. Before long the Sanusi had established a post atop a distant hill to signal others not to use the

[16] Williams, Claud H. (n. d.), p. 16.
[17] S. C. Rolls (1937), pp. 135–6.   [18] Ibid., pp. 136–7.   [19] Ibid., p. 137.

Munassib Pass. Unbeknownst to the British there was another pass about four miles south of Munassib, immediately below which were high sand dunes. Sayyid Ahmad and the rest of his retreating army used this other pass and escaped through the dunes.

Due to problems with the wireless sets communications between Mangles' detachment and General Hodgson were intermittent at best. But on the afternoon of 6 February Hodgson was informed of the situation at Munassib, and he ordered Mangles to return to the Point of Concentration.

While at Siwa, Hodgson and his men bivouacked at night four miles outside of town on the track to Qirba. On the morning of the 6th Royle went with several of the armoured cars to bring in all the arms which the sheikhs had collected. On this occasion he was told that Sanusi casualties at the Qirba action were thirty-one killed, including five out of nine Turkish officers, and many wounded; and this information was backed up by the names of the dead. The Siwans also told Royle about Muhammad Saleh Harb having rushed from Siwa to Qirba on the 3rd to take command. On the afternoon of the same day (6 February) the cars left the Oasis and returned to the Point of Concentration. The entire reunited column reached Mersa Matruh on the evening of 8 February.

The Sanusi were no longer a threat to British-occupied Egypt; and they were now a much weaker threat than before to the Italians in Libya. But neither the British nor the Italians wanted to discuss peace with Sayyid Ahmad, even though he was still the Grand Sanusi, both parties preferring instead to negotiate with his nephew, Muhammad Idris. Idris was an obvious choice. He would have become the Grand Sanusi on the death of his father had he not been too young; he was, in any case, the first in line to succeed to the Sanusi leadership; and, importantly, he had been unequivocally against the invasion of Egypt, and he was at least willing to try to negotiate with the Italians.

In May of 1916, when Sayyid Ahmad was still in Dakhla, Idris was already having discussions with the Italians concerning peace in Cyrenaica

[20] FO 371/2670. Letter from Muhammad Idris to Henry McMahon, 28 May 1916.
[21] Rachel Simon (1987), *Libya between Ottomanism and Nationalism: The Ottoman Involvement in Libya during the War with Italy (1911–1919)*, p. 285.
[22] Forty miles south-west of Tobruk.

(the only Libyan province where Idris had any authority) and in contact with the British. He wrote to the British High Commissioner in Egypt, expressing his willingness to take control of Sanusi affairs and to seek a peace settlement. "I am really so sorry for what [Sayyid Ahmad] has done," he wrote. "He shows firstly that he is a fool, and secondly that he is ungrateful. I [did] my best to prevent this fighting, but I failed."[20]

Negotiations took nearly a year to complete. The future of Sanusi-British relations was not a problem, as, apart from demanding that Sanusi *zawiya*s be closed in Egypt, the British wanted little more than a return to the status quo before the war. But the British did insist that Idris had to deal with Britain and Italy together, not separately as Idris would have preferred, and this gave the Italian negotiators greater leverage in the bargaining. Discussions often broke down as Idris found the Italians unyielding and shifty. Once, for example, the parties were on the verge of an agreement, when the Italian negotiators were curtly informed by their own Government that they had no authority to make binding commitments, only proposals.[21] Idris left the talks, and negotiations had to start all over again later.

Finally, at the town of Akramah[22] on 14 April 1917, Idris signed a peace accord with Great Britain, and three days later, with a lot of coaxing by the British representative, he signed with the Italians.

For the British the Sanusi War was over. For the Italians there were five uneasy years of peace in Cyrenaica, and then ten more years of war throughout Libya. They continued to maintain a fragile hold on the country until 1947. That year, under the terms of Italy's peace treaty with the Allies after the Second World War, Italy finally gave up all claim to Libya.

Epilogue

L EO ROYLE RECEIVED some impressive commendations for his services before and during the Sanusi War. One of the most glowing was written by General Maxwell shortly after he had left Egypt:

> Temporary Captain L.V. Royle … received the Military Cross … in the earlier part of the war. But his services were of exceptional value for, besides an intimate knowledge of Beduins and the desert, he was present at every engagement on the Canal and on the Western Frontier. [He] was an aeroplane observer of exceptional value, and flew incessantly both in the Canal area and on the West. It was mainly due to him that the armoured cars of the Duke of Westminster were able to locate and rescue the prisoners of [HMS] "Tara", and he thoroughly deserves a DSO.[1]

Maxwell went on to say that Lord Kitchener (who died in June 1916, when HMS *Hampshire* struck a mine) "was particularly interested in this officer and knew the great value of his services".[2] The commendation was also "warmly endorsed" by the British High Commissioner in Egypt, Henry McMahon.

The War Office completely ignored Maxwell's recommendation, even though it was supported by McMahon. In Whitehall Maxwell – and

---

[1] FO 372/832. Maxwell's list of recommended honours attached to a letter from McMahon to the Foreign Secretary, dated 31 August 1916.
[2] Ibid.

indeed Kitchener himself! – were blamed as the architects of a policy that had led to war in the Western Desert. Believing for too long that the Sanusi would not invade Egypt, the two men had left the western frontier virtually undefended, despite the presence of Turkish soldiers and German agents at the Sanusi camp. Maxwell defended those who sought to carry out the policy – Hunter, Snow and Royle – in a memorandum, in which he wrote that it had been "entirely directed by me, *under orders from the War Office* [author's italics]".[3] The memorandum had no effect. Royle did not receive his DSO. Indeed, he received no medal at all for his work in the Western Desert in 1915 and 1916. Finally, in February 1917 he was awarded a bar to his Military Cross for his services during the Siwa Raid.

The campaign in the Western Desert was over, but Royle's flying career was still subject to interruptions. Following the events at Siwa Royle did, indeed, return to his duties with the RFC, and an account of a solo flight he made to the Hijaz was published by the Arab Bureau on 30 April 1917.

> Captain L. Royle, MC, whose competence in Arabic, and power of gaining Bedouin confidence are well known, spent some days in the country behind Wejh in March last. He was sent up to search for landing grounds for the RFC, and went as far in as Jeyadah, on the southern el-Ala road, and Ugla (Akila) on the Medina road. He reports, that, though there is scarcity of accessible and good water, the country in general is surprisingly well-wooded, and full of game. In the wadis are guinea-fowl and red-legged partridge; the true ring-dove is common, and so is the blue rock-pigeon. Dorcas and Loder's gazelle were seen, as well as ibex, hyaena, and a small jackal. Captain Royle came on tracks of a leopard, and heard much of an animal, probably a wolf or wild dog, which will attack a camel alone and pull it down.[4]

By year's end a new Egyptian Government department called the Frontiers Districts Administration had replaced the Coastguard as the department responsible for administering the Western Desert. The FDA was headed by George Hunter, and Royle was appointed to be the Governor of the province:

---

[3] Quoted in Sir George Arthur (1932), *General Sir John Maxwell*, pp. 222–3.
[4] *The Arab Bulletin: Bulletin of the Arab Bureau in Cairo, 1916–1919* (Published by Archive Editions, 1986), Vol. 2, p. 201.

Before leaving Akramah Mohammed Idris was visited by the Governor of the Western Desert, Major Royle, who had been despatched by the High Commissioner to convey to Idris the news of the Italian concession in the matter of supplying him with certain war material. Idris expressed some dissent at the smallness of the concession and took the opportunity to submit a detailed list of his requirements. He was, however, considerably gratified by Major Royle's visit, no less than by the presence of armoured cars in his camp, which news he took care to inform Major Royle would not be long in getting west and would doubtless be construed by his enemies to mean that the British armoured cars were actually assisting him. The armoured car is what the Arabs chiefly fear these days.[5]

Being desk-bound did not suit Royle at all, and, as soon as he could, he returned to flying. The RFC was in the process of changing its name to the RAF, and Royle now changed from being an observer to being a pilot. He trained on various types of machines: AVRO monoplanes, Bristol Scouts, Nieuports, Sopwith Pups – but, especially, the SE5a, which many considered to be the best British single-seat fighter of the war. In March 1918 he graduated from the flying school at Heliopolis as a Flight Commander and was appointed to No. 111 Squadron, then at Ramleh in Palestine.

When Royle joined the Squadron, several of its pilots had recently distinguished themselves in air combat. In any case, life at Ramleh was never dull. In April, May and June the number of the Squadron's flying hours were more than they had ever been. There were forty-five instances of air combat. Seventeen German aircraft were destroyed. But in the same period three of their own pilots were killed, and one was shot down and taken prisoner. By July the pilots of the 111th had been supplied with bomb sights and were making daily raids on German airbases in Palestine.[6] Royle had joined the RFC in the second month of the war. Now, finally, four years later, there were no more interruptions, no more orders to return to the Western Desert. This period was the high point of his flying career.

[5] *The Arab Bulletin*, Vol. 3, see issue of 3 January 1918.
[6] AIR/1/1949/204/254/4, "The History of No. 111 Squadron, Royal Air Force" (8 typed pages).

Tragically, on 17 August 1918, Royle crashed and died. It is unclear
whether this was the result of air combat or simply an accident. A fellow
pilot, who was nearby when Royle's SE5a went down, claimed that it was
a result of combat.

> On discussing the crash with various fellows in the different units of this
> Brigade, they nearly all state that they distinctly saw two hostile planes
> circle round over Royle and then fly back over the line. They all state that
> the two Bosh [sc. Boche] planes were about 1,000 feet higher than ours,
> and many say they saw the Black Cross. That would account for the AA
> fire heard just after Royle crashed, as it would be just the time they would
> be crossing our line. The planes were only visible at intervals – when they
> passed across openings in the clouds.[7]

Sources on the ground reported hearing several loud explosions, "when
the machine nose dived very steeply and the wings eventually fell apart".[8]
In any case, Royle was reported to have been "killed in action", although
the exact circumstances of the crash were never determined. He is buried
at Ramleh War Cemetery.

There is this postscript to the story of Royle. In the 1920s, his friend
and fellow intelligence officer, Wilfred Jennings Bramly, conceived and
built an attractive, walled-town, called Borg al-Arab. Located a half-hour's
drive to the west of Alexandria, it was essentially a modern caravanserai for
the Bedouin – a *zawiya*, but without any connection to the Sanusi
Brotherhood. In the central courtyard, amid the stone buildings, Jennings
Bramly placed a monument to the memory of Leopold Royle – a 10 ft-
high pillar. The caravanserai still exists as a minor tourist attraction.
Unfortunately, the monument has not survived, although the locals are
happy to point out the plinth on which it stood. Some of the oldest of
them even remember the name of the extraordinary British officer for
whom it was built.

---

[7] AIR/1/1949/204/254/4, letter of 20 August 1918 by Alan [name illegible].
[8] AIR/1/1949/204/254/4, "The History of No. 111 Squadron, Royal Air Force".
[9] *The New York Times*, 7 April 1941, article cited by Teichmann et al., *Faszination Orient*,
p. 91.
[10] Brandt-Mannesmann (1964), p. 160.

Sayyid Ahmad returned to Jaghbub after his army's defeat at Siwa, but his influence in Cyrenaica steadily declined. In August 1918 he left Libya aboard a German U-boat and was taken to Pola (near Trieste), and from there he made his way to Constantinople. Although he had given up the political leadership of the Brotherhood, he remained its spiritual leader. He died at Medina in Arabia in 1933.

Nuri returned to Turkey, and at the war's end he was commanding guerrilla operations in the Caucasus. He eventually returned to private life, running an ammunition factory on the Golden Horn. On 2 March 1949 he died in an explosion at his factory.

Max von Oppenheim survived the war and devoted the rest of his life to archaeology. He remained in Germany throughout the Second World War and, despite his Jewish origins, was left alone by the Nazis. They apparently considered him to be an "honorary Aryan" because of his past services to Germany. [9] He died in 1946.

Otto Mannesmann was shot and killed on 10 April 1916, while travelling west across Libya with a caravan. An enquiry held by the German Foreign Office concluded that the deed had been carried out by Sanusi soldiers who were "in league with the English". [10]

Ja'far al-'Askari was sent to Cairo as a prisoner of war. A few months after Ja'far was captured, Jemal Pasha shocked the world by ordering the execution of twenty-two well-known Arab nationalists and intellectuals in Beirut and Damascus. Influenced by the savagery of that event, and with the encouragement of his friend and brother-in-law Nuri al-Said, Ja'far joined the Arab Revolt against the Ottomans. He trained and commanded a force of Arab regulars under Prince Faysal bin Husayn in Arabia, working with T. E. Lawrence. After Faysal became the king of Iraq, Ja'far joined the Iraqi government, in which he served five times as Minister of Defence and twice as Prime Minister. He was assassinated in 1936.

Muhammad Saleh Harb accompanied Sayyid Ahmad to Constantinople. After the war he was allowed to return to Egypt where, in 1939, he became the Director-General of the Egyptian Coastguard Administration.

APPENDICES

Appendix 1

Captain Gwatkin-Williams' account of his attempted escape from Bir Hakim

Extract from "A Brief Record of Proceedings of Survivors of HMS *Tara* from the time of their being made prisoners at Port Suleiman, Cyrenaica, on 5th November [1915]" by Captain Gwatkin-Williams[1]

Sunday 20th February

Our mails left for Sollum at 9 a.m. We went through the usual farce of writing home though we have never yet had any assurance that our letters have gone through or that our countrymen have any knowledge of our existence. But it eases our minds. This was the day on which I had for some time determined to escape, and which if I succeeded would end an intolerable situation. The Senoussi were obviously of opinion it was quite impossible and had almost ceased to guard us, and we were rarely mustered. They had brought us by an 11 days' march round three sides of a square, and geometry was to them unknown. We had never traversed the direct track, or anywhere near it, to Sollum. The country was almost waterless, and the rare wells guarded by soldiers. The natives were hungry and hostile, and the chances were that any European met with would at once be killed for the sake of his clothes or anything he had. Their marvellous eyesight at once detects any moving thing while miles away, and our fairer skins and ignorance of Arabic were an additional difficulty, not to mention our lack of money to bribe,

[1] WO 106/1543.

and weakness and lack of shoes for walking. My plans were as follows, and though my mess-mates at first believed the whole affair madness on my part, and did their level best to dissuade me, yet later they came round to my views, gave their whole-hearted assistance, and believed as firmly in its practicability as I did. Ever since landing I had kept a careful diary of distances covered, and I knew the distance of Port Suleiman [Bardia] from Sollum within 10 miles or so, and had a general idea of the configuration of the coast. Plotting these out, I made a rough map, showing Sollum to bear ENE some 80 miles only. Secondly, we had heard gun fire on several occasions and seen a searchlight, which we believed came from the direction of Sollum. These bore exactly ENE. Thirdly, by carefully questioning (through others) camelmen and the two Indian prisoners who had been sent back from there, the average time taken by camels (not going in a straight line but from well to well) was 5 days, or about 100 miles, and probably 80 as a crow flies. Fourthly, the general direction of caravans known to be going there was ENE. From all these I felt perfectly confident of the general direction and distance of Sollum, and my ability to at least strike the coast in its vicinity. The two Indians also gave descriptions of the country which tallied exactly with each other, and stated they had met no one on the whole journey. This removed much of the danger of discovery, and I intended to lessen it still more by travelling only at night and hiding during the day. If I saw anyone I could slightly alter my direction and trust to my Arab clothes and sun burnt face hiding my identity. If, however, I were really caught, I had several sentences written out in Arabic, by which I would state that although I had no money on me then, if they would guide me safely to Sollum they would receive much gold. I had no doubt of Sollum being in British hands, as the Indians had themselves witnessed it, and the repeated assurances of Selim that there was a two months' truce with England made murder at sight less probable. I determined to strike a course which would take me a little Eastward of Sollum into Egyptian territory, and when I believed I had passed it, strike north for the coast. If, however, I had underestimated the distance, and struck north too soon, I knew that sooner or later I must strike the road running west from Sollum in Senoussi territory, and by keeping to the southward of it and moving East, readjust my position and obviate the danger of getting into the area on the West side of the Sollum Gulf. The moon was nearly full, and there would to-night be just an hour's darkness between sunset and moonrise, giving me just the chance I wanted to slip away. I would then have a full moon to walk by for several nights, and however cloudy, its position could generally be seen sufficiently to give me an indication of the course to be steered, though on clear nights the stars would of course be a much better guide. By observing carefully, I knew exactly the positions occupied nightly by the "Bear" or "Huntsman's Clock" and so could tell the time and from that judge the distance covered, as I had been a great pedestrian all my life. For shoes, I borrowed Lieut. Apcar's. He had been sick ever since he landed and they were the only pair in the camp not worn out, and fitted me to a nicety. For food, I had been saving a little rice from each meal all the week, although a bitter pinch it was. Rice rations for two days were issued that morning, so I was able to draw two more days in advance, and I drew another from the general supply. By shamming dysentery I was able to cajole a little flour out of Selim and make a pound of bread, and as he never went near sick people, the chances of my absence being discovered at once were very much decreased. Indeed I had every hope of 3 or 4 days' start before my absence was discovered and that then they would think I had escaped towards the Italian town of Tabrouk which was closer. Thus I had four days rations of rice, weighing, boiled, over 12 lbs. (rice requires exactly twice its own volume of water to cook it) and two days smaller rations of bread. These I tied carefully as separate one day rations, 3 in each leg of my cotton Arab drawers, with the rice to come first as I was afraid it might be sour before the first 4 days were up. The mess contributed to me generously a large piece of meat, which I cut up, and put 1 piece with each ration, and I had also some dates I had saved in a bag at my girdle, also added to generously by my messmates from their scanty store. For water, I carried a half filled kid skin on my back containing, I suppose, 1.5 gallons. The trouble was all our skins were leaking badly, but I got the best, and hoped that with economy it would last me at least 8 days. Thus I had six days full provisions (but of a terribly heavy type and weighing at least 30 lbs.) and I knew I could go for many days more without food if necessary, living on snails and roots. I calculated I could walk at least 20 miles a day (in spite of weakness and impossibility of training) so that if Sollum were only 80 miles as I believed I had a very ample margin. I did not attempt to escape sooner in the year because there was then every prospect of our release or exchange, and besides there was the matter of my parole. But I felt that if I put it off longer I would be losing strength all the time. The nights would be shorter, giving less time to walk, and the heat greater, making exertion greater and water more necessary. I was the only one in the camp who had never known a moment's sickness or had a sore foot, and I had unlimited faith in my own endurance. Going alone was far safer, and two people would only hamper each other as much as leashed grey-hounds. Besides, I fancied a change of scenery and the whole prospect was delightful. It was a case of then or never. So off I started about 6.30 that Sunday evening, well up to programme time, with a very light heart and many a hearty hand grip from those I had not known were my friends. I slipped away without the sentry having a ghost of an inkling. The fires were made to blaze extra high so as to help to dazzle him and in some 20 minutes I lost sight of them behind a rise and was stumbling over the stones in the darkness. Besides my provisions I carried a few letters for home, a list of the crew, my diary, a small tomato tin for a drinking cup, my lucky horse shoe, my bone needle and thread for mending shoes, Tarrick Bey's letter (in case I were accused of breaking parole) a stout staff and a few other odds and ends. Also half my "bernous", which originally was some 14 ft. long. My tailored Naval uniform I wore under the Arab clothes, for showing in an emergency, and I think the safety of my life was greatly increased by it. At first my pack felt very heavy, the ropes feeling hard on shoulders which were little but skin and bones, and the water leaking steadily away soon soaked me through behind. But the stones were so bad in the dark, I soon had little thought of anything else and I gradually became more accustomed to it. As the moon rose walking became better, but the night was full of alarms, and every now and then I had to lay flat under my sand coloured bernous to see if an object moved or not – the only way of deciding whether it were a bush or a human being. I could steer an accurate course by rising stars, East at first and East by North later, and took short rests at as far as I could judge 9 p.m. and midnight, when I ate a few dates and licked the outside of my wet water-skin.

Monday 21st February

I began to get a bit done with my heavy weight and the awful stones towards morning, but managed to keep going pretty steadily. My shoes were a little small, and both my big toe nails worked loose and had to be tied on with a piece of rag, and I got somewhat of a blister on my left heel, not having worn shoes for two months. I tumbled right into a caravan of 80 or 90 camels about 4 a.m., and lay flat in the dust while the driver went chanting past me at a distance of 4 yards, quite unsuspicious. Then the moon became so totally obscured by clouds that I had to wait about an hour before I could again determine my course. But on the whole I calculated I had done well and made good 25 miles, East by North, when day broke. Here I found myself in an area of very stunted bushes only a few inches high, so after a short rest and a good look to see the coast clear, I moved on a mile or so to where they were higher. Here, however, I seemed to be in a very populous neighbourhood. Several very large caravans passed with much noise, and isolated persons as close as 30 or 40 yards. It was anxious work, as I crawled from side to side to get the bush between me and them, but later I became more confident and dozed for a little. My chief anxiety was about the water, as the skin still leaked terribly, and I seemed to have already lost nearly half its contents, though there was no apparent hole. An hour and a half before sunset, there being apparently no one about, and feeling much refreshed, I ventured out and found myself at once in the immediate vicinity of an Arab camp of some 8 tents right in my course. But trusting to my disguise, and making as big a detour as I dared to avoid it, I passed it without mishap. Many fires were visible after dark, so this was evidently not the uninhabited desert I had imagined from the Indians' descriptions – but they probably went an entirely different route. It is very disquieting though. Tramped on until midnight averaging, with stops, some 2.5 miles per hour.

Tuesday 22nd February

Plodded, on at something under 2.5 miles an hour with short rests until dawn, until I fairly dropped from exhaustion into the nearest bush, being quite unable to lift my feet further. A leopard was making night hideous by his caterwauls in the near vicinity, but I was too done to notice him, and after a few brief calculations dozed off happily with the knowledge that I had covered in all some 51 miles in the 36 hours since leaving El Hakkim. More than half way to Sollum. But my water skin was now nearly empty and dripped continuously as I watched it. I hung it from the bush and left my tin cup under it to try and catch some of the precious drops and then fell fast asleep. It must have been an hour later when I awoke with a start and found the whole country around me alive with men and camels moving in all directions. I lay as flat as possible, and trusted that providence would help me again as she had done so often so that I had begun to get careless or I would never have been trapped like this. But the water-skin was my undoing. Evidently its unfamiliar appearance in the bush attracted their attention, and I saw three men making their way with guns and loud ejaculations. I covered my face with my bernous and pretended to be asleep, hoping they would not like to awaken me. But It was no good, and I soon felt myself roughly seized and shaken. I opened my eyes lazily, and then attempted to go to sleep again. But the game was up, and I was pulled on to my feet, while the three villainous looking rascals stared and shouted at me loudly. My captors, who were of a very low type of Bedouin, soon went through my belongings and stripped me, and I should have been in a bad way had not more powerful thieves appeared on the scene, who, assuring me that the first would cut my throat, took me away from them and went over my person even more carefully. I was soon the centre of some 20 or 30 cut-throats, the leaders of whom eventually took charge of me, as being their special prey. All this time I was working in my carefully prepared Arabic sentences about my having nothing of value on me, but that if I could be conducted to Sollum there would be much gold. This was readily understood, and when they discovered I really had nothing of value, beyond my clothes, began to have its effect, though I was in some danger at one time by laughing and displaying my gold tooth; they appeared to think removing my head was the easiest way of getting it. I was then marched off to the nearer encampment, some 30 large tents, on the journey to which they displayed the usual Arab and Turkish idea of humour by firing guns over my shoulder or in my direction. But this not appearing to answer expectations, they later contented themselves by exhibiting me for the rest of the day, much as dancing bears used to be in England. They displayed great curiosity in my diary, and treated it with great respect. I kept on quoting the name of the Grand Senoussi and Nouri Pacha, &c. about any article for which they showed a special acquisitiveness and in the end I had nothing taken from me except my much prized steel needle. This I resisted by force and then later gave it to its would-be purloiner as a present. This made him very ashamed, and I thereby gained a friend, who saved me much annoyance and who at one time I had great hopes would conduct me to Sollum, (Until we were rescued by the Armoured Cars on St. Patrick's Day we all believed Sollum to have remained in the hands of the British since Xmas and that there was peace between them and the Senoussi. Both of these surmises were contrary to fact.) Late in the afternoon I was turned over to two Turkish soldiers (Cretans) who appeared to be billeted in the camp. Ali Hassan, thick set, vulgar and of a negroid type. Mahmoud, well set up & good looking, more refined, and able to read and write. They always reminded me of the two comic villains of a pantomime, and their talents being complementary, they had become quite indispensable and inseparable, the one from the other. As I spent a whole week in their society, I had some opportunity of studying them. When any robbing or threat was necessary, Ali Hassan, the old campaigner was much to the fore. But when it was a matter of finesse and diplomacy he kept his ungainly person out of sight and Mahmoud came to the fore to cajole a night's lodging, a bowl of milk or a feed of dates. Between them they appeared to get on very well, but having no idea of direction they came to rely almost entirely on me to pilot them to unknown places of which I never so much as even knew the name. In fact, I was quite a "Star" turn wherever I went. I was always asked to tell the inhabitants the direction in which different places lay, and which after a glance at the stars and the rough map I had made, I was easily able to do, to their undisguised astonishment. These two soldiers having gone over my person with a dexterity evidently acquired from long practice (and realising that what the Senoussi had left couldn't be worth much) then listened to my story and were sympathetic on the subject of gold at Sollum. My hopes of successful bribery again rose, and I displayed my uniform (worn under my Arab shirt) and Medal ribbons, to emphasize my importance. But I soon discovered they were only "kidding" me, which they indicated by whistling loudly, to show I was a "bird", or someone who had flown. Their incredulity they also expressed by pulling down the corner of one bloodshot eye. Facial expression appears to be very limited, among the Arabs, and I soon fell into the spirit of the game by doing my "tricks", which generally got us a more liberal supply of food. The "tricks" being no more than assuming an expression of hauteur, superciliousness, contempt or vanity. These caused unfailing yells of laughter and had to be many times repeated, and after displaying my gold tooth, tattoos, medal ribbon and diary the show was considered finished and we were generally well repaid with dates and milk. Civilized dental treatment always aroused great interest in this land of perfect teeth, and I well remember an occasion when Lieut. Tanner put the whole of our guards to flight by opening his mouth and letting his upper plate of false teeth suddenly fall. The night I spent in this camp between my two soldier friends, each with his Martini [rifle] at his side a hand on my shoulder and a big camel rug over us. We had the usual supper of dates and milk, and soon I learned the etiquette. The large wooden bowl of milk goes from hand to hand, and you may only drink it with a loud in-drawing of the breath. An exhausting process, but equalizing the amount you all get. Dates you eat as fast as you can, stoning them with one hand all the time, and it is "de rigueur" to throw back the debris in the bowl. I broke my best tooth trying to eat fast enough for my share, but never had a chance, though among my fellow prisoners I had at one time been very unpopular on account of the rate at which I bolted my food. Shoes you always took off, and hats you always kept on. This annoyed me much in bed, where my feet were cold and my head hot, but there was no appeal. The evenings were always spent round the bright fire at the entrance of the tent, well screened from the cold winds and where I was made to display my "tricks". The women, who are never veiled, and generally very well dressed in red and other bright colours, squat round as interested spectators in the background. They always appeared to me to be treated with the greatest kindness and consideration, but to have a definite place in the order of things, which they never try to exceed. They are generally very small compared with the men, but generally well-proportioned and comely, but invariably disfigured by tattoos or slit nostrils. I was much struck by the luxury and richness of most of the tents, which by firelight appeared like vaulted Gothic buildings inside. They were all quite new and very large and covered with magnificent carpets and rugs of wonderful colour and thickness. But food, beyond kids, dates, and milk appeared to have disappeared from the country, and in most camps the whole population appear to subsist entirely on roots, herbs and snails. To see a whole family gorging the latter, cracking the shells on stones, and with smeared faces from the brown juice, is a very disgusting sight. The bowls we ate from were invariably filthy beyond measure, water being too rare a commodity for any form of washing to be ever indulged in, and its lack is, of course, never noticed. The village doctor was generally one of our guests. (Whoever happened to be present always joined in the feed.) He is generally a powerful, saturnine-looking man, and was invariably introduced by drawing a finger across the throat, which I gathered was intended to inform me that he combined the gentle art of medicine with the more trying duties of Lord High Executioner. And this I believe to be the case, since my friend Dr Bechie Fouad had told me he was compelled by Achmed Shereef to amputate the hands of 5 culprits guilty of smoking. Catching "lodgers" and throwing them in the fire was an invariable evening amusement, in which all joined, so that the lack of bridge and other games was not felt.

Wednesday 23rd February

Had a very disturbed night, thanks to the two rifles in my ribs, cold feet, and the noise of camels and dogs, and the fact that my two friends' "lodgers" evidently considered me "fresh fields and pastures new" and moved accordingly. When one is already weak, the loss of this blood and sleep nightly is a serious consideration. We turned out at earliest sunrise and then spent the morning moving from tent to tent, getting dates at one and milk at another, and showing my "tricks". This continued until about 2 p.m. The country as far as I could see in every direction was covered with lines of tents and the great frames for weaving carpets, &c., countless camels, sheep and goats. There appeared to be no water supply, and the few pints I saw were bright yellow from the clayey soil, and I fancy had been gathered from shallow holes dug in the ground to catch the rain. Taking a hawk with us (these beautiful birds can be purchased for a shilling or so) we moved along and soon loosed it at a hare, with the only result I have ever seen in this country – the loss of both the bird and quarry. Soon we came to a deserted part where to my surprise I found a camel, 2 men and a girl, evidently waiting for us. The soldiers mounted and the procession started and once more I was happy in the belief that my bribes had prevailed and that they were thus secretly taking me to Sollum. We passed a man mercilessly beating his wife on the ground, but I was prevented from interfering, which perhaps was wisest, and then to my surprise the soldiers got down and moved off leaving me in charge of the strange camelman. I felt rather disquieted again in this lonely spot, as it somehow looked like a prelude to murder and the division of the spoils between the soldiers and camelman. But then I felt reassured by the fact of a woman being present. They would hardly have brought her to witness it. We moved on on a devious course, saw someone, and coming closer, I discovered to my surprise that it was my two soldier friends, with a very fat lamb just killed, and a bright fire which they had recently lit. In an incredibly short time the animal was skinned, hewn in pieces and cast on the fire, and as each part was cooked it was taken out, portioned and devoured. The first part cooked was the feet, then the liver, lights and kidneys, then the entrails and stomach and head, and lastly the carcass and limbs. The whole animal disappeared in less than half an hour from the time of my arrival, and I have enjoyed many a good dinner at home far less, though we had neither salt nor bread. The Arabs tore the flesh like wolves, and cracked the bones with their teeth to extract the marrow, and I followed their example as well as I was able. So cooked, the entrails (quite uncleaned) were by far the best part of the animal, and filled with its mother's milk, and deliciously crisp and tender. The liver and lights have a seductive taste no frying pan can give them, the feet (hoofs, hair and all) not at all bad, and the stomach decidedly palatable. In fact it was all very good, and I felt very much better after such a quantity of nourishing food, and after this never had any doubts as to the good intentions of Ali and Mahmoud with regard to myself. After eating, we at once departed, but I was able to gather this was the solution of the provisioning problem that had been troubling my soldier hosts. They had again and again asked me for money to buy food for the journey, and failing this, had commandeered the animal. The camelmen were then sent ahead to fill my water-skin at a well, whose yellow mound was plainly visible, while the soldiers and I went off in another direction. Their intentions soon became evident. Another large flock of sheep and goats was passing. A very simple process of acquisition was then gone through. Guns were levelled at the shepherd by Ali, until he ran for his life, while Mahmoud carried on and tried to pacify the irate shepherd's wife. Ali suddenly sprang on the fattest lamb, and bore it off bleating on his shoulders. We then joined the camelmen again, and proceeding a mile or so, a fire was lit, the lamb killed, and another orgy commenced. This time we only half did the job, and the remainder of the flesh was put on the camel. Soon after dark we arrived at an Arab camp, and after being accommodated with the usual dates and milk, the lamb's carcase was put into a large iron pot and boiled. The resulting broth (only about two quarts was made from three quarters of a sheep) was very good, but being evidently despised by my hosts, was given to the woman. We six persons had then eaten two complete sheep within about 4 hours. That night I felt no hunger but very decided pains. My Arab friends, however, were in no way inconvenienced and were quite surprised and annoyed when I wished to curtail the usual evening pantomime. Though I had been kept walking since sunrise, our apparent progress this day was only some 16 miles to the NE and I had no idea yet where they were taking me.

Thursday 24th February

Dragged out at sunrise feeling very *piano*, the result of excessive mutton. We visited tents for some hours, whereby Mahmoud was able to get us invited to partake of several bowls of milk, but no dates. We then proceeded to do the usual robbery of a fat kid, it taking a little longer this time, as its owner was not to be intimidated by Ali Hassan, or his wife to be cajoled by Mahmoud with a signed paper. It was only when the animal had been completely cooked and eaten as before that they ceased their protests. While we ate, the camel strayed and it took us a weary 3 hours' march in the hot sun before we came up with it. We were still in the vicinity of the yellow well mound seen the previous afternoon, and happening on another flock, again seized the fattest lamb without either explanation or apology. The appetite seemed to grow with the eating. This was the fourth, but last, however, for as we bore it off on the camel at a great pace to the NW we saw eight sturdy shepherds with guns following us in skirmishing order. We increased our pace, which I found pretty hard going, in my footsore and weary condition. Firing soon commenced on both sides, and the bullets were soon merrily knocking up spurts of sand all around us, but without anyone being the worse. The girl was put on the camel, and with a kick I was told [to take] off as camel-driver, which I readily did. The whole situation was so humorous, with the girl holding the struggling, bleating lamb on the camel (the latter tacking in every direction) and myself sweating, beating and limping behind, that I fairly yelled with laughter, in which the girl merrily joined. Eventually the shepherds came up and I was told to disgorge the prey. The man who received it, evidently well satisfied, saluted me courteously, but was followed later by a hail of bullets from my robber friends as soon as he had retreated some 300 or 400 yards. This again fortunately without any accidents. We then marched off NW once more in a hot sun, passing the Sollum road and telegraph posts about 3 p.m. until we got to another Arab camp, where we spent the night and got an excellent date and milk supper. Apparent progress only 16 miles NW, though we must have actually covered close on 30 miles in various directions. The country here not so thickly populated as the place where I was re-captured, and where the lines of tents stretched for miles in every direction. But even here there were immense flocks of sheep and goats, mostly moving to the west. The soil is a firm clayey sand, with thick scrub, and dead level, with large numbers of dried up Roman wells or cisterns.

Friday 25th February

Had a cold night of it, my bernous having been on the camel the previous day, which did not arrive before dark, being very slow. Out at sunrise, and Mahmoud having cajoled 3 lots of dates or milk, we started off at 5 miles an hour to the WNW, as though determined to make up for the time wasted on previous days. I found the pace very killing in my weak and footsore condition and with burst shoes. Fortunately the day was cloudy. We continued all day, at never less than 4 miles an hour, with hardly a rest of any kind, pulling herbs and roots as we went along on very zigzag courses between West and NNW, happening suddenly on the Arab camp we sought one and a half hours after dark, and when I was utterly done. The lights suddenly shone out in a hollow, as we topped the rise. Apparent distance made good only some 20 miles WNW, but we must have covered well over 30 miles; the soldiers had no idea of direction. The country here is the same firm sand and clay soil, covered with scrub. There are several low ridges of hills, and a higher one, running E and W, and which gradually receded, lay to the Southward of us. There are many small valleys running towards the coast, green and full of grass and large bushes, with signs of many recent camps in them. But the country was then nearly bare of inhabitants except some very small flocks, whose impoverished owners were busy eating snails and roots and could give us no other food, but indicated the direction we should go in. At the camp where we slept we were given rice, the first I had seen since my escape. All this land must be very fertile and well watered in the winter months, and edible roots and plants were especially abundant. Went to bed very hungry, not having then learned the rules as to eating rice. The latter is brought in, smeared round the sides of a large wooden bowl. Each diner at once scoops all he can with his hands and rams it down his throat, and it is all gone in ten seconds. I was not quick enough and got hardly any. Our host was a very kind, white bearded old gentleman, of a refined type, who spent the evening nursing his family, and with whom I made great friends. We spent the night warm, under luxurious rugs.

Saturday 26th February

Out at sunrise and at once started, again on our wild zigzag at a very fast pace. We had neither breakfast nor water but I had had a refreshing night's sleep, and we gathered what roots we could as we went along. The country was much the same as on previous days, but the valleys flatter and broader and the hills to the South gradually were lost to sight. To the northwest the land appeared more uneven, and I noted what resembled very large well mounds. The whole gave me the impression that the coast was not far away. I had a bad day of it, with no food or water, and covering at least 35 miles; the lack of water I did not feel, only the hunger. Towards 3 p.m. it became obvious that my guides were utterly lost, as they were then heading due North, so I took the matter in my own hands and made them follow me to the WSW, where I saw what I thought were tents. On nearer approach they proved to be a very large number of well mounds, with a kind of pharos and what had evidently been a Roman town. The soldiers evidently recognised it and were overjoyed, and we found an Arab tent near by, whose owner was able to put us on the right track. Going a couple of miles about SE, across a couple of valleys filled, with large lilies in flower, we came on numbers of telegraph posts and, if my memory serves me right, saw a road. A little further on we came upon the huts and tents of the Turkish Camp. Judging by the debris this had apparently at one time been of a considerable size, but at this period, did not contain more than, I think, some 20 soldiers, clad in their tattered khaki uniforms. The officers' quarters was a rough board building of two stories, like a very small railway signal box, from whose upper story ran the telephone wires, and through whose chinks whistled the bitter wind. The upper story was reached by a rough outside stairway, under which was the sentry box. At the entrance I was met by Capt. Achmed, clad in an English khaki uniform, of which, he being somewhat short and stout, the knees were buttoned round his ankles, and Mahomet Effendi, late our Senoussi commandant. They regarded me with stern faces, and Achmed said to me "This is very bad" while Mahomet repeated in broken English "Captain no good". I told Achmed it was nothing of the kind; and that if he had been a prisoner in Egypt he would have been only too glad to escape himself. He said "But why you try to escape … You are mad I believe. What shall we tell the English government if you had been killed by Arabs?" I replied that he could tell them the truth for once, that I quite realised he had the right to kill me now if he wished, that I was no more mad than he was, and that the reason I tried to escape was that we had no news of home since we landed, and I wished to get to Sollum to inform the British of the real state of affairs and how we were treated. He said, "You believed then that Sollum was in the hands of the English?" I said that I knew it was, and at this he smiled. His relief at my safe recapture was obviously great and the atmosphere had become less thundery. I was conducted upstairs to the telephone room, where there was a bed and a dozen or so of Russian magazine rifles. The joyful news of my safe recapture was then telephoned through to all parts of the country, my ears catching the names of Matruh, Bomba [Sidi Barani], and Sollum, which I thought to be only a "bounce" on his part. (I was not then aware that the British had really evacuated Sollum for the time being.) Towards dark I sank in a comatose condition on the floor, worn out. To my surprise I was soon afterwards woken up and brought a delicious bowl of peppered and saffroned rice, followed by the sweet syrupy Arab tea, which I had not tasted since Christmas. In my pocket I had what I called my "liberty pipe" (a pipe which I had in my pocket since I swam for it when the "Tara" sank) which I had sworn not to smoke until I had had liberty. Some kind Senoussi officer giving me cigarettes (very strong and vile Italian tobacco) I now indulged in this luxury to commemorate the two days' freedom I had had. Later in the evening I was allowed downstairs with the other officers (some 5 or 6 Senoussi, mostly elderly men, and Achmed) and was indulged with more tea, while they listened to as much of my adventures as I thought it wise to give them. They were much amused at the story of the soldiers and the sheep, and this way of raising food especially pleased Achmed. I told him how good they had been to me, and specially commended their loyalty in refusing all my bribes. At night I slept with all the officers on the ground floor my head on what I could feel to be a sack of macaroni.

Sunday 27th February

Every one extremely civil to me in the morning, especially a young and good looking Senoussi officer, absurdly like Lewis Waller[2] in appearance. He gave me dates and innumerable cigarettes, and then he and the cook Mohammed shaved and generally preened and decorated themselves. Even Achmed unbent so far as to give me a cigarette and converse in a friendly way and give me the latest Turkish War news, some of the items being that the canal had been crossed in two places near the centre some 10 days previously; that the Germans were within 15 kilometres of Paris; and that the French Government had been moved to Bordeaux. I assumed successfully an air of respectful belief, which evidently pleased Achmed, and he further informed me that the British had been driven back beyond Matruh, and now only held Dabaa at the end of the Egyptian Railway. Later in the morning my two soldier friends were brought forward, and each being rewarded with a silver dollar departed, after a hearty handshake with myself. Achmed informed me that the name of the camp where we were was Arkoma [Akramah], and that our last day's march had been 30 miles. As far as I could understand my soldier guides had called it Tabrouk – which I took to mean the Turkish camp covering the Italian town of that name. But I never had any opportunity of judging how far we really were from the sea, but I was told we were close to Zebla. Achmed, however, never erred on the side of truthfulness. Achmed also told me that the Italians would not fight; that they only had 100 black soldiers at Tabrouk (the rest having been withdrawn for the European War) and that Sollum being closed the Italians were letting through provisions for the Turks. I, however, saw practically nothing to confirm this, except very small quantities. Mahomet Effendi departed during the morning, and Achmed told me he was going West, but would later return to the Wells of El Hakkim. I spent this day resting, washing, and trying to get some of the vermin off my person, having no desire for these mementoes of my soldier guardians. There is a very good well

[2] Lewis Waller (1860-1915) was an English actor of the period.

here full up to the top with water. A prisoner was brought in during the day by two soldiers, an Arab found with modern weapons in his possession. These, by Turkish orders, should have all been given up, the natives being allowed only firearms of obsolete pattern. Of the latter there seems to be a fine collection in the country – flintlocks dating from the Napoleonic wars, fitted with a fixed bayonet, Minié rifles of 1875, percussion rifles and double-barrelled sporting guns of all varieties. The prisoner having had his face well smacked was put in the sentry box under the stairway and left there for the night. I do not know what his subsequent fate was. The soldiers who had brought him in were each rewarded with a small silver coin. The rifle, a Russian magazine, very popular with the Turks, was added to the store in the telephone room. This telephone station is evidently of importance, as there is always an officer on duty there and he sleeps beside it at night. Messages are continuously coming and going all day long. Achmed is commandant here, being busy and important and evidently enjoying life, he seemed to have the handling of a good bit of money. I was allowed to wander within 50 yards of the telephone station during the day and was amused to see the stampeding of an Arab horse. Those I had seen hitherto had always been too old and infirm for such frolics. But they are wonderfully adapted for the country in which they live, and seem to be able to endure thirst for periods approaching those of a camel. Five days without water is quite a common thing, and one which I had often observed in Mahomet Effendi's ancient steed. Selim Effendi arrived during the afternoon with 4 soldiers from El Hakkim and sat in the dust outside looking much depressed. But seeing me smoking amiably with Achmed, soon tumbled to the altered state of affairs, and all spent a merry evening together quaffing tea, to which I was not invited. Macaroni and oil for breakfast and peppered rice in the evening, joyful luxuries but in very small quantities, owing to the, from my point of view, unfortunate advent of guests, who ate the share I might otherwise have had. I was locked in the lower room for the night by myself, the whole place having been cleared of officers and the sacks of provisions it originally contained. I lay down in the dirt, and as soon as the last flickering flames from the box of embers I had been given as a light expired, the fleas literally descended on me in showers and shovelfuls. I never knew anything like it, and there was no sleep for me. But my kind friend Lewis Waller visited me at some late hour and filled my pockets with dates and my heart with gratitude. There are kind hearts everywhere, but there is none more generous than the Arab, or chivalrous than the true Turk. The trouble is that their memories are so short.

Monday 28th February

I left at sunrise, escorted by Selim, the 4 soldiers, a camel, and an old woman driver, after an early bowl of milk. Selim, who was kindness itself and very thoughtful, made me feel somewhat shamefaced, for I could not but be aware that had I not been recaptured, he himself would have been punished by disrating from officer to private, an apparently fixed rule. We trudged steadily South at a good 4 miles an hour over a nearly level country until at 11 a.m., we came on a small Arab camp, where we stopped for dates and milk. Once again due South, good going over the firm soil and bushes, but weary work for me with my raw and aching feet, and the fatigue of 8 days' marching and uncertain food.

On, up to the E and W Sollum road, here 20 ft. wide, and on up the incline which, miles away, had looked like mountains, but is merely a slight plateau-like elevation of the ground. On this rise we heard a great sound of firing, and saw a small party (4 or 5) of Turkish soldiers, but I did not ascertain the cause. Stopping, we were soon joined by them, and I found them to be commanded by a fine specimen of Albanian, fierce looking and clad in flowered silks, a magnificent great silver ring on his finger, with a large mysterious looking stone in it. On his breast he wore a very large decoration, which he informed me was Turkish. We soon made friends and I was proffered the inevitable cigarettes, though I found them a very poor substitute for food. On parting, we turned back to the North, re-crossed the Sollum road, and found an Arab camp close by, where we spent a very comfortable night, boiled mutton being forthcoming as well as milk and dates. Distance covered 28 miles South.

Tuesday 29th February

A very refreshing night's sleep, with soft lying and warm rugs to cover me; spared also the prolixity of rifles and strong-odoured soldiers as bed-mates, to which my former captors had made me almost resigned. Out with the sun, we crossed the Sollum road about 7 a.m., heading ESE at 4 miles an hour. It soon became very bad going over the red and black soapy flints and limestone rocks so familiar round El Hakkim, and I was very glad when at 11 a.m. we pulled up near an Arab camp. The soldiers ware sent in as usual, but returned soon after to my great disappointment, with no food. Apparently there was none to be had there. There were an enormous number of old Roman wells in this neighbourhood, one of which had apparently been recently repaired. After half an hour we moved on, this time to the SSW, looking at first for some other camp but without success. We continued thus at 4 miles an hour over stony ground for the rest of the afternoon. I was utterly done and had been foodless and waterless all day except for part of a small tortoise the soldiers gave me and three hard set larks' eggs which I found and ate warm and raw. There were enormous numbers of hares about in this bare country and the soldiers in vain tried to stalk them with their rifles. A hawk was also loosed and lost. I was soon too utterly done to go a step farther, and Selim again showed his kindness by getting off his camel, which I rode for nearly two hours. This was all the more remarkable, as I found afterwards his feet were blistered from end to end caused by his forced march to Arkoma for me. The soldiers also loudly protested against a culprit like myself being so honoured. About 4.30 p.m., when I had quite given up hope of reaching our destination (as we had apparently made no landmarks) we saw the stone beacon and water wells of El Hakkim. Selim and his soldiers fired a fusillade of rifle shots in the air, and very soon the whole garrison, now reinforced to 16, came running to meet us headed by the black priest Osman and followed by the women and children. Osman greeted me by a blow on the shoulders with his rhinocerous-hide whip, and followed it up by some 7 or 8 more on the head and back. Someone else smacked my face, and the women threw ill-aimed stones and spat. But I seemed hardly to feel it. I was driven forward to the blockhouse and then confined in the sheep-pen at the back. My coat, shoes, possessions and precious diary were taken from me, the four sentries put on guard making a parade of loading their rifles, and no one was allowed to approach. I do not believe Selim intended actual violence should be done to me, but he was ever weak, if kind-hearted, and they all seem to hold their priest (who had no real temporal authority) in great awe. Here in the sheep-pen I remained the night, apparently half naked and hungry. But as soon as it was dark, and the other British prisoners could no longer see, my clothes and bernous were brought back, two mats were given me (one of which I made a roof of) and I was given water and a liberal supply of dates. With a thankful heart I was asleep in a few minutes to be woken a little later by Mahmoud, the bright-eyed 9-year-old body servant of Selim. In his hand he brought a huge bowl of rice and watched delightedly while I ate it. It was, in fact, Selim's own supper, and so liberal that I could not finish it (the first and last time while I was a prisoner), and I often thought regretfully in still hungrier days later on of the part I had left, instead of putting it in my pocket. The sentry himself also gave me a cigarette to smoke and a large fire burned all night to keep me warm. Such is the Arab character.

Appendix 2

A selection of Sanusi correspondence

1
[February 1915][1]

[From General Maxwell to Sayyid Ahmad al-Sharif al-Sanusi]

After Greetings,

Bimbashi Royle has seen me and has told me the result of the interview which you were good enough to accord to him. It has given me great pleasure to learn again of the sentiments of esteem and friendship which you have towards the British and Egyptian Governments and of which I was already fully assured.

There are always evil disposed persons and intriguers who make it their business to spread baseless rumours and to attempt to create misunderstandings between friends, but I do not listen to such stories and I look only at the deeds by which you have proved your affection.

You will have heard that the Turkish Army, urged on by German officers, did actually advance to the Canal and made the great attack which has so long been threatened. By seizing the camels, horses and provisions of the inhabitants of Syria they succeeded in accumulating enough supplies to enable them to bring between 20,000 and 30,000 men across the desert and on the night of the 2nd and 3rd of February they delivered an attack against our forces defending Egypt on the Suez Canal.

---

[1] Although this English draft of a letter which Maxwell had translated into Arabic is undated, the contents indicate that it was written in February 1915.

About 15,000 men were actually employed in the attack and advanced at several points. Of these a large force advanced with boats and bridges towards the Canal opposite the villages of Tussum and Serapium and made an attempt to cross into Egypt.

In the battle that ensued the Turks were defeated at every point. Their bridging material was captured, over 600 prisoners were taken and we have found and buried on the field more than 1,000 dead. The number of wounded is unknown as the majority were carried away on camels. The Turks failed to make any impression whatever upon our defences which is shown by the fact that our losses only amount to nineteen killed and about eighty wounded.

Thus the attack on Egypt, which has been talked of for so long, has failed completely and the enemy have retreated back across the Sinai Peninsula and no signs of them are to be found anywhere within fifty miles of the Canal.

It is unknown whether the Turks will attempt any fresh attack but what has happened shows that it could only result in complete failure. It is possible that the German officers, who care nothing for the sufferings of the Turkish soldiers, may force them to attack again, but from the information given by the prisoners whom we have taken it appears that the soldiers are tired of this war and have no wish to lose their lives in any attack on Egypt. Deserters who have come over to us from the Turkish army confirm this opinion.

I shall not fail to inform you if I receive any news regarding your cousin [al-Sayyid Muhammad al-Idris al-Sanusi] and if I have an opportunity of assisting him in his return journey from the Holy Places you may be sure that I shall spare no pains in doing so.

I am always pleased to receive letters and messages from you and to answer them, as such communications prevent misunderstanding and strengthen the bonds of affection between friends.

With salutations,
[General John Maxwell]

2
6 Jumada II 1333 [21 April 1915]

To the General Officer Commanding in Egypt,

Your telegrams have pleased us very much. They show that you are looking after our interests. We thank you for this, which confirms the good relations between us, but we find it necessary to inform you that certain officials and others at al-'Aqabah [the general area around Sollum] wish to intrigue against us by telling you untruths. God will deal with them. Our desire to avoid any friction or unpleasantness is proved by the behaviour of our men who went to visit their relations [in Egypt] and were challenged and threatened with rifles [by the coastguards]. It would have been perfectly proper and legal had these men responded in kind. According to the laws of any country their action would have been seen as self-defence.

There can be no better proof of our good intentions and sincerity towards you. In conclusion we offer you our thanks and greetings.

[Sayyid Ahmad al-Sharif al-Sanusi]

3

14 Jumada II 1333 [29 April 1915]

To His Excellency General Maxwell,
General Officer Commanding the troops in Egypt of His Majesty the King of Great Britain

I have received your letter dated the 12th of this month and was pleased by your expressions of friendship. We also want [good relations with Egypt], as our actions have shown.

I thank you for the arrangement you have made with the Coastguard for facilitating procedures [at the border] for us. With regard to those of our soldiers who crossed the frontier bearing arms, I wish to inform you that they did this without our permission, but they were merely visiting their relations, who are followers [of the *Sanusiyya*] and live at al-'Aqabah. You say that [to try to take arms across international borders] is contrary to the customs of all nations. Yes, but these are people who are unaware of the usages of Governments and States; they are simple desert Arabs, and we are doing our best to teach them. God willing, only good will come of it. You also refer in your letter to certain evil-doers and intriguers, like Zafer and others. God will judge them. We prefer not to deal with such people. We leave it to God to deal with those who commit evil ...

The written card, which you enclosed with your letter, is nothing but a forgery perpetrated by intriguers.

I would be grateful if you would send to me Hamad, the son of 'Uthman Habbun, of whom I have previously written.

[Sayyid Ahmad al-Sharif al-Sanusi]

4

15 Jumada II [30 April 1915]

From the slave of God and the servant of his Master, Al-Sayyid Muhammad al-Mahdi, Ahmad bin Sayyid Muhammad al-Sharif al-Sanusi al-Khattabi al-Hasani al-Idrisi;
To His Excellency, the discerning, wise, brave and honourable General Maxwell, Commander-in-Chief of British Forces in Egypt (May his happiness last forever).

After greetings,

Our master, Sayyid Muhammad Idris has returned. He has praised you and spoken highly of the kind treatment you have accorded him and the signs of friendship you have shown towards the Sanusi Brotherhood.

We have received your letter and understood its contents. We are keeping our promise, and nothing will ever make us break our word, once given.

That is what we have to say, and may you enjoy long life, and may honour and peace be with you.

5

[Seal of the Sanusi Government]

16 Rajab 1333 [30 May 1915]

To His Excellency General Maxwell, Commander-in-Chief of British Forces in Egypt

After greetings,

I thank you for your expressions of pleasure and congratulations on the arrival of [the new Sanusi agent in Egypt] Sayyid Muhammad al-Sharif [al-Idrisi] and his brother ... The Sayyid arrived here [at Amsa'id] most grateful for the care you had taken on his behalf ...

You mention that the [Western Frontier] is now under the command of Colonel Snow Bey, a senior Coastguard official, because you think him suitable for the post and because you wish to have an important official as head of this region. We are aware of his capabilities, and we hope that he will continue to do his best, as he always has.

As to the rumours which have reached you, that munitions and arms have reached us by sea for use against Egypt – which, you say, you do not believe, but in our promises – if certain intriguers have deliberately spread these rumours, you know that they are false. There has never been war between you and me ..., but I am at war with another country [Italy], and it is not surprising that I have to be prepared and ready while I am fighting that enemy ...

As for the son of 'Uthman Habbun, I mentioned him only because Lord Kitchener himself promised to release him ... When Lord Kitchener knew of my request, he wrote to me, saying that if I so wished, he would release him for my sake. That was his promise and you can ask him if that is not so.

I shall look after our friendship and good relations until something happens from your side to change this. Then you will be the aggressor ...

[Sayyid Ahmad al-Sharif al-Sanusi]

6

14 Ramadan 1333 [26 July 1915]

To the noble and respected General Maxwell

After greetings,

I write this letter to Your Excellency as a reminder of our friendship and an affirmation of our good relations in times past; and to erase that which has since happened, which has affected the friendly relationship which I hold dear in the depth of my heart. You look upon these events from Egypt. Here they have resulted in some men being executed and others imprisoned. In any case, you are aware of the facts and know the circumstances in which we were placed ..., and I see in Your Excellency the best means of correcting any adverse opinion of us that may have become established in the minds of the Government officials of Great Britain.

   We learn from the newspapers that Italy wants to annex Jaghbub to Libya, and I take this opportunity to beg you to communicate with Great Britain in this matter to try to prevent this annexation. As you know, Jaghbub and Kufra are holy places and religious centres for us. They must not be allowed to come under Italian administration. As the head of the Sanusi family and the chief sheikh of the *Sanusiyya* by succession ..., I demand this ...

   Jaghbub and Kufra should be placed under the Egyptian Government. Jaghbub relies entirely on the Siwa Oasis. Great Britain has always been a friend, and her custom has always been to respect our holy places. In these difficult circumstances, Great Britain is the best protector of the interests of Muslims, in general, and Arabs, in particular. She should not deprive us of her support now ... I shall never forget her past favours and her friendship for the Sanusi ...

[Sayyid Ahmad al-Sharif al-Sanusi]

7

20 Shawwal 1333 [31 August 1915]

To His Excellency General Maxwell, Commander-in-Chief of British Forces in Egypt

After greetings,

I have received your telegram stating that some of our men had transgressed the area near the fort of Sollum. I have looked into this, and my conclusion is that these men did nothing wrong and that they were a night patrol merely carrying out their duties. Furthermore, the patrol was only sent out because we had learned that machine guns had been mounted, mines had been laid, soldiers had arrived at Sollum port, and roads were being worked on. These actions on your part give us the impression that you are preparing for war. I understand also that you have prevented some of the Awlad 'Ali sheikhs from visiting me.

Only then did we take the precaution of sending out this patrol, and it was under specific orders not to cross the boundary. The report that you received that guns had been sent out for use against the fort is not true. I have been careful not to allow any irregularities, as I have informed Snow Bey.

As you have embarked on these military preparations, I have had to send an armed force ... to defend the tomb of my grandfather at Jaghbub. Nevertheless, I am doing my best to keep the peace and to maintain communications so long as that is mutually beneficial ...

We place our trust in God and in the sincerity of our intentions. For four years all are efforts have been directed against Italy alone. However, if we perceive a threat elsewhere, it is only natural that we should prepare to counter it. We place our faith in God, who shows the right course to take and gives support.

[Sayyid Ahmad al-Sharif al-Sanusi]

8
11 Dhu l-Qa'da [20 September 1915]

To His Excellency General Maxwell, Commander-in-Chief of British Forces in Egypt

After greetings,

We are still waiting for the son of 'Uthman Habbun to be released.

We have heard that certain married Sudanese women have arrived at Sollum and re-married with men there. This is against the law of Islam. We have made our complaint to Snow Bey, but he has taken no action. I am doing my best to keep our relations on a friendly basis.

Today Abu Bakr bin 'Umran, a Libyan and a relative by marriage of Wasfi Bey, arrived here, having been ordered out of Alexandria, where he has family. This man is a merchant, not a soldier, and he should be allowed to stay in Egypt. I ask you therefore to allow him to return ...

Sheikh al-Tukhi [my astrologer] is waiting for permission to visit me ...

[Sayyid Ahmad al-Sharif al-Sanusi]

9
1 Dhu l-Hijja 1333 [10 October 1915]

To His Excellency General Maxwell, Commander-in-Chief of British Forces in Egypt

After greetings,

I have received your letter and noted its contents. With regard to securing the release of the son of 'Uthman Habbun, I agree to the restriction that he not be allowed to return to Siwa. Your efforts in this regard are most appreciated.

As to Sheikh al-Tukhi, I trust you will assist him to come here in the company of [the Sanusi agent in Egypt] Sayyid Muhammad al-Sharif [al-Idrisi]. Sheikh al-Tukhi [the astrologer] would be staying for about one week, for we are in great need of his services ...

We have now sent Abu Bakr bin 'Umran back to his relations in Alexandria ...

[Sayyid Ahmad al-Sharif al-Sanusi]

10
17 Muharram 1334 [25 November 1915]

To His Excellency General Maxwell, Commander-in-Chief of British Forces in Egypt

I have received your letter of 5 Muharram 1334 [13 November 1915] and noted its contents. Please note that I do not take the side of any of the Great Powers, nor do I seek to confront any except those who transgress against me. I work only for the welfare of Muslims.

I do not approve of the disturbances which have taken place [at Sidi Barani]. They are the actions of foolish people. I have already told you that if I wished to wage war [against Egypt] I would declare it officially and not begin it in this manner. You know that I keep my word and that I want my communications with Egypt to continue and be strong to our mutual benefit.

The incidents which have take place at Sollum and Sidi Barani need to be explained. One foolish officer from our Muhafizin Battalion had a quarrel with the Arabs of Sidi Barani, which eventually turned into a major disturbance. This greatly displeased me. I immediately sent for him, but when he heard that he would be severely punished, he was afraid to come and see me. Satan then took hold of him. He decided to attack Sollum in order to create a disturbance. Then he would be able to steal some camels and run away. If fact, he did create a disturbance and he and his men stole what they could. Meanwhile they spread the rumour that they were acting according to my orders – even though I was at that time trying to have him arrested and brought to me. I did not even hear about all this until noontime on 15 Muharram [23 November].

I then sent an armed force to put matters right. It never occurred to me that Snow Bey would evacuate Sollum. In order to show him that I keep my word I sent Sayyid Muhammad [Idrisi] with the force. When they arrived at Sollum they found that the steamer had already left and could not be recalled. Muhammad

Idrisi will explain this to you more fully.

I say again that if I wish to do something, I come straight to the point and say that that is what I want to do. The reason for my coming [to Amsa'id] was not to fight with Egypt. As you know, in this region and in Egypt, I have followers, both Arab and non-Arab. I cannot neglect them. As their leader, I must defend them as honour requires ... I also wish to communicate with my followers in Arabia, and I hope you will enable me to do this by affording me the necessary facilities ...

I regret very much that communications have been cut between here and Egypt, and I hope that things will return to normal. Mistakes sometimes happen when two armies are near each other, the more so when one of them is made up of Bedouin Arabs ...

With regard to the men who were landed in boats from the ship which sank, I have made enquiries and learned that they came ashore in the western Bomba region, and that they are now at Ghurayyat. They are all well, and they will remain so until they are safely returned to Egypt when our relations return to normal ...

I hope you will soon send me Hamad bin 'Uthman Habbun, as both you and Lord Kitchener have promised you would. I have also asked several times that al-Tukhi be sent to me ... I am very displeased that he has been incarcerated ...

[Muhammad al-Idrisi] has spoken to me about the post at Qirba. You know that years went by during which I never interfered with it ..., but when I perceived ambitions [on your part] in my parts of the country, I sent guards [there]. I cannot be blamed for placing guards in my own locations ...

Muhammad al-Idrisi will explain everything to you. In God is our sufficiency.

[Sayyid Ahmad al-Sharif al-Sanusi]

11
3 December 1915

To Sayyid Ahmad al-Sanusi

After greetings,

On my return to Egypt from visiting the Allied Armies at Gallipoli, I am astonished to find that the situation between us has undergone a change, and that your followers have been guilty of acts of hostility against the Egyptian Government.

I was gratified to learn that you sent one of your chief advisers to Barrani to endeavour to recall such of your adherents as had flagrantly disobeyed your orders, but was surprised to learn that these were so far out of hand that, not only did they disobey, but actually fired on Jaafar Effendi. I have also learnt with concern that some 70 British subjects, survivors from off a ship that had been torpedoed by enemy submarines, are detained west of our frontier.

I must ask you, as a proof of the friendly sentiments that you have professed, to cause these unfortunate people to be brought at once without harm to Mersa Matruh.

The influences at work, headed by Nuri Bey and his German friends, appear to be working, in regard to your person, on similar lines to those on which Enver Pasha treats His Majesty the Sultan of Turkey, which sinister influence has plunged Turkey into the present disastrous war, the end of which will inevitably be the break-up of the Turkish Empire.

As you are aware, the Egyptian Government, and the British Government have invariably treated you with the greatest consideration and respect, but now, owing to the evil intentions of those around you, I have been obliged to withdraw our post at Sollum, and take up a position at Mersa Matruh; the responsibility for what follows is on your shoulders, and it is for you to prove, by the actions of yourself and your followers, whether you wish to remain on the same friendly terms, or not.

I will now be obliged to view any of your followers that enter Egyptian territory with arms, as having hostile intentions, and will treat them accordingly. I asked you to show your friendly intentions by removing from your entourage those persons who are known to be hostile to us: I regret that you have not been able to do this.

I have no doubt that Muhammad Sherif El Idrisi has handed you my letter, and spoken to you on all the affairs that were entrusted to him. He must have explained to you that our intentions have been invariably friendly, and you must realize that it is acts from *your* side − *not* from ours − which have brought about the change in our relations.

I cannot but think that you have been told stories of the European situation which are not true. I can only tell you this in all truth: that the German Emperor and his Allies are slowly but surely losing all along the fighting fronts; but the future will reveal to you what God directs. I ask you to pause and consider that, if you unfortunately take the wrong line, you will have against you, not only Italy, but France, England and Egypt. You will have to take the responsibility of all the lives that will be lost, your people will suffer from starvation (for all supplies will be cut off), the coasts will be blockaded, and if your advisers trust in enemy submarines, they will depend on nothing. I am telling you these things, not as threats, but as a friend, who would be sorry to see misfortune overtake you and your people.

The situation cannot continue as it is; and I ask you to prove your good intentions by acts, not words, and to return to me at once at Mersa Matruh the shipwrecked Englishmen whom I know are West of our frontier, and to re-establish friendly relations with us, by dismissing from your territory those Turkish and German Advisers − Nuri Bey, Manesmann [sic], and others − who will most certainly bring you and your people into great trouble.

I hope, therefore, that you will give these matters your earnest consideration, before such harm is done as cannot be remedied.

John Maxwell, General Officer Commanding in Egypt

12
26 Muharram 1334 [4 December 1915]

To His Excellency General Maxwell, Commander-in-Chief of British Forces in Egypt

After greetings,

Because of the relations between us, I beg to inform you that I wish for nothing but to guard the honour of Islam, and to maintain our religion and our influence [as a member of the Sanusi family] among our people.

We know perfectly well that for us peace can be secured only through maintaining friendly relations with a Great Power, especially one in close proximity to us.

We do not want to wage war or to quarrel with any neighbouring country; and we do not deny the benefits which come to us from Egypt.

Therefore, I wash my hands of those who perpetrate evil or wish to stir up dissension or cause the shedding of blood for their own personal ends... Especially, we abhor any dissension which might lead to cutting of communications between us and the stopping of those benefits [which the Sanusi Brotherhood needs so badly]. Furthermore, I wash my hands of any war which brings harm to Muslims and weakens our country. I cannot approve of any acts which are destined to lead us to misfortune.

I am now leaving [Cyrenaica] and heading west in order to have nothing to do with these disturbances, which I abhor. Nor do I wish any of the blame for them to fall upon me. The bearer of this message will explain my sincere intentions.

Sayyid Muhammad Idris bin al-Mahdi

13
3 Safar 1334 [11 December 1915]

To His Excellency General Maxwell, Commander-in-Chief of British Forces in Egypt

After greetings,

You know it to be true that a leader is valued among his people in accordance with how well he supports them and directs their affairs; and you know that I have many followers who, by God's will, firmly believe that I guard their faith and bring back its lost glory, and that I do that by following in the footsteps of the Prophet (may God bless him and grant him salvation).

A year has now passed since I came to Sollum in order to meet Sayyid Muhammad Idris, after the battles in which we successfully checked the assaults of the Italians and their transgressions upon our country and our people. During that year I carefully maintained good relations and kept the roads between us open. Food and goods came to us from you; sheep and camels went from us to you. I always kept you informed of my intentions.

Recently the words which we exchanged became futile. You began to engage in military preparations and made roads, while I said nothing because you said that you meant no harm. But as soon as your preparations were completed, you sent armed automobiles down those roads, while armed soldiers arrived by sea. Their purpose is to threaten the Arabs and to make those who are here [at Amsa'id] think that I want to benefit myself alone [and not my people]. First you want to alienate them from me, and then you will resort to political tricks. You will render service to Italy by [bribing?] my soldiers, who are dispersed between here and Tunisia ...

Yet I stood by my word. I punished those of my people who transgressed, although they knew no better. I did this to keep my promises [to you] and for the good of the Muslims, thinking that you would help to maintain our good relations; that is, until Snow Bey evacuated Sollum without even telling me beforehand. All this I have already explained in my previous letter brought to you by [Muhammad Idrisi].

Because confusion now reigns in al-'Aqabah, I have had to come to Sidi Barani despite the fact that I had been planning to go to Jaghbub. I have done this to restore order and to calm down the Muslims, whom you have upset.

Upon my arrival at Sidi Barani I learned that you were preparing to wage war on us. I then realized that the purpose of Snow Bey's departure was to break relations with us ... Therefore, I am now obliged to continue to Mersa Matruh so that I can see for myself what is going on there.

If all of this has taken place without your knowledge and you wish to negotiate, then you can do the following: send to me Bashir al-Tawati, 'Abd al-Wahhab al-Tukhi and the son of 'Uthman Habbun; reopen the trade routes; and henceforth stop upsetting [our people] ...

[Sayyid Ahmad al-Sharif al-Sanusi]

14
3 January 1916

To Sayyid Ahmad al-Sanusi

After greetings,

I have received your telegram and one for [Muhammad al-Idrisi]. You acknowledge that you have received my letter. I have now to tell you that until you comply with my demands there can be no further discussions. I warned you that would happen, [but] you have chosen to take the advice of those around you and I am forced to my great regret to say that your assurances to me have not been acted on. I have letters written in your own hand urging Egyptians to rebellion, promising them decorations, titles, and rewards. I have had brought to me papers that Gaafar left behind when he hurriedly retired from his camp at [Wadi] Majid that clearly prove how completely you have allowed yourself to be influenced by Nuri Bey and his German friends.

Since I wrote my letter to you, you have advanced as an enemy to attack Egypt. You have been responsible for a great many lives, your people are now starving and will starve, for I will prevent any foodstuffs from leaving Egypt until you comply with the following conditions:

1) You will deliver up safely all British, Indian, or European prisoners in your hands. These are to be delivered at Mersa Matruh;

2) Nuri Bey, Baruni, Gaafar and all Turks or Germans must be removed. If you have any difficulty in doing this, they could be, as prisoners of war, handed over to me;

3) You must undertake that no armed men enter Egyptian territory. If they do they will be treated as enemies wherever found.

4) You must withdraw altogether from Sollum or [Amsa'id] and establish yourself in peace at Jaghbub, which is also in Egyptian territory.

When these conditions are complied with, I will be prepared to discuss the situation further.

John Maxwell, General Officer Commanding in Egypt

15
8 Rabi' al-Awal [13 January 1916]

To His Excellency General Maxwell, Commander-in-Chief of British Forces in
Egypt

After greetings,

I have read your letter of [3] January 1916, and, I must say, I had never expected
to be addressed by you in such strong language. I wish to reply in detail.

You say in your letter that you warned me what would happen, and that I
followed the advice of those around me. But if you had wanted to be fair towards
me, you would not have said that, for had I listened to others and not the voice
of my own conscience, relations between us would have been cut long ago.

You accuse me of inciting the Egyptians to revolt and that you have documents
which prove this. You conclude that I chose to be your enemy. However, that was
never my intention. Had I intended that, I would have cut relations first and things
would have turned out differently.

But how do you explain the agreement concluded between Great Britain and
Italy against us, a copy of which was left behind by Snow Bey when he left Sollum
in haste. I wonder if you have ever been sincere in your attitude towards us. Was
that worthy [of a representative] of a Power like Great Britain ...?

You say that we began hostilities against you. But what are you referring to?
Were you not the first to cause this state of affairs? The cutting of a few telegraph
wires between Sollum and Sidi Barani and the attack by an irresponsible party of
Arabs at Barani – both acts were immediately put right by the severe measures we
took [against the perpetrators], precisely so that you would not have grounds for
complaint. But you made matters worse by sending cars, armoured and non-
armoured, which greatly upset the Arabs and made my position among them very
difficult. Yet we were patient, until you evacuated Sollum for no reason and
without telling us in advance – despite the fact that we had assured Snow Bey of
our good intentions. We even waited a few days, hoping to receive some
explanation from you for your activities and that you would put matters right. But
you neither explained your actions nor tried to correct them, and fearing a clash
between my soldiers and the Arabs, as well as further disorder in Sollum, we
ourselves went to Sollum to re-establish order ...

But let us consider your four conditions:

1) With regard to the prisoners, we do not consider them to be such. They are
   simply hostages delivered to our care by the Ottoman Government, and we
   have treated them in the best possible manner. If you had not broken
   communications with us, we would have already arrived at a solution which
   would have satisfied all parties ...

2) For me to hand over to you [Nuri Bey, Baruni, Ja'far and all Turks or Germans] as prisoners of war would utterly destroy my reputation in the Islamic world. I ask you to look at your own conscience: does it justify your making that demand? Have you forgotten the Italian spy who escaped from us and took refuge in Egypt? When we asked that he be returned to us, you said that you could not because he was now being protected by England. Why do you have one set of rules for yourself, and another set for everyone else? Are we not free to act as we wish in our own land?

3) We had already begun, on our own initiative, to address this problem [of our men carrying arms into Egypt]. We needed only to ensure the safety of all our followers.

4) As regards our leaving the area of Sollum, by what right do you ask this of us? And since when has Jaghbub belonged to Egypt? If you ever try to take Jaghbub over, you will find that not to be as easy as you might think. And since when has Amsa'id been part of Egypt, that I should leave it in your hands?

If these are your conditions, I regret to have to inform you that some of them, at least, are out of the question; also, that the responsibility for any loss of life will fall upon the side responsible for the present state of affairs. I feel quite at ease with my conscience ... do not blame me, rather blame yourselves.

If you desire peace, I would suggest that you moderate your conditions. Then we could discuss them and arrive at a satisfactory conclusion for both parties. I am writing to Lord Kitchener on this subject, asking him to arbitrate between us ...

[Sayyid Ahmad al-Sharif al-Sanusi]

16
9 Rabi' al-Awal [14 January 1916]

To the Minister of War of Great Britain, the highly respected Lord Kitchener

After greetings,

I wish to convey my best and most sincere wishes ...

The friendly relations which exist between us and the kindness which you have shown me in the past make me certain that you will regret the state to which my relations with the military authorities in Egypt have sunk.

Enclosed is a copy of my letter to General Maxwell, which I am sending to you lest its contents be conveyed differently. From it you will be able to grasp the real state of affairs. I am greatly astonished at everything that has happened. Snow Bey had hardly left Sollum when my messengers in Alexandria were arrested and treated as enemies. We do not understand ... what hostile action has occurred on our part which calls for such treatment. Such action is not necessary even between enemies. We consider the Italians to be our greatest enemy and a savage people, but our men have been able to go to them as messengers, transact their business, and return to us without any interference whatsoever. In fact, the Italians treat them with kindness. But the military authorities in Egypt are treating us outrageously, even though we have always thought the British to be the most honourable and humane of all the Great Powers.

If you consider your country to be honourable, you will not be pleased by such behaviour; and for the sake of your country's honour you will order the authorities to set our messengers free ... They should be returned to me with all their belongings – for they took with them nothing which could be considered contraband of war.

We ask this of you, wishing to prove that your past friendship for us still exists. If you feel they were in possession of anything that might help your enemies, then I agree that such things should not be handed back ...

Once our messengers are set free, we can then negotiate (i) over the mistakes that have occurred; (ii) over the prisoners, both those with us, and also those in your custody; and (iii) over such matters as are in the interest of our followers in Egypt, and other matters of interest to both parties. Then the good relations which [until recently] existed between us can be restored ...

[Sayyid Ahmad al-Sharif al-Sanusi]

NOTE
Letters 1 through 9 in Appendix 2 are from the John Grenfell Maxwell Papers, Manuscripts Division, Department of Rare Books and Special Collections, Princeton University Library. Letters 10, 12, 13 and 14 are from the Sudan Archives, Durham University. Letters 11, 15 and 16 were found in both the Maxwell Papers and the Sudan Archives.

The author is grateful to both Princeton University Library and the University Library at Durham for permission to reproduce these letters.

BIBLIOGRAPHY

Bibliography

Adam, C. F. (1948), *The Life of Lord Lloyd* (London: Macmillan).

Anonymous, "In the Western Desert of Egypt", *Blackwood's Edinburgh Magazine*, (Edinburgh), February, 1917, pp. 206-222.

Arab Bureau (1986), *Bulletin of the Arab Bureau in Cairo, 1916–1919*, 4 vols. (Gerrards Cross: Archive Editions).

al-'Askari, Ja'far (1988), *Mudhakkirat Ja'far al-'Askari* (London: Dar al-Lam)

Al-Askari, Jafar (2003) (eds. William Facey and Najdat Fathi Safwat) *A Soldier's Story: The Memoirs of Jafar Pasha Al-Askari* (London: Arabian Publishing).

Arthur, George (1932), *General Sir John Maxwell* (London: John Murray).

Badcock, G.E. (1925), *A History of the Transport Services of the Egyptian Expeditionary Force, 1916–1918* (London: Hugh Rees, Ltd).

Barlow, Ima Christina (1940), *The Agadir Crisis* (Chapel Hill, NC: University of North Carolina), Ch. 6 "The Mannesmann Brothers".

Belgrave, C. Dalrymple (1923), *Siwa: The Oasis of Jupiter Ammon* (London: The Bodley Head Ltd).

Blaksley, J. H. (n. d.), "Charge of the Dorset Yeomanry at Agagia", proof copy of published letter, National Army Museum, London (Acc. No. 8201-23).

Bluett, Antony (1919), *With our Army in Palestine* (London: Andrew Melrose Ltd).

Brandt-Mannesmann, Ruthilt (1964), *Dokumente aus dem Leben der Erfinder* (Remscheid).

Briggs, Martin S. (1918), *Through Egypt in War-Time* (London: T. Fisher Unwin, Ltd).

Brown, Malcolm (1988) (Ed.), *The Letters of T. E. Lawrence* (London: J. M. Dent & Sons).

Buchan, John (1920), *The History of the South African Forces in France* (London: Thomas Nelson and Sons, Ltd).

Burnell, Richard (n. d.), "134 Days in the Libyan Desert", booklet (Holyhead Maritime Museum).

Butt, M.T. and Cury, Alec R. (n. d.), *Mersa Matruh: How to see it, plus a vivid account of the operations of 1915–1917* (booklet, printed in Egypt, held at Royal Geographical Society library).

Caillard, Mabel (1935), *A Lifetime in Egypt* (London: Grant Richards).

Candole, E. A. V. De (1988), *The Life and Times of King Idris* (London: Mohamed Ben Ghalbon).

Cosson, Anthony de (1935), *Mareotis* (London: Country Life Ltd).

Coury, Ralph M. (1998), *The Making of an Egyptian Arab Nationalist: The Early Years of Azzam Pasha, 1893–1936* (Reading: Ithaca Press).

Davies, William (n. d.), *The Sea and the Sand* (privately printed).

Djemal, Ahmad (1922), *Memories of a Turkish Statesman, 1913–1919* (New York, NY: Doran).

Dumreicher, André von (1931), *Trackers & Smugglers in the Deserts of Egypt* (London: Methuen & Co. Ltd).

—— (1931), *Le Tourisme dans les Déserts d'Égypte* (Alexandria: La Cité du Livre).

Elgood, P. G. (1924), *Egypt and the Army* (Oxford: Oxford University Press).

Enver Pascha (1918), *Um Tripolis* (Munich: Hugo Bruckmann Verlag).

Evans-Pritchard, E. E. (1954), *The Sanusi of Cyrenaica* (Oxford: Oxford University Press).

Fakhry, Ahmed (1973), *Siwa Oasis* (Cairo: AUC Press).

Falls, J. C. Ewald (1913), *Three Years in the Libyan Desert* (London: T. Fisher Unwin).

Fischer, Fritz (1967), *Germany's Aims in the First World War* (New York: Norton).

Fletcher, David (1987), *War Cars: British Armoured Cars in the First World War* (London: HMSO).

Garnett, David (1938) (ed.), *The Letters of T. E. Lawrence* (London: Jonathan Cape).

Graves, Robert (1927), *Lawrence and the Arabs* (London: Jonathan Cape).

Gwatkin-Williams, R. S. (1919), *Prisoners of the Red Desert* (London: Thornton Butterworth, Ltd).

Halpern, Paul (1987), *The Naval War in the Mediterranean, 1914–1918* (Annapolis, MD: Naval Institute Press).

Hamilton, Ian (1920), *Gallipoli Diary*, 2 vols. (London: Arnold).

Harold, Jim, "Deserts, Cars, Maps and Names", paper published in the University of Glasgow online journal *eSharp*, issue 4 (spring 2005).

Hassanein, A. M. (1925), *The Lost Oases* (London: Thornton Butterworth Ltd).

Herbert, Aubrey (n. d.), *Mons, Anzac and Kut* (London: Hutchinson & Co.).

Huwaydi, Mustafa 'Ali (1988), *Al-haraka l-wataniyya fi sharq libya khilal al-harb al-'alamiyya l-ula* (Tripoli: Markaz Dirasat Jihad al-Libiyin didd al-Ghazu-l-Italiyya).

Inchbald, Geoffrey (2005), *With the Imperial Camel Corps in the Great War* (UK: Leonaur).

Jackh, Ernest (1944), *The Rising Crescent* (New York: Farrar & Rinehart).

Kelly, Alfred Davenport ["Captain Miller"] (1916), *With the Springboks in Egypt* (London: Hodder and Stoughton).

Lawrence, A. W. (1937) (ed.), *T. E. Lawrence by his Friends* (London: Jonathan Cape).

Lawrence, M. R. (1954) (ed.) *The Home Letters of T. E. Lawrence and his Brothers* (Oxford: Basil Blackwell).

Liddell Hart, Basil, (1934), *T. E. Lawrence: In Arabia and After* (London: Jonathan Cape), repr. 1948.

Magnus, Philip (1958), *Kitchener: Portrait of an Imperialist* (London: John Murray).

Mansfield, Peter (1971), *The British in Egypt* (London: Weidenfeld and Nicolson).

Massey, W. T. (1918), *The Desert Campaigns* (London: Constable and Co. Ltd).

McCullagh, Francis (1912), *Italy's War for a Desert* (London: Herbert and Daniel).

McKale, Donald (1998), *War by Revolution* (Kent, OH: Kent State University Press).

—— "'The Kaiser's Spy': Max von Oppenheim and the Anglo-German Rivalry Before and During the First World War", *European History Quarterly*, Vol. 27, No. 2, April 1997, pp. 199–219.

MacMunn, G. and Falls, C. (1928), *Military Operations: Egypt & Palestine* (London: HMSO).

Morgenthau, Henry (1918), *Ambassador Morgenthau's Story* (New York: Doubleday).

Murray, G. W. (1935), *Sons of Ishmael: A Study of the Egyptian Bedouin* (London: George Routledge & Sons, Ltd).

Rolls, S. C. (1937), *Steel Chariots in the Desert* (London: Jonathan Cape), repr. 1988.

Russell, Thomas (1949), *Egyptian Service, 1902–1946* (London: John Murray).

Sheffy, Yigal (1998), *British Military Intelligence in the Palestine Campaign, 1914–1918* (London: Frank Cass & Co. Ltd).

Simon, Rachel (1987), *Libya between Ottoman and Nationalism: The Ottoman Involvement in Libya during the War with Italy (1911–1919)* (Berlin: Klaus Schwarz Verlag).

Sonbol, Amira (1998) (ed.), *The Last Khedive of Egypt: Memoirs of Abbas Hilmi II* (Reading: Ithaca Press).

Spaulding, Jay and Kapteijns, Lidwien (1994), *'Ali Dinar and the Sanusiyya, 1906–1916* (Evanston, IL: Northwestern University Press).

Starkey, Janet, "Perceptions of the Ababda and Bisharin in the Atbai", paper presented to the Fifth International Conference on Sudan Studies, Durham University, 31 August–1 September 2000.

Stirling, W. F. (1953), *Safety Last* (London: Hollis and Carter).

Storrs, Ronald (1937), *Orientations* (London: Ivor Nicholson & Watson Ltd).

Stürmer, M., Teichmann, G. and Treue, W. (1994*), Striking the Balance: Sal. Oppenheim jr. & Cie.: A Family and a Bank* (London: Weidenfeld & Nicolson).

Swanson, Glen W., "Enver Pasha: The Formative Years", *Middle East Studies* (London), 16 No. 4, October 1980, pp. 193–99.

Sykes, Mark (1915), *The Caliph's Last Heritage* (London: Macmillan).

Teichmann, Gabriele and Völger, Gisela (2001) (ed.), *Faszination Orient: Max von Oppenheim, Forscher–Sammler–Diplomat* (Cologne: Max von Oppenheim-Stiftung).

The Times (1916), *History of the War*, Vol. 9, "The Senussi and Western Egypt" (Chap. 145) (London: The Times).

Thompson, C. W. (1921), *Records of the Dorset Yeomanry, Queen's Own, 1914–1919* (Sherborne: Bennett & Co.).

Trumpener, Ulrich (1968), *Germany and the Ottoman Empire, 1914–1918* (Princeton, NJ: Princeton University Press), repr. 1989, Caravan Books.

Vaglieri, L. Veccia, "Al-Baruni, Sulayman", *Encyclopedia of Islam*, Vol. 1, 1960.

Vivian, Cassandra (2000), *The Western Deserts of Egypt* (Cairo: AUC Press).

Weldon, L.B. (1926), *Hard Lying: Eastern Mediterranean 1914–1919* (London: Herbert Jenkins Ltd).

Westrate, Bruce (1992), *The Arab Bureau: British Policy in the Middle East, 1916–1920* (University Park, PA: Pennsylvania State University Press).

Wild, Auguste (1954), *Mixed Grill in Cairo* (Bournemouth: Sydenham & Co.).

Williams, Claud H. (1919) *Report on the Military Geography of the North Western Desert of Egypt* (London: HMSO).

Wilson, Jeremy (1989), *Lawrence of Arabia* (London: William Heinemann Ltd), Minerva edition 1990.

Winstone, H. V. F. (1982), *The Illicit Adventure: The Story of Political and Military Intelligence in the Middle East from 1898 to 1926* (London: Jonathan Cape).

Wright, John (1969), *Libya* (London: Ernest Benn).

Principal Non-published Sources

Davies, David John (Engineer of HMS *Tara*), "Diary", Anglesey County Record Office.

El-Horeir, Abdulmola S. (1981), "Social and Economic Transformations in the Libyan Hinterland During the Second Half of the Nineteenth Century: The role of Sayyid Ahmad al-Sharif", unpub. Ph.D thesis (University of California, Los Angeles).

Gwatkin-Williams, R. S., "Brief Record of Proceedings of Survivors of HMS *Tara* …", 21 March 1916, WO 106/1543, National Archives, Kew.

Hamilton, Major A. S. (City of London Yeomanry), "Diary", Department of Documents, Imperial War Museum, London.

Kophamel, Kapitänleutnant Waldemar, *U-35* logbook, Bundesarchiv, Freiburg.

Lewis, N. S. (1977), "German Policy in Southern Morocco during the Agadir Crisis of 1911", unpub. Ph.D thesis, University of Michigan.

Marsh, Sub-Lt. Albert (officer, HMS *Tara*), "Diary", Department of Documents, Imperial War Museum, London.

Maxwell, General Sir John, Papers, Manuscripts Division, Department of Rare Books and Special Collections, Princeton University Library.

Newbold, Lt. Douglas (17th Machine Gun Squadron, assigned to Queen's Own Dorset Yeomanry), "Diary", Sudan Archive, Durham University.

Oppenheim, Max Freiherr von, "Denkschrift Oppenheim über Revolutionierung der Islamischen Gebiete unsere Feinde", written autumn 1914, Politisches Archiv des Auswärtigen Amts, R26319, Schuldreferat 131.

Stoddard, Philip Hendrick (1963), "The Ottoman Government and the Arabs, 1911 to 1918: A Preliminary Study of the Teshkilat-ı Mahsusa", unpub. Ph.D thesis (Princeton University).

War Diary 15th Sikhs, WO 95/4428, National Archives, Kew.

War Diary Western Frontier Force, WO 95/4437, National Archives, Kew.

Western Desert Intelligence, Sept.–Dec. 1915, FO 371/2356, National Archives, Kew.

Williams, Claud H. (n. d.), "Light Car Patrols in the Libyan Desert", 85-page typed document, Royal Geographical Society, London.

Newspapers

The Egyptian Gazette (Cairo)

The Times (London)

Offical Records

British National Archives (formerly the Public Record Office) at Kew:

ADM 137/(Admiralty: First World War)
   ADM 137/193.

ADM 137/334.
AIR 1/(Air Ministry: Historical: RFC and RAF)
    AIR 1/691/21/20/30.
    AIR 1/1753/204/141/4.
    AIR 1/1949/204/254/4
FO 141/(Foreign Office: Embassy and Consulates: Egypt: General
Correspondence)
    FO 141/732.
FO 371/(Foreign Office: Political Departments: General Correspondence)
    FO 371/59.
    FO 371/65.
    FO 371/1971.
    FO 371/2202.
    FO 371/2353.
    FO 371/2354.
    FO 371/2356.
    FO 371/2670
    FO 371/27432.
FO 372/(Foreign Office: Treaty Department: General Correspondence)
    FO 372/717.
    FO 372/832
FO 383/(Foreign Office: Prisoners of War: General Correspondence)
    FO 383/238
PRO 30/57(Kitchener Papers)
    PRO 30/57/47
WO 33/(Telegrams: First World War: General)
    WO 33/714.
    WO 33/731.
    WO 33/747.
    WO 33/750
WO 95/(War Office: First World War and Army of Occupation War Diaries)
    WO 95/4360.
    WO 95/4428.
    WO 95/4437.
    WO 95/4438
WO 106/(War Office: Directorate of Military Operations and Military
Intelligence: Correspondence and Papers)
    WO 106/218
    WO 106/1543
WO 157/(War Office: Intelligence Summaries: First World War)
    WO 157/697.
    WO 157/687.
    WO 157/688.

INDEX

Index